T0339546

Organization outside Organizations

The book explores how various social settings are partially organized even when they do not form part of a formal organization. It also shows how even formal organizations may be only partially organized. Professors Göran Ahrne and Nils Brunsson first established the concept of partial organization in 2011 and in doing so opened up a ground-breaking new field of organizational analysis. An academic community has since developed around the concept, and Ahrne and Brunsson have edited this collection to reflect the current state of inquiry in this burgeoning subject and to set an agenda for future research. Its chapters explain how organization is a salient feature in many social settings, including markets, interfirm networks, social movements, criminal gangs, internet communication and family life. Organization theory is much more relevant for the understanding of social processes than previously assumed. This book provides a new understanding of many social phenomena and opens up new fields for organizational analysis.

GÖRAN AHRNE is professor emeritus at the Department of Sociology, Stockholm University and also affiliated with Stockholm Centre for organizational research (Score). He has written a number of books in various fields of sociology and organization theory including: *Agency and Organization* (1990), *Social Organizations*: *Interaction Inside, Outside and Between Organizations* (1994), and *Meta-Organizations* (2008).

NILS BRUNSSON is professor of management and affiliated with the Department of Business Studies, Uppsala University and with Stockholm Centre for organizational research (Score). He has published almost thirty books in the field of organization studies, including *Mechanisms of Hope* (2006), *The Consequences of Decision-Making* (2007), *A World of Standards* (2000), *Reform as Routine* (2009), *Meta-Organizations* (2008), and *Organizing and Reorganizing Markets* (2018), as well as numerous articles.

Organization outside Organizations

The Abundance of Partial Organization in Social Life

Edited by

GÖRAN AHRNE
Stockholm University, Sweden

NILS BRUNSSON
Uppsala University, Sweden

CAMBRIDGE
UNIVERSITY PRESS

CAMBRIDGE
UNIVERSITY PRESS

University Printing House, Cambridge CB2 8BS, United Kingdom

One Liberty Plaza, 20th Floor, New York, NY 10006, USA

477 Williamstown Road, Port Melbourne, VIC 3207, Australia

314-321, 3rd Floor, Plot 3, Splendor Forum, Jasola District Centre, New Delhi - 110025, India

103 Penang Road, #05-06/07, Visioncrest Commercial, Singapore 238467

Cambridge University Press is part of the University of Cambridge.

It furthers the University's mission by disseminating knowledge in the pursuit of education, learning and research at the highest international levels of excellence.

www.cambridge.org
Information on this title: www.cambridge.org/9781108468268
DOI: 10.1017/9781108604994

© Cambridge University Press 2019

First published 2019
First paperback edition 2022

A catalogue record for this publication is available from the British Library

Library of Congress Cataloging in Publication data
Names: Ahrne, Goran, 1944– editor. | Brunsson, Nils, 1946– editor.
Title: Organization outside organizations : the abundance of partial organization in social life / edited by Goran Ahrne, Nils Brunsson.
Description: New York : Cambridge University Press, 2019.
Identifiers: LCCN 2019002560 | ISBN 9781108474986 (hardback)
Subjects: LCSH: Organizational sociology. | Organization. | BISAC: BUSINESS & ECONOMICS / Organizational Behavior.
Classification: LCC HM786 .O743 2019 | DDC 302.3/5–dc23
LC record available at https://lccn.loc.gov/2019002560

ISBN 978-1-108-47498-6 Hardback
ISBN 978-1-108-46826-8 Paperback

Contents

Preface

Within the scientific field called organization studies, it is virtually taken for granted that formal organizations constitute the object of study: how formal organizations function internally and how they relate to the rest of the world – to their "environment", to use a favourite metaphor from the field. What is more, it is a standard, implicit assumption that organization happens within formal organizations, whereas their environments, and thus society in general, is not organized. Consequently, organizational environments have been regarded as a terrain set aside for other social sciences: economics, sociology, political science, or social anthropology. In these disciplines, theories of organization have been neglected, crowded out, and seen as irrelevant or perhaps banal or disenchanting. With this book we want to demonstrate that there is much organization outside organizations, a fact that is highly relevant for social science in general. If the world is becoming increasingly organized, and the boundaries of formal organizations are no longer as sharp, science should be mirroring this circumstance. The distinction between what is and is not organized is a crucial one, and we believe that many social settings could be better understood if one recognizes how they are partially organized.

Scholars in the field of organization studies have long experience in the useful importing of concepts and theories from other disciplines, including theories about culture, institutions, and networks. We believe that the time has come for organization studies to be exporting. Many of the insights gained from a half-century of research on formal organizations can be used in understanding wider social phenomena. In a paper published in *Organization* in 2011, we suggested a specific conceptualization of organization that allows studies of organizing activities and how they may lead to the specific order that we call organization.

Since that paper was published, many studies using this perspective have been conducted. In this book, we and a number colleagues report on some of them, ranging from inter-firm networks to families, from markets to social movements, from organized crime to international relations. And not only are organizational environments more or less organized, so also are formal organizations. In all, we see this book as an early step and hope that it will inspire others to study organization in even more social settings and to develop more detailed theories of how the social world is organized.

We are grateful for support we received for this project from many sources. Stockholm Centre for Organizational Research (Score) not only provided us with an excellent research setting, but also supported the project with financial resources and in other material ways. Mikaela Sundberg and Adrienne Sörbom, both at Score, arranged workshops and, together with other Score members, contributed with useful comments in an almost continuous discussion over several years. Nils Brunsson benefitted from a generous grant from Riksbankens Jubileumsfond (Grant No M2007-0244:1). And last but not least, Nina Colwill not only turned the text into proper English, but also raised many questions that forced us to clarify and develop our reasoning.

Stockholm and Uppsala March 2019
Göran Ahrne Nils Brunsson

Contributors

Göran Ahrne is professor of sociology at Stockholm University and affiliated with Stockholm Centre for Organizational Research (Score).

Sanne Bor is a postdoctoral researcher at Hanken School of Economics, Department of Marketing in Helsinki and a researcher at LUT School of Business and Management in Mikkeli, Finland.

Nils Brunsson is professor of management and affiliated with Uppsala University and Stockholm Centre for Organizational Research (Score).

Daniel Castillo holds a PhD in sociology and is associate professor of business administration at the Academy of Public Administration, Södertörn University.

Frank den Hond is the Ehrnrooth professor of management and organisation at Hanken School of Economics in Helsinki, and affiliated with Vrije Universiteit FSW/ORG in Amsterdam.

Leonhard Dobusch is professor of business administration with a focus on organization at the University of Innsbruck.

Peter Edlund is a postdoctoral researcher at the Department of Business Studies, Uppsala University.

Christina Garsten is professor of social anthropology at Stockholm University and chair of Stockholm Centre for Organizational Research (Score).

Michael Grothe-Hammer is a postdoctoral researcher at the Institute of Social Sciences at Helmut Schmidt University in Hamburg.

Cecilia Gullberg has a PhD in business studies from Uppsala University, and is assistant professor at Södertörn University.

Ingrid Gustafsson holds a Phd in public administration from the School of Public Administration, Gothenburg University. She is affiliated to Stockholm Centre for Organizational Research (Score).

Kati Järvi is affiliated as a researcher and lecturer to Hanken Scool of Economics in Helsinki.

Dieter Kerwer is a lecturer of International Relations at the University of Munich.

Stefan Kirchner is professor of sociology at Technical University, Berlin

Mikko Laamanen is a lecturer at the School of Management, Royal Holloway University of London.

Josef Pallas is professor at the Department of Business Studies, Uppsala University.

Andreas Rasche is professor of business in society at the Centre for Corporate Social Responsibility at Copenhagen Business School (CBS) and co-director of the CBS World-Class Research Environment on "Governing Responsible Business." He is also visiting professor at Stockholm School of Economics.

Amir Rostami holds a PhD in sociology from Stockholm University. He is currently researcher at the Institute for Future Studies in Stockholm.

Lambros Roumbanis holds a PhD in sociology from Stockholm University and is affiliated to Stockholm Centre for Organizational Research (Score). He is also a lecturer in sociology at the Department of Social Work, Stockholm University.

Dennis Schoeneborn is professor of organization, communication, and CSR at Copenhagen Business School (CBS). He is also visiting professor of organization and management at Leuphana University, Lüneburg.

Elke Schüßler is professor of business administration and head of the Institute of Organization Science at Johannes Kepler University, Linz

David Seidl is professor of management and organization at the Department of Business Administration at the University of Zurich and is a research associate at the Centre for Business Research (CBR) at Cambridge University.

Mikaela Sundberg is associate professor in sociology at the Department of Sociology, Stockholm University and director of research at Stockholm Centre for Organizational Research (Score).

Jörg Sydow is professor of management and chair for Inter-firm Cooperation at the School of Business & Economics at Freie Universität Berlin. He is currently the director of the Research Unit "Organized Creativity", sponsored by the German Research Foundation (DFG).

Adrienne Sörbom is professor of sociology at Södertörn University in Stockholm, and senior researcher at Stockholm Centre for Organizational Research (Score).

Kristina Tamm Hallström is associate professor of management at Stockholm School of Economics, and senior researcher at Stockholm Centre for Organizational Research (Score).

Jaakko Turunen holds a PhD in political science from Uppsala University, and is a lecturer in political science at Södertörn University.

Noomi Weinryb, has a PhD in business studies from Uppsala University, and is an associate senior lecturer at the Academy of Public Administration, Södertörn University.

Linda Wedlin is professor at the Department of Business Studies, Uppsala University.

Liisa Välikangas is professor of innovation management at Aalto University and Hanken School of Economics.

Introduction

I   Organization Unbound

Göran Ahrne and Nils Brunsson

How can an airplane land on another continent? How can we know that exotic fruits at the grocery shop have been produced in a relatively fair way? How is it that we can learn about some universities being better than others – even universities on the other side of the globe? How are we able to know which scientists are among the most outstanding in the world? In order to answer such questions, one must realize that all these phenomena rely on organization.

Contemporary everyday life is rife with organization. Working life contains much organization, but consumers also encounter various forms of organization in shops and restaurants. Leisure activities such as sports or tourism involve a substantial degree of organization, as does the Internet. One can even speak of 'hyper organization' as a characteristic of the contemporary world: 'Faced with any problematic situations, the modern impulse is to create more organizational structures' (Bromley & Meyer, 2015: 4).

Much organization takes place within formal organizations; they constitute an extremely common element of contemporary social life. There are states, firms, and associations everywhere, taking care of almost every aspect of society. The abundance of organizations has motivated ever-expanding research and academic education about these entities. A special academic field of organization studies has been formed, involving many thousands of scholars studying formal organizations in all their complexity, including research on how they organize their activities.

One effect of this development is the fact that the study of formal organizations has overshadowed other forms of organization. Organization seems to happen only in formal organizations. And although scholars specializing in the study of organizations have been interested in wider aspects of society, their conceptualizations have reinforced the image of organization as tied only to formal organizations. What happens outside the context of formal organizations has been dubbed 'organizational environments', and organizational environments have seldom been seen as organized. Rather, they have been described as resources, as markets, as institutions, or as networks within which a focal organization is a part.

In this book, we take another stance. We believe that there is more organization than is contained in formal organizations. Or, more precisely, we believe that it is easier to understand many aspects of contemporary society by seeing them as organized. And organization happens not only inside, but also outside the context of formal organizations. Organizations are more similar to their environments than most organizational scholars have acknowledged.

Yet, our concept of organization is conservative, in the sense that it is closely connected to the ways in which early students of organization distinguished formal organizations from other social phenomena, and it connects to common, contemporary perceptions of the specificities of formal organizations. We define organization as a decided order – an order created by people having made decisions about others. We see some decisions as more fundamental than others when it comes to organization and have dubbed these decisions 'organizational elements'. These are decisions about who can participate, about rules for how people shall behave, about ways to monitor others' behaviour, about how to issue positive or negative sanctions, and decisions about who can make decisions for others and in what way. But organizers do not necessarily use all organizational elements, and all settings are not organized by all elements. There is much *partial organization* within – but above all outside – formal organizations (Ahrne & Brunsson, 2011).

Individuals or organizations can use organizational elements to organize other individuals or organizations, even if they do not belong to the same organization. In this book we give examples of how organizations consider part of their environment as members;

how they set rules in the form of standards for how other organizations shall behave and for what they shall produce; and how other organizations distribute sanctions in the form of awards. Yet others monitor other organizations by rating or ranking them. We also demonstrate how we can find elements of organization where it is usually not expected – in markets, families, or social movements, for instance.

Organization is one base of social order: It can create predictability and facilitate interaction among individuals or organizations. But it is essential to distinguish organization from other forms that contribute to social order – forms such as institutions or networks that are much discussed in social science. Those forms are not decided by anyone, but have emerged out of processes of mutual adaptation among individuals or organizations. Their effects differ from organization, and they change in different ways. Organization is more transparent and is more likely to be challenged than emerging forms are. It is also crucial to distinguish among various forms in order to make it possible to analyse transitions from one form to another – how organization sometimes becomes institutionalized and how networks become organized, for instance (Ahrne & Brunsson, 2011; Ahrne, Brunsson, & Seidl, 2016).

The concept of organization is salient for understanding many social phenomena that happen outside formal organizations, not least many aspects of globalization – like those we mentioned in the first paragraph. Air travel is dependent on a huge number of rules in the form of international standards, goods are marked with fair trade labels, universities all over the globe are monitored and ranked by ranking organizations, and scholars are awarded by organizations such as the Nobel Foundation.

Because there is little systematic research about organization outside organizations, there are many remaining questions about organization. Under what circumstances can we expect organization? Why is organization often partial? Why are some organizational elements used rather than others? When does organization succeed to create order and when does it fail? What difference does organization make and what consequences does it have? The purpose of this book is to discuss these types of issues, in order to develop greater knowledge about a crucial aspect of contemporary society. We base our arguments on a large number of empirical studies of a wide array of social settings and situations.

After this short overview of our main arguments, we now turn to a more detailed account. In the next section, we use the concepts of social relationship and formal organization to specify further what we mean by organization and organizational elements. We compare organizational elements as they are used within formal organizations with other ways by which social relationships are formed. We then give examples of partial organization outside formal organizations. Thereafter, we discuss the special characteristics of organization that require us to distinguish organization from other forms of order. Finally, we introduce a number of questions about how organization outside formal organizations works in practice and provide an overview of the chapters that follow.

ORGANIZATION AND ORGANIZATIONAL ELEMENTS

In the field of organizational studies there is relatively general agreement over what shall count as a formal organization. When it comes to defining the more general concepts of organization and organizing, there is more variation, less agreement, and a certain lack of clarity. Sometimes organization and organizing are given a broad meaning, identical or close to the concepts of coordination or co-operation (Weick, 1979; Lindberg & Czarniawska, 2006). In this book we use a more narrow and specific definition, which covers a smaller part of social reality but allows us to highlight what we think is a special but crucial phenomenon in contemporary society. Our concept of organization can be understood as describing a special form for achieving coordination or co-operation, but organization may also be used for other purposes and may exist without giving rise to those effects.

We begin our analysis of organization by using the concept of social relationships and relating it to existing knowledge about formal organizations. This analysis of organization inside organizations we then use in the next section for describing our main theme: organization outside organizations.

According to Max Weber, a *soziale Beziehung* (social relationship) exists as soon as people act with each other in mind and orient themselves to each other, when 'the action of each takes account of the others and is oriented in these terms' (1968: 26). Yet Weber's definition seems to include both what is nowadays called interaction (see, e.g., Goffman, 1972) and more permanent social relationships. Interaction is occasional and merely presupposes the co-presence of those involved. Relationships, on the other hand, are expected to last for some time. A relationship can continue even through periods of isolation and may exist even if the parties seldom or never interact with each other.

Rather than being dependent on co-presence and interaction, relationships are supported by other factors. There are at least five elements that help link people together in a relationship: (1) They know who is involved in the relationship; (2) they have some common ideas about what the relationship involves and what they are expected to do; (3) they have the means to acquire some knowledge about the extent to which the others do what they are expected to do; (4) they have some possibility of influencing each other in a way that makes them fulfil the expectations; and (5) they have common ideas about who can take initiatives and who can act in order to maintain and develop the relationship.

These aspects of relationships may arise in various ways. In formal organizations, they can be decided. By creating a formal organization, one creates a specific type of relationship among the people involved – a relationship that is decided upon to a large extent. The organization is created by a decision, and decisions are fundamental in organizations (March & Simon, 1958; Luhmann, 2003, 2005). People in organizations not only make decisions for what they shall do themselves; some of them make decisions for what others shall do. Organizational decisions are communications about the way people should act or the distinctions or classifications they should make.

Organizational decisions are ubiquitous. But most significantly, the five aspects of relationships constitute objects for decisions in organizations. Organizations are expected to make decisions about (1) who can be a member; (2) rules that specify expectations for what the members shall do; (3) monitoring of what the members do; (4) positive or negative sanctions connected to the members' tendencies to meet the decided expectations; and (5) how decisions shall be made and who shall make them.

These organizational elements bind an organization together and constitute the fundamental relational decisions in organizations. Formal organizations are expected to make decisions on these elements, or at least be able to do so. If they don't, they run the risk of not being considered organizations or 'true' organizations, and scholars tend to characterize them as networks. Yet, these decisions typically constitute only a small part of all decisions in organizations; in Kemper's (2012: 12) terms, relational activities in organizations can be contrasted to 'technical' activities that tend to be more common.

We now discuss the organizational elements in more detail. We systematically contrast the organizational elements to other ways of creating and maintaining relationships – to their functional non-decided equivalents. For each element we start by exemplifying its non-decided equivalents and then show how organization is different.

Membership

In life in general, with whom one has a relationship often emerges as a result of interaction. People meet each other because they get involved in common activities. They have children in the same school class; they share a hobby or the like. Or friends or colleagues introduce them to other people. Such interactions, especially if they are repeated, sometimes lead to relationships that evolve when people get to know each other.

People sometimes categorize themselves or are categorized by others as belonging to a certain group on the basis of ethnicity, nationality, age, preferred music style, and the like. Such categorizations may lead to relationships as well, as people orient themselves to the actions of their peers and 'think of themselves as equivalent and similar to, or compatible with, others' (Lamont & Molnár, 2002: 188). Such perceived similarities create symbolic boundaries.

In contrast, organizational *membership* is not something that merely emerges in complex and implicit social processes. People in organizations decide who is to be a member. Those who want to become members must usually apply for membership, which is conditional on the approval of existing members. Membership provides a more distinct and less floating categorization of affiliation than do other forms, like friendship. Citizenship in a state is a much more distinct category than nationality is. The duration of a membership may be short, but is often expected to be long, and the decision about membership is often lacking a time frame. For the membership to cease, a new decision is required. Members are not anonymous. They are usually asked to provide a name, address, e-mail address, and telephone number, thereby facilitating further contact. Moreover, new members may increase the importance and strength of those who are already members, because it is possible to communicate how many members there are and who they are.

Members are treated differently than non-members by other members and by non-members. This relationship can be referred to when one wants to interact with other members, thus facilitating the beginning of an interaction. But membership can be upheld without any interaction with other members. As an employee in a firm or a state, one does not interact with all other members. Most members in large contemporary organizations interact only with a few other members, and the task of some members, such as salespeople, may be to interact primarily with non-members. Management control systems may have an enormous impact on members in subsidiaries of multinational companies without requiring much interaction between the subsidiary and the head office. And as a member of a political party or the Red Cross, one need not interact with any other member.

Rules

Many expectations about how people should behave are controlled by social norms. Norms have slowly emerged, are taken for granted, and have no clear origin, their origin is forgotten, or their origin is seldom brought to mind. They differ across societies and are bound to specific social situations. There are norms for such salient aspects of social life as justice, equality, or reciprocity, but also for such mundane behaviour as the way people greet each other, how they talk to each other, or who shall be invited to a wedding. Norms are sometimes described in terms of their behavioural effects, such as ceremonies, rituals, or traditions. These can even be understood as whole packages of norms.

Many scholars like us make a sharp distinction between norms and decided expectations. In the introduction to an anthology about various ways of defining and explaining norms, the editors describe the difference between norms and laws:

> Social norms, by contrast, often are spontaneous rather than deliberately planned (hence, of uncertain origin) unwritten (hence, their content and rules for application are often imprecise) and enforced informally (although the resulting sanctions can sometimes be a matter of life and death).
>
> *(Hechter & Opp, 2001: xi)*

Although Hechter and Opp talk about laws in contrast to norms, their distinction applies to all types of rules. Rules are decisions about how people are expected to behave: when they shall meet, what they shall do, how they shall do things together, and the goals they are expected to achieve. Organizations such as states or firms typically issue many rules. For achieving internal coordination, they cannot rely only on shared social norms among their members.

The source of a rule is virtually always known. Most rules are in written form, and they often include a statement about who decided what and when – which does not preclude the fact that people often learn about rules from their colleagues' oral communications. Rules can be specific to certain people. And they are useful for people who do not share norms that are common among the majority.

One can often find a distinction in the organizational literature between rules on the one hand and goals or objectives on the other hand. But as the literature on management by objectives tells us, this distinction is easier to uphold in principle than in practice (Sundström, 2003). A goal or objective is described as an expectation of what shall be achieved, whereas a rule is described as a script for how it shall be achieved; but the difference between ends and means is often vague and open to interpretation. In the context of this book, we do not have to enter this debate, but simply categorize goals and objectives as constituting one form of rules.

Monitoring

People observe each other in their interactions, but in a relationship interaction is often infrequent (or even non-existing), which makes direct observation of what the others are doing virtually impossible. In relationships including more than two people, the parties gossip about each other instead: One person informs another about what others have done or about rumours of what they have done. People tell stories that describe and evaluate the behaviour of the others (Burt, 2005: 105; Gambetta, 1994).

In organizations, principals regularly decide to monitor what members do and how they meet expectations, deciding who and what shall be monitored and by what means. Monitoring systems vary among organizations (Edwards, 1979; Mintzberg, 1983). They can be relatively simple, as when one monitors attendance at work or at a meeting. Or they can be more complicated, as when the organization monitors whether job instructions have been complied with or what results have been achieved. Some organizations, such as schools, regularly use tests and other detailed examinations as monitoring tools.

Monitoring can be done secretly, and even the decision to monitor is not necessarily communicated to the person to be monitored. But most often organizations inform their members about their monitoring decisions, as they may have implications for discipline or may have a motivational effect (Focault, 1977). The 'monitorees' may even demand monitoring – as when students take tests in order to obtain diplomas.

Sanctions

People's (perceived) behaviour in relationships may lead others to pay respect to and honour them, or, conversely, to show contempt for and despise them. Such reactions may, in turn, incite pride or shame with those concerned. But it may also lead others to become more or less interested in contacting them or may cause them to be finally squeezed out of the relationship (Burt, 2005: 105). If it is difficult to avoid meeting a despised person, bullying may arise.

There are many ways to decide about positive sanctions that are appropriate to an observed performance: by giving grades, bonus payments, wage rises, or awards to the employee of the month, or by appointing someone as an honorary member. Negative sanctions may take the form of warnings or lowered pay. Decisions about sanctions are communicated to the person involved – and often to other members as well, in order to demonstrate the preferred behaviour or performance.

Hierarchy

The power of people in relationships may be unevenly distributed. Some have more power than others and are better able to take initiatives and influence the others. Power may be based on superior access to resources that others want, centrality in a multiperson relationship (Borgatti & Halgin, 2011: 1173), or high status. People considered high status, whether by tradition or because of their individual qualities, can even expect voluntary compliance from others (Kemper, 2012).

Some relationships engender leaders – people who, because of their charisma, motivate others to follow them of their own free will. As history has recorded, strong leadership may lead to many disasters, but it may also coordinate a group of people into achieving complicated and difficult tasks.

In contrast, an organization's principals decide who shall have the power to influence others by their decisions and how their decisions shall be made – decisions about how to make decisions, sometimes called constitutions or corporate governance schemes but here called hierarchy. For firms, part of the organization's constitution is decided in law. Instead of relying on leaders, organizations can appoint principals such as chairpersons, presidents, prime ministers, or executives, and they are allowed to delegate their decision-making capability in some issues to hordes of managers or officials. The term 'hierarchy' is often used with reference to that situation. But here we also use the term for constitutions that alternatively or additionally stipulate that all organization members can participate in decision making, at least about some issues.

Hierarchy also includes decisions about the issues that can be decided by the appropriate decision makers. Organization members have a limited zone of indifference, within which they are expected to abide with decisions by their principals – a zone that may be wide or narrow (Barnard, 1968; Stinchcombe, 1990; Ahrne, 1994). In democratic states or bureaucracies, constitutions may be relatively detailed, but the zone of indifference is narrow.

The role of organizational elements in organizations

In conclusion, we argue that fundamental aspects of relationships are the objects of decisions in formal organizations. Organizational elements are functional equivalents of non-organized aspects of relationships. Membership is a functional equivalent of friendship, rules an equivalent of norms, monitoring an equivalent of gossip, sanctions an equivalent of bullying, and hierarchy an equivalent of leadership.

By saying that organizational elements are key aspects of and even constitutive of formal organizations, we do not argue that they

exclude their non-organized equivalents. On the contrary, it is difficult to imagine a relatively large, functioning, formal organization
where these do not exist. Weber constructed an ideal type of bureaucracy in which everything was decided, but actual organizations work
differently. People form non-decided groups in organizations; they
develop norms; they observe and gossip about each other; bullying
happens; and leaders who are not appointed managers emerge, gaining
authority from their status or charisma.

In fact, much of the organization theory literature has been
concerned with non-decided phenomena that can be seen as either
problematic dysfunctions, even corruption, or as necessary for making
a complex organization function and fulfil its task. The management
literature tells us that the art of management does not consist merely
of organizing, but of many other ways of influencing people, including
a selective spread of information, attempts at convincing people of
certain ways of understanding situations, setting good examples. In
addition, organizations are embedded in wider societal institutions
providing patterns of behaviour that organization members take for
granted (Meyer & Rowan, 1977).

These aspects are often called 'informal' in the organizational
literature, which is also rife with the term 'formal'. Rarely are either of
these terms defined. Our strong impression is that 'formal' most often
stands for what we have called 'decided' in this book. Rules, for
example, are defined as formal, whereas norms are described as informal. Law is often described as a formal institution, whereas customs
are considered informal. The extremely common use of the terms
'formal' and 'informal' is a sign that there is, in fact, a strong need
for distinguishing between orders that were decided and not decided.
Our aim is to make this distinction more explicit and clearer.

We do not use the terms informal and formal – with one exception. For practical reasons, we adhere to the common use of the expression 'formal organization' – a term that denotes firms, states, and
associations, and connotes something that has been created by decision.

ORGANIZATION OUTSIDE ORGANIZATIONS AND PARTIAL ORGANIZATION

Although much organization can be found in formal organizations, it is a mistake to assume that formal organizations have a monopoly on organization. There is organization outside formal organizations as well. The fundamental decisions on membership, rules, monitoring, sanctions, and hierarchy are made without assuming or prescribing that those to whom the decisions are directed belong to the same organization as the decision makers.

Indeed, there is research indicating that the five organizational elements are used in many forms for collective action all over the world and have been used for centuries. In a large research programme conducted over decades, Elinor Ostrom and colleagues studied so-called common pool resource projects, some of which have been functioning for thousands of years – mountain grazing and forests in Switzerland and Japan and irrigation systems in Spain and the Philippine Islands, for instance. Ostrom (1990) has argued that these projects have resolved the problem of efficient use of common resources (the tragedy of the commons) through the use of five so-called design principles: clearly defined boundaries; congruence among appropriation, provision rules, and local conditions; and collective choice arrangements, monitoring, and graduated sanctions. These principles reflect our five organizational elements. Boundaries were constructed through membership; there were clear rules and an agreed-upon procedure for making common decisions and also monitoring and sanctions. In the successful projects, people had been able to apply all the principles; in less successful projects, those involved had been able to use only a few.

Even if Ostrom did not recommend it, her analysis illustrates that all five organizational elements need not be used together. We have dubbed this phenomenon 'partial organization' (Ahrne & Brunsson, 2011), a common form outside formal organizations. Outside organizations there are typically many who act as organizers, and they often specialize in one element. In what follows, we provide some examples of situations in which elements are used separately in a context outside formal organizations.

Membership is not necessarily connected to other elements. People or organizations may have decided who can belong to a certain group without deciding on other elements. Whether new-comers are to be accepted or not may be their only decision. When and where they meet (if they ever do) may be decided on an ad hoc basis without any decided rules, monitoring, sanctions, or hierarchy. Even if members care about what the others do and they observe each other, they do not have to do this in an organized way. Customer clubs provide one example of such isolated membership. When customers become members, they are no longer anonymous, and they agree to be contacted with offers and invitations, but that is the extent of the organization.

Rules as a single element do not have to be about members; they can just as well pertain to various types of interaction. Common rules facilitate interaction; people know what they can expect of each other. Standards issued by national or international standardization organizations are examples of rules that do not presuppose other elements. The standards are directed at anyone for whom they are relevant. In most cases the standardization organizations do not arrange sanctions, and they rarely arrange for the monitoring that determines who does or does not comply. And there is no generally agreeed constitution for who can set standards or how; official standardization organizations often meet competition from other standardizers such as consortia formed by leading firms in an industry.

In other cases, rules are aimed at those who visit a certain place or those who are performing a certain activity that is open for anybody. Those who own or are responsible for a park, a beach, a playground, or a shop may issue rules. The aim of the rules can be to facilitate interaction among those who visit the place, to protect the area from damage, or to protect people living or staying in that place. Many laws are valid for anyone who is present on a state's territory, even though they are not citizens of that state, and even if there has been no decision to allow them in – as in cases in which there are no border controls between states.

Decisions concerning *monitoring* can be directed towards individuals or organizations, even without previous bonds in the form of membership or without rules. Rating institutes monitor the creditworthiness of firms and states, and many organizations rank universities without necessarily being explicit about the specific rules used. The aim of such decisions is often to try to influence an individual or organization that is being the object of observation to do things in other, ideally better, ways. Or the aim may be to influence the interactions of other people or organizations with the monitored actor through the communication of decisions about results of the monitoring.

Such decisions are often presented in the form of a grade. For creditworthiness, that could be a letter grade like A+ or B; for films or books, it is usually a number of stars or other symbols. Ranking is another form for presenting the results of monitoring, involving a direct comparison among similar objects, such as universities, schools, hospitals, or restaurants. Decisions presented in the format of grades or ranking are more accessible and comprehensible ways of comparing organizations, films, or books than are short reports or reviews.

Decisions about *sanctions* can be directed at individuals or organizations without any previous membership, without any rules or monitoring. Probably the most common form for positive sanctions is the awarding of a prize to a person or to an organization. And no hierarchy needs to be involved, because a prize can be given to someone without any previous contacts or relationship, and anyone is free to give out prizes.

Outside organizations, positive sanctions seem to be more common than negative ones. But there are also negative sanctions in the form of prizes awarded for the worst movie of the year or for bad behaviour, such as environmental pollution. Boycotts are another type of negative sanction in the form of a decision that recommends others not to interact with a certain organization or person.

Hierarchy can be used without other organizational elements in situations in which a loosely defined group of people or organizations is in need of a way to make certain necessary decisions in order to carry on, as when states decide that one state shall be responsible for chairing their next meeting. A chairperson who has been delegated the authority to lead an open meeting can decide who has the right to talk, thereby providing the possibility for others to listen to what every speaker has to say and the opportunity of having their say. The convener occupies a hierarchical position with the authority to make decisions about future meetings or agendas.

Missing elements

An isolated element is just one form of partial organization. Partial organization can also be described by giving examples of when almost all – but not all – elements are used. Rewards can be combined with rules and monitoring, for instance, providing a way of observing people or organizations to determine their fit with predetermined rules, but not necessarily using membership or hierarchy. In the same way, standardization is sometimes supplemented by monitoring and positive sanctions in the form of certifications for those who comply with the standards (conducted by organizations other than the standardization organizations), but hierarchy and membership are lacking. And membership can be combined with monitoring and sanctions, as in a gang with a strong leader but no hierarchy or rules.

Organization may increase over time. Some people who tend to show up at a bar playing darts may start organizing themselves with membership by making a list of those who participate. Over time the group may form a team in order to participate in tournaments, a decision that may require additional elements such as hierarchy and monitoring.

In a similar way, organization may start with the issuing of standards, and only later does a need develop for monitoring who does or does not comply with the standard – a situation that gives rise to certification schemes. The issuing of the ISO 9000 standard was followed by an entire industry of firms spread across the globe, monitoring compliance and issuing certifications and awards for the organization with the highest quality (Tamm Hallström, 2004). Another development may start with the issuing of an award that leads people to ask, over time, why certain persons or organizations have received the prize and claim that there should be clear rules for who shall be awarded.

This is not to say that there is a general tendency towards more organization. A situation with only one organizational element may persist. And sometimes the development is in the other direction: from much organization to less. A group of people may lose interest in most of its collective actions, for instance, and no longer need as many organizational elements.

Formal organizations as partially organized

Partial organization exists not only outside the context of formal organizations. Although formal organizations must be represented as having access to all organizational elements, they may not use all of them, a situation that renders them partially organized. Managers of formal organizations may not have such lofty ambitions that they need to use every organizational element. When membership is used as a marker of status, for example, an organization may offer only membership or members can choose to be members only. Members then gain high status because they belong to a high-status club, but they do not have to comply with any rules or participate in any activities. The organization has few or no activities on its programme, and thus has little need for other organizational elements.

In other cases, the functional equivalents of organization may be enough to satisfy some of an organization's purposes. A firm may abstain from monitoring its employees because management is confident that customers will immediately complain if the quality of service declines. Organizations may also be embedded in such strong institutions that they lack both the need and ability to organize. Many aspects of teaching and research are so heavily institutionalized that academics have little need or ability for much organization. Many aspects of running a research or teaching seminar are taken for granted, and few decisions need to be made; in fact, any decision that goes against the institutionalized way runs the risk of being met with lack of understanding or even resistance.

The fact that there can be much organization outside formal organizations and little inside and vice versa makes the difference between organizations and their environments less dramatic than is usually assumed in organization studies. It is not the existence of organization that makes organizations differ from their environments. Rather, the difference is due to the special social construction of formal organizations that is typical of modern times. A formal organization is constructed as a type of entity, not unlike the way individuals are constructed, as a kind of person (usually a legal person) who can own resources, can be addressed by others, and is thought of as an actor, able to act as one entity; such persons are responsible for their actions (Brunsson & Sahlin-Andersson, 2000; Meyer & Jepperson, 2000; Dobusch & Schoeneborn, 2015).

Arguably, the expectation that organizations have access to all organizational elements makes the construction as one actor seem more realistic because the use of these elements is believed to lead to a high degree of coordination. If one wants something to be unambiguously perceived as a formal organization, therefore, one cannot completely deny that this entity has access to every organizational element. Organizations that are weak in organizational elements but are under pressure to prove that they are indeed formal organizations can be expected to produce much hypocrisy (Brunsson, 2007, Ch. 7). They represent themselves as more organized than they are. This is a likely situation for contemporary states (Krasner, 1999), but also for universities.

Although there is a relationship between organizational elements and the constituting aspects of a formal organization, it is noteworthy that a situation in which all organizational elements are used does not alone produce a formal organization. Many markets are organized by all five elements, yet they are markets rather than formal organizations (Brunsson & Jutterström, 2018). In a previous paper (Ahrne and Brunsson, 2011), we have called a situation in which all elements are used 'complete' rather than 'partial', but a complete organization does not necessarily create an entity in the form of a formal organization.

THE SIGNIFICANCE OF ORGANIZATION

There is great interest in contemporary social science for bases of social order other than organization – primarily for institutions and networks, which are substantially different from organization and from each other. It is crucial to distinguish between these forms when studying and analysing stability and change of social structures. Institutions and networks that come into existence in a way other than organized order are affecting people's behaviour for other reasons, and their patterns of change are different. In order to specify further the special characteristics of organization, it is useful to compare it with institutions and networks.

An institution can be defined as a stable, routine-reproduced pattern of behaviour, combined with norms and conceptions that are taken for granted by larger or smaller groups of people (Jepperson, 1991). Institutions emerge from long processes of mutual adaptation among people (Berger & Luckmann, 1991: 75); they develop slowly (Czarniawska, 2009) and are difficult to change (North, 1998: 498).

The term 'network' has been used in social science for describing almost any relationship among people (Thompson, 2003: 2; Borgatti & Hagin, 2011: 1168). Yet there are more stringent definitions that describe a network as a special social form with specific characteristics (Marsden, 2000: 2727; Granovetter, 1985). A network, then, consists of non-decided structures of relationships linking social actors. Like institutions, such pure networks are emergent structures. They are established and expanded through people meeting in various contexts and getting to know each other. But this is a slow process (Burt, 2005: 99). Networks are embedded in other social relationships; they do not have any natural boundaries; it is the researcher that defines the network (Borgatti & Haglin, 2011: 1169). Networks have no names or identities and do not announce what they are doing; they are 'silent' (Bommes & Tacke, 2005). Networks are generally assumed to be non-hierarchical and are maintained through reciprocity, trust, and social capital (Borgatti & Foster, 2003; Podolny & Page, 1998; Bommes & Tacke, 2005). Just like the concept of institution, the concept of network describes results rather than attempts, and it is difficult to point to some one person as responsible for these results.

Like networks, organization has to do with relations and inter-actions among people or organizations; and just like institutions, organization can produce common patterns of behaviour among peo-ple. But in many other respects, organization can be seen as the opposite of networks and institutions.

Organization is not an emerging order but is based on decisions. Organization comes into being through the communication of deci-sions (Schoeneborn et al., 2014: 309). An organized order has certain qualities that mark its difference from emergent orders. It is more likely to be controversial; it implies other mechanisms of change; it is more visible; it concentrates responsibility; it can be more specific; and it can introduce a comparison between intentions and results.[1]

Decisions are far from taken for granted. A decision presupposes that there are options: A decision could have been different; another option could have been chosen. Thus, decisions can always be con-tested and they regularly are. By signalling their own contingency, decisions tend to dramatize uncertainty – uncertainty about their appropriateness and their chances of implementation (Brunsson, 1982; Luhmann, 2000). Decisions may be changed by new decisions, which may happen quickly.

Those expected to be affected by the decision need to know that the decision was made. Decisions must be communicated. Furthermore, the decision makers are visible and perceived as responsible for the decision. There is someone who can be blamed if one dislikes a decision and someone to whom protests are to be directed. Quests for transparency, accountability, and democracy involve quests for decisions – an order that is not decided is more difficult to challenge. One fundamental argument for state constitutions, for example, is to avoid power stemming from centrality, status, or leadership (cf. Perrow, 1986).

According to March and Simon (1958: 3), a distinctive quality of decisions is their specificity in contrast to the diffuseness of other influence processes in society. Decisions can be adjusted to specific situations and be more detailed than institutions.

Organization constitutes an attempt to create a specific order, but much organization fails (Brunsson, 2009), and these failures are visible for those who know and remember what was decided.

Identification of the differences among organization, institution, and networks is salient not only because of the different effects and dynamics that characterize these forms, but also because it makes it possible to analyse transitions among them. Organization is sometimes institutionalized – when a standard becomes taken for granted, for instance, and its origin in a decision is forgotten or seen as irrelevant. A pure network may become organized, perhaps starting with a listing of members and then with the introduction of more organization. Institutions may become organized – when professional norms are formulated in explicit rules, for example. All such transitions are examples of crucial changes that produce new orders with different conditions for further development, but they can be understood only if we have concepts that differentiate among the types of order.

Organization as attempt

Decisions in general are attempts, and it is an old observation in decision and organization theory that their implementation is uncertain. Not least is this true for decisions directed towards others. The purpose of such decisions is to influence others' decisions – to make the decision makers make decisions for themselves that are consistent with the first decision. Such decisions can be described as compliance with or acceptance of the decisions of others.

It is far from certain that everyone complies with rules decided by others, that they agree to become and remain members, that they accept prizes, that they tolerate and do not sabotage monitoring, or that they recognize the rights of others to make decisions for them at all. Indeed, people may not even notice that others have made decisions that they think should concern them. All these problems may exist within formal organizations, but they are even more acute with organization outside organizations.

As we have argued here, creating a formal organization is one way of establishing a relationship among the organization's members, one implication being that the members are expected to be informed about organizational decisions and consider them as relevant for them – although those expectations are not always met.

Organization outside organizations can sometimes build on an existing relationship, such as when people knowing each other begin organizing their relationship, or when firms interacting in a market start organizing their relations. In other cases, organizers try to organize people with whom they have no previous relationship. Such organizing is more difficult because it must be combined with attempts to make the decisions not only known, but also relevant for the target group – who should at least consider the organizers' decisions when making their own decisions.

The connection can sometimes be made at a specific place: A shop may inform customers of the fact that they are monitored by cameras; a set of rules can be announced on a billboard in a park; a brochure can be given to people crossing a state border to inform them about national traffic rules. The organizer in these cases builds on the assumption that the people targeted share the institutions of ownership and state.

In other cases, the organizer has no such assistance, but must try to establish a mutual relationship with those they want to organize – a relationship that means that the people being organized find the organizers' decisions to be relevant. A standardizing organization tries to make other organizations consider its standards when developing new products and processes, for example. Amnesty International wants its decisions to be considered relevant by all state governments. A common idea behind a prize is not only that the winner shall decide to accept it, but also that others shall think of the possibility of receiving a prize or at least consider the values that the prize expresses when making their decisions. Retail chains try to establish a relationship with their customers by sending them membership cards.

The task of these organizers may not be as hopeless as it seems, however. They can build on the relationships that exist within their target groups. Because of the relationships among firms in a value chain, it may be enough that one dominant firm accepts a standard for the others to do the same. Small Amnesty groups in various countries have relationships with journalists or lobbyists who, in turn, have strong relationships with key politicians.

Even if people observe the decisions of others and consider them relevant, there is no guarantee that they comply with them in making their own decisions. But their decision to comply with earlier organization decisions may constitute premises that make it more likely that they comply with future decisions. Within formal organizations, the decision to accept membership or hierarchy becomes a premise that increases the likelihood for accepting further decisions that are made within the context of this organization, because members are expected to comply with such decisions. If one decides not to comply, one questions one's earlier decision to become a member and transforms the decision into two decisions: to comply or not and to revoke one's membership or not.

Similarly, organizational elements outside organizations can form positive premises for each other. The decision to accept hierarchy, for instance, makes it more likely that decisions made according to a constitution are complied with; decisions to accept a rule makes it more likely that monitoring according to the rule is accepted. Such links among decisions create a certain path dependence that supports organizers. But it also means that the organizer who can or wants to use only a few elements has a more difficult time making an impact than do organizers who are willing to and expected to use all five elements – the management of formal organizations, for example.

PUZZLES OF ORGANIZATION

Organization happens in both the small world and the big world. Friendship relationships and marriages can become organized; protest groups and social movements are partially organized; relationships among firms in a value chain can be more or less organized; and almost all markets are organized to some extent. In the big world, formal organizations are the main organizers, active in organizing not only themselves, but also their environments. To do so, they need not merge with other organizations. They can expand their control of the environment with decisions on one or a few organizational elements, sometimes on their own, sometimes in co-operation with other organizations in meta-organizations or co-operative networks (Ahrne & Brunsson, 2008; Sydow, 2005).

Yet, the social sciences have demonstrated limited interest in organization. The emphasis in most fields has been on such emerging orders as institutions, cultures, and networks. And we believe that organization has often been overlooked in the social sciences other than organization studies. One indication is that concepts from the world of organizations are often used metaphorically rather than analytically. The language of organizations and organization studies is used for describing other phenomena. Institutionalized norms for behaviour are described as 'scripts' (Tilly, 1998), for instance – a bewildering metaphor, because there are, in fact, no scripts in these situations – no decisions about how things should be – yet people know how to behave. The term 'membership' has been used to describe the characteristic of belonging to a culture (Lamont & Molnár, 2002); by using this term, the authors use the language of organizations in a rather misleading way, while completely ignoring the fact that organizations are major creators of social boundaries in the modern world. Social norms for gender are described as 'negotiated' (Finch & Mason, 1993), and agency is described as distributed (Garud & Karnøe, 2003). All these terms indicate that there are decisions behind them – that someone has decided on a script or on membership, that people have come to a common decision after a negotiation, or that someone has distributed agency to some persons and not to others. But characteristic of all these phenomena is the fact that they are *not* decided or do not lead to a decision. Were they actually decided, the world would be different indeed. Gender inequality, for instance, could be abolished simply by a new negotiation leading to a new decision! Using organization concepts as metaphors indicates that the authors do not consider it important to uphold the distinction between the organized and non-organized. For those who think differently, the metaphors are likely to produce more confusion than clarity.

An investigation of the occurrence of organization can serve as a bridge between organization theory and more general social theory. Through studying partial organization, we can learn when, how, and why social interaction and social relationships become organized, and we can observe the consequences of organization. But because we are dealing with partial organization, we can also explore the limits of organization: why organization is sometimes partial rather than complete, and why some organizational elements are not used in specific situations. And it will also be possible to see when organization fails.

For understanding such issues, it is useful to look at the development of partial organization. Which elements were organized first and in which combinations? What triggers more or less organization? Do demands for more organization come from organizers, from those organized, or from others? What is achieved by organization? Is something lost? Are there risks? What are the options to organization? The answers to these questions and more are discussed in this book.

The aim of the book is threefold. First, we demonstrate the existence of organization in many settings, including intimate relationships, social movements, criminal gangs, networks, corporations, and markets. Second, we offer at least tentative explanations for why there is more or less organization in various situations and when and why organization is sought and when and why it is not. Third, we discuss the ways in which our concept of partial organization helps offer better explanations for a large number of social phenomena than existing explanations do.

In **Part 1** of the book we discuss the use of specific organizational elements. In Chapter 2 (*Standards between Partial and Complete Organization*), Andreas Rasche and David Seidl analyse rules in the form of standards. Standards are probably the most powerful organizational element for organizing the contemporary world. In this chapter, the authors demonstrate why standards are sometimes combined with other organizational elements and the dynamics among elements are discussed.

Prizes are ubiquitous today, and the awarding of prizes is expanding into virtually every area of social life. A prize is a positive sanction sometimes combined with other organizational elements. In Chapter 3 (*Prizes and the Organization of Status*), Peter Edlund, Josef Pallas, and Linda Wedlin explore three ways in which prizes vary: through the uses of rules, membership, and the ways in which prize decisions are communicated. A lack of rules and membership allow the decision maker greater freedom to choose the winner. It also makes it more difficult for others to predict to whom a prize will be awarded, thereby giving the prize an aura of mystery.

Membership is often regarded as fundamental in all types of organization. In Chapter 4 (*Membership or Contributorship? Managing the Inclusion of Individuals into Organizations*), Michael Grothe-Hammer compares membership to contributorship, which is another way of organizing participation. Based on two case studies, he demonstrates how contributorship can be understood as a matter of decision concerning the ways in which individuals can contribute. An absence of membership does not necessarily make the boundary of an organization open or fluid. Contributorship may generate more organization for a short time, but it is more volatile than membership.

Markets are often described as being decidedly different or even the opposite of organizations. Yet, markets and organizations are similar in the sense that they are both organized. In **Part 2** of the book we analyse organization in and around markets.

In Chapter 5 (*The Partial Organization of Markets*), Nils Brunsson demonstrates how markets are organized by different combinations of organizational elements and by different organizers. He distinguishes among four types of market organizers: sellers, buyers, profiteers (those who profit from organizing the market activities of others), and 'others' (those who try to organize markets in the interest of anyone other than themselves). He further discusses how market organizers contribute to the uncertainty and changeability of many markets.

In Chapter 6 (*The Organization of Digital Marketplaces: Unmasking the Role of Internet Platforms in the Sharing Economy*) Stefan Kirchner and Elke Schüßler analyse digital marketplaces as a relatively new form of market organization. By drawing on two exemplary cases, Lyft and Airbnb, they show how profiteers succeed in organizing consumers, turning them into sellers, while legitimizing their activities by using the somewhat romantic but unrealistic label of the 'sharing economy'.

In Chapter 7 (*Organizing for Independence*), Ingrid Gustafsson and Kristina Tamm Hallström ask how market profiteers such as certification and accreditation organizations can use one or a few organizational elements in order to argue that they are independent evaluators of sellers and their products. The authors analyse how the search for independence results in the addition of elements to elements, driving more and more organization and forming a complex system of interdependent organizations, which resembles a rational, authoritative Weberian bureaucracy.

Organization and institution are different forms for social order, but they also exist side by side. Institutions may be reinforced by organization, but organization may also be a threat to an institution. In Chapter 8 (*Queues: Tensions between Institution and Organization*), Göran Ahrne, Daniel Castillo, and Lambros Roumbanis use queues as an example. The idea of how to form a queue has strong legitimacy as an institution. The authors discuss why queues are sometimes supported by organization, in the form of monitoring, for instance. But when an organization decides the order in which people are admitted, little remains of the institution of the queue.

Social relationships such as networks, families, kinship or brotherhood are not usually regarded as organized. But they often rely on one or several organizational elements. In **Part 3** we examine a number of social relationships and compare the organizational elements with their functional equivalents and discuss the consequences of and obstacles to organization.

We begin with two chapters analysing organization of networks. In Chapter 9 (*The Inter-Firm Network as Partial Organization?*), Jörg Sydow argues that the concept of partial organization assists in the understanding of the development of inter-firm networks from initial market relationships and from hierarchical organizations. With many examples, he analyses the management of inter-firm networks through various combinations of organizational elements.

In Chapter 10 (*An Organized Network: World Economic Forum and the Partial Organizing of Global Agendas*), Christina Garsten and Adrienne Sörbom demonstrate how the World Economic Forum (WEF) organizes a global network of representatives for large business firms and states. They argue that WEF representations of the network downplay its high degree of organization. The decision for anyone to become a member of any type of WEF group lies primarily in the hands of WEF staff, and they keep their invited participants under close supervision. Monitoring and sanctioning is built into the organization at all levels.

In Chapter 11 (*Organizing Intimacy*), Göran Ahrne compares three types of intimate relationships: families, friendship, and kinship. There are considerable differences among them not only in their degree of organization, but also in the elements present. But there are also differences within the same type of relationship regarding the amount of organization and the ways in which the relationship is organized. An investigation of organizational elements in intimate relationships also provides an awareness of the limits of organization and why intimate relationships remain partially organized.

Organized crime is a concept that covers many types of criminal actions. Law enforcers and the media often discuss whether a crime is organized or not, but rarely do they address the question of how it is organized. In Chapter 12 (*How Is 'Organized Crime' Organized?*) Göran Ahrne and Amir Rostami explore the usefulness of applying the idea of partial organization in order to find variations in how and to what extent crimes are organized. They examine three examples: outlaw motorcycle gangs, street gangs, and mafias, and explain why some of them are formal organizations, whereas others are organized to a limited extent.

Brotherhood is a social relationship that is associated with strong affectual bonds. But in Chapter 13 (*Brotherhood as an Organized Social Relationship*), Mikaela Sundberg argues that brotherhood presupposes decisions about membership and is connected to formal organizations, and thus differs from friendship. The analysis is based on three cases: outlaw motorcycle gangs, armed forces, and Catholic monasteries.

People in social movements and similar types of collective action often do not want to be regarded as formal organizations, yet most movements must struggle with the dilemma of organization. In **Part 4**, we discuss the partial organization of social movements and collective action.

Chapter 14 (*The Dilemma of Organization in Social Movement Initiatives*) is a study of a local social movement – timebanking – that examines the tensions around hierarchy and leadership; why and how hierarchy is resisted. Mikko Laamanen, Sanne Bor, and Frank den Hond illustrate how a group vested in the idea of horizontal, non-hierarchical collective action is dealing with the coordination and decision-making challenges they meet over time.

The following two chapters demonstrate how the use of Internet and social media has changed the preconditions for organization. In Chapter 15 (*Alternating between Partial and Complete Organization: The Case of Anonymous*), Dennis Schoeneborn and Leonhard Dobusch develop a process perspective on partial organization and how the various organizational elements interrelate jointly, to constitute organizational phenomena. They show how a temporary use of all elements occurred in and through a communicative event when Anonymous publicly 'celebrated' a decision to exclude a 'member', thereby demonstrating the social collective's ability to mobilize all five elements when needed – elements that were absent most of the time.

Noomi Weinryb, Cecilia Gullberg, and Jaakko Turunen wrote Chapter 16 (*Collective Action through Social Media: Possibilities and Challenges of Partial Organization*). It builds on a story of the organization of a fundraising campaign for refugees through social media. The unorganized character of an initial call led to rapid development. The technological affordances of the social media platform served as a substitute for hierarchy, and there were no members or rules. The initiators were soon forced to introduce several rules for the collection and distribution of donations, however, and the activists and donators made demands for monitoring how the donations were being used.

In **Part 5** we analyse the partial organization of formal organizations.

In Chapter 17 (*Partial De-Organizing for Innovation and Strategic Renewal? A Study of an Industrial Innovation Programme*), a continuum from emergent to decided order is used to create an understanding of the dynamics in formal organizations, using a case of 'de-organization' of a large industrial firm. Frank den Hond, Kati Järvi, and Liisa Välikangas investigate the extent to which the partial deconstruction of its hierarchy led to innovation and strategic renewal.

Along with Dieter Kerwer, we discuss the difficulties of organizing meta-organizations in Chapter 18 (*The Partial Organization of International Relations: International Organizations as Meta-Organizations*). Meta-organizations – organizations with other organizations as their members – are paradoxical constructions; they are autonomous actors with autonomous actors as members, which explains why they are often unable to use all organizational elements. We take the example of international government organizations to explain why meta-organizations tend to be weak organizations, but we also point to some of their strengths. We argue that membership is a key element in international government organizations.

In the **concluding Chapter** 19 (*More and Less Organization*), we highlight the empirical findings, and use the analysis of the preceding chapters for discussing origins and motives for partial organization and what triggers the process of adding or eliminating organizational elements: why there is more or less organization. We discuss why people's interests in organization do not always lead to the formation of a formal organization. We argue that partial organization outside formal organizations tends to become more extensive and salient in a globalized world – partial organization should be a major research topic for students of organization.

REFERENCES

Ahrne, G. (1994) *Social Organizations. Interaction, inside, outside and between Organizations.* London: SAGE.

Ahrne, G. & Brunsson, N. (2008) *Meta-Organizations.* Cheltenham: Edward Elgar.

Ahrne, G. & Brunsson, N. (2011) Organization outside Organizations: The Significance of Partial Organization. *Organization* 18(1): 83–104.

Ahrne, G., Brunsson, N. & Seidl, D. (2016) Resurrecting Organization by Going beyond Organizations. *European Management Journal* 34(2): 93–101.

Barnard, C. (1968) *The Functions of the Executive.* Thirtieth Anniversary Edition. Cambridge, MA: Harvard University Press.

Bommes, M. & Tacke, V. (2005) Luhmanns System´s Theory and Network Theory. In Seidl, D. & Becker, K. (eds.), *Niklas Luhmann and Organization Studies.* Malmö: Liber. 282–304.

Borgatti, S. P. & Foster, P. C. (2003) The Network Paradigm in Organizational Research: A Review and Typology. *Journal of Management* 29(6): 991–1013.

Borgatti, S. P. & Hagin, D. S. (2011) On Network Theory. *Organization Science* 22 (5): 1168–81.

Bromley, P. & Meyer, J. (2015) *Hyper-Organization. Global Organizational Expansion.* Oxford: Oxford University Press.

Brunsson, N. (1982) The Irrationality of Action and Action Rationality: Decisions, Ideologies and Organizational Actions. *Journal of Management Studies* 19(1): 29–44.

Brunsson, N. (2007) *The Consequences of Decision-Making.* Oxford: Oxford University Press.

Brunsson, N. & Jutterström, M. (eds.) (2018) *Organizing and Re-Organizing Markets.* Oxford: Oxford University Press.

Brunsson, N., & Sahlin-Andersson, K. (2000) Constructing Organizations: The Example of Public Sector Reform. *Organization Studies* 21(4): 721–46.

Burt, R. S. (2005) *Brokerage and Closure. An Introduction to Social Capital.* Oxford: Oxford University Press.

Czarniawska, B. (2009) Emerging Institutions: Pyramids or Anthills? *Organization Studies* 30(4): 423–41.

Dobusch, L. & Schoeneborn, D. (2015) Fluidity, Identity and Organizationality: The Communicative Constitutions of Anonymous. *Journal of Management Studies* 52(8): 1005–35.

Edwards, R. C. (1979) *Contested Terrain: The Transformation of the Workplace in the Twentieth Century.* New York: Basic Books.

Foucault, M. (1977) *Discipline and Punish. The Birth of the Prison.* Harmondsworth: Penguin Books.

Gambetta, D. (1994) Godfather's Gossip. *European Journal of Sociology* 35(02): 199–223.

Garud, R. & Karnøe, P. (2003) Bricolage versus Breakthrough: Distributed and Embedded Agency in Technology Entrepreneurship. *Research Policy* 32(2): 277–300.

Goffman, E. (1972) *Encounters. Two Studies in the Sociology of Interaction.* Harmondsworth: Penguin Books.

Hechter, M. & Opp, K.-D. (eds.) (2001) *Social Norms.* New York: Russell Sage Foundation.

Jepperson, R. L. (1991) Institutions, Institutional Effects, and Institutionalism. In Powell, W. & Di Maggio, P. (eds.), *The New Institutionalism in Organizational Analysis.* Chicago: Chicago University Press. 143–63.

Kemper, T. D. (2012) *Status, Power and Ritual Interaction. A Relational Reading of Durkheim, Goffman and Collins*. Farnham: Ashgate.

Krasner, S. D. (1999) *Sovereignty: Organized Hypocrisy*. Princeton: Princeton University Press.

Lamont, M. & Molnár, V. (2002) The Study of Boundaries in the Social Sciences. *Annual Review of Sociology* 28: 167–95.

Lindberg, K. & Czarniawska, B. (2006) Knotting the Action Net, or Organizing between Organizations. *Scandinavian Journal of Management* 22(4): 292–306.

Luhmann, N. (2000) *Organisation und Entscheidung*. Opladen: Westdeutscher Verlag.

Luhmann, N. (2003) Organization. In Bakken, T. & Hernes, T. (eds.), *Autopoietic Organization Theory. Drawing on Niklas Luhmann's Social System Perspective*. Oslo: Abstrakt Forlag AS. 31–52.

Luhmann, N. (2005) The Paradox of Decision Making. In Seidl, D. & Becker, K. (eds.), *Niklas Luhmann and Organization Studies*. Malmö: Liber. 85–106.

March, J. & Simon, H. (1958) *Organizations*. New York: John Wiley.

Marsden, P. (2000) Social Networks. In *Encyclopedia of Sociology*. 2nd edition, volume 4. New York: MacMillan Reference USA. 2727–35.

Meyer, J. & Rowan, B. (1977) Institutionalized Organizations: Formal Structure As Myth and Ceremony. *American Journal of Sociology* 83(2): 340–63.

Meyer, J. W. & Jepperson, R. L. (2000) The 'Actors' of Modern Society: The Cultural Construction of Social Agency. *Sociological Theory* 18(1): 100–20.

Mintzberg, H. (1983) *Power in and around Organizations*. Englewood Cliffs: Prentice Hall.

North, D. C. (1998) Where Have We Been and Where Are We Going? In Benner, A. & Putterman, L. (eds.), *Economics, Values and Organization*. Cambridge: Cambridge University Press. 491–508.

Ostrom, E. (1990) *Governing the Commons. The Evolution of Institutions for Collective Action*. Cambridge: Cambridge University Press.

Perrow, C. (1986) *Complex Organizations. A Critical Essay*. 3rd edition. New York: McGraw-Hill.

Podolny, J. M. & Page, K. L. (1998) Network Forms of Organization. *Annual Review of Sociology* 24: 57–76.

Schoeneborn, D., Blaschke, S., Cooren, F., McPhee, R. D., Seidl, D. & Taylor, J. R. (2014) The Three Schools of CCO Thinking: Interactive Dialogue and Systematic Comparison. *Management Communication Quarterly* 28(2): 285–316.

Stinchcombe, A. (1990) *Information and Organizations*. Berkeley: University of California Press.

Sundström, G. (2003) *Stat på villovägar: resultatstyrningens framväxt i ett historisk-institutionellt perspektiv.* Dissertation, Stockholm University.

Sydow, J. (2005) Managing Interfirm Networks: Towards More Reflexive Network Development? In T. Theurl (ed.), *Economics of Interfirm Networks.* Tübingen: Mohr Siebeck. 217–36.

Tamm Hallström, K. (2004) *Organizing International Standardization. ISO and the IASC in Quest of Authority.* Cheltenham: Edward Elgar.

Thompson, G. F. (2003) *Between Hierarchies and Markets. The Logic and Limits of Network Forms of Organization.* Oxford: Oxford University Press.

Tilly, C. (1998) *Durable Inequality.* Berkeley: University of California Press.

Weber, M. (1968) *Economy and Society.* Volume 1. Berkeley: University of California Press.

Weick, K. (1979) *The Social Psychology of Organizing.* Reading: Addison-Wesley.

NOTE

1. A more detailed account of differences among organization, institution, and network can be found in Ahrne and Brunsson (2011).

PART I Rules, Sanctions, Membership

2 Standards between Partial and Complete Organization

Andreas Rasche and David Seidl

The modern world is increasingly governed by standards. There is hardly any domain of private or public life that is not affected in one way or another by standards prescribing specific behaviours or their outcomes (Brunsson & Jacobsson, 2000b; Timmermans & Epstein, 2010). Standards can be defined as 'rule[s] for common and voluntary use, decided by one or several people or organizations' (Brunsson, Rasche, & Seidl, 2012: 616). Like laws and norms, standards are rules that are meant for common use; but unlike laws they are voluntary, and unlike norms they are the product of decisions (Brunsson & Jacobsson, 2000b). Given that many standards are either produced by organizations (e.g., the International Organization for Standardization (ISO), industry consortia, and governmental regulators) or directed at organizations (e.g., corporate social responsibility (CSR) standards, corporate governance codes, and accounting standards), standards have long been of central concern to organization scholars (Egyedi & Blind, 2008; Brunsson & Jacobsson, 2000a). More recently, scholars have drawn attention to the fact that standards not only constitute input into and output from organizations, but can also be considered forms of organization themselves (Brunsson *et al.*, 2012; Ahrne, Brunsson, & Seidl, 2016). Even though standards may not always possess all elements of a complete organization, they fulfil at least the minimal definition of organization as 'decided orders'. As Ahrne *et al.* (2016: 96) have written: 'Standardization is based on decided rules but other elements of organization are often missing.'

This perspective on standards as (partial) organization holds great promise, not least because it allows for the conceptual apparatus of organization analysis to be applied to standards. The aim of this chapter is to explore the fruitfulness of this new approach to the study of standards. In particular, we describe how the concept of partial organization can be applied to standards and the types of research questions this raises. We illustrate our argument with examples of standards in the area of CSR and corporate governance, as these types of standards are particularly prominent in the organization studies literature (Aguilera & Cuervo-Cazurra, 2004; Gilbert *et al.*, 2011; Haxhi & van Ees, 2010; Seidl, 2007). We do not focus on product or technical standards in our analysis, because they solve the problem of coordination through the mere existence of rules, and usually, given their exclusive nature, do not allow for deviations (Farrell & Saloner, 1988). For example, manufacturers who produce screws that do not comply with existing standards would be unable to sell them. So additional organizational elements such as sanctioning for deviations from technical standards are rarely necessary. By contrast, CSR and corporate governance standards allow for higher degrees of deviation and are less exclusive (i.e., competing standards often exist). This makes additional organizational elements like monitoring and sanctioning more relevant.

The remainder of this chapter is structured into six sections. We begin by discussing the different degrees of partiality of standards. We show that standards can range from extremely partial to (almost) complete organization. We then elaborate on reasons for the partiality of standards as organization. We demonstrate that partiality is sometimes the result of restrictions in the design of standards, whereas, in other cases, it is the result of an explicit choice due to partiality having several distinct advantages. This section is followed by a discussion of possible dynamics between the partiality and completeness of standards. We suggest that there are often pressures for standards to adopt additional organizational elements, and we also suggest that there are sometimes power struggles and conflicts over the adoption of additional elements. We next discuss the dispersed nature of standards as organization, demonstrating that different actors often provide different organizational elements of standards without any central coordination, and how this lack of central coordination has several unintended consequences. We close with a short recapitulation of our argument and an outline of an agenda for future research.

THE DEGREE OF PARTIALITY OF STANDARDS

Organization is a type of decided social order, in which one or more of the following five organizational elements may exist: *rules, hierarchy, membership, monitoring,* and *sanctions.* (See Chapter 1.) Formal organizations possess all five of these elements and can thus be characterized as 'complete' organization: (1) They usually coordinate their activities by issuing rules about what members of the organization are expected to do and not to do; (2) they decide who can join the organization and thus constitute its membership; (3) they assign decision making authority to certain individuals, thereby creating hierarchy (Child, 2005); (4) they often install monitoring mechanisms to ensure compliance with the rules (Weber, 1968); (5) and they contain some form of positive or negative sanctioning mechanism to enforce relevant rules. These five elements can be viewed as the outcome of deliberate decisions. The extent to which they are implemented in any given formal organization remains an empirical question, however. Organization also exists if one or more of these elements is missing. Standards, for instance, exist within the environment of formal organizations, but they use a number of organizational elements.

The distinction between complete and partial organization is not based on a strict dichotomy. Rather, standards (and other forms of decided orders) differ with regard to the number of organizational elements. Some standards have only one element (rules), whereas other standards have all organizational elements and thus reflect complete organization. It can be expected that the degree of partiality of a certain standard can be the outcome of a deliberate choice of the standard setter (e.g., to position the standard vis-à-vis other standards or to respond to criticism from stakeholders). What characterizes standards as forms of partial organization is not merely the existence of a combination of organizational elements, but the fact that these elements have been decided upon, rendering decision 'the most fundamental aspect of

Table 1 *Degrees of Partiality/Completeness of CSR and Corporate Governance Standards*

Organizational Elements	Rules	Rules Hierarchy	Rules Hierarchy Membership	Rules Hierarchy Membership Monitoring	Rules Hierarchy Membership Monitoring Sanction
Example	German Code of Corporate Governance (Berlin Initiative Group)	Global Reporting Initiative	UN Global Compact	Equator Principles	Forest Stewardship Council

organization' (Ahrne & Brunsson, 2011: 85). In the following, we discuss different degrees of partiality in the context of CSR and corporate governance standards. (See Table 1 for an overview.) We do not assume that the different organizational elements necessarily build upon each other, and we also believe that other combinations are possible (e.g., rules, hierarchy, and monitoring). The combinations depicted in Table 1 should be viewed as reflecting typical examples that exist in the area of CSR and corporate governance standards.

Rules

Some CSR and corporate governance standards contain just one organizational element: the rules themselves. In 2000, for example, a group of German academics, consultants, lawyers, and business leaders – the so-called Berlin Initiative Group – drew up a list of corporate governance rules that, they suggested, German corporations should follow voluntarily: the German Code of Corporate Governance (GCCG: www.ecgi.org/codes/documents/gccg_e.pdf). As stated in the preamble to the Code: '[t]he standards of the GCCG should attain authority through the voluntary unilateral application by the company' (p. 5); the rules were not linked to any monitoring and sanctioning, however. Neither did the standard assume any type of membership for those companies that followed the Code. In contrast to the standards discussed in the following section, this standard did not involve either a hierarchy or a governance mechanism: The initiative was established as a temporary group and dissolved after the Code was issued. Even though the standard setters highlighted the necessity of revising the rules contained in the Code from time to time, they left it open as to who should be responsible for that revision. Besides initiatives of this type, we often find that individual academics or consultants issue standards in books or articles (e.g., Pohl & Tolhurst, 2010; Lipton & Lorsch, 1992) without linking them to any other elements of organization.

Rules and hierarchy

In addition to voluntary rules, some standards contain hierarchical elements of steering. 'Hierarchy', in its general sense of the term, refers to the use of 'authority (legitimate power) to create and coordinate a horizontal and vertical division of labor' (Adler, 2001). In the case of standards, hierarchy indicates the existence of an explicit governance mechanism (e.g., a Board) that oversees the creation, maintenance, and adoption of the standard. The Global Reporting Initiative (GRI), for instance, outlines a commonly accepted framework for disclosing social and environmental information to a firm's stakeholders. (See www.globalreporting.org.) The standard is not based on any explicit membership mechanisms; rather, it is free for anyone to use, and the GRI has no control over who uses the framework or in what ways it is used. The GRI does articulate clear rules, however, about what 'good' reporting means in disclosing a firm's social and environmental performance. It also contains an element of hierarchy, as there is a Board of Directors and a Stakeholder Council that make centralized decisions that are relevant for the GRI as a whole. The lack of membership, monitoring, and sanctioning elements can be interpreted as a deliberate choice by the standard setter. After the launch of the first version of the guidelines in 2000, the GRI was interested in the rapid institutionalization of its standard (Etzion & Ferraro, 2010). The inclusion of membership and monitoring as organizational elements would have prevented a swift diffusion of the standard, as these elements would have acted as entry barriers for small and medium-sized enterprises (SMEs) that often lack the financial resources to pay for monitoring.

Rules, hierarchy, and membership

Whereas the GRI remains 'open' in the sense that there is no control over who uses the rules of the standard, other CSR standards deliberately add membership as an organizational element. The UN Global Compact, for example, defines ten principles to which those firms that sign up to the initiative must publicly commit themselves. (See www .unglobalcompact.org.) Being a member of the UN Global Compact comes with certain obligations. The standard expects behaviour from members that is not expected from non-members. For instance, standard adopters are asked to report annually on implementation progress. The UN Global Compact does not monitor the behaviour of its members, however; nor does it contain any direct sanctioning mechanism in the event of non-compliance with the ten principles. The Compact's lack of monitoring and sanctions as organizational elements has been strongly criticized by NGO leaders, who argue that members can easily misuse the standard to 'bluewash' their operations: to wrap their dirty corporate image in the blue UN flag (Rasche, 2009). Yet the absence of monitoring and sanctioning was an explicit strategic choice by the architect of the UN Global Compact, former UN Secretary-General Kofi Annan. When launching the initiative in 2000, Annan knew that, politically speaking, a UN initiative that monitored and sanctioned private businesses would not find support within the UN system (Coleman, 2003) and would not be attractive to smaller firms.

Rules, hierarchy, membership, and monitoring

Some standards use all organizational elements except sanctions. Launched in 2003, the Equator Principles (EPs) reflect a principle-based voluntary risk management standard for assessing and managing social and environmental risks in project finance. (See www.equator-principles.com.) Financial institutions such as banks use the standard. Members must follow the ten principles and report annually on compliance. Principle Nine explicitly demands that participants monitor their compliance with the principles. The standard setter does not conduct the monitoring; rather, it must be organized by participating organizations – through the appointment of an independent consultant, for example. This leaves implementation and monitoring to the discretion and interpretation of each participant (Goetz, 2013). Currently there is no explicit sanctioning mechanism for non-compliance, other than public delisting from the initiative. Again, the mix of organizational elements reflects the standard setter's deliberate decision. The inclusion of the organizational element of harsh sanctions (like legal follow-up in cases of non-compliance) would have lowered the acceptance of the standard among financial institutions. This argument is backed by the analysis of Haack, Schoeneborn, and Wickert (2012), who argue that 'relative ease of adoption has been arguably conducive to the diffusion of the EPs, although adoption possibly meant initially professed rather than actual compliance' (p. 837).

Rules, hierarchy, membership, monitoring, and sanctions

Some CSR standards contain all five organizational elements and could therefore be considered examples of complete organization. It is important to note, however, that the five different organizational elements are usually not performed by a single organizational entity; rather, they are dispersed among several organizations, which, as a whole, comprise the standard. Examples of CSR standards that contain all five organizational elements include the Forest Stewardship Council, Social Accountability 8000, and the Fair Labor Association.

These initiatives are organized in similar ways. (See, for example, Gilbert & Rasche, 2007.) They all contain voluntary rules that guide the behaviour of adopters; they all have centralized decision-making bodies that govern the standard; and they all differentiate clearly between members and non-members. If firms want to use these standards, they must publicly commit to the relevant rules and must usually pay for being associated with the certification standard. In addition, they all monitor the compliance levels of adopters through independent audits. Accredited certification bodies perform the audits, whereas the standard setters determine only the quality criteria that such bodies must meet (Bartley, 2014). Finally, in order to punish members who have violated the rules, they all use sanctions – sanctions that usually take the form of revoked certificates and terminated memberships.

REASONS FOR THE PARTIALITY OF STANDARDS

There are various reasons for the partiality of standards as organization. In many cases, this partiality is the result of a deliberate choice by the standard setters, either because they do not see (or are unable to see) the need to add other organizational elements or because they value the advantages of partiality: legitimacy, accountability, plasticity, flexibility, and the facilitated diffusion of standards (Ahrne *et al.*, 2016: 94–5).

First, partiality can grant *legitimacy* to a standard, and especially to the standard setter. As Brunsson (2000: 23) writes, 'legitimacy is claimed . . . for standardization on the ground that in principle these forms are voluntary'. Standard setters often do not occupy accepted positions of authority that would enable them to issue binding rules for others. In the area of transnational regulation, for example, the regulatory bodies typically have no formal rights to enforce rules vis-à-vis national states and their actors (Ahrne & Brunsson, 2006; Kerwer, 2005). We also find that industry consortia (Leiponen, 2008), private initiatives (Gilbert *et al.*, 2011), and individual actors (Constance & Bonanno, 2000) often attempt to set new rules despite lacking a legal mandate. If the rules were binding, the rule setting would be chal-lenged as illegitimate. By proclaiming rule compliance to be volun-tary, however – by omitting any legal sanctioning of non-compliance – the standard setters can legitimize their activity (Brunsson, 2000: 23). Standard setters typically claim that the rules are in the interests of those who adopt them and that they therefore need to be viewed as legitimate and beneficial for users. In this sense, 'standardization [without formal enforcement] may be regarded as a way of regulating in a situation where there is no legal center of authority' (Jacobsson, 2000: 48). Even where such a centre does exist, however, those who possess formal authority, including states, may delegate rule setting to actors who do not possess the same degree of authority (Brunsson & Jacobsson, 2000: 3). The German government delegated the develop-ment of corporate governance rules to a commission comprising legal experts and representatives of the business world (Werder *et al.*, 2005). As Seidl (2007: 621) observed, issuers of corporate governance codes 'emphasize the voluntariness of the code, arguing that anyone can issue rules as long as they are not binding' (e.g., Ringleb *et al.*, 2004: 51–65).

Second, the partiality of standards can also reduce the *account-ability* of standard setters for the consequences of the rules they issue. By proclaiming standard compliance to be formally voluntary – by leaving out the sanctioning and often omitting the monitoring element – standard setters can shift accountability for the effects of the rules to standard adopters. Adopters thus become answerable for the effects of implementation. As Jacobsson (2000: 46) writes: 'The voluntary aspect – no one is forced to follow a standard – makes it relatively easy for those who draft standards to disclaim responsibil-ity.' Standard setters can do this even when the standards have become de facto binding because, for example, third parties, such as consumers, may base their decisions on how to interact with potential standard adopters on the degree to which those adopters follow the rules. (We discuss this point in the next section) As Kerwer (2005: 622) has pointed out, even when standard followers have no real choice but to adopt the standard, 'it will be hard to hold standard setters accountable because they will deny any responsibility for the fact that their standards have become compulsory'. For instance, the GRI has developed into the de facto standard for CSR reporting over the past fifteen years. Although corporations are often criticized for producing poor reports (Dennis, Connole, & Kraut, 2015), the GRI is not held accountable for the quality of these reports, especially given that it neither monitors nor sanctions the use of the standard.

Third, partiality can increase the *plasticity* of standards. To the extent that sanctioning (and possibly monitoring and membership) is missing, potential adopters have greater freedom in tailoring the standards to their local needs. It is often argued that this helps to avoid the problem of one-size-fits-all: the issuing of rules that need to fit all adopters in the same way. As Rasche (2010a) demonstrated, deviations from the rules established by the standard setters are sometimes unavoidable and even desirable, because rules can never perfectly regulate all possible local particularities. Plasticity also makes it easier for standard setters to devise rules, because they do not have to account for all possible circumstances of application. In some cases, standard setters even explicitly call for their adopters to consider the idiosyncrasies of their situation when deciding whether and in which ways to adopt the standards. This is particularly evident in codes of corporate governance. For example, the official commentary on the GCCG states that the plasticity of the code:

> is meant to prevent companies affected by the code from being corseted into regulations that are too inflexible. Companies should have the possibility of tailoring the modalities of corporate governance to their individual situations and of optimizing them with regard to efficiency criteria.   *(Ringleb et al., 2004: 89; our translation)*

Fourth, the partiality of standards can also increase their *flexibility*, in the sense of making it easier to change the underlying rules. It is often argued that a lack of the elements of monitoring, sanctioning, and membership make it easier and faster for standard setters to modify the rules (Ringleb *et al.*, 2004). On the one hand, standard setters need not be concerned about the consequences of changes to the rules for the design of monitoring and sanctioning processes and for its membership base. On the other hand, because formal voluntariness tends to grant legitimacy to standards, standard setters are not as dependent on complex formal processes to legitimize changes to the rules (Rasche, 2012). This flexibility in rule changing is often one of the main reasons presented for regulating corporate governance through formal, voluntary standards, rather than through binding laws (Gregory, 2003). For example, the Berlin Initiative Group wrote in the preamble to the GCCG that 'the formulation of governance principles in a code below the legal level, offers the advantage of being able to adapt standards more flexibly to altered conditions and fresh experiences by way of forward projection of the code' (p. 4). One could also argue that on a more macro level the absence of monitoring, paired with the absence of hierarchy, facilitates the replacement of one set of standards with another, because actors who are unhappy with existing standards can issue other standards (Brunsson *et al.*, 2012; Rasche, 2010a). Sometimes we also find that different standards co-exist, so that potential adopters can choose between competing initiatives rather than changing the standards (Reinecke *et al.*, 2012).

Finally, partiality can also *facilitate the diffusion* of standards. As indicated, leaving out monitoring and sanctioning elements increases the flexibility of the standard vis-à-vis the idiosyncrasies of its potential adopters. Flexibility increases the fit with potential adopters, and thereby the potential reach of the standard (Seidl, 2007). Not including any formal monitoring and sanctioning mechanisms also makes it possible for potential adopters to experiment with new standards or adopt them only superficially without being held accountable to them. Some studies have shown that this lack of formal enforcement makes standards more attractive to potential adopters (Haack *et al.*, 2012). To the extent that a standard setter is more interested in the diffusion of the standard rather than its regulatory impact, particularly in the first stages of establishing a new standard, the fact that standards are only superficially applied may not be of particular concern. The UN Global Compact, for instance, has deliberately not included monitoring and sanctioning as organizational elements, in order to keep entry barriers low and to ensure the swift diffusion of the standard. The lack of a membership requirement may also contribute to an increased diffusion of a standard, because the introduction of membership requirements limits the reach of a standard to those who are willing to become members (Ahrne *et al.*, 2000), whereas the relinquishing of membership increases the potential reach of standards. Even when membership is open to everyone, the fact that one must first become a member means that greater effort and higher degrees of accountability are involved when adopting the standard (Rasche & Kell, 2010). Typically, membership-based standards also require long-term commitment from members, to ensure that it is not too easy to enter and exit membership repeatedly.

THE DYNAMICS OPERATING BETWEEN THE PARTIALITY AND COMPLETENESS OF STANDARDS

Because standards operate on a continuum between partial and complete forms of organization, there are also significant dynamics between the ends of the continuum. Standard setters often add organizational elements over time, and they have the ability to eliminate elements if, for example, they want to increase the diffusion of the standard. We distinguish between two types of dynamics: (1) those dynamics that occur *between* different types of organizational elements; and (2) those dynamics that occur *within* certain types of organizational elements. We understand partial organization to be a dynamic phenomenon that develops over time.

Dynamics between organizational elements

Standard setters usually experience pressures to adopt more complete forms of organization when their own legitimacy is questioned. Standard setters depend on a high level of perceived legitimacy;

otherwise it would be difficult for them to convince potential adopters that complying with the standard is the right thing to do. The case of the Equator Principles highlights some of the underlying dynamics. (See the more elaborate discussion by Schoeneborn *et al.*, 2012.) The Equator Principles began as a set of rules, with no explicit reference to other organizational elements. Adopters initially saw the high degree of partiality of the standard as a clear advantage. Over time, however, the Equator Principles Association was challenged on moral grounds by various NGOs. The analysis undertaken by Schoeneborn *et al.* (2012) has shown that this criticism was directly linked to the absence of certain organizational elements – above all, those of clear membership rules and a hierarchical governance mechanism. Once the Equator Principles Association realized that these criticisms posed significant constraints on its own legitimacy and therefore its social licence to operate, a strategic review process was initiated to assess whether the introduction of additional organizational elements would be feasible. As a result, other organizational elements were added to the standard; today, the Equator Principles have a clear membership, monitoring requirements, and a certain level of hierarchical steering.

In other cases, standard setters may deliberately choose to begin by including only a few organizational elements, with a view to subsequently ratchetting up the standard by adding certain elements. Working with only a few organizational elements in the beginning is likely to have a positive influence on adoption behaviour. Working without monitoring, sanctioning, or a clearly defined membership structure, for instance, reduces the costs of adoption for interested parties and requires lower levels of commitment, all of which can positively influence the diffusion of standards. The UN Global Compact, for example, started out in 2000 as a CSR standard that drew upon rules, hierarchy, and membership as organizational elements. It was a strategic choice to leave out monitoring and sanctioning. The UN wanted the standard to be somewhat open, in the sense that various types of firms in all countries and sectors could adopt it and in order to meet the UN's demand for inclusiveness and universality (Rasche, 2009). A certifiable standard would have been counterproductive in this context, given that smaller and non-Western firms would have had to bear significant implementation costs. Although these low entry barriers supported a quick diffusion of the standard in the early days, from 2003 onwards the Compact required an annual implementation report from all members. This mandatory report reflects self-monitoring by adopters, with the goal of creating higher levels of transparency (Rasche & Kell, 2010).

It is also possible for standards to move on a pathway towards more partial organization – by excluding certain organizational elements over time, for example. We believe such 'partialization' (Schoeneborn et al., 2012) to be rare in practice, however. Standards that move towards partial organization endanger their perceived legitimacy in the eyes of such external parties as critical NGOs. The exclusion of certain organizational elements (e.g., monitoring or sanctions) from a standard is likely to weaken the enforceability of the underlying rules and can result in lower degrees of output legitimacy (Mena & Palazzo, 2012).

Conflicts often arise as to whether a certain standard should become more or less partial. Different actors prefer different forms of organization, and the final outcome may not perfectly suit all the actors directly or indirectly involved in setting the standard. Conflicts among various parties are particularly likely to arise in the case of standards that are established as multi-stakeholder initiatives. For example, a number of conflicts have arisen in the Forest Stewardship Council about the Council's underlying rules and about the choice of relevant enforcement practices, and these conflicts have led to the withdrawal of some NGO supporters from the standard (Moog, Spicer, & Böhm, 2015). The development of a standard typically involves struggles over whether certain organizational elements should be added at all and how certain organizational elements should be defined (e.g., the specificity of the underlying rules). Schouten and Glasbergen (2012), for example, have demonstrated how different organizers in the context of the Roundtable for Sustainable Palm Oil were unable to agree on ways of conceptualizing the link between palm oil production and poverty. Such conflicts are often an outcome of the different ideologies of organizers, as when unions, which are traditionally sceptical of voluntary CSR, and corporations, which favour non-binding agreements, meet within the context of a single standard.

Dynamics within organizational elements

It is also possible for the design of certain organizational elements within standards to change over time and create pressures to develop more complete or more partial organization. Returning to the example of the UN Global Compact's mandatory requirement to submit an annual implementation report, this requirement was initially implemented such that all submitted reports were simply acknowledged by the UN as long as they met certain minimum criteria, regardless of their underlying quality (Rasche *et al.*, 2013). Some of the larger companies that already had advanced CSR reporting in place and had submitted more comprehensive reports than had many of the smaller firms started to complain about the lack of differentiation and the one-size-fits-all approach to reporting. The UN Global Compact responded to this criticism in 2010 by introducing a differentiation framework that placed participants in categories – learner, active, advanced, and LEAD – depending on the quality of their report. This example shows that the standard moved from a relatively simple to a more fine-grained and contextualized model of self-monitoring. This change in monitoring was accompanied by a change in membership rules, whereby participants could not simply enter into the LEAD category, even if they fulfilled the formal requirements, but had to be invited by the Compact. In addition, LEAD participants had to pay a membership fee, whereas participants in the other categories could use the standard free of charge. Interestingly, this created a self-selection mechanism, as only relatively large companies with sufficient financial resources could enter the LEAD category.

THE DISPERSED ORGANIZATION OF STANDARDS

As discussed in the preceding sections, standards are often partial, to the extent that they contain only some of the five elements of organization. Beyond this, they are often partial in another sense: Different organizational actors provide different elements, without any central coordination between these elements. In other words, standards often represent a dispersed form of organization. Some scholars speak of so-called third parties (Brunsson & Jacobsson, 2000a) – parties beyond the standard setters and standard followers who become involved by providing specific organizational elements. There is often one body that issues the rules, for example, another that monitors compliance, and a third that sanctions deviations from the rules (Kerwer, 2005; Hülsse & Kerwer, 2007).

In some cases, standard setters explicitly encourage certain actors to contribute other organizational elements. For example, standard setters often set up separate organizations that monitor and certify compliance with the rules. Kerwer (2005: 618) highlights how 'there are private firms, which by auditing and certifying compliance with a certain standard, act as a deliberately designed monitoring structure'. Fairtrade International (FLO) and the Marine Stewardship Council (MSC) both collaborate with independent certification bodies to monitor compliance with their standards (Abbott, Levi-Faur, & Snidal, 2017; Auld & Renckens, 2017; Loconto, 2017). In other cases, the standard setters expect adopters to engage in self-regulation – to monitor their own compliance with the rules. The issuers of the GCCG, for example, stress that adopters must publicly declare each year which rules they have followed. As the issuers write on the Code's website (www.dcgk.de/en/home.html): 'The recommendations and suggestions are not mandatory. However, deviations from the recommendations – not the suggestions – have to be explained and disclosed with the annual declaration of conformity (Comply or Explain).' This self-monitoring function is, in itself, part of statutory law. The sanctioning function, in turn, should be accomplished by shareholders who are expected to base their decisions on whether to buy or sell the stocks of the respective company on the degree of a company's conformity with the code. As Seidl (2008) wrote:

> Unjustified deviations from the code provisions are expected to be 'sanctioned' through negative share-price reactions. It is assumed that shareholders will take the level of compliance into consideration when they make a decision to buy, sell, hold, or vote. Accordingly, unjustified deviations from code provisions that appear significant to shareholders are expected to result in lower share prices. *(Seidl 2008: 623; see also Gregory, 2003: 68–9)*

In this case, the sanctioning appears highly dispersed, as the overall sanction – the share price reaction – is a result of the decisions of multiple actors.

Actors other than the standard setter may also add other elements of organization. In some cases, associations require their members to follow particular standards set by bodies external to the association, as when certain industry associations expect their members to follow specific CSR standards. Sometimes we also find that a standard's governance body is established in such a way that it is independent from the actors who issued the standards. Temporary committees of experts have instituted numerous national corporate governance standards. The Cadbury Committee was formed temporarily to develop standards for corporate governance in the UK, for instance (Spira & Slinn, 2013), but it was not part of the London Stock Exchange as the relevant governing body for the code.

The dispersed nature of organization is particularly relevant in the context of global governance. Here we witness a relatively low degree of decided order (Ahrne & Brunsson, 2011: 100), as neither nation states (the jurisdictions of which are territorially bound) nor international organizations (which usually depend on nation states for implementation) can set adequate rules (Scherer *et al.*, 2016). Multinational corporations often work in a regulatory vacuum, and standards are increasingly filling this vacuum. The dynamics that exist within and between organizational elements are helpful in this .context, because they allow standard setters to find the right mix of elements when trying to regulate issues across borders. Regulating social and environmental conditions in global value chains is difficult for a single organizational actor to achieve. Global standard setters often collaborate with local or regional actors (e.g., certification bodies and consultants) in order to enforce a standard. Some scholars have noted that monitoring requires knowledge of the local business environment, the customs, traditions, and local norms rendering it necessary to understand monitoring as a participatory process in which local and regional actors interact with global standard setters (Hale & Opondo, 2005).

Although standard setters often specify which organizational actors should provide additional organizational elements, we sometimes find that some actors simply start to provide organizational elements of their own accord and without any coordination. After the publication of the GCCG, for example, one financial magazine began to monitor levels of compliance with the rules, awarding prizes to organizations that demonstrated high levels of compliance and offering a platform for naming and shaming those that deviated significantly from the code provisions. The UN Global Compact experienced a similar situation. After it was announced that the standard would require mandatory annual reports from all adopters, but that the UN would not monitor these reports, an alliance of NGOs decided to expose cases in which participants did not live up to the underlying rules. This 'social vetting' mechanism proved difficult to sustain, however, as the negative impact of naming and shaming was limited.

The dispersed organization of standards has both advantages and disadvantages. The possibility of capitalizing on different competencies is one significant advantage of separating organizational functions among various actors. Many standard setters may be good at developing rules but do not have the competencies and capacities to monitor or even sanction deviations from those rules. Monitoring is known to be a complicated and resource-intensive process that requires expert knowledge and experience, but standard setters in the areas of CSR and corporate governance are often newly created entities lacking both experience and financial and non-financial resources. Separating organizational functions among different actors can also increase the flexibility and responsiveness of standards, particularly when facing specific local contingencies. By having compliance monitored and sanctioned by local actors (e.g., by shareholders in the case of corporate governance codes), for example, the local context can better be taken into account. In addition, dispersed organization may often be the only way to ensure that other organizational elements are enacted when the code issuers themselves lack the necessary formal authority. The dispersed organization of standards is beneficial in some cases, because there is a need for actors who provide additional organizational elements to be independent of the standard setter. For example, in order for monitoring to be truly effective, it is important that relevant organizational actors be independent of the standard setter and the adopter (Abbott *et al.*, 2016).

There are also disadvantages to the dispersed organization of standards. Most importantly, dispersed organization often has unintended consequences, to the extent that the actors who add other organizational elements do not share the same intentions or understandings as the standard setters. Actors who monitor or sanction the degree of standard adoption, for example, often undermine the intended plasticity of the rules (Seidl, 2007; Brunsson & Jacobsson, 2000a). The dispersed organization of standards can thus lead to an uncontrolled drift in the meaning of the underlying rules (Seidl, 2007). In this respect, Kerwer (2005: 618) has noted that dispersed organization 'can result in complex, unplanned control structures'. Separating organizational elements can also undermine accountability for any consequences – or lack of consequences – that standards create. Once third parties are involved, it becomes more difficult to judge which actor can be assigned responsibility for the (lack of) functioning of a standard. Standards may lack impact because of poor monitoring, poor sanctioning, and/or poorly defined rules. When organizational elements are dispersed, it can be difficult to assign accountability clearly. Adding organizational actors can also make a standard more easily subject to regulatory capture. Adopters often lobby for the inclusion of third parties (e.g., monitoring organizations) within the overall organization of a standard. Their inclusion can lead to regulatory capture, as adopters may find it easier to influence third parties (e.g., to soften rule implementation) or to use third parties as a channel for recommending rule changes to the standard setter (see Abbott *et al.*, 2016).

REFERENCES

Abbott, K., Levi-Faur, D., & Snidal, D. (2017) Theorizing Regulatory Intermediaries: The RIT Model. *Annals of the American Academy of Political and Social Science* 670(1): 14–35.

Adler, P. S. (2001) Market, Hierarchy, and Trust: The Knowledge Economy and the Future of Capitalism. *Organization Science* 12(2): 215–34.

Aguilera, R. & Cuervo-Cazurra, A. (2004) Codes of Good Governance Worldwide: What Is the Trigger? *Organization Studies* 25(3): 415–44.

Ahrne, G. & Brunsson, N. (2006) Organizing the World. In M.-L. Djelic and K. Sahlin-Andersson (eds.), *Transnational Governance: Institutional Dynamics of Regulation*. Cambridge: Cambridge University Press. 74–94.

Ahrne, G. & Brunsson, N. (2011) Organization Outside Organizations: The Significance of Partial Organization. *Organization* 18(1): 83–104.

Ahrne, G., Brunsson, N., & Garsten, Ch. (2000) Standardizing through Organization. In N. Brunsson and B. Jacobsson (eds.), *A World of Standards*. Oxford/New York: Oxford University Press. 50–68.

Ahrne, G., Brunsson, N., & Seidl, D. (2016) Resurrecting Organization by Going beyond Organizations. *European Management Journal* 34(2): 93–101.

Auld, G. & Renckens, S. (2017) Rule-Making Feedbacks through Intermediation and Evaluation in Transnational Private Governance. *The Annals of the American Academy of Political and Social Science* 670(1): 93–111.

Bartley, T. (2014) Transnational Governance and the Re-Centered State: Sustainability or Legality? *Regulation & Governance* 8(1): 93–109.

Brunsson, N. (2000) Organizations, Markets, and Standards. In N. Brunsson and B. Jacobsson (eds.), *A World of Standards*. Oxford/New York: Oxford University Press. 21–39.

Brunsson, N. and Jacobsson, B. (eds.) (2000a) *A World of Standards*. Oxford/New York: Oxford University Press.

Brunsson, N. & Jacobsson, B. (2000b) The Contemporary Expansion of Standardization. In N. Brunsson and B. Jacobsson (eds.), *A World of Standards*. Oxford/New York: Oxford University Press. 1–17.

Brunsson, N., Rasche, A., & Seidl, D. (2012) The Dynamics of Standardization: Three Perspectives on Standards in Organization Studies. *Organization Studies* 33(5–6): 613–32.

Child, J. (2005) *Organization: Contemporary Principles and Practice*. Malden: Blackwell.

Coleman, D. (2003) The United Nations and Transnational Corporations: From an Inter-Nation to a 'Beyond-State' Model of Engagement. *Global Society* 17(4): 339–57.

Constance, D. H. & Bonanno, A. (2000) Regulating the Global Fisheries: The World Wildlife Fund, Unilever, and the Marine Stewardship Council. *Agriculture and Human Values* 17(2): 125–39.

Dennis, P., Connole, H., & Kraut, M. (2015) The Efficacy of Voluntary Disclosure: A Study of Water Disclosures by Mining Companies Using the Global Reporting Initiative Framework. *Journal of Legal, Ethical & Regulatory Issues* 18(2): 87–106.

Egyedi, T. M. & Blind, K. (2008) *The Dynamics of Standards*. Cheltenham: Edward Elgar.

Etzion, D. & Ferraro, F. (2010) The Role of Analogy in the Institutionalization of Sustainability Reporting. *Organization Science* 21(5): 1092–107.

Farrell, J. & Saloner, G. (1988) Coordination through Committees and Markets. *RAND Journal of Economics* 19(2): 235–52.

Gilbert, D. U. & Rasche, A. (2007) Discourse Ethics and Social Accountability: The Ethics of SA 8000. *Business Ethics Quarterly* 17(2): 187–216.

Gilbert, D. U., Rasche, A., & Waddock, S. (2011) Accountability in a Global Economy: The Emergence of International Accountability Standards. *Business Ethics Quarterly* 21(1): 23–44.

Goetz, A. (2013) Private Governance and Land Grabbing: The Equator Principles and the Roundtable on Sustainable Biofuels. *Globalizations* 10(1): 199–204.

Gregory, H. J. (2003) *International Comparison of Selected Corporate Governance Guidelines and Codes of Best Practice*. New York: Weil, Gotshal & Manges LLP.

Haack, P., Schoeneborn, D., & Wickert, C. (2012) Talking the Talk, Moral Entrapment, Creeping Commitment? Exploring Narrative Dynamics in Corporate Responsibility Standardization. *Organization Studies* 33(5/6): 815–45.

Hale, A. & Opondo, M. (2005) Humanising the Cut Flower Chain: Confronting the Realities of Flower Production for Workers in Kenya. *Antipode* 37(2): 301–23.

Haxhi, I. & van Ees, H. (2010) Explaining Diversity in the Worldwide Diffusion of Codes of Good Governance. *Journal of International Business Studies* 41(4): 710–26.

Hülsse, R. and Kerwer, D. (2007) Global Standards in Action: Insights from Anti-Money Laundering Regulation. *Organization* 14(5): 625–42.

Jacobsson, B. (2000) Standardization and Expert Knowledge. In N. Brunsson and B. Jacobsson (eds.), *A World of Standards*. Oxford: Oxford University Press. 40–9.

Kerwer, D. (2005) Rules That Many Use: Standards and Global Regulation. *Governance* 18(4): 611–32.

Leiponen, A. E. (2008) Competing Through Cooperation: The Organization of Standard Setting in Wireless Telecommunications. *Management Science* 54 (11): 1904–19.

Lipton, M. & Lorsch, J. W. (1992) A Modest Proposal for Improved Corporate Governance. *The Business Lawyer* 48(1): 59–77.

Loconto, A. M. (2017) Models of Assurance: Diversity and Standardization of Modes of Intermediation. *The Annals of the American Academy of Political and Social Science* 670(1): 112–132.

Mena, S. & Palazzo, G. (2012) Input and Output Legitimacy of Multi-Stakeholder Initiatives. *Business Ethics Quarterly* 22(3): 527–56.

Moog, S, Spicer, A., & Böhm, S. (2015) The Politics of Multi-Stakeholder Initiatives: The Crisis of the Forest Stewardship Council. *Journal of Business Ethics* 128(3): 469–93.

Pohl, M. & Tolhurst, N. (2010) *Responsible Business: How to Manage a CSR Strategy Successfully*. Chichester: John Wiley & Sons.

Rasche, A. (2009) 'A Necessary Supplement' What the United Nations Global Compact Is and Is Not. *Business & Society* 48(4): 511–37.

Rasche, A. (2010a) Collaborative Governance 2.0. *Corporate Governance: The International Journal for Business in Society* 10: 500–11.

Rasche, A. (2010b) The Limits of Corporate Responsibility Standards. *Business Ethics: A European Review* 19(3): 280–91.

Rasche, A. (2012) Global Policies and Local Practice: Loose and Tight Couplings in Multi-Stakeholder Initiatives. *Business Ethics Quarterly* 22(4): 679–708.

Rasche, A. & Kell, G. (2010) *The United Nations Global Compact: Achievements, Trends and Challenges.* Cambridge/New York: Cambridge University Press.

Rasche, A., Waddock, S., & McIntosh, M. (2013) The United Nations Global Compact: Retrospect and Prospect. *Business & Society* 52(1): 6–30.

Reinecke, J., Manning, S., & von Hagen, O. (2012) The Emergence of a Standards Market: Multiplicity of Sustainability Standards in the Global Coffee Industry. *Organization Studies* 33(5/6): 791–814.

Ringleb, H. M., Kremer, Th., Lutter, M., & Werder, A. von (2004) *Kommentar zum Deutschen Corporate Governance Kodex.* München: Beck.

Scherer, A. G., Rasche, A., Palazzo, G., & Spicer, A. (2016) Managing for Political Corporate Social Responsibility: New Challenges and Directions for PCSR 2.0. *Journal of Management Studies* 53(3): 273–98.

Schouten, G. & Glasbergen, P. (2012) Private Multi-Stakeholder Governance in the Agricultural Market Place: An Analysis of Legitimization Processes of the Roundtables on Sustainable Palm Oil and Responsible Soy. *International Food and Agribusiness Management Review* 15(B): 63–88.

Schoeneborn, D., Haack, P., & Kuhn, T. R. (2012) The Communicative Constitution of Partial Organizations in the Global Realm. Paper presented at the Academy of Management Meeting, August 3–7, Boston, MA.

Seidl, D. (2007) Standard Setting and Following in Corporate Governance: An Observation-Theoretical Study of the Effectiveness of Governance Codes. *Organization* 14(5): 705–27.

Spira, L. F. & Slinn, J. (2013) *The Cadbury Committee: A History.* Oxford: Oxford University Press.

Timmermans, S. & Epstein, S. (2010) A World of Standards but Not a Standard World: Toward a Sociology of Standards and Standardization. *Annual Review of Sociology* 36: 69–89.

Weber, M. (1968) *Economy and Society.* Berkeley: University of California Press.

Werder, A. von, Talaulicar, T., & Kolat, G. L. (2005) Compliance with the German Corporate Governance Code: An Empirical Analysis of the Compliance Statements by German Listed Companies. *Corporate Governance: An International Review* 13(2): 178.

3 Prizes and the Organization of Status

Peter Edlund, Josef Pallas, and Linda Wedlin

A major foundation of social life rests on the need for approval (e.g., Goode, 1978; Henrich & Gil-White, 2001). Although approval can be given or achieved in many ways, we focus in this chapter on the role and function of prizes as a way of organizing approval.

Prizes are ubiquitous today. Consider, for example, the 37th edition of *Awards, Honors & Prizes*, a directory listing more than 24,000 prizes from over 130 countries (Gale, 2008). This is, presumably, only the tip of the iceberg. Keeping track of the continuous expansion of more and more prizes in virtually every area of social life would seem to be an impossible task. We are, in the words of Best (2008: 1), witnessing a 'prize proliferation'.

The spread of prizes has received a great deal of scholarly attention. Sociologists have focused on the diffusion of prizes into such previously sacred areas of social life as the arts, sculpture, and architecture, noting the attention commanded by prizes and arguing that they are significant drivers of an increasingly commercialized aesthetic realm (e.g., Best, 2008; English, 2005; Street, 2005). Economists (e.g., Frey & Neckermann, 2009; Nalebuff & Stiglitz, 1983) have examined the rapid expansion of prizes within the private sector, viewing prizes as common incentive tools with which to raise the extrinsic motivation and, ultimately, the performance of employees in firms. And management theorists (e.g., Schein, 2010; Trice & Beyer, 1984) have, in a slightly different approach, analysed prizes as parts of 'cultural toolboxes' that leaders increasingly use to steer the values, beliefs, and perceptions of subordinates.

Pointing to the potential disciplining effects of prizes, previous research has not focused extensively on the factors that produce those effects and on the unintentional effects that may follow from the proliferation of prizes. An alternative way of understanding prizes and their implications is to approach them as a form of partial organization. Partial organization is referred to here as elements that structure relationships among individuals, groups, and/or organizations in social life. From this perspective, prizes are one way in which approval procedures are organized, using one or more of the organizational elements discussed in this volume. A basis for this view is that prizes are based on decisions – decisions about who or what is worthy of approval. Based on these decisions, prizes constitute a sanctioning mechanism that primarily provides positive sanctions to actors in the form of awards. Prizes represent instances in which individuals, groups, or organizations receive positive recognition. Although prizes could potentially provide negative sanctions as well – when used to point out bad performances or characteristics – these types of prizes appear much less prevalent.

The proliferation of prizes can be understood in relation to the emergence of a so-called 'audit society' (Power, 1997, 2007), in which public measures of performance have become increasingly popular and influential ways of handling uncertainties. Performance measurements of various kinds have come to be influential means of monitoring, comparing, and positioning individuals, groups, and organizations against each other or against pre-set criteria. As organizational mechanisms providing positive sanctions, prizes are similar to but distinct from other such mechanisms. Setting standards, as discussed in Chapter 2, relies extensively on the use of rules and the principles of rule setting as ways of ordering social relations. Although standards can also make use of and be interrelated to sanctioning, it appears that those sanctions are more often negative: a fine for not complying with rules or a revoking of previously awarded certificates. (See Chapter 2.) Another mechanism closely related to a prize is a ranking that appears to provide positive sanctions in a similar way: recognition of and approval to those achieving a top-ranking position. Unlike prizes, however, rankings render fine-grained orders of many individuals, groups, and/or organizations positioned in relation to each other;

they have significant effects for the lower-ranked actors as well (Wedlin, 2006; cf. Sauder & Espeland, 2009). Because prizes direct the attention to one or a few winners, it is the behaviours and characteristics of those individuals, groups, or organizations that are celebrated. This is the winner-take-all aspect of prizes (cf. Frank & Cook, 1995).

Our aim in this chapter is to explore the characteristics and effects of prizes as partial organization. How do prizes create approval? What are some of the potential outcomes? We use prizes in the field of science as empirical examples to address our questions and compare them with sports prizes. Science prizes have been around since the Enlightenment, but the number and size of these prizes has grown exponentially over the past ten years (e.g., Brumfiel, 2012; Merali, 2013). Prizes in sports are well known and ubiquitous, and provide a solid comparative ground for illustrating the varying characteristics of prizes and their effects.

Contrasting examples from sports and science help us to elaborate on the use of different organizational elements and the degree of organization of prizes and to discuss the implications of these variations. Our chapter is organized into three main sections. First, we elaborate on the distinct characteristics of prizes and what sets them apart from other ways of signalling approval. Second, we discuss variations in the way prizes are organized and make use of organization elements. Third, we discuss some potential implications of the varying forms of organization identified in different prizes and prize-giving procedures. We end the chapter with some concluding points on prizes as partial organization.

PRIZES: PUBLICLY COMMUNICATED DECISIONS OF APPROVAL

Acts of deference in everyday life, such as compliments or praise, are largely spontaneous gestures of approval. They normally take place in private, in a relationship between two parties – a giver and a receiver. Such general acts of praise may or may not be planned, but they are generally not communicated to others in advance. Imagine hearing that a colleague is going to be complimented by the boss on Wednesday next week. Most of us would probably react with suspicion. In clear contrast, prizes represent a form of approval distinct from these more everyday forms. This example suggests that at least three characteristics of prizes make them different: They are decided; they are communicated to others; and they are normally planned in advance. We now elaborate on these three features in order to set the frame for understanding prizes as partial organization.

Prizes are based on decisions. Prizes consist of decisions aimed at distinguishing behaviours and characteristics that are worthy of deference (cf. Allen & Lincoln, 2004; Goode, 1978). The decision to award a prize is commonly made by an assigned organization, group, or subgroup, such as a jury or an appointed judge. The distinctions produced by the decisions involved in awarding a prize are, however, embedded to varying degrees in social life: According to Bourdieu (1991: 120), the 'most efficacious socially are those which give the appearance of being based on objective differences'. This would clearly seem to be the case for distinctions that have, over time, become ingrained into the fabric of social life. Bourdieu (1991) referred to them as 'rites of institution'. But prizes seldom, if ever, reach the stage of becoming 'objective' distinctions. Decisions are at the root of prizes, and decisions also mean that there are options to the paths of actions that have been chosen in specific situations. Thus, prizes inherently communicate their own contingency (Luhmann, 2000; Seidl, 2006).

The decision to bestow approval to somebody or something through a prize has to become known; it has to be *communicated to others*. Unlike such everyday acts of approval as compliments, the decision to award someone a prize is communicated not only to the receiver of the prize, but also to a third party – an audience – thereby affecting the status of the receiver. From the works of Speier (1935) and Goode (1978) on status and the status-conferring processes involved in prizes, we know that status exists through public acts of deference. Speier (1935: 74–6) argued that there had to be bestowers, bearers, and observers, and Goode (1978: 13) similarly emphasized the role of others – persons and groups or communities providing status through prizes. Whereas status may be but one potential outcome of prizes and the approval procedures involved in prize giving, we note that the potential benefits of receiving a prize require the involvement of an audience that can place value on the act of approval. Both Speier (1935) and Goode (1978) suggest that a certain degree of consensus among givers, recipients, and audiences for the behaviours or characteristics worthy of deference enhances the likelihood of status being conferred through a prize. This means that less status is likely to follow from a prize when the audience does not value or care about the activities or features being recognized.

A third central feature of prizes is that the result of the decision tends to be *presented on specifically organized formal occasions*, such as ceremonies or award galas, often in conjunction with public announcements. To underline the worth ascribed to the decision to approve or appraise certain behaviours and characteristics, prizes thus draw on facets from rituals – the 'periodic events removed in some culturally well-defined way' (Appadurai, 1986: 21), or a kind of 'social magic' that 'produces discontinuity out of continuity' (Bourdieu, 1991: 120). In this way, prize givers seek to pause the flow of social life, hoping to catch the attention of possible recipients and the audience or audiences. The ritualistic aspects of prizes often take the form of more or less elaborate and pompous ceremonies, organized so as to celebrate the behaviours and characteristics of recipients publicly.

VARIATIONS IN THE ORGANIZATION OF PRIZES

Although we have outlined some common features of prizes, at least in their most distinct form, prizes may also vary in the way they are organized and how decisions are made and communicated. This variation has implications for the capacity of prizes to influence the social order of which they are a part. In this section, we explore three of the dimensions on which prizes can vary: the uses of rules, membership, and communication of prizes and prize decisions.

The use of rules

A central dimension in the variation of prizes is connected to the way the decisions are made: the decision to award a prize and the decision about who should receive it. We consider such decisions to be rule based – that there are explicit criteria for deciding what is to be awarded and who is the winner. These rules can be either highly detailed or more vague in their articulation and execution. Vagueness leaves room for some degree of subjectivity in determining who can be considered for a prize, what is recognized as good performance, and who or what decides on the winner of the prize. To illustrate this variation, we turn to the case of prizes in science and sports.

The field of science has relatively few specific rules for what constitutes a good performance and what makes a prominent scientist – at least few generally accepted and acknowledged rules. Such rules vary among scientific fields (Whitley, 2000), and are likely to be dependent upon context and time. Science is characterized by plentiful measures and standards of performance, including prizes, the most prominent of which are the Nobel Prizes. They have the 'unique distinction of being regarded as the supreme symbol of scientific excellence not only by the general public but by scientists as well' (Zuckerman, 1978: 420). The Nobel Prizes thus serve both a scientific audience and the general public.

There are no rules or specific criteria for what shall be awarded a Nobel Prize. Nobel Prizes celebrate activities that have 'contributed the greatest benefit to mankind' (Nobel Prize, 2017a), but any further principles or potential rules remain unspecified. Lack of specificity opens the door for the awarding body to make a decision, but also leaves room for audiences to contest or refute the decision. The Nobel Prize in Economics[1] serves as an example of such debates. In 1976, Milton Friedman received the prize for his work on consumption, monetary history, and stabilization policy (Nobel Prize, 2017b). The decision stirred a mixture of feelings: It was openly supported by the International Monetary Fund and the World Bank, but strongly opposed by leftist organizations throughout Europe and the USA (Cohen, 2008). Because there are no rules to make the Nobel decisions indisputable, audiences know that the prizes *could* be given to someone other than the eventual recipients. This gives the Nobel Prize a certain aura of mystery.

In contrast to the field of science, sports appear to be an area of social life with many examples of clear and explicit rules for prize giving and other means of status competition. In many sports, we find rules for what constitutes a good performance and a good athlete. Sports are organized mainly through sports events that involve competition, with set rules for who can compete, what they compete on, and who is the winner (Brunsson & Wedlin, 2018). Runners, long-jumpers, and tennis players could be expected to have a strong grasp of the rules in the races, heats, and matches they enter. Prizes follow from the competition, and it is relatively easy for all involved, including the audiences, to judge the performances and the results. Because of the precise rules of the competition, then, competitors, prize givers, and audiences have already figured out who the winners are by the time the prize is awarded. One of the implications is that the drama is removed from the prize giving and is located in the competition as such, rendering the process less mysterious.

The use of membership

Related to the setting of rules is the extent to which prize giving is dependent on decisions related to membership. Membership is thus another organizational element that can be used more or less extensively in the prize-awarding process. In the most extreme case, the awarding of a prize is completely dependent on being a member of the organization giving the prize or a member of a group otherwise specified.

We find examples in science of both membership requirement and no membership requirement. The European Commission (EC), for example, awards the Descartes Prize to projects and researchers that have made 'Outstanding Scientific and Technological Achievements Resulting from European Collaborative Research'. This prize has been awarded since 2000 by the EC to researchers who work in public–private consortia within the frameworks of their collaborative projects' funding schemes (EC, 2006). Thus, only research team members of the specific funding programme of the EC can win the prize. The Nobel Prizes, on the other hand, have no obvious membership criteria for their awards.

With the lack of membership-based criteria for awarding a prize comes the question of how potential prize recipients are to be identified? With membership, the basis for selection is relatively clear, but without that criterion, the scope for who could potentially be a winner is much greater. Here the relationship to other mechanisms that provide approval or recognition, such as other prizes, may play a role. Many organizational mechanisms exist in the field of science for counting academic publications or citations as measures of performance, including the Clarivate Analytics ranking lists of highly cited researchers and such professional or popular bibliometric mechanisms as Google Scholar or Microsoft Academic (Adler & Harzing, 2009) – measures that could potentially be used for the selection of candidates. Membership in scholarly networks, societies, academies of science, and other professional organizations also help to form perceptions of elite scientists (Engwall, 2015). From what is known of the prize decisions, these other forms of status organization appear to have little direct connection to the Nobel Prizes, however, although the decisions of the Nobel committees and the considerations involved in their decisions become public only fifty years after the decision has been made (Feldman, 2001). We can assume, however, that the Nobel Prizes in science are relatively independent of membership in other evaluating and measuring bodies and processes in which academics acquire their status. This limited dependency is another factor that renders the nomination and selection of winners and the entire competition shrouded in a bit of mystery.

In contrast, winners in many areas of sports are intimately linked to several decisions made in such contexts as world cups, leagues, and tournaments. Decisions made in these contexts create not only necessary conditions for status competition, but decisions also become interlinked with each other, thereby embedding sport prizes in other decisions. Membership is a common decision base in these competitions. Almost all sports are organized in national and international meta-organizations that set many of the rules for competition (Brunsson & Wedlin, 2018), and membership in these organizations is, in most cases, a necessity. Performance in previous competitions may limit the possibility of entering other competitions. The UEFA Champions League nicely illustrates this membership. Winners of national leagues are invited to participate in international leagues. But there are other conditions (see Article 3 in UEFA's 2017 regulations) that decide who else can or cannot join the competition. Similarly, there are three ways of determining who can play tennis in the major Grand Slam tournaments: rankings, qualifying, and wildcards. It is a system set by the International Tennis Federation, but in which each tournament utilizes its own merit-based system (Paragraph G, Article 1 in the Grand Slam's 2017 official regulation).

As with rules, when it comes to membership, we can locate prizes on a continuum ranging from (1) having little or no reliance on membership or being relatively independent of other forms of competition to (2) dependence on membership or being relatively dependent on being connected (by way of rule-generating membership) to other forms for organization competition and to other prize-giving attempts. The greater the use of membership, the less mysterious the prize appears to be.

What is communicated? Prizes may also vary in the amount of information provided in connection to the prize decision – to audiences and to potential (and real) prize recipients – in terms of offering more or less transparent accounts of what has been decided, on what basis, and to whom. In some cases, only the final decision is communicated, making the prize-giving process relatively opaque. Take the example of the Nobel Prize: Nominations are kept secret, as are discussions about the final candidates and the rationale for making a particular decision. Although the Nobel Prizes appear particularly noteworthy in this respect, other prizes in science are relatively opaque and mysterious. The new Breakthrough Prize, established in 2012 by Google co-founder Sergey Brin, social media investor Yuri Milner, and Facebook co-founder and CEO Mark Zuckerberg is also silent on the rationale for decisions and the selection of candidates. The prize represented a complement to the Nobel Prizes, in an attempt to acknowledge many significant discoveries and contributions that go unnoticed in the field of physics and life sciences (Brumfiel, 2012). Unlike the Noble Prizes, the nominations are publicly communicated, opening some space for audiences to make their own judgment of candidates and their performances.

In other cases, the decisions, the rules for participation and evaluation, and, in some cases, the specific rationales behind the decision are communicated. Examples from the world of sports, where the use of rules is abundant, seem appropriate here. In soccer, the decisions and the rules by which the referee makes decisions are clear, explicit, and communicated, and the prize competition is therefore transparent. Decisions about which team wins are rarely contested: The team that scores the most goals is the winner. There may be other decisions involved that can be contested, however: the referee's decisions about fair play made during the game, what is accepted as a goal, and whether the rules of the game have been followed. In some sports, such as figure skating, the judges' decisions are more prominent, and are more influential in the decision about the winner. In this case, the criteria for decisions are less well communicated, at least to the audience, and the prize can be described as somewhat less transparent (Zitzewitz, 2006). Decisions are often debated long and hard by the audience and the sports journalists. In both soccer and figure skating, however, there are extensive rules and membership criteria for competition, and they are communicated to a greater extent than for many other prizes. This influences whether the prize is perceived as formal, rational, and just. The aura of mystery thus decreases with the increase in communication of the rules and criteria limiting the decision.

Another aspect of communication in connection with prizes is *how* the prize and the final decision of a winner are communicated. The goal is often for the prize and the prize-giving organization to become known and widely accepted by one or more audiences of a prize. Such recognition is important for the legitimacy of the prize and acceptance for the decisions behind it.

Looking at the Breakthrough Prize and the Nobel Prizes, money and tradition appear to be two obvious ways that these prizes gain legitimacy and acceptance. The Breakthroughs' founders have used large economic clout as one of their arguments for legitimacy, with a purse containing more than USD 25 million (~EUR 20.3 million) (*New York Times*, 2015) for the three categories. In comparison, the Nobel Prize currently awards 'only' USD 1 million (~EUR 822,000) for each prize category, and this amount is often shared among several recipients (e.g., Johansson & Zemlianichenko, 2014; Merali, 2013). The generous monetary rewards associated with the Breakthrough Prize have, however, been met with some degree of suspicion in the scientific community. It has been suggested that the prizes are nothing more than attempts at strengthening the 'personal brands' of Brin, Milner, and Zuckerberg and that the Breakthroughs, being connected to Google, Facebook, and other social large media companies, are inherently riddled with conflicts of interest. Thus it seems as if large purses would not in themselves be conducive to audience acceptance. In the case of the Nobel Prize, in contrast, money as a source of legitimacy is downplayed. The Nobel Assembly argues that the 'Nobel legacy' is enough to make their prizes the most important in science. 'We have a steady place in the boat', as Lars Bergström, Secretary in the Nobel Physics Committee, put it. 'We have the tradition, the others do not have it' (Bergström, as quoted in Johansson & Zemlianichenko, 2014).

Although money and tradition may be most important for those immediately concerned, perhaps particularly for potential prize recipients, other means for gaining recognition from a wider audience are often performed. This involves a process of popularization (Pallas, Wedlin, & Grünberg, 2016), which often means creating or connecting prizes to rituals (Couldry, 2003) and creating media attention for the prize and the winners (Friedman, Dunwoody, & Rogers, 1999). Media can also be involved in the specific organization of prizes and the accompanying rituals of prize giving.

Our two examples of prizes in science share the ritualistic aspects of large award ceremonies involving media actors and continuous efforts to attract attention to the prize, aiming to elicit positive responses towards the behaviours and characteristics of prize recipients (cf. Fombrun & Van Riel, 2004). The Nobel Prize uses the legacy of Alfred Nobel, the Swedish Royal family, and other means of connecting the prize to tradition and authority and organizes public lectures, speeches, and other events during Nobel week to celebrate and recognize the activities and the characteristics of the laureates. Similarly, the Breakthrough Prize has developed its ceremonies in close collaboration with the National Geographic TV Channel, engages entertainment celebrities as guests or hosts, and has deliberately placed the ceremonies in famed venues in and around Silicon Valley, in order to build public recognition for the prize. Furthermore, its ceremonies feature long lists of prominent invitees, lengthy acceptance speeches, and outbursts of joy – all of which are explicitly modelled on the Oscars. Collaboration with the media has also ensured that the Breakthrough ceremonies are distributed through several media channels: prime-time television slots, homepage website coverage, and 'best of' clips in social media outlets (National Geographic, 2017). In this sense, prizes have become significant media products, extensively followed, written about, and reported on (Pallas et al., 2016), not only in cultural production (Anand & Watson, 2004), but also in other fields.

From the variation of prizes in the use of rules, membership, and communication, we can identify two main strategies for prize giving: one more organized and the other more 'mystical'. One possible strategy for gaining acceptance and recognition for a prize is to use elements of formal organization to formulate explicit rules or clear membership criteria and to communicate them to both the potential prize recipients and the audience. But we also see that a lack of rules and membership can engulf prizes with an aura of mystery, leaving more room for the prize giver to decide on the prize and the winner. Whereas this strategy may increase the room for contestation, it is a strategy used for a number of recognized prizes, including the Nobel Prize.

EFFECTS OF PRIZES

Considering the large number of prizes in many fields and the proliferation of prizes to seemingly new areas of activity, we must also ask about the effects or potential effects that prizes have on actors and activities in these fields. The effects can be intended, in that the prize givers explicitly state their goal of changing, altering, or modifying activities and actors within a particular field. We also find prizes that do not express such goals, more modestly stating their desire to 'acknowledge' or 'reward' people or practices. It is reasonable to assume that whether an expressed goal or not, instigating prizes have an effect on potential or real prize recipients. In the rest of this section, we explore some potential intended or unintended effects of prizes from three perspectives: the effect on actors' behaviours, the effect on status and status positions in the relevant fields, and the effects on prize givers.

Effects on behaviour: forming templates for action

Prizes can be used to shape or influence the behaviours of actors in a desirable direction, thereby functioning consistently with other management tools. This is because the prize awards or recognizes specific activities, characteristics, or properties, providing guidance to actors about what is deemed valuable and desirable. This knowledge can be used deliberately to shape or influence actors' behaviours in a desired direction – by promoting work in areas such as human rights or environmental protection, for example (e.g., Right Livelihood Award), or encouraging innovativeness and new business ventures (e.g., Di Gasell Award; see Pallas *et al.*, 2016). Even when it is not an explicit aim, however, shaping behaviour may be an unintended effect of prizes.

Comparing briefly with another form of recognition – a ranking – studies show that these measures are often used by actors to form identities or comparisons and to shape reform activities inside the ranked organizations (Martins, 2005; Espeland & Sauder, 2007; Wedlin, 2007). Mechanisms such as rankings thus form what can be described as templates for organizations and activities. These templates can be used by actors when comparing with others and when reforming (Wedlin, 2007). In similar ways, prizes target individuals, groups, and organizations, pitting their behaviours and characteristics against each other in public and providing cues for what are considered appropriate and desirable characteristics and behaviours of these actors. Thus, prizes can form templates for actors and actions that can potentially influence behaviours of both potential and actual prize recipients.

The likelihood of a prize forming a template for action will be influenced by the use of the different organizational elements. The extensive use of rules for deciding a prize, for instance, is likely to increase the potential of a prize to form templates for action. With increasing rules and a clear communication of those rules to potential prize recipients, the cues for action are both more specific and more accessible for actors. Prizes associated with greater mystery are, on the contrary, less likely to form templates, as they provide less guidance on the behaviour or characteristics awarded and are less accessible for actors to use. Explicit membership rules for a prize, however, may restrict the effect of the template, reducing the impact to members; if only members have the potential to win, the template is useful only for member organizations. This may, in turn, promote membership in these settings.

Effect on status: prize givers, prize receivers, and prize audiences

A second potential effect of a prize is status, which follows naturally from the recognition associated with receiving a prize. There are likely several potential status effects, the most obvious being the status that may be granted to the prize recipients – the winners. Winning a prize or an award implies recognition of the characteristics, activities, or behaviours of an organization, individual, or group, given that the audience accepts the claims made by the prize and the prize giver. The aim of the Breakthrough Prize is explicitly to create 'science superheroes' similar to the world's foremost sports or music celebrities (Merali, 2013), although it is not obvious that this is (yet) the accepted status of these winners. The winners of prizes in which status is accepted may enjoy status boosts that are long lasting: The Nobel Prize gives life-long recognition as a Nobel Laureate, and an Olympic gold medal forever puts the winner in the group of Olympic Champions. Other prizes may have more temporary status effects, such as being recognized as the 'best player of the year'.

From our examples, it seems that both mysterious and organized prizes can have status effects for recipients, and it is not clear that either provides more or less status. The mystery of the Nobel Prizes provides high status, and Olympic prizes are highly organized and have clear status effects. Because status is dependent on audience acceptance, we can hypothesize that the organizational elements play a more indirect role for the evaluation of status and status claims in response to prizes. We point to the indirect role of these organization elements for two processes: audience assessment of the status or authority of the prize giver and audience assessment of the status claims in relation to previous status positions.

As to a first aspect, *audience acceptance of status claims* are likely to be influenced by their assessment of the status or authority of the prize giver. Audiences will be more inclined to accept status claims made by what they perceive to be legitimate and trustworthy assessors. In this process, organizational elements may be one way for prize givers to create legitimacy and authority for their evaluations – having clear rules, specific criteria, and high transparency. More mysterious prize decisions, however, will depend on other means for gaining authority. It is possible to obtain legitimacy and authority by drawing on traditions or proven track records of prize recipients judged as worthy, or by liaising with actors and organizations with high status or authority, in order to build a position as prize giver. This may be easier for established prize givers, and thus those who – like the Nobel Foundation argues – already have 'a steady place in the boat'. In some cases, the mysteriousness may even help to create legitimacy by providing a means of protecting the discretion of the prize jury (or judge) to make the decision. Fewer rules and limited communication thus allow greater leeway in the decision process and would, for instance, mean that interpretations of performance could be allowed to vary over time.

As a second aspect, *audience acceptance depends on previous status orders*. New claims for status and changes to status orders are always related to pre-existing status structures. Audiences evaluate status claims in relation to other assessments and to previously held notions of status. An assessment practice, such as a prize, needs to challenge existing orders in order to influence and contribute to change, but it cannot challenge existing status orders too much, or there is a risk that it will not be taken seriously (cf. Wedlin, 2006). Clear rules, explicit membership criteria, or extensive communication may serve to increase the acceptance of new or revised status claims resulting from a prize: When previous status orders are unclear or when no clear rules exist for the factors that provide status, creating rules or membership criteria may promote acceptance of the prize. If the prize giver does not significantly break or challenge existing status orders, however, less organization may be necessary to legitimate the results.

One way that prizes or other assessment principles modify existing status orders is to redefine or alter groups for comparison or to set new membership criteria. With clear membership criteria and a clearly defined group for a prize – such as the Book of the Year award offered by various publishers – a prize could limit the comparison to a particular group or change the definition of this group. Again, the Breakthrough Prize provides a good example. In its category of theoretical physics, the prize has upset traditional understandings of the research that is deemed valuable within the domain: 4 out of the 9 initial Breakthrough Prizes went to scientists active in the area of string theory (Breakthrough, 2017), to the critical evaluation of parts of the physics community (Brumfiel, 2012). Similarly, prizes in the life sciences seem to have reinforced pre-existing intra-disciplinary separations between the biology of cells and the biology of organisms. Whereas fifteen prizes have been awarded for work on cell biology, none were awarded for evolution, ecology, botany, zoology, or parasitology, which are significant branches in organism biology. In this way, prizes can shift attention to new activities and characteristics of performances and actors within a particular group or category or, in a more extreme case, even shift the definition of membership criteria. It could be noted that membership criteria that are too restricted may reduce the scope of the status claims. Perhaps the recognition gained is most important – or the only important recognition – for that particular group or for a limited and specific audience.

We also note that there are different possibilities for status effects of prizes. Apart from giving status to actors or winners and their activities, prizes can also have status effects on the entire field of activity. This is often also an explicit aim of prizes: to promote a field of actors or an area of activity in need of recognition. Yuri Milner, co-founder of the Breakthrough Prizes, repeatedly emphasized that his intention with the prize was to 'say that science is as important as shares trading on Wall Street' (Milner, as quoted in Brumfiel, 2012). Similar arguments are often heard for other prizes, in an attempt to raise the status of a particular field of activity or one set of actors relative to others. Even when this is not an explicit aim, increasing the status of a field or area of activity is likely an effect of much of prize organization. Sports – an area in which prizes abound – provide one example. This field is generally considered a prominent and popular one, attracting significant attention and money among the general public, sports organizations, sponsors, media, and other actors. One reason for this interest and the importance attached to the field of sports could be its abundance of prizes and prize-driven competitions.

Effects on the prize givers

It is not only other recipients that may receive status boosts from prizes, however. The prize giver can also receive a status boost, which can, in fact, be a reason for establishing a prize: to enhance its reputation as an organization. A prize created or backed by a high-status organization is more likely to enjoy high status and to influence status and behaviours to a greater extent than are prizes launched by an organization with low status. High-status prizes are also more likely to produce high-status award winners, which is likely to produce feedback effects on the prize giver – as the Nobel Prize and the Olympics exemplify.

As noted, it is not clear that recognition for the prize giver is dependent on the use of rules and membership, and decision procedures involving rules and membership may play an indirect role providing prize givers with legitimacy for their decisions. The way in which the prize is communicated plays a more prominent role in this process, however. Popularizing a prize through rituals and media is one way that prize givers increase the legitimacy and acceptance of a prize decision, which in turn increases the likelihood that the prize-giving organization will be well regarded and will reap reputational benefits from giving a prize.

ORGANIZATION OF STATUS AND BEYOND

Throughout this chapter, we have viewed prizes as decisions of approval. Prizes vary in the extent and use of organizational elements, and we have discussed potential ways that this variation influences the function and effect of prizes. Further pushing our argument about the way status is organized, we can go beyond the function of an individual prize giver and the effects on individual prize receivers and specific audiences. As argued, prizes do not appear and function in isolation. Rather, prizes – whether in cultural fields or in sports – are connected to each other, thereby constituting an ecology of prizes. This ecology is often explicit – by acknowledging other prizes when deciding its winners, for example, or by building status hierarchies of prizes in popular media, where prizes themselves can be ranked. Therefore, prizes and the way they organize status need to be addressed in terms of the way prizes relate to and influence other prizes, and how such interconnectedness taps into status effects at an individual level.

REFERENCES

Adler, N. J. & Harzing, A.-W. (2009) When Knowledge Wins: Transcending the Sense and Nonsense of Academic Rankings. *Academy of Management Learning & Education* 8(1): 72–95.

Allen, M. P. & Lincoln, A. E. (2004) Critical Discourse and the Cultural Consecration of American Films. *Social Forces* 82(3): 871–93.

Anand, N. & Watson, M. R. (2004) Tournament Rituals in the Evolution of Fields: The Case of the Grammy Awards. *Academy of Management Journal* 47(1): 59–80.

Appadurai, A. (1986) Introduction: Commodities and the Politics of Valu. In A. Appadurai (eds.), *The Social Life of Things. Commodities in Cultural Perspective*. Cambridge: Cambridge University Press. 3–63.

Best, J. (2008) Prize Proliferation. *Sociological Forum* 23(1): 1–27.

Bourdieu, P. (1991) *Language and Symbolic Power*. Cambridge: Polity Press.

Breakthrough (2017) Rules. Retrieved 28 March 2017 from https://breakthrough prize.org/Rules/2.

Brumfiel, G. (2012) Physics Prize Dwarfs All Others. *Nature* 488(7410): 144.

Brunsson, N. & Wedlin, L. (2018) *Organizing competition for status*. Unpublished paper.

Cohen, P. (2008) On Chicago Campus, Milton Friedman's Legacy of Controversy Continues. Retrieved 29 March 2017 from www.nytimes.com/2008/07/12/bo oks/12milt.html.

Couldry, N. (2003) *Media Rituals: A Critical Approach*. London: Routledge.

English, J. F. (2005) *The Economy of Prestige: Prizes, Awards, and the Circulation of Cultural Value*. Cambridge, MA: Harvard University Press.

Engwall, L. (2015) Academies and their Roles in Policy Decisions. In L. Wedlin & M. Nedeva (eds.), *Towards European Science. Dynamics and Policy of an Evolving European Research Space*. Cheltenham: Edward Elgar. 147–74.

Espeland, W. N. & Sauder, M. (2007) Rankings and Reactivity: How Public Measures Recreate Social Worlds. *American Journal of Sociology* 113 (1): 1–40.

European Commission (2006) 6 Years of Descartes Prize Winners. Excellence in Scientific Collaborative Research and Science Communication. Retrieved 12 May 2017 from https://ec.europa.eu/research/science-awards/pdf/6_years_descartes_en.pdf.

Feldman, B. (2001) *The Nobel Prize: A History of Genius, Controversy*, and Prestige: Arcade Publishing.

Fombrun, C. J. & Van Riel, C. B. M. (2004) *Fame and Fortune: How Successful Companies Build Winning Reputation*. Upper Saddle River, NJ: Pearson Education.

Frank, R. H. & Cook, P. J. (1995) *The Winner-Take-All Society*. New York: Free Press.

Frey, B. S. & Neckermann, S. (2009) Awards: A View from Economics. In G. Brennan & G. Eusepi (eds.), *The Economics of Ethics and the Ethics of Economics*. Cheltenham: Edward Elgar. 73–88.

Friedman, S. M., Dunwoody, S., & Rogers, C. L. (1999) *Communicating Uncertainty: Media Coverage of New and Controversial Science*. London: Routledge.

Gale (2008) Awards, Honors, and Prizes. Retrieved 24 March 2017 from http://assets.cengage.com/pdf/fs_AHP.pdf.

Goode, W. J. (1978) *The Celebration of Heroes: Prestige as a Social Control System*. Berkeley: University of California Press.

Grand Slam (2017) *2017 Official Grand Slam Rule Book*. London: Grand Slam Board.

Henrich, J. & Gil-White, F. J. (2001) The Evolution of Prestige: Freely Conferred Deference as a Mechanism for Enhancing the Benefits of Cultural Transmission. *Evolution and Human Behavior* 22(3): 165–96.

Johansson, R. & Zemlianichenko, A. (2014) Fler priser utmanar Nobels status. Retrieved 27 March 2017 from www.svt.se/nyheter/vetenskap/fler-priser-utmanar-nobels-status.

Luhmann, N. (2000) *Organisation und Entscheidung*. Opladen: Westdeutscher Verlag.

Martins, L. L. (2005) A Model of the Effects of Reputational Rankings on Organizational Change. *Organization Science* 16(6): 701–20.

Merali, Z. (2013) The New Nobels. *Nature* 498(7453): 152–4.

Nalebuff, B. J. & Stiglitz, J. E. (1983) Prizes and Incentives: Towards a General Theory of Compensation and Competition. *Bell Journal of Economics* 14(1): 21–43.

National Geographic (2017) 2017 Breakthrough Prize Ceremony: Scientists Changing the World. Retrieved 28 March 2017 from http://channel .nationalgeographic.com/breakthrough-prize/.

New York Times (2015) Breakthrough Prizes Give Top Scientists the Rock Star Treatment. Retrieved 28 March 2017 from www.nytimes.com/interactive/201 5/11/06/science/breakthrough-prize-winners-2016.html?_r=0.

Nobel Prize (2017a) Alfred Nobel. Retrieved 15 May 2017 from www.nobelprize .org/.

Nobel Prize (2017b) Milton Friedman – Facts. Retrieved 29 March 2017 from www.nobelprize.org/nobel_prizes/economic-sciences/laureates/1976/fried man-facts.html.

Pallas, J., Wedlin, L., & Grünberg, J. (2016) Organizations, Prizes, and Media. *Journal of Organizational Change Management* 29(7): 1066–82.

Power, M. (1997) *The Audit Society. Rituals of Verification*. Oxford: Oxford University Press.

Power, M. (2007) *Organized Uncertainty. Designing a World of Risk Management*. Oxford: Oxford University Press.

Sauder, M. & Espeland, W. N. (2009) The Discipline of Rankings: Tight Coupling and Organizational Change. *American Sociological Review* 74(1): 63–82.

Schein, E. H. (2010) *Organizational Culture and Leadership*. Hoboken: John Wiley & Sons.

Seidl, D. (2006) The Basic Concepts of Luhmann's Theory of Social Systems. In D. Seidl & K. H. Becker (eds.), *Niklas Luhmann and Organization Studies*. Copenhagen: Copenhagen Business School Press. 21–53.

Speier, H. (1935) Honor and Social Structure. *Social Research: An International Quarterly* 2(1): 74–97.

Street, J. (2005) 'Showbusiness of a Serious Kind': A Cultural Politics of the Arts Prize. *Media, Culture & Society* 27(6): 819–40.

Trice, H. M. & Beyer, J. M. (1984) Studying Organizational Cultures Through Rites and Ceremonials. *Academy of Management Review* 9(4): 653–69.

UEFA (2017) *Regulations of the UEFA Champions League 2015–18 Cycle*. Nyon: Union of European Football Associations.

Wedlin, L. (2006) *Ranking Business Schools. Forming Fields, Identities and Boundaries in International Management Education.* Cheltenham: Edward Elgar.

Wedlin, L. (2007) The Role of Rankings in Codifying a Business School Template: Classifications, Diffusion, and Mediated Isomorphism in Organizational Fields. *European Management Review* 4(1): 24–39.

Whitley, R. (2000) *The Intellectual and Social Organization of the Sciences:* Oxford: Oxford University Press on Demand.

Zitzewitz, E. (2006) Nationalism in Winter Sports Judging and Its Lessons for Organizational Decision Making. *Journal of Economics & Management Strategy* 15(1): 67–99.

Zuckerman, H. (1978) The Sociology of the Nobel Prize. Further Notes and Queries: How Successful are the Prizes in Recognizing Scientific Excellence? *American Scientist* 66(4): 420–5.

NOTE

1. Technically named the Sveriges Riksbank Prize in Economics in Memory of Alfred Nobel.

4 Membership or Contributorship? Managing the Inclusion of Individuals into Organizations

Michael Grothe-Hammer

Do organizations need members? In recent years, scholars have observed the increasing emergence of new forms of organization that challenge established assumptions about what an organization is (Barley, 2016; Schreyögg & Sydow, 2010). These new forms include terrorist networks (Stohl & Stohl, 2011), hacker collectives (Dobusch & Schoeneborn, 2015), and certain social movements (den Hond, de Bakker, & Smith, 2015). In these forms, membership is described as becoming fluid or unclear, most often leading to 'open or permeable' boundaries (Dobusch & Schoeneborn, 2015: 1006; see also, e.g., Bartel & Dutton, 2001; Miles & Snow, 1986; Schreyögg & Sydow, 2010).

In this context, several scholars have introduced proposals to broaden the notion of organization to include new – looser or more fluid – organized phenomena (Ahrne & Brunsson, 2011; Ahrne, Brunsson, & Seidl 2016, Dobusch & Schoeneborn, 2015). Two research streams are particularly interesting in this respect: the Communicative Constitution of Organizations (CCO) perspective (Bencherki & Snack, 2016; Dobusch & Schoeneborn, 2015; McPhee & Zaug, 2000; McPhee & Iverson, 2009; Schoeneborn & Scherer, 2012) and decision-based organization theory (as outlined in this book). Both attempts include one crucial issue: how to deal with established assumptions on membership and its relevance.

The decision-based perspective sees decisions as the constitutive elements of organization. (See Chapter 1.) Consequently, because organizations are based on decisions – not on members – Ahrne, Brunsson, and Seidl (2016) propose that membership should no longer be seen as a defining criterion for a formal organization. Yet, even if organizations are treated as systems of decisions rather than systems of people, it is necessary to remember that 'there can be no organization without persons' (Barnard, 1938: 83). Therefore, people must be somehow related to the organizational decision processes, even if these people are not members.

In this respect, the CCO perspective provides some recent insights that seem fruitful. Most noteworthy, Bencherki and Snack (2016) reintroduced the concept of 'contributorship' into organization studies. For them, there are not only members of an organization, but also contributors, who belong partially to the organization as long as they share communicative actions with it. Consequently, Bencherki and Snack call for subsequent studies on contributorship, the forms it can take, and how contributions are to be identified. I acknowledge this call, and want to combine it with the decision-based perspective. As I demonstrate, the concept of contributorship and the framework of decision-based organization theory can fruitfully complement each other.

Combined with the idea of organizations as decision-based systems, contributorship can be understood as a matter of decision. Even if organizations do not decide about membership, I assert that it is their decisions that distribute the possibilities of contributorship. Treating organizations like decision systems implies that the attribution of rights to contribute to those decisions is, in itself, a matter of decision (Blaschke, 2015). Therefore, a decision-based informed perspective can deepen the understanding of contributorship and lead to the following question: How do organizations decide about the distribution of possibilities to contribute to the organizational processes?

To answer this question, I draw upon two qualitative case studies. The first case covers the establishment of an organization concerned with the distribution of refugees from incoming trains to refugee camps; in doing so, it relied partly on non-affiliated volunteers. The second case shows the work of a voluntary organization that had no official membership but existed as an addressable actor running a news blog and organizing congresses and other events on behalf of itself.

As demonstrated here, both cases involve individuals that contributed to organizational processes without being members. Both organizations under study decided to manage contributorship in other ways. Instead of defining specific members, these organizations decided on spatial, temporal, attributional, resource-related, and/or quantitative-limitational premises for distributing possibilities of contributions. I learned, for example, that organizations can decide that individuals may contribute to organizational processes if they are physically present at a specific place and time. Organizations can further decide that anyone having a particular set of skills or access to certain resources may contribute to organizational processes, and more. It does not necessarily matter so much *who* participates in decision processes, therefore; rather, it matters *when, where,* and *how* people contribute, *how many* contribute, and the *backgrounds* of those contributors.

This study makes at least three contributions to the existing literature. First, it adds to recent developments in decision-based organization theory that dropped membership as a defining criterion of organization. In this respect, I present a way of maintaining a distinctive notion of formal organization without relying on established assumptions of membership. Second, this study adds to recent calls for subsequent studies on contributorship, by outlining specific forms of contributorship and ways in which an organization can decide on their distribution. Third, I argue on this basis that organizations that renounce the possibility of deciding about membership need not be treated as boundaryless or fluid systems.

A DECISION-BASED VIEW OF CONTRIBUTORSHIP

Most organization theories do not treat formal organizations as fixed entities, but as systems of activities (Barnard, 1938), actions (March & Simon, 1993), communication (Schoeneborn et al., 2014), decisions

(Luhmann, 2003), interactions (Haas & Drabek, 1973: 8) or practices (Nicolini, 2012). Although none of these scholars see organizations as mere assemblages of people, the issue of how to understand the relationship between organizations and those individuals that somehow participate in the organizational processes tends to challenge these established theories (Barley, 2016). This challenge occurs because, although based on the assumption that organizations do not consist of members, many modern organization theories do have a membership bias, asserting that the organization has to make a distinction 'between members and non-members' (Aldrich, 2008: 4), 'has to control who its members are' (King, Felin, & Whetten, 2010: 292), or must select its members before they can participate (Ahrne, 1994: 7). Membership is seen as the 'premise for deciding on the premises for making decisions' (Luhmann, 2013: 143), and even from the CCO perspective, membership is often taken for granted (Bencherki & Snack, 2016). Although definitions of membership differ, of course, there does seem to be a common ground: Membership implies that an organization must know *who* its members are by pre-selecting specific individuals who join the organization consciously under certain conditions (Ahrne, 1994; Kühl, 2013).

In the context of an increasing emergence of new forms of organization, this membership bias has become problematic. New organizational phenomena such as hacker collectives are described as fluid or boundaryless, making it difficult to identify members clearly. (See Chapter 15.) In this respect, several CCO scholars have already tried to re-establish a distinctive notion of organization by going beyond the existing ideas of membership. Schoeneborn and Scherer (2012) have noted that membership is attributed retrospectively in terrorist organizations. Wilhoit and Kisselburgh (2015) inquired into the case of what they call a 'proto-organization' – a collective capable of mutual action but which participants do not identify as members. McPhee and colleagues (McPhee & Zaug, 2000; McPhee & Iverson, 2009) have argued that membership is not one fixed decision, but a constant flow of on-going negotiation. As

Dobusch and Schoeneborn (2015) have illustrated, organizations can establish asymmetric memberships – cases in which there is no guided pre-selection of members but in which people can be excluded if they do not comply with organizational decisions. And Bencherki and Snack (2016) have demonstrated that organizations can implement partial inclusions of individuals who are not members, but who participate as contributors to the organizational processes.

This development corresponds to the recent work of Ahrne, Brunsson, and Seidl (2016), who build on a decision-based view of organizations (see also Ahrne & Brunsson, 2011; Luhmann, 2000, 2003; March & Simon, 1993), according to which formal organizations can be defined as 'social systems constructed and run by decision making' (Ahrne, Brunsson, & Kerwer, 2016: 9). Within these systems, decisions make reference to previous decisions and facilitate subsequent decisions, thereby creating an interconnected network that includes certain decisions and excludes other elements in the environment. Organizations can therefore be understood as operatively closed, recursively connected networks of on-going decision processes on behalf of a collective (Apelt et al., 2017; Luhmann, 2000, 2003; Nassehi, 2005; Seidl & Becker, 2006). As decision systems organizations can decide about five structural elements: rules, hierarchies, compliance monitoring, sanctions, and membership. (See Chapter 1.) Organizations can also decide not to decide on these elements, however, thereby including the possibility of not deciding on membership. In this sense, formal organizations can remain partially organized on a structural level. (See Chapter 1.) This view allows for the possibility of considering phenomena of organization that do not match the broadly established idea that organization must always include these five elements.

The proposal to drop membership as a defining criterion for organizations is consistent with the classical work of March and Simon (1993), who, in turn, were in the tradition of Chester Barnard (1938). Both works treated organizations as systems of activities or actions by 'participants' (March & Simon, 1993) or 'contributors'

(Barnard, 1938) – not necessarily by members. These participants or contributors subsumed members, but also involved any other individuals who contributed to the organizational activities. As mentioned, Bencherki and Snack (2016) have recently revived this idea, by turning back to the classical assumption (and wording) that an organization is better understood as having 'contributors' rather than 'members' (Barnard, 1938). What is more, Bencherki and Snack (2016: 285), and Ahrne and colleagues highlight the fact that membership includes the possibility that members can belong to an organization – in terms of having an administrative tie with it – without actually participating in the organizational processes. Prominent examples would be 'customer clubs' like the IKEA Family Club, in which membership does not include actual participation in internal decision processes of the formal organization. This view allows one to distinguish between actual contributors and members, therefore, yet not neglect the possibility that membership will often include contributorship.

Consequently, the question of who is to be regarded as a contributor becomes crucial (cf. Scott & Davis, 2007: 24). Like Barnard (1938), March and Simon (1993) treated organizations as open systems, which led to the problem of highly blurred boundaries. For March and Simon (1993: 3), even supporters and customers had to be considered contributors to an organization, because in a very broad sense they provided 'contributions to its existence' (March & Simon, 1993: 108). Consequently, a precise distinction between the organization and its environment was not possible (cf. Hernes & Bakken, 2003: 1519–20). Bencherki and Snack (2016) solve this problem by clarifying that contributors do not only contribute in some way to organizational existence, but that they must participate in communicative actions on behalf of the organization.

But how is this participation managed? Returning to a decision-based perspective on organizations, if organizations are treated as systems of recursive decision processes, they do not necessarily need members, but persons that somehow *contribute* to these decision processes. In this respect, Steffen Blaschke (2015) recently noted that organizations as decision-based systems decide about the distribution of internal decision rights to certain individuals. Therefore, the management of contributorship can also be understood as a matter of organizational decision. In order to contribute, one must have been granted the right to contribute. Organizations can decide how and to what extent rights to contribute in internal decision processes are assigned to individuals. Indeed, the classical way of distributing decision rights would be by usual membership decisions: the identification of certain individuals as members (deciding on *who* participates) in combination with a decision on certain rights to participate (e.g., via work contracts). As studies on contributorship (Bencherki & Snack, 2016) indicate, however, there are other ways to distribute these decision rights.

CASE DESCRIPTIONS

Case 1: Voluntary organization

The first case covers a voluntary organization that is, by self-description, an initiative that criticizes the educational system and demands better inclusion of learners at all levels of the educational system. The initiative runs a website with a blog that applies peer review with at least two reviewers and one editor, coordinates several campaigns, and organizes congresses with several hundred participants. The organization consists of approximately thirty contributors ('activists') and has established hierarchies, rules, compliance monitoring, functional positions, and even denominated departments. It also has a basic corporate design – for example a logo – and has acquired funding grants. The voluntary organization can be treated like a formal organization, therefore, because it is constituted as an actor that can be addressed by others. (See Chapter 1.) Nevertheless, for several years it was not officially founded, nor did it have denominated members.

During this time, top-level decisions were made in a monthly meeting, announced on the website and on the online social networking service, Facebook, and open to everyone. Everyone who joined the meeting in person had the right to participate in decisions, which meant that even people who showed up only once were able to participate in decision making or even introduce a new idea that was then decided upon. And they did just that!

There were three other departments located in the hierarchy below the monthly meeting, one of which was the blog. Although it had no official members either, the blog department had established three editorial positions with assigned persons and was organized via an e-mail distribution list and an online voting system. People who wanted to contribute to the blog could subscribe to the e-mail distribution list and make proposals for blog articles that were reviewed by at least two reviewers under the supervision of an editor. After the review, at least three anonymous people voted via the voting system for acceptance or rejection of the proposed blog article. This voting system was open to everyone, although the link to access was published only via the e-mail distribution list. Noteworthy in this respect is the fact that subscription to the list did not mean that one had to sign up by name. So the e-mail distribution list must not be confused with a list of members.

Case 2: Refugee distribution station collective

The second case covers an organization concerned with the distribution of refugees from incoming trains to refugee camps. During the peak of the European refugee crisis in 2015, several cities in Germany were picked to function as hubs for refugee distribution. Trains with refugees were sent from southern Germany and Austria to these hubs, where the refugees were distributed into busses headed for their specific refugee camps. These hubs had to be organized – at first on an ad hoc basis, and then over a period of several months.

Regarding the specific hub that forms the basis of this case, the organization included more than the mere distribution of refugees. Up to a thousand refugees per train were provided with food and refreshments, limited medical attention, bathroom equipment, childcare, communication devices, and more. To ensure the running of this operation, several organizations under the leadership of the local fire service established an organized collective. It included state and federal police, the municipal office for public order, the German rail service, four emergency medical service (EMS) agencies, several charitable organizations, the state district administration, the municipal Office of the Commissioner for Refugees, a private security service, several city administration departments, and other organizations.

This collective established an organizational structure for the distribution of refugees at a railway station; it included rules for procedures, hierarchies, and compliance monitoring. The railway station collective for the distribution of refugees was in operation for six months, but a significant drop in the number of incoming refugees in 2016 resulted in its disbanding. During its operation, the station collective established a strong hierarchy: A joint decision board – called a task force – under the leadership of the fire service and with representatives from involved organizations met every two days to decide upon general aspects, like rules and shift lengths. Head staff at the railway station comprised representatives of the fire service who were supported by a committee of representatives from involved organizations.

Many of the additional staff members were representatives of the collective's member organizations, although the lower levels included hundreds of volunteers. Of the 168 personnel per 24-hour shift, between 40 and 50 were explicitly 'non-affiliated' volunteers, the inclusion of whom was organized by two member organizations of the collective. On the one hand, the municipal Office of the Commissioner for Refugees called for volunteers. The Office placed two lists online for every duty shift, and volunteers signed up if they wanted to participate. One list was for miscellaneous volunteers; the other was established a bit later and was for interpreters. Only a given number of volunteers could sign each list. At least in the first weeks, volunteers did not have to state their real names or provide any other information; they merely had to identify themselves by stating the name or pseudonym used on the list. Eventually, however, the collective began checking the passports of contributors for security reasons.

On the other hand, a charitable organization included non-affiliated interpreters in the railway station collective. The selection of these interpreters was not a guided process. In a first phase, interpreters could just show up and participate, if they spoke a language that was needed. Non-affiliated volunteers contributed to the decisions of the collective for the entire time it was active. They had limited decision rights and also participated in broader decision processes. They acted as stewards and nurturers, for example, and actively contributed to the decisions of the collective.

Is the station collective an organization? Although an inter-organizational committee led the station collective, several interview partners explained to me that the station collective gained a certain degree of decision autonomy and was recognized as a distinctive actor:

> So very many participants perceived this station – it was soon just called 'the station' – as an autonomous organization. So one did not address the task force. Instead, it was always the station ... The autarkical status was strongly emphasized ... A strong process of emancipation that factually became an organization of its own.
>
> (Interviewee 1, Case 2)[1]

Furthermore, the station collective had its own rules, hierarchies, some identifiable members (member organizations), monitoring of rule compliance, and even sanctions for contributors. Consequently, all possible structural elements of an organization can be identified. (See Chapter 1.) Because it is possible to find a certain level of autonomy, perceived actorhood, and contributors to a distinctive system, the station collective can be treated as a formal organization.

METHOD

I applied a comparative case study using an interpretive and exploratory research design (Lincoln & Guba, 1985; Yin, 2009). Data was gathered from three main sources: observations, interviews, and documents. In Case 1, observations were retrospectively extracted from participation as an active contributor in several meetings and events and on other occasions, during a period of approximately one year in 2014 and 2015. In order to validate and expand upon these observations, I held interviews with nine individuals in 2016. Documents cover meeting protocols and complete conversations from two e-mail distribution lists. For Case 2, I conducted two weeks of direct observation in 2015, conducted interviews with fifteen individuals, and collected several documents, including operational documents, checklists, protocols, and presentations.

MANAGING CONTRIBUTORSHIP VIA DECISIONS

I found four instances of the way organizations used forms other than membership to manage potential contributions. The organizations under study made several decisions to distribute possibilities of contributions, and these findings are illustrated in what follows, using evidence from both cases.

Decisions on time and space

Both of the organizations I observed decided on temporal-spatial determinations for potential contributions. The voluntary organization and the station collective decided when and where contributions could be made. The voluntary organization applied this way of managing contributorship in its highest decision committee: the monthly meeting. This meeting served as the board meeting of the whole organization – setting the general conditions for the lower departments, deciding about expenses and overarching rules, and discussing the main identity and organizational presentation. The location of the monthly meeting was announced to the public on the website and via Facebook, and held at a specific time and in a specific place. All participants had a vote, even if they were attending for the first time.

> The situation is that everyone can come there [to the monthly
> meeting] and can participate. We also announce that in our
> newsletter, for example. We create a Facebook event and share it on
> our website. Sometimes people come who are interested. Sometimes
> people we already know, sometimes people we don't know yet ...
> Everyone can participate and co-decide at this monthly meeting.
>
> *(Interviewee 1, Case 1)*

It is noteworthy that regular contributors were aware that this
modus of decision making fosters some difficulties (cf. Cohen, March,
& Olsen, 1972), one of which was a problem with the permanency of
decisions. Although the organization was able to remember decisions
that had been made, there were written protocols of the monthly
meetings spread via an e-mail distribution list; sometimes certain
decisions were quickly revised at the next meeting, when another
set of individuals attended. Nevertheless, the organization decided
not to change the overall rule that everyone who happened to be at
the monthly meeting had a vote:

> It is controversially discussed from time to time that if decisions are
> revised – which does not happen very often – if that is somehow
> legitimate. Or if a decision, once made, somehow persists. And then
> there is the argument: Well, the people that are now here are
> actually the association and this is how we decide ... So
> theoretically, if one would want to take over our association, one
> could come with ten people and decide anything.
>
> *(Interviewee 2, Case 1)*

A different but similar picture unfolds in the case of the refugee
distribution station. Non-affiliated contributors in the station collective were included only at lower hierarchical levels. Nevertheless,
they were not mere executors of working tasks, but contributed to
organizational decision processes. On the one hand, contributors had
to make instant decisions during their work – regarding which refugees were to be supplied with clothes, for example. On the other hand,

contributors contributed to more general and higher-level decisions, making requests to higher-ranking decision makers, leading occasionally to corresponding decisions.

> We had the children's drawing table organized by the volunteers. Then there is the baby-changing facility. That was a small room in which mothers could come for milk ... swaddle and something of that sort. And ... volunteers ... established a clothing stock for children up to five years. ... And they ran that completely by themselves.
>
> *(Interviewee 14, Case 2)*

> We have a clothing stock and we said [to the volunteers] that if you see someone, who is dressed desolately ... then you could give them something ... Within this frame, they made the decision ... In the baby-changing facility we had ... in fact, a paediatric nurse ... she was professionally qualified. And within her assigned area of responsibility, she indeed made decisions respectively, even requested things. For example, she wanted specific small syringes ... And these were either granted or not. And she decided ... that child gets a diaper and this one does not. And here we have a baby shoe and this one is for you and not for you.
>
> *(Interviewee 6, Case 2)*

The basic condition for the illustrated contributions was that individuals had to be physically present in the train station during a defined period for defined working shifts (around 12 and up to 24 hours), and only during these shifts were contributions possible. It was not possible for non-affiliated persons to participate outside the train station; nor could they contribute during the non-operational phases of the station. This situation differs from usual membership, which implies that one does not stop being a member when one takes a sick day.

In both cases, individuals were permitted certain rights to contribute to decision processes. Being in a certain place at a certain time did not mean that individuals could make every type of decision; time and space of contributorship were coupled with certain decision rights.

In the case of the voluntary organization, these were board decisions; the station collective partially included individuals with certain rights to decide specific issues on the scene or make requests to people in higher-ranking positions in the hierarchical decision-making processes.

Decisions on specific resources potential contributors must have access to

I also discovered that both organizations made decisions about specific resources to which potential contributors must have access. In the case of the voluntary organization, the blog department turned out to be a good example. As I learned from the observations, to be able to contribute to the decision processes of the blog – writing and publishing articles, reviewing article proposals, voting for acceptance or rejection of articles – one had to be signed into a specific e-mail distribution list. Everyone who wanted to could sign in on this list; there were no regulations in this respect. If one wanted to contribute, however, it was necessary to be able to access the Internet and an e-mail account, and to understand the technical aspects of using an e-mail distribution list. Moreover, to be able to write, review, or vote for articles, one had to have access to word processing software.

A similar picture unfolds in case of the station collective. Miscellaneous helpers and many interpreters had to enrol on online lists to be allowed to show up at the station as a helper on a shift. These contributors also had to have access to the Internet, and know how to use a web browser and how to sign in on specific web-based tools for coordinating meetings.

It is noteworthy that in both cases it was not necessary to use real names in order to be allowed to contribute. In the case of the blog, I observed that contributors could write anonymously, sign in on the e-mail distribution list using pseudonyms, and subsequently review articles. The voting system also worked anonymously. To contribute to the station collective, pseudonyms could be used to sign in for at least several weeks:

> So I had friends of mine from France here several times. And they
> brought someone with them and I didn't know the full name. So
> I just wrote something like Maxi M. into the list.
>
> *(Interviewee 14, Case 2)*

Although the expectation that contributors must have specific resources to contribute may sound banal, in both cases large parts of humanity are actually excluded from contributing – a situation that should be taken seriously. The organizations decided on the implementation of specific structures – in both cases specific communication media the contributors were required to use – and these decisions restrict possibilities of contribution significantly. In both cases, it would have been possible to allow other forms of managing contributions. The voluntary organization could, for example, have allowed postal submissions of articles and the station collective could have selected potential contributors directly on the scene instead of using an online tool. Again, organizational decisions managed the possibilities of contributorship.

Decisions about certain skills and characteristics of potential contributors

In addition to the resources that potential contributors must be able to access, I discovered a closely related but different type of decision: the requirement of certain skills and characteristics that contributors had to have. In case of the station collective, helpers who wanted to contribute as interpreters *had to* speak one of the languages of the arriving refugees. In the first phase of the station collective, interpreters could just arrive and be granted access by the charitable organization. Representatives of the charitable organizations let them contribute because they spoke a required language:

> I see some post in the Internet ... 'Refugees Welcome'. And they
> would be in [train station] ... Maybe they need [an interpreter] ...
> I asked when and where ... go there and I see [Johann] and
> [Charitable Organization A] and ask him, 'How can I help?'
>
> *(Interviewee 8, Case 2; English in original)*

This way of contributing was eventually restricted, however. On the one hand, the charitable organization would then allow only interpreters they knew, which I construed as a membership decision that admitted only certain individuals. On the other hand, the Office of the Commissioner for Refugees started to use a specific online tool to manage inclusion, as described in the next section. Nevertheless, I see the decision about specific skills as one way of managing contributorship.

Decisions about quantitative limitations

The train station collective applied even more restrictive conditions for potential contributorship. Because too many people wanted to contribute – around 3,000 according to interviewees – the station collective decided to manage the number of contributors by limiting to 25 per shift the number of people who could sign in online:

> We tried to organize that a little. Because a hundred volunteers, non-affiliated, are too much for one evening. So we tried somehow to limit this by Doodle lists [a web-based tool for coordinating meetings] ... Tried to organize the volunteers ... So we essentially worked in a shift system. First shift from 6 PM until midnight and then from midnight until 6 AM.
>
> *(Interviewee 10, Case 2)*

Although this decision was implemented via an online tool, there are other ways that quantitative limitations could have been applied. The station collective could have decided to limit the potential contributors on the scene by counting the contributors, for example, and admitting a certain number. Nevertheless, like the other three types of decisions outlined here, the limitation of potential contributions poses yet another way of successfully managing potential contributions to the organization.

Combinations of decisions

Four potential ways of managing contributorship other than classical membership decisions have been identified – decisions that can be used separately or in parallel with other decisions to regulate potential contributions. As illustrated, the voluntary association used decisions about time and space to manage contributions to their board meetings, whereas decisions about the specific resources to which contributors must have access were used to manage contributions to the blog department. Similarly, the station collective combined classical members – representatives of the collective's organizations – with other forms of contributorship.

There is one other crucial aspect yet to be highlighted: the observed decisions were not only used in parallel; they were also combined to increase limitations on contributorship. Take, for example, the interpreters of the station collective who were included via an online list: They had to speak the required language (decision about skills), had to ensign the online list (decision about resources), and had to show up at a specific time in a specific place (decisions about time and space). Through the combination of several types of decisions, possibilities of contributorship are further restricted, because the number of potential contributors decreases more than would be the case using only one possibility.

POTENTIAL EXCLUSION

I have identified several ways of managing the access of potential contributors to organizational decision processes; yet the contributions are not arbitrary. That contributors are partially included into organizational decision processes does not mean that they can contribute whatever they want. They must comply with the rules and hierarchies of the organization or face the consequences, a situation that could be observed in the case of the station collective. Several contributors were later excluded because they did not comply with organizational decisions, rules, and hierarchies.

> We observed that there were some problems with the non-affiliated helpers ... That they were not willing to follow the rules on the scene. And these we had to sort out ... At first we had a talk with

them. But if it was obvious that she was not perceptive, we declared a ban on entering the station.

(Interviewee 10, Case 2)

After certain individuals had been excluded, security personnel were informed and were ordered to deny access. The possibility of excluding contributors acknowledges that even contributorship is subject to certain conditions, and that even non-members can be excluded from an organization if they fail to comply.

CATEGORIZING DECISIONS ON CONTRIBUTORSHIP POSSIBILITIES

What could be a more general concept of the relationship between an organization and those individuals contributing to it? Both of these cases show organizations that did not decide about membership – at least to a certain extent. In both cases, data indicate that the attribution of rights to certain individuals for contributing to the organizational processes can be distributed in several ways other than classical membership. This investigation therefore confirms the latest proposals that organizations do not necessarily build on membership (Ahrne, Brunsson, & Seidl, 2016) and can be captured more adequately by treating them as contributorship-based systems (Bencherki & Snack, 2016). As demonstrated, organizations can establish a broad variety of other forms of inclusion that go beyond the possibility of membership decisions.

In the following, I build on these insights and outline a more general understanding of the management of contributorship. Drawing on the underlying framework of decision-based organization theory presented in this chapter, it is possible to distinguish between the actual decisions of an organization and the structures that frame these decisions. These structures can be understood as the premises for decisions, and these premises are thereby a matter of decision (Luhmann, 2003; Seidl & Becker, 2006). In this broader sense, the illustrated possibilities of managing potential contributions can be understood as *premises for contributorship* on which an organization can decide. In this respect, the notion of membership can be combined with the notion of contributorship quite fruitfully. On the one hand, I agree with Bencherki and Snack (2016) and Ahrne and Brunsson (see Chapter 1) that membership in its basic form merely describes a decision about who belongs to an organization administratively, without necessarily combining this administrative tie with certain rights to contribute to the organizational processes. If this 'who-decision' were combined with participation rights in internal decision processes (Blaschke, 2015), it could be referred to as 'active membership', which I see as the classical decision premise managing contributorship. Taking the possibility of active membership into account and combining it with these findings, it is possible to identify six general categories of premises on which organizations can decide in order to manage contributorship:

(1) *Social*: Organizations decide on who is to be regarded as a contributor – understood as active membership (cf. Luhmann, 1995: 196).
(2) *Spatial*: Organizations decide on specific places at which contributions can be made.
(3) *Temporal*: Organizations decide on specific time frames during which contributions can be made.
(4) *Attributional*: Organizations decide on specific skills and characteristics one must possess in order to contribute.
(5) *Resource-related*: Organizations decide on specific resources that one must have access to in order to contribute.
(6) *Quantitative-limitational*: Organizations decide that a specific number of people can contribute, on a first-come–first-served basis.

As illustrated in this chapter, these premises for contributorship can be combined to increase the degree of limitation. Especially in the case of the station collective, spatial, temporal, attributional, resource-based, and quantitative-limitational premises were combined to reduce the number of volunteers to a certain extent.

The identified premises determine the possibilities for an organization to decide on how to include individuals into its decision processes. In this respect, the horizon of possible forms of inclusion can be broadened. Whereas the notion of (active) membership implies that an organization can decide *who* can participate in the organizational decision processes, other possibilities for contributorship management show that it is also possible to decide *when, where, how,* and based on *what background* contributions can be made, and by *how many.*

FROM CONTRIBUTORSHIP TO EXPLICIT NON-MEMBERSHIP

As outlined, I understand organizations to be decision systems that decide on the distribution of internal decision rights to certain individuals. To this point the discussion has focused on how the possible premises of contributorship can be used to distribute the right to potentially contribute to the organizational decision processes. However, organizations also decide *which* decision rights they distribute in this respect (Blaschke, 2015); contributors therefore have certain boundaries for what they may do and what they must not do. In the case of the monthly board meeting of the voluntary organization, for example, contributors could participate only in board decisions; they could not vote for blog articles. Contributors of the blog department could participate in writing, reviewing, and voting for blog articles via an e-mail distribution list, but they could not participate in board decisions without attending board meetings.

Furthermore, there were limits to these decision rights in the case of the station collective: Contributors could be and were excluded by failing to comply with organizational decisions. Thus partial inclusion does not mean that the contributions can be arbitrary. Contributors must contribute within their decided boundaries or face exclusion.

At first glance, the possibility of exclusion looks similar to classical membership. Similar to a usual member, contributors can be excluded if they do not comply with organizational decisions. There is a crucial difference, however. In a usual organization–

membership relationship, members are known and identifiable to the organization as individuals (Ahrne, 1994), which implies that an organization does not usually have to know who its non-members are. When it comes to contributorship, this relationship seems to be turned upside down. Although contributors are not necessarily known by name, organizations need to make a list of explicit non-members as soon as contributors are excluded. To exclude people permanently from contributing, the organization must be able to recognize them if partial inclusion is to be denied. In the case of the station collective, security staff members were informed about excluded contributors, in order to keep them away. An excluded contributor therefore becomes an *explicit non-member* of an organization, confirming insights gained by Dobusch and Schoeneborn (2015; also see Chapter 15), who call this phenomenon 'asymmetric membership negotiation' (p. 1029). I would agree with this view. In usual membership, an organization 'has to control who its members are' (King *et al.*, 2010: 292); in cases of excluded contributors, however, it has to control who its non-members are. Otherwise, organizations could not prevent excluded contributors from contributing again. I see this difference as an asymmetric version of membership – that contributorship implies the possibility of explicit non-membership.

FLUID BOUNDARIES?

Does lack of membership decisions lead to fluid or open boundaries? As discussed here, unclear, ambiguous, or absent decisions on membership in organizations are often associated with open, fluid, or permeable boundaries (Bartel & Dutton, 2001; Dobusch & Schoeneborn, 2015; Miles & Snow, 1986; Schreyögg & Sydow, 2010). In these two cases, I observed organizations that at least partly renounce the decision on membership and identified several other possibilities of managing access to organizational decision processes.

Neither organization needs be understood as having open boundaries. Rather, all the identified premises for contributorship can be understood as boundary-maintaining decisions of an organization. Even if not a member, an individual must match one or more certain premises set by an organization to be able to contribute to the organizational processes. Therefore, even with lack of membership, contributions are not arbitrary. Moreover, not everyone that matches the premises for contributorship is automatically a contributor; not everyone who could contribute actually contributes. As seen in the case of the monthly board meeting of the voluntary organization, for example, only relatively few people showed up, although many more people could theoretically attend. The majority of potential contributors do not attend. Consequently, contributorship not only requires management by the organization, but individuals must also contribute. Contributorship thus encompasses two aspects: First, a contributor must match certain premises on which an organization has decided; and second, a contributor must actually participate in organizational decision processes.

From the point of view of the organization, therefore, it is clear which acts of participation are to be considered internal. If an organization is treated as a system consisting of an on-going stream of decision making, the boundary is marked by exactly these decisions. Only certain decisions refer to previous decisions and facilitate subsequent decisions. This stream therefore includes certain decisions and excludes other elements in the environment. By deciding on possibilities of contributorship, an organization knows that if an individual makes a certain contribution under certain social, spatial, temporal, attributional, resource-related, and/or quantitative-limitational conditions, these contributions can be considered organizational in the sense that they are accepted as contributions to the internal decision process. I conclude that although an organization may not necessarily know who its contributors are, it can nevertheless recognize and distinguish contributions from non-contributions. Moreover, if contributions do not comply with organizational decisions, contributors can be excluded and become explicit non-members. Even with unclear or absent memberships, therefore, the boundary of an organization is not necessarily fluid or open. Both inclusion and exclusion can still be effectively managed by substitutes for membership.

CONTRIBUTORSHIP: A NOTE ON POSSIBLE REASONS, CONDITIONS, AND CONSEQUENCES

This study demonstrates how organizations that renounce decisions on membership establish substitutes for managing contributions to their organizational decision processes. Combining the concept of contributorship with decision-based organization theory therefore allows for a better understanding of the ways in which organizations distribute opportunities to contribute, thereby enabling scholars to look differently at the ways in which organizations include persons in their internal decision processes. Although this study is primarily concerned with the organizational possibilities of managing contributorship, I did not ask the question of 'why' organizations renounce decisions on membership; nor did I expend much effort on looking at the contexts enabling organizations to operate without membership decisions.

Regarding the context, it is noteworthy that in both cases organizations could rely strongly on institutionalized organizational elements and ideas of how organization works (Bromley & Meyer, 2015). The organizations in these two cases did not have to do much to 'organize' the contributors. In fact, contributors partly organized themselves (as in cases of different functional areas of the station collective) or relied on their professional backgrounds to do their work (as in case of the paediatric nurse). Moreover, the organizations relied on established organizing tools – e-mail distribution lists, meeting coordination tools, and more – and started to produce checklists under the assumption that everyone had an idea of what a checklist is, or established a peer review system adapted from well-known models of scientific publishing.

Another important condition in this respect is that organizations that renounce decisions on membership seem to need a constant flow of people contributing to the organizational processes. Although, on a basic level, this is true in usual membership relations, this aspect seems to be more prevalent in organizations that renounce membership decisions. Specifically, through decisions on membership, organizations can achieve a certain degree of reliability of expectations by binding specific demands to it that must be fulfilled if one wants to remain a member (Luhmann, 1996). An organization therefore usually knows who it can 'count on' and what it can minimally expect by those it calls 'members'. And, as is usual in many organizations, it can make the expectation of contributions a condition for membership. This characteristic is missing in membership-less contributorship, because an organization cannot rely on specific, known individuals, and it becomes dependent on a constant flow of incoming contributors (even if this includes recurrent contributions by the same individuals).

Regarding the aspect of 'why' organizations renounce decisions on membership, I can only speculate about underlying intentions – if there were any – but it is possible to discuss some potential advantages and difficulties stemming from the renouncing of membership decisions. Perhaps organizing without membership makes it easier to organize temporarily. By relying on institutionalized ideas of organization and lowering the threshold for contributions, it may be possible to generate much greater organization in and for a short time than would be possible in conventional ways. I would assume, however, that this situation could pose difficulties for the possible persistence of an organization. In the context of this study, I was unable to explore this aspect systematically. The station collective, at least, poses an interesting case in this respect. The research on conventional organizations indicates that they often do not cease to exist after goal achievement, but tend to persist merely by changing their goals (Kühl, 2013). However, the station collective ceased after six months exactly because it achieved its goal – not because of a lack of contributions.

The persistence of organization, I argue, is possible through membership. By applying membership, it is possible to achieve a generalization of expectations. Membership creates a 'zone of indifference' for members (Barnard, 1938), within which they are willing to accept a broad variety of expectations and changes as long as the general inducement for the membership remains stable (Luhmann, 1996). Many organizations can change their goals, therefore, while keeping their members, as long as the goal change lies within the members' zones of indifference. When it comes to contributorship, however, this generalization of expectations seems not to be possible – at least not to the degree it would be in a membership relationship. Through membership, individuals can be bound to an organization on a long-term basis, but contributorship is much more volatile. I assume, therefore, that persistence is somewhat more difficult for organizations without membership, especially when it comes to goal flexibility.

In context of this paper, I have been able to discuss only briefly the aspects of contextual conditions and their possible advantages and difficulties. In both respects, however, I see the need for future inquiries exploring the conditions under which and the reasons for organizations to renounce membership decisions and the consequences. Moreover, there seems to be a general need for further studies exploring the inclusion of individuals into organizations, apart from a narrow focus on membership.

REFERENCES

Ahrne, G. (1994) *Social Organizations: Interaction inside, outside, and between Organizations*. London/Thousand Oaks, CA: SAGE.

Ahrne, G. & Brunsson, N. (2011) Organization Outside Organizations: The Significance of Partial Organization. *Organization* 18(1): 83–104. DOI:10.1177/1350508410376256.

Ahrne, G., Brunsson, N., & Kerwer, D. (2016) The Paradox of Organizing States: A Meta-Organization Perspective on International Organizations. *Journal of International Organizations Studies* 7(1): 5–24.

Ahrne, G., Brunsson, N., & Seidl, D. (2016) Resurrecting Organization by Going beyond Organizations. *European Management Journal* 34(2): 93–101. DOI:10.1016/j.emj.2016.02.003.

Aldrich, H. (2008) *Organizations and Environments*. Stanford: Stanford University Press.

Apelt, M., Besio, C., Corsi, G., von Groddeck, V., Grothe-Hammer, M., & Tacke, V. (2017) Resurrecting Organization without Renouncing Society: A Response to Ahrne, Brunsson and Seidl. *European Management Journal* 35(1): 8–14. DOI:10.1016/j.emj.2017.01.002.

Barley, S. R. (2016) 60th Anniversary Essay: Ruminations on How We Became a Mystery House and How We Might Get Out. *Administrative Science Quarterly* 61(1): 1–8. DOI:10.1177/0001839215624886.

Barnard, C. I. (1938) *The Functions of the Executive*. Cambridge, MA: Harvard University Press.

Bartel, C. & Dutton, J. (2001) Ambiguous Organizational Memberships: Constructing Organizational Identities in Interactions with Others. In M. A. Hogg & D. J. Terry (eds.), *Social Identity Processes in Organizational Contexts*. Philadelphia: Psychology Press. 115–30.

Bencherki, N. & Snack, J. P. (2016) Contributorship and Partial Inclusion: A Communicative Perspective. *Management Communication Quarterly* 30 (3): 279–304. DOI:10.1177/0893318915624163.

Blaschke, S. (2015) It's All in the Network: A Luhmannian Perspective on Agency. *Management Communication Quarterly* 29(3): 463–8. DOI:10.1177/ 0893318915584824.

Bromley, P. & Meyer, J. W. (2015) *Hyper-Organization. Global Organizational Expansion*. Oxford: Oxford University Press.

Cohen, Michael D., March, James G., Olsen, Johan P. (1972) A Garbage Can Model of Organizational Choice. *Administrative Science Quarterly* 17(1): 1–25. DOI:10.2307/2392088.

den Hond F., de Bakker, F. G., & Smith, N. (2015) Social Movements and Organizational Analysis. In D. Della Porta & M. Diani (eds.), *The Oxford Handbook of Social Movements*. Oxford: Oxford University Press. 291–305.

Dobusch, L. & Schoeneborn, D. (2015) Fluidity, Identity, and Organizationality: The Communicative Constitution of Anonymous. *Journal of Management Studies* 52(8): 1005–35. DOI:10.1111/joms.12139.

Haas, J. E. & Drabek, T. E. (1973) *Complex Organizations: A Sociological Perspective*. New York: Macmillan.

Hernes, T. & Bakken, T. (2003) Implications of Self-Reference: Niklas Luhmann's Autopoiesis and Organization Theory. *Organization Studies* 24(9): 1511–35. DOI:10.1177/0170840603249007.

King, B. G., Felin, T. & Whetten, D. A. (2010) Finding the Organization in Organizational Theory: A Meta-Theory of the Organization as a Social Actor. *Organization Science* 21(1): 290–305. DOI:10.1287/orsc.1090.0443.

Kühl, S. (2013) *Organizations: A Systems Approach*. Farnham: Gower.

Lincoln, Y. S. & Guba, E. G. (1985) *Naturalistic Inquiry*. Beverly Hills: SAGE.

Luhmann, N. (1995) *Social Systems*. Stanford: Stanford University Press.

Luhmann, N. (1996) Membership and Motives in Social Systems. *Systems Research* 13(3): 341–48. DOI:10.1002/(SICI)1099-1735(199609)13:3<341::AID-SRES 92>3.0.CO;2-5.

Luhmann, N. (2000) *Organisation und Entscheidung*. Wiesbaden: VS Verlag für Sozialwissenschaften.

Luhmann, N. (2003) Organization. In T. Bakken & T. Hernes (eds.), *Autopoietic Organization Theory: Drawing on Niklas Luhmann's Social Systems Perspective*. Oslo, Norway: Abstrakt forlag. 31–52.

Luhmann, N. (2013) *Theory of Society: Volume 2*. Stanford: Stanford University Press.

March, J. G. & Simon, H. A. (1993) *Organizations*. Cambridge: Blackwell.

McPhee, R. D. & Iverson, J. (2009) Agents of Constitution in Communidad: Constitutive Processes of Communication in Organizations. In L. L. Putnam & A. M. Nicotera (eds.), *Building Theories of Organization: The Constitutive Role of Communication*. New York: Routledge. 49–87.

McPhee, R. D. & Zaug, P. (2000) The Communicative Constitution of Organizations: A Framework for Explanation. *Electronic Journal of Communication* 10(1–2).

Miles, R. E. & Snow, C. C. (1986) Organizations: New Concepts for New Forms. *California Management Review* 28(3): 62. DOI:10.2307/41165202.

Nassehi, A. (2005) Organizations as Decision Machines: Niklas Luhmann's Theory of Organized Social Systems. *The Sociological Review* 53: 178–91. DOI:10.1111/j.1467-954X.2005.00549.x.

Nicolini, D. (2012) *Practice Theory, Work, & Organizations: An Introduction*. Oxford: Oxford University Press.

Schoeneborn, D., Blaschke, S., Cooren, F., McPhee, R. D., Seidl, D., & Taylor, J. R. (2014) The Three Schools of CCO Thinking: Interactive Dialogue and Systematic Comparison. *Management Communication Quarterly* 28(2): 285–316. DOI:10.1177/0893318914527000.

Schoeneborn, D. & Scherer, A. G. (2012) Clandestine Organizations, al Qaeda, and the Paradox of (In)Visibility: A Response to Stohl and Stohl. *Organization Studies* 33(7): 963–71. DOI:10.1177/0170840612448031.

Schreyögg, G. & Sydow, J. (2010) Organizing for Fluidity? Dilemmas of New Organizational Forms. *Organization Science* 21(6): 1251–62. DOI:10.1287/orsc.1100.0561.

Scott, W. R. & Davis, G. F. (2007) *Organizations and Organizing: Rational, Natural, and Open System Perspectives*. Upper Saddle River, NJ: Pearson Prentice Hall.

Seidl, D. & Becker, K. H. (2006) Organizations as Distinction Generating and Processing Systems: Niklas Luhmann's Contribution to Organization Studies. *Organization* 13(1): 9–35. DOI:10.1177/1350508406059635.

Stohl, C. & Stohl, M. (2011) Secret Agencies: The Communicative Constitution of a Clandestine Organization. *Organization Studies* 32(9): 1197–215. DOI:10.1177/0170840611410839.

Wilhoit, E. D. & Kisselburgh, L. G. (2015) Collective Action without Organization: The Material Constitution of Bike Commuters as Collective. *Organization Studies* 36(5): 573–92. DOI:10.1177/0170840614556916.

Yin, R. K. (2009) *Case Study Research: Design and Methods*. Los Angeles: SAGE.

NOTE

1. All interviews are translated from German, if not declared otherwise.

ACKNOWLEDGEMENT

I want to thank Maja Apelt, Cristina Besio, Svenja Hammer, and Karoline Helbig for their helpful suggestions and comments. The chapter also benefitted from extensive discussions during a research stay at Score (Stockholm centre for organizational research) in 2017 and from invaluable feedback of participants in the subtheme 'The Communicative Constitution of Organizing: Toward and Beyond (Formal) Organization' at the 33rd EGOS Colloquium 2017 in Copenhagen and of the participants of the session on work and organization 4.0 at the 38th Congress of the German Sociological Association 2016 in Bamberg. Last but not least, I want to thank Olivier Berthod and Jörg Sydow for their constant support in the research process. This work was supported by the German Research Foundation (DFG) (grant SY 32/6–1 supervised by Jörg Sydow).

PART 2 Organization in and around Markets

5 The Partial Organization of Markets

Nils Brunsson

Ideal types can be fruitfully used for comparisons with and analysis of empirical phenomena (Weber 2012: 125). But when they are used as concepts for defining empirical phenomena, they may produce more confusion than clarity. There has been a tradition of defining 'market' as an ideal type and a form of governance with peculiar characteristics – as a system of exchange in which the exchanging parties have no dependency relationship with each other (Williamson, 1996), the benefits exchanged are clearly specified and no trust is required (Powell, 1990), or buyers and sellers are not connected to and dependent on specific buyers and sellers but can choose freely among all available partners (Håkansson & Johanson, 1993). In order that the concept of 'market' be used, it has even been required that sellers be private firms with the goal of maximizing profits and that the buyer is the end consumer of the product (Le Grand, 1991). Scholars using such narrow definitions in empirical studies would find relatively few examples – and if they combined the requirements, they would find even fewer. And, indeed, the supporters of narrow definitions need more concepts to describe what many others would characterize as markets. Systems of exchange that do not fulfil the criteria have been defined not as markets but as something else: 'hybrids' of markets and formal organizations (Williamson, 1996), 'networks' (Powell, 1990; Håkansson & Johanson, 1993), or 'quasi-markets' (Le Grand, 1991; Walsh, 1995), for example. It is not difficult still to find traces of this tradition in economic literature.

Using such a narrow definition of a fundamental social phenomenon does not seem fruitful. Applying a wider definition with older roots, markets can be seen as systems for exchange under competition (Aspers, 2011). Using that definition, it is possible to see that markets are not a rare phenomenon, but that modern society is rife with markets. Although one can find markets that function in rough accordance with the narrow definitions, many or perhaps most markets are lacking in some or all of these characteristics. Furthermore, a broader definition allows one to observe that markets have become even more salient in many countries over the last few decades of marketization, privatization, and outsourcing, although the new or expanded markets seldom fulfil the requirements of an ideal-type market. And one can observe that different markets function differently – not only to the extent that they are close or distant to an ideal type, but in many other respects as well. It is important to investigate the processes that lead to these differences.

MUTUAL ADAPTATION, INSTITUTIONS, AND ORGANIZATION

In the discipline of economics, scholars have traditionally been fascinated by the way markets develop as the result of mutual adaptation among sellers and buyers (Lindblom, 2001). These processes may lead to relatively stable equilibria, but also to highly dynamic situations, to power concentration or power diffusion, and to the efficient or inefficient use and allocation of resources. Over the past few decades, economists have demonstrated increased interest in institutions (North, 1990) – particularly in institutions that are fundamental to the existence and expansion of markets, such as property rights and a stable monetary system. Such institutions vary among countries and epochs and influence the functioning of markets. The importance of institutions has been a topic in economic sociology as well, but here also the varying institutions in different markets have been observed (Fligstein, 2001). Patterns of behaviour have emerged historically and are now taken for granted, rendering large differences among markets: the market for diamonds compared to the fashion market, for example (Bernstein, 1992; Aspers, 2010). Business-to-business markets tend to follow patterns that differ from most consumer markets (Håkansson & Johanson, 1993).

The fact that markets are *organized* differently has also been observed (Fliegstein, 2001; Abolafia, 1996). Basic neo-classical theory is based on Walras's and Marshall's studies of stock exchanges, which Marshall called 'the most highly organized exchange' (Marshall, 1920: 256–7) and Walras called 'perfectly organized markets' (Walras, 1954: 83–4). Attempts at achieving this type of organization have been described by the so-called performativity literature (MacKenzie, Muniesa, & Siu, 2007). But the concept of organization in these arguments remains wide and vague; it indicates a certain order that can be actively created by people and organizations, but not much more.

In the literature on 'market regulation', the basic imagery is one of markets formed mainly by mutual adaptation but open to occasional interventions. Even if there are tendencies to broaden the regulation approach (Baldwin, Cave, & Lodge 2010; Braithwaite & Drahos, 2000), it has been traditionally assumed that the interventions are made by states (or meta-organizations of states) and have consisted primarily of new or changed rules in the form of law, whereas other market interventions have been described with such sweeping concepts as self-regulation or soft law.

In order to understand differences among markets and how markets change, it is not enough to study mutual adaptation and institutions. The organization of markets is also a key factor. And to analyse how markets are organized, a concise concept of organization is needed – a concept that is complex enough to reflect sufficiently the multifarious nature of this empirical phenomenon. The organization concept suggested in this book can be used for illustrating how markets are organized differently, how their organization changes over time, and who are the organizers. Different elements of organization are used in different markets and by different organizers.

ORGANIZATION AND ORGANIZERS OF MARKETS

Other chapters in this book provide many examples of organizational elements that are used in markets. Markets have *rules*, some of which are set by states or international government organizations and consist of or are connected to compulsory state laws. Even more common are standards – non-compulsory rules (Brunsson & Jacobsson, 2000). There are standards for the way sellers and buyers should perform their activities, as exemplified in Chapters 2 and 7. And there are international standards for how firms should design their accounting systems to make it easier for trading partners to judge each other's financial robustness.

Other standards concern the products for exchange, one purpose of which is to facilitate coordination. When firms design their products according to international standards, they are able to trade with a large number of other firms in extensive global 'value chains', whereby each firm makes one component in what will be a complex end product.

Other standards promote moral principles in markets (Dubuisson-Quellier, 2013; Alexius & Tamm Hallström, 2014) for both products and production processes, in order to protect the physical environment or to guarantee acceptable workplace conditions and fair pay for workers. Products with an acceptable design or origin are often marked with a label that makes it easy for consumers to judge their compliance with standards, the idea being that people and organizations that exhibit strong morals will avoid buying from firms that do not fulfil those standards – in the hopes that non-compliers will eventually be forced to comply or disappear from the market.

As illustrated in Chapters 2 and 7, standards are often connected to *monitoring*; certification firms can certify sellers' and buyers' application of standards. Certification firms are sellers that compete with each other in a market for certifications, and their ability to conduct fair certification processes is assisted by accreditation organizations. In other cases, monitoring is not connected to standards. A few rating firms – Standards and Poor's, Moody's, and Dun & Bradstreet – monitor the creditworthiness of sellers and buyers around the globe, which strongly affects markets for credits but can also affect other markets, as was demonstrated in the 2008 financial crisis. Consumer organizations monitor the quality of consumer products, and digital platforms such as PriceRunner monitor prices in many consumer markets.

Certifications, accreditations, and permission to use prestigious labels can be seen as a form of *sanctions* – positive if received and negative if denied. Prizes are common not only in science and sports (see Chapter 3), but also in markets. Beer manufacturers boast about their gold medals, even those obtained decades or even a century ago, and newspapers give prizes to successful start-ups. Michelin stars have an impact on the demand for restaurants and the prices they can charge. Consumer boycotts constitute negative sanctions.

Membership in markets is a significant factor where people under a certain age are not allowed to buy alcohol, cigarettes, or weapons, or when sellers of taxi rides or train rides must have a license in order to operate. Membership in industry associations provides a seller with an image of acceptance and seriousness. Dissatisfied consumers of commuter transports can establish and join associations that require greater supply and higher quality from the service providers. Membership in associations for employers and for employees is crucial for achieving good terms in many labour markets.

An agreement among firms that possible future disputes shall be handled by a certain arbitration institute or by the courts in a certain country constitutes an example of *hierarchy*. And members in industry, employers' or employees' associations, or in cartels accept that their associations make decisions about the members' behaviour.

As demonstrated, many aspects of markets can be organized, such as the design of goods exchanged, the characteristics of sellers and buyers, their internal processes, and their behaviour in their market. Sometimes even prices or supply are decided not by the individual sellers or buyers, but by others: by cartels or states, for instance. Cartels decide about how much each member can deliver, to whom, or at what price. States may decide that a seller must deliver to all interested buyers, and they may forbid certain forms of price discrimination.

In summary, there are many ways to organize markets. Markets differ not only in the structures produced by mutual adaptation or in their institutions, but also in the way they are organized.

Organization is often necessary for the creation of a market, whether a new marketplace or a market for a new product. Market organization is an essential part of the innovation process – when sellers establish a market for a new product or set of products (Brunsson & Tyllström, 2018). Organization can begin even before it is clear exactly what products will be sold, as exemplified by the organization of the market for nano-products, in which both prospective sellers and buyers were engaged (Delemarle & Larédo, 2012).

Organization is also an instrument for changing an existing market. As exemplified in other chapters, it can be an attempt to change traditional and highly institutionalized forms of behaviour, as sustainability standards did when they were a new phenomenon and as platform owners do when they transform into sellers people who traditionally were consumers. (See Chapter 6.) The formation of an industry association can be an attempt to challenge traditional networks that have emerged in an industry over time. Alternatively, organization is a disrupting reaction to previous or pending organization, as when new standards or prizes can be developed in order to challenge existing standards or prizes. An industry association can be formed or used to protect the members from organization attempts they dislike. The association decides on its own rules, monitoring system, and sanctions, arguing, whether successfully or unsuccessfully, that no more organization is required. In other cases, existing organization can be supported by more organization, as when certification and accreditation are added to standards.

Organizers

These examples demonstrate that there are many organizers of markets. Almost all of them are formal organizations. Based on their positions in the markets one can distinguish four types of organizers: sellers, buyers, profiteers, and 'others' (Ahrne, Aspers, & Brunsson, 2015).

Sellers and *buyers* form associations, sometimes cartels, with the purpose of organizing their markets. They engage in standardization work, monitoring, and sometimes boycotts. In fixed-role markets

(Aspers 2009), the most common form of market in which sellers and buyers permanently stick to their roles, the parties often have contrary interests. Interests are more harmonious in switch-role markets, such as exchanges, where people or organizations frequently switch between the role of seller and the role of buyer.

Profiteers include organizers of physical or virtual marketplaces and intermediaries such as brokers, agents, auction houses, or digital platform owners. They all work in the market that represents their offerings, but their business concept is to organize another market on which they are dependent for their own economy. They set rules for how exchange shall be conducted, for instance, and they establish systems for monitoring. Although they bring sellers and buyers together, they do not want sellers to trade without their own participation. Their income is often dependent on the volume of trade, which influences their way of organizing. (See Chapter 9.)

Sellers or buyers in one market sometimes engage themselves in the organization of other markets on more of an ad hoc basis. Markets are typically interconnected (Aspers, 2011), and the way Market B is organized may negatively affect the situation in Market A – an incentive for actors in Market A to try to reorganize Market B. Alexius (2018) demonstrated, for instance, how hotels and travel terminal owners began organizing the Swedish 'deregulated' taxi market when they found that this market functioned so poorly that it disturbed their own businesses. In other cases, the effect that sellers or buyers have on other markets may merely be an unintended side effect. When newspapers or magazines publish rankings of producers or products or establish prizes for firms, their primary interest is probably not in organizing these markets, but they hope that their initiatives will get more people interested in reading and buying their own product. Yet they contribute to market organization.

Another type of profiteer is an organization that does not initiate market organization, but supports and adds to the organizing efforts of others. The whole notion of certification provides room for a large number of firms around the world to make money by offering that service – firms that implement this idea and have an interest in supporting it. (See Chapter 7.) Credit ratings are the basis for profitable market activities for a few powerful rating agencies.

Others are organizations that claim to work in the interest of others or everyone (Meyer, 1996), and many of them are active in organizing markets. International government organizations such as the Organisation for Economic Co-operation and Development, the International Monetary Fund, and the World Bank are deeply involved in organizing markets or giving advice to other organizers. A great number of national and international organizations set standards for what they argue are morally acceptable products and production processes and they monitor firms' compliance to these standards.

In summary, there are many more market organizers than states – the category that is emphasized in the market regulation literature. Yet, states as a general category are also significant market actors and always have been. States and princes established market-places early on, in order to profit from taxable dependents (Weber, 1981; Masschaele, 1992). Because states are still profiteers in almost all markets through their various forms of consumption taxes, an interest in high trade volumes follows. States are active sellers – in markets for welfare services that have been created by partial privati-zation over the last few decades in many countries, for instance. States are big buyers of goods and services; in Sweden, for example, public purchases represent almost 15 per cent of GNP. For the past two centuries, states have assumed the role of 'other', trying to make sellers and buyers take social or other considerations into account (Poliyani, 1957). This work is increasingly conducted in symbiosis or in competition with idealistic organizations.

When it comes to market organization, it is rarely useful to conceive of a state as one actor, however. Rather, the diversity of state activities in markets is reflected in their own organization, with a large number of agencies involved in different aspects of and different, often competing interests in market organization (Andersson, Erlandsson, & Sundström, 2017).

Market dynamics

Organization brings certain dynamics to markets. Institutions imply stability, and mutual adaptation sometimes leads to relatively steady states, whereas an organized order is fundamentally unstable. (See Chapter 1.) It builds on decisions, and the order can quickly be changed by new decisions – perhaps even made by new decision makers. A boycott may drastically reduce demand for a certain product overnight. A decision about accepting or excluding a firm as a member in an association for employers may swiftly change an employer's position in the labour market. Decisions about new standards can render products obsolete at a stroke.

Decisions about markets are as difficult to predict as other decisions are. And decisions by people and organizations trying to organize markets are not guaranteed to be effective. It is difficult to predict which decisions will be implemented and have an effect, and which will not. Suggestions for different decisions are easily evoked, but it is difficult to predict if those new decisions will be made – and if they were, if they will be effectual.

All in all, organization adds to the uncertainty that characterizes many markets for other reasons (Knight, 1921). No wonder it is common that firms demand 'stable rules of the game'. The problem is that in a certain sense there are no stable rules: Any rule can be unstable, and its endurance is difficult to predict.

Uncertainty is increased by the fact that there are many organizers with different interests, ideas, and ways of organizing. And organizers often compete among one another. In the area of environmental protection, for example, there is an abundance of labels within Europe alone. 'Industrial consortia' compete with such standardization organizations as ISO in creating standards. Prize givers and rankers compete with each other for attention for their prizes and rankings (Wedlin, 2006; see also Chapter 3).

All in all, there is a strong tendency in contemporary markets for inconsistencies and changeability. It is unlikely that anyone is satisfied with every organizational element in a given market – which is a reason for more organization attempts and even more inconsistencies and more changes. Most markets that are not organized within a formal organization (such as an exchange) are lacking the organizational element of an overall hierarchy that could limit the amount of other organizational elements.

This situation is likely to make formal organization attractive. Hierarchy in a formal organization is generally used to avoid competing organizers by specifying exactly who has the right to make decisions. And organizations are expected to organize in a way that does not allow competition among organizational elements. Members are regularly seen as having the right to demand that rules do not conflict with one another and that managers must respond to those demands. States expend considerable effort to prevent or handle inconsistent laws in the legislation process and by courts. So, forming an industry association or another type of meta-organization may be an attempt to avoid competition among organizers, and thereby among organizational elements. The same is true for moving markets into formal organizations by creating exchanges or for turning them into internal markets within states or firms.

MARKETS AND ORGANIZATIONS

Markets and formal organizations constitute the two basic forms of the economy (Marshall, 1920). Contemporary Western society can be characterized as both a market society and an organization society (Simon, 1991). Markets and organizations are sometimes discussed as if they constitute very different forms, even opposites, easily distinguished from each other. Yet they are interrelated and similar in several ways.

Markets and organizations are closely interrelated in at least three ways. *Organizations are key market actors.* They are the only entities other than individuals that are equipped with the identity, property rights, autonomy, and responsibility necessary to be a seller or a buyer. In an overwhelming majority of market relationships, organizations are present on at least one side. *Organizations are the main organizers of markets*, and they often organize other organizations as well – organizations that are the target for market organization. Most significantly, *markets and organizations can be combined*, as is the case in stock exchanges and other exchanges and in various forms of internal markets in states and firms. This combination is not a threat to either form. Rather, as Marshall's (1920) and Walras's (1954) studies demonstrate, it seems difficult to create anything like what economists have called a 'perfectly competitive' or 'perfectly organized' market without integrating it into a formal organization. Samuelson argued that textbook economic theory is valid only to 'a perfectly competitive market where some kind of standardised commodity such as wheat is being auctioned by an organized exchange' (Samuelson, 1969: 69).

Social science traditions have contributed to a distinction between markets and organizations that is often exaggerated. They have been studied in different disciplines, with the study of markets allocated primarily to economics, and the study of organizations concentrated in sociology and management research. And these disciplines have had different traditions. The tradition in economics, to emphasize mutual adaptation, can be contrasted to early organization theory that concentrated on what we have here called organization. This tradition launched the still-widespread idea that the environment of organizations is fundamentally different from their inner life – a perspective that is likely to produce an emphasis on differences.

In later years, organization theorists have been much more interested in mutual adaptation and institutions in organizations. If that interest is combined with increased interest in organization in markets, the differences seem less far-reaching. Both a market and an organization can be instances of 'complete organization', in the sense that all organizational elements are used. Some markets have a great deal of organization (see Chapter 9), and some formal organizations have relatively little organization. (See Chapters 17 and 18.) Because market organizers do not normally have access to management techniques other than organization, markets are more likely than most contemporary organizations to be dominated by organization and bureaucratic logic (Castillo, 2018). Markets and organizations are different social and judicial forms – or different fundamental institutions – but they support each other, and they are not opposites.

Whether common research perspectives affect popular images of markets and organizations is another issue. The idea of control in organizations being exerted by decisions concentrates responsibility on the decision makers, particularly those at the top. When markets are perceived as being primarily the result of mutual adaptation and institutions, responsibility is less clear and more diffused: Although sellers and buyers tend to be responsible for their own behaviour, it is difficult to find someone responsible for the market as a whole.

How markets and organizations are analysed and perceived has implications for the complex question of why markets rather than organizations are sometimes created. Why are some activities performed in markets and others performed in formal organizations without any market mechanisms? And what motivates redistribution between these forms – marketization and outsourcing on the one hand, and expansion of the organizational sphere and insourcing on the other?

Transaction cost analysis has provided answers to these questions, based on an analysis of what is seen as fundamental differences between markets and formal organizations (called 'hierarchies' in this tradition) – in handling the risk for opportunistic behaviour, for instance (Coase, 1937; Williamson, 1996). But if one observes organization in both markets and organizations, it opens things up for a wider perspective on the market or organization issue. Managers can try to organize not only their own organizations, but also their relevant markets, although the result is uncertain in both cases. To diminish the risk for opportunistic behaviour in a market, for instance, a firm may, alone or with others, engage in standardization work and require certifications from customers. Such measures may sometimes be more effective than similar ones directed at members of one's own organization and lead the firm to prefer a market solution rather than an in-house solution. Furthermore, at least in some situations, managers are likely to consider responsibility effects when choosing between organization within their organization and market organization.

From a wider perspective than that of an individual firm, the attractiveness of formal organization and market seem to be connected to the general images of these forms. The mutual adaptation perspective emphasizes the freedom of sellers and buyers to choose what and with whom to exchange goods or services, whereas the organizational perspective emphasizes the subordination of organization members to decisions made by others. So formulated, propagators of market solutions can refer to the freedom of the individual for their case, whereas propagators of formal organization must defend their case with other arguments. When the existence of mutual adaptation, institutions, and organization is observed in both markets and organizations, the picture becomes less clear and the situation more complex for both parties.

Market democracy

It is fair to say that scholars have paid less attention to organization in markets than to mutual adaptation and institutions. Among people seeking political influence, market organization has been more salient. Traditionally, politics has been conducted mainly with reference to formal organizations in the form of states, but during the last few decades a great deal of political activism has moved to markets (Micheletti, 2003), particularly at the global level, where there is no state to criticize or mobilize. In order to secure decent conditions for labour, standards and labels such as Fair Trade were developed, and similar standards and labels have been decided upon in an attempt to save the physical environment from pollution. In some cases, boycotts are arranged – even worldwide boycotts – the idea being that people should be able to exercise their power as consumers in markets rather than as citizens of states.

Many traditional conceptions tie democracy closely to such formal organizations as states and the ways in which they are organized. But markets can also be organized in order to offer another form of democracy. It does not presuppose the engagement of states – neither a non-existing world state nor other existing states. 'Market democracy' is different in that it builds on markets, but similar in the sense that it is exactly the organizational aspects of markets that make it work. Organization increases transparency and makes it easier to form an opinion and more likely that many others have the same information. Without an environmental standard and a monitoring system, for example, few people would know or agree on the products they should avoid, and it would be difficult to mobilize common, effective buyer behaviour. If there were only mutual adaptation, institutions, and state regulation in markets, there would be less space for this type of transnational politics.

REFERENCES

Abolafia, M. (1996) *Making Markets*. Cambridge, MA: Harvard University Press.

Ahrne, G., Aspers, P., & Brunsson, N. (2015) The Organization of Markets. *Organization Studies* 36(1): 7–27.

Alexius, S. (2018) 'The Most Regulated Deregulated Market in the World': Sellers Organizing across Markets. In N. Brunsson & M. Jutterström (eds.), *Organizing and Reorganizing Markets*. Oxford: Oxford University Press. 101–14.

Alexius, S., & Tamm Hallström, K. (eds.) (2014) *Configuring Value Conflicts in Markets*. Cheltenham: Edward Elgar.

Andersson, C., Erlandsson, M., & Sundström, G. (2017) *Marknadsstaten. Om vad den svenska staten gör med marknaderna – och marknaderna med staten*. Stockholm: Liber.

Aspers, P. (2009) Knowledge and Value in Markets. *Theory and Society* 38: 111–31.

Aspers, P. (2010) *Orderly Fashion. A Sociology of Markets*. Princeton: Princeton University Press.

Aspers, P. (2011) *Markets*. Cambridge: Polity Press.

Baldwin, R., Cave, M., & Lodge, M. (2010) The Future of Regulation. In R. Baldwin, M. Cave, & M. Lodge (eds.), *The Oxford Handbook of Regulation*. Oxford: Oxford University Press. 613–27.

Bernstein, L. (1992) Opting out of the Legal System: Extralegal Contractual Relations in the Diamond Industry. *The Journal of Legal Studies* 21(1): 115–57.

Braithwaite, J. & Drahos, P. (2000) *Global Business Regulation*. Cambridge: Cambridge University Press.

Brunsson, K. & Brunsson, N. (2017) *Decisions. The Intricacies of Individual and Organizational Decision Making.* Cheltenham: Edward Elgar.

Brunsson, N., Jacobsson, B., & associates. (2000) *A World of Standards.* Oxford: Oxford University Press.

Brunsson, N. & Jutterström, M. (eds.) (2018) *Organizing and Reorganizing Markets.* Oxford: Oxford University Press.

Brunsson, N. & Tyllström, A. (2018) When Sellers Organize Markets: Dilemmas and Strategies in Markets for Professional Service Markets. In N. Brunsson & M. Jutterström (eds.), *Organizing and Reorganizing Markets.* Oxford: Oxford University Press. 82–100.

Castillo, D. (2018) Creating a Market Bureaucracy: The Case of a Railway Market. In N. Brunsson & M. Jutterström (eds.), *Organizing and Reorganizing Markets.* Oxford: Oxford University Press. 32–45.

Coase, R. (1937) The Nature of the Firm. *Economica* (Blackwell Publishing) 4(16): 386–405.

Delemarle, A. & Larédo, P. (2012) *Organizing Markets for Nanotechnology Products: Investigating Firms' Collective Actions in ISO and the European Code of Conduct.* Paper presented at The Organization and Re-Organization of Markets, Stockholm.

Dubisson-Quellier, S. (2013) A Market Meditation Strategy: How Social Movements Seek to Change Firms' Practices by Promoting New Principles of Product Valuation. *Organization Studies* 34(5–6): 683–703.

Fligstein, N. (2001) *The Architecture of Markets: An Economic Sociology for the Twenty-First Century Capitalist Societies.* Princeton: Princeton University Press.

Håkansson, H. & Johanson, J. (1993) The Network as a Governance Structure: Interfirm Cooperation beyond Markets and Hierarchies. In G. Grabher (ed.), *The Embedded Firm. On the Socio-economics of Industrial Networks.* London: Routledge. 35–51.

Knight, F. (1921) *Risk, Uncertainty and Profit.* Boston: Houghton Mifflin.

Le Grand, J. (1991) Quasi-Markets and Social Policy. *The Economic Journal* 101 (408): 1256–67.

Lindblom, C. (2001) *The Market System: What It Is, How It Works, and What to Make of It.* New Haven: Yale University Press.

MacKenzie, D., Muniesa, F., & Siu, L. (eds.) (2007) *Do Economists Make Markets: On the Performativity of Economics.* Princeton: Princeton University Press.

Marshall, A. (1920) *Industry and Trade: A Study of Industrial Technique and Business Organization; of Their Influences on the Conditions of Various Classes and Nations.* London: Macmillan.

Masschaele, J. (1992) Market Rights in Thirteenth-Century England. *The English Historical Review* 107(422): 78–89.

Meyer, J. (1996) Otherhood, the Promulgation and Transmission of Ideas of the Modern Organizational Environment. In B. Carniawska & G. Sevon (eds.), *Translating Organizational Change*. New York: Walter de Gruyter. 241–52.

Micheletti, M. (2003) *Political Virtue and Shopping: Individuals, Consumerism, and Collective Action*. New York: Palgrave Macmillan.

North, D. (1990) Institutions and Their Consequences for Economic Performance. In K. Cook & M. Levi (eds.), *The Limits of Rationality*. Chicago: Chicago University Press. 383–401.

Polanyi, K. (1957) *The Great Transformation*. Boston: Beacon.

Powell, W. (1990) Neither Market nor Hierarchy: Network Forms of Organization. *Research in Organizational Behavior* 12: 295–36.

Samuelson, P. (1969) *Economics, An Introductory Analysis*. 6th edition. New York: McGraw Hill.

Simon, H. (1991) Organizations and Markets. *The Journal of Economic Perspectives* 5(2): 25–44.

Walras, L. (1954) *Elements of Pure Economics, or The Theory of Social Wealth*. London: George Allen and Unwin Ltd.

Walsh, K. (1995) *Public Services and Market Mechanisms*. Basingstoke: Macmillan Press.

Weber, M. (1981) *General Economic History*. New Brunswick: Transaction Publishers.

Weber, M. (2012) *Collected Methodological Writings*. Bruun, H. & Whimster, H. (eds.). London: Routledge.

Wedlin, L. (2006) *Ranking Business Schools: Forming Fields, Identities, and Boundaries in International Management Education*. Cheltenham: Edward Elgar.

Williamson, O. (1996) *The Mechanisms of Governance*. Oxford: Oxford University Press.

ACKNOWLEDGEMENT

This chapter draws from Ahrne, Aspers, and Brunsson (2015) and Brunsson and Jutterström (2018).

6 The Organization of Digital Marketplaces: Unmasking the Role of Internet Platforms in the Sharing Economy

Stefan Kirchner and Elke Schüßler

Established economic practices and social relations currently face the pressures of what has recently become known as the *platform economy* (Kenney & Zysman, 2016). The word 'platform' is used in a variety of ways (Langley & Leyshon, 2016) and refers to what Evans and Gawer (2016) generally term 'transaction platforms'. Some social media platforms such as Facebook or YouTube post content mainly to host user communities. Other Internet platforms provide digital marketplaces for paid transactions, ranging from crowdsourcing of creative ideas to the digital sale of products and services (Langley & Leyshon, 2016; Aspers & Darr, 2017). Focusing on digital marketplaces, the platform economy provides sociotechnical infrastructures that facilitate new forms of Internet intermediation between buyers and external sellers that are not directly employed or contracted by the platform. Many of these digital marketplaces introduce novel economic practices.

Several prominent and successful organizers of digital marketplaces depict themselves as a part of the *sharing economy* – a general term that evokes non-market notions of a community orientation, empowerment, and social transformation (Schor, 2014; Mair & Reischauer, 2017) and revolves around the basic idea that existing goods and services are shared or traded with others in a peer-to-peer fashion, eliminating intermediaries from value distribution (Schor & Fitzmaurice, 2015). In stark contrast, platforms such as Airbnb (for temporary accommodation), Rover (for pet sitting), Getaround (for car sharing), Uber and Lyft (for ride sharing), TaskRabbit (for freelance handy home tasks and driving), or Vinted (for second-hand clothes and accessories) are regularly equated with the sharing economy and often display a clear for-profit orientation. These for-profit platforms shift such transactions as ordering a ride or renting short-term lodging away from the established, orderly, and regulated world of formal organizations. Numerous platforms exist transnationally and locally. Precise figures are difficult to acquire, but global revenues derived from the sharing economy in five sectors – travel, car sharing, finance, staffing, and music and video streaming – are estimated to increase from about USD 15 billion (~EUR 12 billion) in 2015 to some USD 335 billion (~EUR 275 billion) by 2025 (PricewaterhouseCoopers, 2015). These sharing economy marketplaces depart from a world of internal labour markets and state-regulated market rules. Instead, transactions are performed in the form of largely unregulated, individualized market relationships that quickly scale up because they thrive on monopoly-prone network effects (Cusumano, 2015; Kenney & Zysman, 2016). With their underlying business model built upon monetizing consumer assets and human effort, these for-profit sharing-economy platforms constitute a radical shift away from established social orders (Kenney & Zysman, 2016).

From the perspective of economic sociology, market actors need to solve central coordination problems to facilitate a sufficiently stable market order (Fligstein, 2001; Beckert, 2009). Yet stabilizing a viable digital market order is significantly more complicated than creating stabilization in traditional markets because of the specific properties of the Internet. Market participants face high uncertainty, for example, because it is difficult to build mutual trust as a basis for co-operation, because competition is fierce, and because demand can fluctuate substantially (Brinkmann & Seifert, 2001; Diekmann & Przepiorka, forthcoming; Belk, 2014; Dolata, 2015; 2017; Hartl, Hofmann, & Kirchler, 2016; Kirchner & Beyer, 2016). Whereas these conditions theoretically inhibit orderly market transactions, sharing-economy platforms operate successfully because their providers have found a way to create and operate a new kind of market order.

We posit here that the key to understanding the social structures of sharing-economy platforms is to analyse them as digital marketplaces created and operated by market organizers. According to this understanding, digital marketplaces constitute an extended case of general market models (Beckert, 2009). Whereas general market models comprise at least three actors – one buyer and two competing sellers, for example – market orders of digital marketplaces require an additional fourth actor: the market organizer. The market organizer facilitates market transactions by creating and operating a market order for external sellers and buyers. (See Evans, 2011; Langley & Leyshon, 2016.) Thus the digital marketplaces of the sharing economy also represent a specific case for the organization-of-markets approach (Ahrne, Aspers, & Brunsson, 2015). This approach suggests an investigation of specific organizational elements in order to reveal underlying mechanisms of coordination and social order in markets.

In this chapter we address the question of how digital marketplaces are organized by drawing on two exemplary cases – Lyft and Airbnb – both adequately described as 'profiteers' (Ahrne et al., 2015) because they earn money by raising fees for market transactions. We first consider the efforts of market organizers to create new market orders on their digital marketplaces by mobilizing participants and resources. We then analyse the elements of organization that these market organizers install in order to operate their digital marketplaces continuously. All in all, we show that although they use the rhetoric of sharing, Internet platforms in the sharing economy generate enormous profits by establishing order on digital marketplaces using the five elements of organization. Specifically, and noteworthy from the perspective of partial organization, all five organizational elements are implemented in a specific configuration that allows these market organizers to scale up their operations quickly and cheaply, simultaneously securing a powerful intermediary position.

CREATING A NEW MARKET ORDER: THE CASES OF AIRBNB AND LYFT

Following our proposed perspective, the market organizers of the sharing economy face a challenging problem of creating a new market order. Whereas 'regular' digital marketplaces like Booking.com or online services for regular taxi drivers often merely apply a digital format to extant professional sellers, the sharing economy challenges established market orders more substantially. Market organizers of the sharing economy like Lyft and Airbnb primarily organize sellers with no specific qualifications to offer services using such private resources as a car or a spare bedroom. This process transforms previously non-market resources into market objects. The attempt to construct amateurs as competitive sellers and to commodify their private resources for a digital marketplace constitutes a considerable departure from established market orders.

Established market orders do not change easily, however. Market orders typically exhibit a taken-for-granted character because they build on a shared understanding of who the market actors are and how they should interact with each other (Fligstein, 2001). So how do market orders change? Fligstein (2001) and Rao (2008) argue that social movement-like activities can bring about substantial change in markets and facilitate the creation of new market orders. (See also Davis & Thompson, 1994; Schneiberg & Soule, 2005; Schneiberg, King, & Smith, 2008; Schneiberg & Lounsbury, 2008.) To subvert established taken-for-granted models, challengers need to theorize an alternative market order and mobilize participants and resources to facilitate diffusion. *Theorization* involves the development of 'abstract categories' and 'patterned relationships' (Strang & Meyer, 1993). Thus, theorization constructs specific types of actors, including specific identities and roles, and provides an alternative frame to make sense of new activities. Theorization ties in with opportunities for mobilization. Social movement studies (Snow, Rochford, Worden *et al.*, 1986; Schneiberg & Lounsbury, 2008) posit that certain frames (see

Goffman, 1977; Snow *et al.*, 1986) or, more precisely, active *framing* processes, allow for an effective mobilization of participants and resources (e.g., funding, political support). If orientations of potential participants resonate with a provided frame, they are more likely to contribute (Snow *et al.*, 1986).

For a short illustration of how market organizers of the sharing economy created their market orders through theorization and framing, we draw on transcripts of two National Public Radio interviews from the radio show 'How I built it' (NPR, 2016, 2017). Both interviews provide official self-descriptions of the co-founders of Lyft and Airbnb as they narrate for a national radio audience the processes and obstacles of setting up their marketplaces for a national radio audience.

Lyft, which originated in San Francisco, USA, operates a ride-sharing service in some 300 US and Canadian cities. Amateur drivers who are screened by Lyft register themselves on the platform and offer rides via the Lyft app using their private car, and riders request rides using the app. Lyft regulates prices, and riders rank drivers on a scale of 1 to 5 through the Lyft app. The company began as an online service for ride sharing to and from US universities and shifted in the middle of 2012 to a general Internet platform for private taxi services (NPR, 2017), turning a digital infrastructure for ride sharing at universities into a general service for individual transport. According to co-founder John Zimmer, this expansion of services was driven by Lyft's vision to create a 'better use for underused cars' (NPR, 2017: 16:00). To accomplish this vision, the company needed to combine two resources: a personal car and a car owner willing to drive other people around. In the interview, Zimmer describes the difficulties the company faced in establishing the digital marketplace and presents several corner-stones of his model, which conflicted with taken-for-granted beliefs of potential sellers (drivers) and buyers (riders). He explains that taxicabs are considered to be 'safe' to ride in. People do not want to ride in 'someone else's vehicle', and few people are willing to drive a taxi. When the general notion of car-based transport is shifted to 'share a ride', however, many more people would be willing to participate as drivers and customers rather than driving for or riding in a regular taxi. The co-founder elaborates more extensively:

> But also you have to remember what is now accepted as normal. Getting into someone else's vehicle was not at all normal at the time [mid-2012]. In fact, we had to work to change people's behaviour. And in the early days, we suggested sitting up front. And ... creating this ... 'your-friend-with-a-car hospitality' environment ... And if you go in a room with a hundred of our friends and you ask: 'How many of you are willing to drive a taxi?' A couple of hands maybe go up. When you say: 'How many of you are willing to share a ride?' Ah you know – 75 hands would go up. And so ... We wanted to create the experience around that.
>
> *(our simplified transcription from NPR, 2017: 16:46)*

So, the co-founder described that in order to enable the Lyft market model, they needed to alter the framing of the paid service to foster a new practice that breaks away from taken-for-granted beliefs and routine behaviour. They reframed the service with a community notion: 'your-friend-with-a-car hospitality environment'. This community-based reframing is also illustrated by his example that, initially, riders were asked to sit up front and not in the back. In order to facilitate trust between drivers and riders, Lyft encouraged drivers to link their Lyft profiles with their Facebook profiles. The example describes an approach to denote the everyday-life practical difference between a regular taxi ride and the novel Lyft service. Conversely, applying a community framing to the service also increased the drivers' willingness to provide shared rides. After developing the model further, Lyft eventually secured venture capital funding and expanded the service.

Airbnb, which also originated in San Francisco, now operates internationally, providing a digital market infrastructure for short-term lodging in private properties (Constantiou, Eaton, & Tuunainen, 2016; NPR, 2016). Similar to the Lyft platform, individuals offer their private resources for rent on the Airbnb Internet platform – a bedroom, a flat, a condominium, or a house – and potential guests search for and book suitable accommodation. Safety and service quality is assured through verified personal profiles accompanied by an extensive user-review system. In our interview, the co-founder of Airbnb, Joe Gebbia, describes how the service evolved. After several unsuccessful attempts to launch the website, the founders serendipitously discovered a viable business model: making Airbnb a digital marketplace by collecting transaction fees. Gebbia elaborates extensively on how Airbnb evolved through a trial-and-error process that involved many setbacks. Early in the process, the founders faced adverse conditions because their idea of renting out private homes to strangers on a commercial basis was an uncommon notion that potential investors rejected out of hand.

Gebbia indicates that the Airbnb model disrupted taken-for-granted beliefs in such a substantial way that it was difficult to mobilize venture capital from investors: 'They look you square in the eyes and go: "This is weird. I am not investing in this."' (NPR, 2016: 16:33). Eventually, and again serendipitously, Airbnb secured funding from an investor to develop the Airbnb platform further. Building on this initial funding, the founders tried to overcome the remaining obstacles that were preventing the platform from working properly. Gebbia describes the key problem of enabling amateurs to become good competitive actors in the marketplace:

> As we start going through the search results and looking at the hosts, we identified a pattern. And the pattern was this: People just generally didn't know how to take a good photo of their home. So the photos were really bad . . . Well people were just using their camera phones. At the time it was like flip camera phones, which is even worse. They were taking pictures at night. It just wasn't [good] . . . They weren't merchandizing their home in a way that you'd wanna stay there. So therefore no one was booking them.
> *(our simplified transcription from NPR, 2016: 29:56)*

Poor presentation impeded a smooth marketization of sellers' homes as offerings on the digital marketplace. The solution was to go directly to some of the early sellers and take professional photos of their accommodations with greater attention to lighting, composition, and staging. These changes facilitated bookings. Eventually, international guests – especially guests traveling back to their home countries from the USA – diffused the Airbnb model globally and soon requested that the service be implemented in their city. Following this salient user-mobilization success, more investors entered the company and provided additional venture capital.

As the interview quotes illustrate, the sharing economy represents a specific case of the way a new market order is actively created by market organizers. In both sharing-economy cases, market organizers needed two vital ingredients: capital and framing. They first secured venture capital to develop and expand their models. This step was more pronounced in the Airbnb case, in which elaborate and tailored *theorizations* of different models were necessary to pitch the concept to and convince investors. The mobilization of amateur sellers was achieved next by *framing* the sharing-economy marketplace through the use of non-market notions of 'sharing' and 'community'. This notion was more pronounced in the Lyft interview. The Airbnb case also demonstrated the market organizers' efforts to position the amateurs as proper competitive actors, advising them on how to commodify their private resources in the best way (e.g., improved pictures for the offers). The need to rally participation and support from participants and investors explains the contradictory framing strategy combining market-orientated theorizations primarily for investors and the non-market, sharing-oriented ideas for potential participants.

In this sense, the sharing economy with its non-market connotations indicating that equal users would perform transactions in a peer-to-peer fashion effectively conceals the central role of market organizers as profiteers at the core of the phenomenon. Whereas sharing-economy marketplaces tend to present themselves as part of a quasi-social movement, respective theorization and framing presents only an initial step in creating a new stable market order. Thus the structural basis of sharing-economy marketplaces differs strongly from the notions that are evoked by the appealing term 'sharing'. To run smoothly, these new marketplaces require careful and continuous organization in a way that firmly establishes Internet platforms as powerful intermediaries in their marketplaces. In the next section, we elaborate on the ways in which the two companies establish this market order.

ORGANIZATIONAL ELEMENTS AND THE MARKET ORDER ON DIGITAL MARKETPLACES

Providing a general perspective on the interrelation of sociotechnical shifts and emerging digital marketplaces, Kirchner and Beyer (2016) argue that digital technology reshapes established transactions through three basic mechanisms: delocalization, delegation, and digital market organization. (1) *Delocalization* loosens strong ties to a particular physical place of objects or activities. For example, MP3 files can be more easily transferred than a regular audio CD can, and mobile digital technologies enable workers to perform their work outside their designated workplaces. (2) *Delegation* allows the reassignment of work tasks from regular employees to external actors. This development ranges from early examples of IT outsourcing to more recent phenomena, such as paid crowd sources and unpaid Internet users that perform essential tasks in novel value-creation processes (Kleemann, Voß, & Rieder, 2008; Bauer & Gegenhuber, 2015). (3) *Digital market organization* represents a market-bound form of intermediation on the Internet. Here, market organizers combine opportunities of delocalization (e.g., using a worldwide mobile IT infrastructure) and delegation (e.g., using contributions to user-evaluation systems) to establish a sociotechnical infrastructure for digital marketplaces. In this sense, digitalization systematically enables and fosters the rise of market organizers as specialized intermediaries on digital marketplaces.

A market organizer is not exceptional, of course. Historically, many marketplaces were organized to allow for a safe exchange of goods (Aspers & Darr, 2017), the most salient example being stock exchanges, which are formal organizations, yet serve as prime examples of markets in general (Ahrne et al., 2015; Langley & Leyshon, 2016). Considering markets from a field perspective, Fligstein and McAdam (2012) and Dombrowski (2016) similarly argue that formal organizations often provide substantial contributions in many markets. As internal governance units, market organizers perform several functions to uphold established market orders – in the form of standardization organizations or trade associations that regulate the properties of goods and services facilitating market processes, for example. In fact, Ahrne et al. (2015) note that scholars often incorrectly conceive of 'organization' and 'market' as mutually exclusive. They argue that organization and market usually mesh, as market transactions require certain organizational elements.

Thus, digital marketplaces of the sharing economy represent a specific form of the organization of markets, because a market organizer (a formal organization) digitally mediates market transactions between sellers and buyers on an Internet platform. To date, however, it remains largely unclear what specific elements market organizers install to operate market orders on digital marketplaces. Ahrne et al. (2015) proposed an analysis of the organization of markets along five key organizational elements that represent elements of a decided order: membership, rules, monitoring, sanctions, and hierarchy. (See Ahrne & Brunsson, 2011; Ahrne et al., 2015; Ahrne, Brunsson, & Seidl, 2016; also Rasche, de Bakker, & Moon, 2013; and a critical response by Apelt, Besio, Corsi, et al., 2017.) According to Ahrne and Brunsson (2011), these five elements represent core features of regular formal organization, which they call 'complete organization'. They also argue, however, that these elements can be found outside formal organizations, including in markets, where the elements define buyers and sellers and their interrelations, rights, and responsibilities. Thus, sharing economy platforms can be investigated according to their specific configuration of organizational elements that underlie the particular elements that characterize their digital marketplaces.

In the following subsections, we use the five elements of organization outlined by Ahrne *et al.* (2015) as a general taxonomy to flesh out the common properties of the market orders in the two sharing-economy marketplaces – Lyft and Airbnb – based on website information, existing studies, and company reports.

Membership: Account Membership

Market organizers require sellers and buyers to create an account to interact on the digital marketplace (van Dijck, 2009). Creating an account requires sellers and buyers to agree to the general rules of the marketplace and to reveal their identities by providing such information as full name, residential address, e-mail address, social media account information, payment information, and telephone number. Airbnb, for example, verifies identities by telephone numbers and profile photos, and sometimes requires additional verification by photo ID. The implications of accounts differ for buyers and sellers: Whereas seller profiles routinely identify buyers, their registration often resembles the rules and procedures of consumer websites, such as those in regular retail Internet businesses. (See Chapter 4.) In contrast, a seller account often entails more extensive rules and responsibilities regarding, for instance, detailed rules on providing a service, the extend of shared and verified personal information, or descriptions of offers. Thus, at least a seller setting up an account constitutes a form of membership that could be called 'account membership'. Account membership serves as a necessary precondition for displaying information, offering goods and services, placing orders, and eventually performing market transactions.

Account membership constitutes a limited and vague form of membership as compared to membership in a regular, formal organization (Luhmann, 2000) – as an employee in a company, for example. A marketplace does not use membership to command members to perform particular actions. It merely grants access to a general frame that enables market-related activities. With these properties, account membership is similar to club membership (Ahrne & Brunsson, 2011) or membership in a voluntary association (Lütz, 2006): Users can perform certain activities that comply with general rules, yet are typically not contractually obliged to routinely perform specific actions, as employees of a company would be.

The boundaries of membership status represent a key issue for sharing economy platforms. It is noteworthy that some market organizers of the sharing economy go to great lengths to ensure that sellers have no formal employment relationship with market organizers. Uber provides prominent examples for this argument, with its currently pending court cases regarding requests that drivers be treated as employees and be granted such rights as minimum wage and holiday pay (Davies, 2017), and the questioning of its regulatory status as a mediator rather than a transport service (Bowcott, 2017).

Rules: Algorithmic Bureaucracy

Market organizers decide on rules that users must comply with (Evans, 2012) – rules defining the type of goods or services that can be offered and the general conditions and processes for user-generated information and market transactions. Marketplaces implement rules on processes by their technical infrastructure operating through algorithms. (See Orlikowski & Scott, 2015; see generally Mittelstadt, Allo, Taddeo, *et al.*, 2016.) Algorithms generate a user interface of apps or websites, allowing users to act according to predefined processes and preselected information and to choose from the options presented.

Digital marketplaces enforce a regime of rules (Butler, Joyce, & Pike, 2008). Developing the idea of algorithmic governance (Müller-Birn, Dobusch, & Herbsleb, 2013), this regime could be termed *algorithmic bureaucracy*. Comparable to traditional bureaucracies, activities in digital marketplaces resemble predefined 'performance programs' (March & Simon, 1958) or 'conditional programs' (see Luhmann, 2000) performing simple bureaucratic if-A-then-do-B rules. Thus, similar to regular formal organizations (Mintzberg, 1979), marketplaces standardize processes by bureaucratic routines to cope effectively with the vast uncertainty and the manifold options of possible user activities. Performance programmes ensure the predictable and routine processing of information and transactions on the digital marketplace.

In clear contrast to formal organizations, digital marketplaces implement these processes through websites or app interfaces. On digital marketplaces, algorithmic interfaces appear as impersonal entities, whereas employees in regular organizations would traditionally perform bureaucratic programmes. Users on digital marketplaces cannot act in a way that is not already included in these technical interfaces.

Monitoring: User Evaluations and Process Data Recording

Market organizers monitor user behaviour through their technical infrastructure to ensure compliance with rules. The technological infrastructure allows for a comprehensive recording, storage, and analysis of the user data generated (van Dijck, 2009: 47). Often referred to as 'big data' (Lazer & Radford, 2017), these data masses create an extensive reservoir for quasi-panoptic observations (see Foucault, 1977) of users by the market organizers. Additionally, online evaluation systems gather comprehensive data about users' activities. (See Orlikowski & Scott, 2014; Orlikowski & Scott, 2015; Diekmann & Przepiorka, forthcoming.) Users generate these data as they rank, rate, describe, or comment on offers, users, and transactions. At Lyft, both drivers and passengers can be ranked on a 5-point scale, and anything below 4.8 is defined by the platform as problematic. The platform also asks for written feedback and sends drivers a weekly passenger feedback summary, flagging potentially problematic issues. Airbnb uses a longer questionnaire for guests and hosts, embracing such dimensions as communication, location, and cleanliness of the property, which are also ranked on a 5-point scale. Guests and hosts also can provide additional written evaluative statements. Airbnb, like Lyft, mediates in case of problems and provides advice for such issues as giving and dealing with negative evaluations.

User evaluation systems facilitate several mechanisms that digital marketplaces require to operate:

(1) Comprehensive evaluation systems create a basic *comparability of offers* (Beckert, 2009; Kirchner & Beyer, 2016; Aspers & Darr, 2017). Offers can be ordered and related to individual preferences, and rankings, ratings, descriptions, and comments become 'judgment devices' (Karpik, 2010).

(2) Evaluation systems also *facilitate trust* between sellers and buyers – a necessary basis of any working market order (Beckert, 2009; Kirchner & Beyer, 2016; Aspers & Darr, 2017; Kornberger, Pflueger, & Mouritsen, 2017). Reputation and the number of completed transactions allow for a more reliable assessment of users' trustworthiness (Diekmann & Przepiorka, forthcoming). To some extent, evaluation systems substitute for prices as the main market signal, rendering them a key mechanism for structuring market transactions on digital marketplaces (Aspers & Darr, 2017), and *terms of trade become terms of evaluation*. This means that evaluations by ratings and rankings provide the basis for successful market exchanges on the marketplaces. Good ratings enable sellers and buyers to participate, whereas bad ratings lower the chances of selling or buying. Evaluations, especially for Airbnb, substantially determine the prices that sellers can charge, because good ratings signal trustworthiness and service quality.

(3) The evaluation system congenially *complements algorithmic bureaucracy*. Whereas the technical infrastructure enforces the rules of algorithmic bureaucracy on the Internet platform, user-evaluation systems cover activities or information that are not processed directly via app or website interfaces. This includes the actual performing of the service, the delivery of the goods, and the experienced quality and accuracy of descriptions. Combining user data and evaluation results allows market organizers to monitor user activities comprehensively, efficiently, and effectively.

Sanctions: Exclusion and Rating Impact on Transactions Terms

Market organizers can sanction users to enforce marketplace rules through such effective forms of sanctioning as market exclusion. Revoking account membership disenables users to perform transactions or take part in other marketplace activities. (See Evans, 2012.) The mere threat of exclusion enforces marketplace rules, which, in some respects, is similar to exclusion and rule enforcement in formal organizations (Luhmann, 2000). A violation of a single rule allows for exclusion – the loss of account membership status. The technical infrastructure limits the need to sanction members negatively, because options are either technically presented or simply not provided. Deviant behaviour in the marketplace is therefore substantially contained. Additionally, user evaluation systems decrease the need for direct sanctioning by the market organizer because bad user ratings result in decreased transaction chances and lower obtained prices. Conversely, good user ratings increase transaction opportunities and raise obtained prices. In combination, these mechanisms enable an effective sanctioning of user behaviour.

Hierarchy: Asymmetrically Decided Order

The market organizer – being a formal organization itself – assumes a strong hierarchical role in the digital marketplace. In this technically enabled power position (see Dolata, 2017), market organizers decide asymmetrically on the organization of the digital marketplace, designing and adapting membership, rules, monitoring, and sanctions. There is usually no routine mechanism of voice, vote, or other forms of direct participation of users in a marketplace.

This obviously strong position of asymmetrical power by market organizers must not be confused with universal power – a critical distinction, because other perspectives may result in accounts that view the unquestionably powerful technology as overly deterministic. Similar to traditional organizations, in which actual work practices often undermine attempts to standardize workflows and control member activities through technology (Orlikowski & Robey, 1991), users of platforms can evade some of the formal rules and monitoring efforts. (See Orlikowski, 2000; Orlikowski & Scott, 2014.) Airbnb, for example, requires full names and suggests that sellers and buyers upload a personal account photo to provide a sense of security and relatability. Users actually employ this information to discriminate, however – on the basis of race, for example (Edelman & Luca, 2014). Additionally, some marketplace users take advantage of the platform's search and communication infrastructure to find accommodations, but then exchange private contact details with the seller in order save the transaction fee by undertaking transactions outside the platform (Aspers & Darr, 2017). In such cases, users employ mechanisms programmed to facilitate market order for unintended purposes. Market organizers must therefore engage in a general process of constant adaption to integrate other user activities (Dolata, 2015; Grenz & Eisewicht, 2015), prevent undesired activities (e.g., deviance, fraud, disorder), and incorporate desired ones (e.g., new process accommodating specific user demands or preferences). Other deviant activities, such as the fake reviews that plague other platforms, including Amazon, TripAdvisor, and Yelp (Orlikowski & Scott, 2014; Luca & Zervas, 2015), seem to be less often associated with Lyft or Airbnb, because the technical infrastructure of the platform ties the reviews directly to transactions.

Additionally, although individual sellers and buyers have practically no direct say in the organization of the marketplace, one could assume that users could collectively pressure the market organizer – in the form of a collective outcry, collective behaviour shifts, or collective reinterpretation of rules, for instance. To date, however, protests come mainly from established competitors, as evidenced by the recent anti-Uber protests by taxi drivers around the world (Schmidt, 2016).

A Digital Market Order Comprising Five Organizational Elements

Summarizing our argument, the hierarchical position enables market organizers to enforce binding decisions about general user activities through membership, rules, monitoring, and sanctions. Table 1 briefly summarizes the five elements and the associated general characteristics of the digital marketplaces.

Table 1 *Five Elements of Organization and Digital Marketplaces*

Element	Description according to Ahrne & Brunsson, 2011	Characteristic of the digital marketplaces
(1) Membership	Decide who joins as member	Account membership
(2) Rules	Require members to comply	Algorithmic bureaucracy
(3) Monitoring	Surveil members' compliance with commands and rules	User evaluations and process data recording
(4) Sanctions	Impose positive or negative sanctions on members	Exclusion and rating impact on transactions terms
(5) Hierarchy	Exercise a right to make binding decisions	Asymmetrically decided order

The combination and interrelation of the five elements enable the organization of a sufficiently stable market order for the users. The rules of the algorithmic bureaucracy predetermine processes on the digital marketplaces and inhibit unwanted activities. These technically implemented rules are complemented by user evaluations that cover aspects of the digital marketplace that cannot be transformed into algorithmic processes. Thus, algorithmic bureaucracy and evaluation systems provide two core mechanisms for market organizers to establish and maintain a new kind of market order on digital marketplaces.

We would like to highlight two important points here.

First, market organizers implement powerful and effective rules on the digital marketplace based on their materiality (Orlikowski, 2000; Orlikowski & Scott, 2015): Digital marketplaces build on an extensive sociotechnical infrastructure that is necessary to process communication and market transactions on an Internet platform. This sociotechnical infrastructure determines processes by inscribing rules into the technology, so that only rule-conforming processes allow for successful user activities on the Internet platform (e.g., market transactions or information sharing). Here, algorithms or 'code, in the form of an operating system, becomes the medium for connecting disparate actors' (Langley & Leyshon, 2016: 5; see Evans, 2011). In this sense, algorithmic code restricts user behaviour and fulfils a law-like function at the expense of other options (Kenney & Zysman, 2016; Orlikowski & Scott, 2015). The rules of the decided order need to be enacted in practice, however. Although market organizers implement formal rules in the platform infrastructure in order to facilitate market transactions, some users employ the same infrastructure to discriminate against other users or to communicate with each other privately, thereby evading marketplace fees. Only in practice does the powerful materiality of marketplace rules meet the opportunities of users to reinterpret and potentially circumvent the decided order implemented in the code (Grenz & Eisewicht, 2015; Aspers & Darr, 2017).

Second, a digital marketplace represents a specific configuration of the five organizational elements that enable a formal organization – the market organizer – to operate a digital marketplace. Digital markets are highly organized, because all five organizational elements are applied. They are not applied in a way that would resemble a full-fledged formal organization with employees, however. Conveniently, the evasion of such a standard formal organization significantly reduces responsibilities (e.g., employee rights, compensation, voice mechanisms, and regulatory responsibilities) that would require substantial resources and coordination efforts from market organizers. At the same time, algorithmic bureaucracy and evaluation systems implemented through the technological infrastructure substitute for more hierarchical and binding structures possible only in full-fledged formal organizations. By employing this specific configuration of organizational elements, digital market organizers are able to scale up and adapt their platform business models. In fact, this effective limbo between partial and complete organization may constitute the very basis for successful market organizers to achieve a quick-growth, low-fixed-cost, high-flexibility business operation with just enough control to extract transaction fees. This may also be the secret of the rapid growth and international success of the sharing economy platforms, pioneered and exemplified by Lyft and Airbnb.

The sharing economy platforms take a generally diffused pattern in the platform economy to a further level, because sharing-economy market organizers deploy a general template of digital market orders (Kirchner & Beyer, 2016) to commodify private resources and harness labour power from amateurs. The sharing-economy platform effectively advances marketization into social arenas that previously were not generally under the pressures of market mechanisms. Thus, market organizers in the sharing economy, like Lyft and Airbnb, do not merely mediate communications between buyers and sellers. By installing the five elements of organization, the market organizers decide on specific rules, and subsequently monitor and sanction these rules. Through these technologically enabled mechanisms, market organizers of the sharing economy govern how the services are offered, categorized, performed, evaluated, and paid for.

TOWARDS AN IRON CAGE OF ALGORITHMIC BUREAUCRACY?

In the so-called sharing economy, market organizers serve as transformative agents installing new market orders with a digital format. In the created market order on digital marketplaces, market organizers constitute an essential fourth actor, providing an infrastructure to intermediate between sellers and buyers for their own interest. Theoretical positions that consider only sellers and buyers would fail to capture this crucial structural difference. By installing organizational elements, market organizers of the sharing economy effectively transform 'peers', 'communities', and 'crowds' into organized participants on a digital marketplace. Furthermore, if the spread of digital technology systematically facilitates the intermediary position of market organizers (see Kirchner & Beyer, 2016), the rise of the platform economy should systematically foster a further rise of market organizers. Thus, instead of viewing digitalization as a mere technological or innovative process, we need to engage more with the *organizers of digitalization* and the emerging *organization of a digital society*. This need for engagement underlines the possible contribution of the five organizational elements for research on digital marketplaces in particular, and for research on the transformative power of the Internet and digital technology for society in general.

Our investigation yields general insights for the perspective of the organization of markets. Digital marketplaces clearly represent a current and perhaps central case for the organization-of-markets perspective. The diffusion of digital marketplaces in many social arenas poses critical questions that call for future investigation: Are we perhaps facing an iron cage of algorithmic bureaucracy, as more and more markets assume a digital format? How does the omnipresence of panoptic evaluation systems on digital marketplaces shape interactions between sellers and buyers? How do digital marketplaces change social arenas that face intensified pressures of marketization? These questions clearly deserve further consideration and empirical analyses in organization studies and beyond.

REFERENCES

Ahrne, G., Aspers, P., & Brunsson, N. (2015) The Organization of Markets. *Organization Studies* 36(1): 7–27.

Ahrne, G. & Brunsson, N. (2011) Organization outside Organizations: The Significance of Partial Organization. *Organization* 18(1): 83–104.

Ahrne, G., Brunsson, N., & Seidl, D. (2016) Resurrecting Organization by Going beyond Organizations. *European Management Journal* 34(2): 93–101.

Apelt, M., Besio, C., Corsi, G., von Groddeck, V., Grothe-Hammer, M., & Tacke, V. (2017) Resurrecting Organization without Renouncing Society: A Response to Ahrne, Brunsson and Seidl. *European Management Journal* 35(1): 8–14.

Aspers, P. & Darr, A. (2017) *A Marketplace in Cyberspace? The Social Infrastructure of Online Trade* – Draft Version.

Bauer, R. M. & Gegenhuber, T. (2015) Crowdsourcing: Global Search and the Twisted Roles of Consumers and Producers. *Organization* 22(5): 661–81.

Beckert, J. (2009) The Social Order of Markets. *Theory and Society* 38(3): 245–69.

Belk, R. (2014) You Are What You Can Access: Sharing and Collaborative Consumption Online. *Journal of Business Research* 67(8): 1595–600.

Bowcott, O. (2017) Uber to Face Stricter EU Regulation after ECJ Rules It Is Transport Firm. *The Guardian*. Retrieves 23 January 2018 from www .theguardian.com/technology/2017/dec/20/uber-european-court-of-justice-ruling-barcelona-taxi-drivers-ecj-eu.

Brinkmann, U. & Seifert, M. (2001) 'Face to Interface': Zum Problem der Vertrauenskonstitution im Internet am Beispiel von elektronischen Auktionen. *Zeitschrift für Soziologie* 30(1): 23–47.

Butler, B., Joyce, E., & Pike, J. (2008) Don't Look Now, but We've Created a Bureaucracy: The Nature and Roles of Policies and Rules in Wikipedia. *Proceedings of the SIGCHI Conference on Human Factors in Computing Systems*. Florence, Italy: ACM. 1101–10.

Constantiou, I., Eaton, B., & Tuunainen, V. K. (2016) The Evolution of a Sharing Platform into a Sustainable Business. *2016 49th Hawaii International Conference on System Sciences (HICSS)*. 1297–306.

Cusumano, M. A. (2015) How Traditional Firms Must Compete in the Sharing Economy. *Communications of the ACM* 58(1): 32–34.

Davies, R. (2017) Uber to Take Appeal over Ruling on Drivers' Status to UK Supreme Court. *The Guardian*. Retrieved 23 January 2018 from www .theguardian.com/technology/2017/nov/24/uber-to-take-appeal-over-ruling-on -drivers-status-to-uk-supreme-court.

Davis, G. F. & Thompson, T. A. (1994) A Social Movement Perspective on Corporate Control. *Administrative Science Quarterly* 39(1): 141–73.

Diekmann, A. & Przepiorka, W. (forthcoming) Trust and Reputation in Markets. In F. Giardini & R. Wittek (eds.), *The Oxford Handbook of Gossip and Reputation*. Oxford: Oxford University Press.

Dolata, U. (2015) Volatile Monopole. Konzentration, Konkurrenz und Innovationsstrategien der Internetkonzerne. *Berliner Journal für Soziologie* 24 (4): 505–29.

Dolata, U. (2017) Apple, Amazon, Google, Facebook, Microsoft Market Concentration – Competition – Innovation Strategies. In U. Dolata (ed.), SOI Discussion Paper. Stuttgart: University of Stuttgart, Institute for Social Sciences.

Dombrowski, S. (2016) Networks, Institutions, Culture and Association? A Case Study on Associative Action in the German Markets for Organic Food. *Centre for Globalisation and Governance Working Paper Series*. Hamburg: Centre for Globalisation and Governance.

Edelman, B. G. & Luca, M. (2014) Digital Discrimination: The Case of Airbnb.com. *Harvard Business School NOM Unit Working Paper*. Harvard Business School.

Evans, D. S. (2011) *Platform Economics: Essays on Multi-Sided Businesses*, Chicago: Competition Policy International.

Evans, D. S. (2012) Governing Bad Behavior by Users of Multi-Sided Platforms. *Berkeley Technology Law Journal* 2(27): 1202–49.

Evans, P. C. & Gawer, A. (2016) The Rise of the Platform Enterprise. A Global Survey. The Emerging Platform Economy Series. New York: The Center for Global Enterprise.

Fligstein, N. (2001) *The Architecture of Markets. An Economic Sociology of Twenty-First-Century Capitalist Societies*. Princeton: Princeton University Press.

Fligstein, N. & McAdam, D. (2012) *A Theory of Fields*. Oxford: Oxford University Press.

Foucault, M. (1977) *Überwachen und Strafen: Die Geburt des Gefängnisses*. Frankfurt am Main: Suhrkamp.

Goffman, E. (1977) *Rahmen-Analyse ein Versuch über die Organisation von Alltagserfahrungen*, Frankfurt am Main: Suhrkamp.

Grenz, T. & Eisewicht, P. (2015) Outlaws in App Stores: die Nebenfolgenanfälligkeit digitaler Dienste als blinder Fleck der Service Science. *Arbeits- und Industriesoziologische Studien* 8(1): 76–94.

Hartl, B., Hofmann, E., & Kirchler, E. (2016) Do We Need Rules for 'What's Mine Is Yours'? Governance in Collaborative Consumption Communities. *Journal of Business Research* 69(8): 2756–63.

Karpik, L. (2010) *Valuing the Unique: The Economics of Singularities*, Princeton: Princeton University Press.

Kenney, M. & Zysman, J. (2016) The Rise of the Platform Economy. *Issues in Science & Technology* XXXII(3).

Kirchner, S. & Beyer, J. (2016) Die Plattformlogik als digitale Marktordnung. Wie die Digitalisierung Kopplungen von Unternehmen löst und Märkte transformiert. *Zeitschrift für Soziologie* 45(5): 324–39.

Kleemann, F., Voß, G. G., & Rieder, K. (2008) Un(der)paid Innovators: The Commercial Utilization of Consumer Work through Crowdsourcing. *Science, Technology & Innovation Studies* 4(1): 5–26.

Kornberger, M., Pflueger, D., & Mouritsen, J. (2017) Evaluative Infrastructures: Accounting for Platform Organization. *Accounting, Organizations and Society* 60 (Supplement C): 79–95.

Langley, P. & Leyshon, A. (2016) Platform Capitalism: The Intermediation and Capitalisation of Digital Economic Circulation. *Finance and Society* EarlyView: 1–21.

Lazer, D. & Radford, J. (2017) Data ex Machina: Introduction to Big Data. *Annual Review of Sociology* 43: 19–39.

Luca, M. & Zervas, G. (2015) Fake It Till You Make It: Reputation, Competition, and Yelp Review Fraud. *Harvard Business School NOM Unit Working Paper.* Cambridge, MA: Harvard Business School.

Luhmann, N. (2000) *Organisation und Entscheidung.* Opladen: Westdt. Verl.

Lütz, S. (2006) Einleitung: Governance in der politischen Ökonomie. In S. Lütz (ed.), *Governance in der politischen Ökonomie.* Wiesbaden: VS Verlag. 13–56.

Mair, J. & Reischauer, G. (2017) Capturing the Dynamics of the Sharing Economy: Institutional Research on the Plural Forms and Practices of Sharing Economy Organizations. *Technological Forecasting and Social Change* online first.

Mintzberg, H. (1979) *The Structuring of Organizations.* Englewood Cliffs: Prentice-Hall.

Mittelstadt, B. D., Allo, P., Taddeo, M., Wachter, S., & Floridi, L. (2016) The Ethics of Algorithms: Mapping the Debate. *Big Data & Society* 3(2): 2053951716679679.

Müller-Birn, C., Dobusch, L., & Herbsleb, J. D. (2013) Work-to-Rule: The Emergence of Algorithmic Governance in Wikipedia. *Proceedings of the 6th International Conference on Communities and Technologies.* ACM.

National Public Radio. (2016) Interview: 'NPR How I Built This'. Airbnb: Joe Gebbia (17 October 2016), downloaded on 16 February 2017. Washington, DC: National Public Radio.

National Public Radio. (2017) Interview: 'NPR How I Built This'. Lyft: John Zimmer (13 February 2017), download on 16 February 2017. Washington, DC: National Public Radio.

Orlikowski, W. & Scott, S. V. (2015) The Algorithm and the Crowd: Considering the Materiality of Service Innovation. *MIS Quarterly* 39(1): 201–16.

Orlikowski, W. J. (2000) Using Technology and Constituting Structures: A Practice Lens for Studying Technology in Organizations. *Organization Science* 11(4): 404–28.

Orlikowski, W. J. & Scott, S. V. (2014) What Happens When Evaluation Goes Online? Exploring Apparatuses of Valuation in the Travel Sector. *Organization Science* 25(3): 868–91.

PricewaterhouseCoopers. (2015) The Sharing Economy, accessed 24 January 2018 at www.pwc.com/cis. In *Consumer Intelligence Series.* Delaware: PricewaterhouseCoopers.

Rao, H. (2008) *Market Rebels: How Activists Make or Break Radical Innovations.* Princeton: Princeton University Press.

Rasche, A., de Bakker, F. G. A., & Moon, J. (2013) Complete and Partial Organizing for Corporate Social Responsibility. *Journal of Business Ethics* 115(4): 651–63.

Schmidt, F. A. (2016) Arbeitsmärkte in der Plattformökonomie – Zur Funktionsweise und den Herausforderungen von Crowdwork und Gigwork. In A.W.-u. (ed.), *Sozialpolitik*. Bonn: Friedrich-Ebert-Stiftung.

Schneiberg, M., King, M., & Smith, T. (2008) Social Movements and Organizational Form: Cooperative Alternatives to Corporations in the American Insurance, Dairy, and Grain Industries. *American Sociological Review* 73(4): 635–67.

Schneiberg, M. & Lounsbury, M. (2008) Social Movements and Institutional Analysis. In *The SAGE Handbook of Organizational Institutionalism*. Thousand Oaks, CA: SAGE. 650–72.

Schneiberg, M. & Soule, S. A. (2005) Institutionalization as a Contested Multilevel Process. In G. F. Davis, D. McAdam, W. R. Scott, *et al.* (eds.), *Social Movements and Organizations*. Cambridge: Cambridge University Press. 122–60.

Schor, J. (2014) Debating the Sharing Economy. *A Great Transition Initiative Essay*. Online: Great Transition Initiative.

Schor, J. B. & Fitzmaurice, C. J. (2015) Collaborating and Connecting: The Emergence of the Sharing Economy. In L. A. Reisch & J. Thøgersen (eds.), *Handbook of Research on Sustainable Consumption*. Cheltenham: Edward Elgar. 410–25.

Snow, D. A., Rochford Jr., E. B., Worden, S. K., & Benford, R. D. (1986) Frame Alignment Processes, Micromobilization, and Movement Participation. *American Sociological Review* 51(4): 464–81.

Strang, D. & Meyer, J. W. (1993) Institutional Conditions for Diffusion. *Theory and Society* 22(4): 487–511.

van Dijck, J. (2009) Users Like You? Theorizing Agency in User-Generated Content. *Media, Culture & Society* 31(1): 41–58.

ACKNOWLEDGEMENT

The authors are grateful to Robert M. Bauer, Tilo Grenz, Otto Hüther, Robert Jungmann, and Lauri Wessel for helpful and provoking comments that contributed to a significant sharpening and improvement of our chapter.

7 Organizing for Independence

Ingrid Gustafsson and Kristina Tamm Hallström

The contemporary world is populated by formal organizations. More and more social orders, such as churches, associations, or family businesses are now transformed into an institutionalized order of a formal organization, which ascribes certain features. They are assumed to have a rationalized and coherent 'inside'; they are assumed to have borders depicting them as separated entities; they are autonomous and sovereign. As such, formal organizations are expected to make their own decisions, to set their own agenda, and to act in their own stated interest (Brunsson & Sahlin-Andersson, 2000; Bromley & Meyer, 2015).

For a growing number of organizations – whether expert, media, or consultancy organizations with a mission of serving the public interest – the list of characteristics to show to the outside world requires an additional feature: These organizations need to demonstrate their *independence*. An increasing number of contemporary organizations appear to be viewing independence as a valuable quality worth organizing for if they are to be perceived as trustworthy actors. We understand the ideal of independence as closely linked to such qualities as autonomy and sovereignty – institutionalized features of the formal organization. Ideally, an independent organization is autonomous and sovereign in relation to its environment. The general idea seems to be that an independent organization is less prone to corruption and illicit behaviour. And indeed, organizations invest heavily in resources in order to construct an image of independence for the outside world to see and endorse.

As discussed in this chapter, however, independence is also a complicated, fragile quality that can be easily questioned. It is far from a binary state of being. Organizations obviously require resource dependencies for their functioning, but they are also dependent on the external world for their credibility. It is difficult for an organization to proclaim its own independence. Independence is constructed through dependency relationships with other formal organizations that grant the organization independence, like the dubbing of knights.

Organizations trying to maintain an image of independence, autonomy, and sovereignty must guard against becoming too dependent on others; they should carefully consider the implications of following the rules of others or being monitored by them. Our analysis demonstrates the construction of independence through partial organization among organizations. We analyse the character of these dependencies with respect to rules, sanctions, hierarchy, monitoring, and membership, how the various elements of organization form a complex system of interdependent organizations, and that this system is constructed in order to secure the independence of those organizations. Through this analysis, we are able to differentiate among the elements and discuss where and why some elements and combination of elements are used. We also discuss the dynamics of partial organization, in terms of escalating structures of elements added to each other – and then coming to a halt – in the organizing efforts of constructing an image of independence.

INDEPENDENCE AND AUDITING

The notion of independence is particularly interesting to analyse in relation to organizations performing audits of other organizations, such as accreditation organizations (hereafter 'accreditors') and certification organizations ('certifiers'). Independence is perceived as a fundamental ideal for organizations that promote 'independent auditing' as a service offered in the public interest. The widespread use of independent auditing is often justified as the right of the general public to obtain more knowledge about the goings-on in organizations. It is claimed that investors, customers, and citizens cannot trust organizations to behave in an acceptable fashion in such matters as the economy, ethics, sustainability, occupational health and safety, and security. We are told that we live in an audit society, characterized by the logic of distrust (Shapiro, 1987; Power, 1997). The general notion that organizations cannot be trusted – that there is always a risk that they work purely in their self-interests – reinforces the demand for external control: auditing, inspection, monitoring, evaluation, certification, and accreditation. It is by these means that organizations endeavour to affirm their credibility (Johansson & Lindgren, 2013).

Independence in the literature on financial auditing

Accounting scholars have long been interested in analysing auditing and auditor independence as a measure of integrity – a distancing from auditing clients (Sikka & Willmott, 1995; Power, 2003, 2011; Kouakou, Boiral, & Gendron, 2013). According to that definition of independence, it is not appropriate for an auditor to be a shareholder in or to have a family or friendship relationship with employees in the audited company or to develop a substantial economic dependence on providing consultancy services to the audited company. The fundamental solution to such threats has been auditors' membership in and dependence on a professional auditors' association, which sets rules for its members and has the ability to sanction its members for non-compliance. Using the partial organization framework, this solution could be understood in terms of de-organization or weakening of the auditing organization that employs the auditors. In other words, although suspicion could exist about an auditing firm prioritizing its self-interests as a profit-making company, the idea is that the auditors it employs, although partially organized with another organization, are loyal to the professional auditors' association with respect to their independence, and thus their capacity to serve the public interest.

The common depiction of 'independent auditing' has been questioned – as objectively defined and performed by neutral experts acting in the public interest. Auditing has, in fact, been described as highly political and contextually dependent (Humphrey & Moizer, 1990; Sikka & Willmott, 1995; Power 2003, 2011). The professional auditors' associations are not perceived as fully credible in their role as endorsers of independence for auditing organizations. Moreover, some audit scholars question the taken-for-granted nature of independence (Chapman & Peecher, 2011; Power, 2011); in some auditing contexts, the expert role of an auditing consultant appears to be valued more for credibility than for independence. Jamal and Sunder (2011) have shown, for instance, how certifiers of baseball cards were more highly valued with regard to such other attributes of the audit as price, competence, expertise, or service. We agree with this line of scholarly work that highlights 'independent auditing' as an idea and an ideal that does not necessarily exist per se, but it is constantly debated, developed, and changed. We also see how an analysis of the social construction of independence could be further nuanced through an organizational perspective that distinguishes among various dependency relationships and elements of organization.

Independence in the literature on certification and accreditation

Another type of auditing that has attracted scholarly attention during the past two decades is found in the area of certification, which, like financial auditing, is a monitoring activity based on standards – but for aspects other than accounting. The standards used for certification are the rules most often drafted, decided, and published by private organizations specializing in developing standards. Compared to rules issued by national parliaments or authorities, standards originate in private organizations and cannot be used as references in the public court system. A standard, as defined by the literature studying standards, 'can be defined as a rule for common and voluntary use, decided by one or several people or organizations' (Brunsson, Rasche, & Seidl, 2012: 616). Standards have become more and more detailed over time (Fouilleux & Loconto, 2016) – from rules of thumb to long, explicit, and complex written documents. Moreover, many current standards have evolved into rules directed towards organizations, such as the management system standard ISO 9001 for quality management – a standard for how organizations are to structure their administrative routines in order to become more efficient and enhance their quality (in whatever area of work they are active). Many organizations have chosen to complement the following of a specific standard by becoming certified by a third-party certifier with reference to that standard. Some people argue that it is through such monitoring mechanisms that standards gain credibility (Boiral & Gendron, 2011).

Linking back to our view on organizations as social actors, an ISO 9001 certification could be seen as a tool for an organization to become more of an actor, because the standard helps the organization to structure its 'inside' to become more rational and hierarchical – a critical feature of the modern actor – and the certification serves as a 'receipt' of that structuration (Meyer & Jepperson, 2000; Meyer, 2010; Bromley & Meyer, 2015). There are similar standards and monitoring devices specifically targeting certifiers and accreditors, but the focus of these standards and monitoring devices is the quality of auditor independence rather than efficiency and quality assurance.

In the emerging literature on certification, some studies specifically examine how independence is debated and managed at the operational level of certification. Contextual factors in audited organizations are highlighted as influential in the audit process and in the way independence is perceived in studies of ISO 9001 certification (Walgenbach, 2001) and ISO 14001 certification (Boiral, 2012; Kouakou et al., 2013), and in studies of certification for agriculture and food products (Hatanaka & Busch, 2008; Renard & Loconto, 2013). One limitation in these studies is the one-sided focus at the operational level, whereas contextual factors of the independence of the auditing organizations are omitted. Because attention has not focused on auditing organizations, these studies are missing an analysis of the independence problems they perceive and of the organizing efforts they engage in to handle such problems.

Other certification scholars have observed tendencies among certifiers to engage in a 'race to the bottom': When competition is tough among certifiers, which are dependent upon customer revenue, the ambition to monitor carefully and report deviations from standards is lowered in the hunt for customers (Bernstein & Cashore, 2007; Bartley, 2011; Marx, 2011; Boiral, 2012; Boiral & Gendron, 2011). A few of these studies mention accreditation as a way to overcome legitimacy and independence problems within certification (Hatanaka & Busch, 2008; Loconto & Busch, 2010; Gustafsson & Tamm Hallström, 2013; Tamm Hallström & Gustafsson, 2014; Hatanaka 2014; Brunsson, Gustafsson, & Tamm Hallström, 2018). In this line of research, the concept of a Tripartite Standards Regime has been developed to problematize and conceptualize contemporary regulatory structures that are organized through a combination of three intertwined practices: standard setting, certification, and accreditation (Loconto & Busch, 2010; Hatanaka, Konefal, & Constance, 2012; Galland, 2017, Gustafsson & Tamm Hallström, 2018).

Again, because few researchers have taken the organizational perspective seriously, neither specific certifiers nor specific accreditors have been studied explicitly. The literature on certification usually refers to the structures developed as emergent: 'hybrid', 'governance' or 'non-state', 'network' orders, with blurred boundaries among the organizations involved and between private and public sectors (Bernstein & Cashore, 2007; Bartley, 2007; Marx, 2008). This means, in turn, that there is a lack of theorizing about the work and organization of accreditation bodies as constructors of independence. There is an equal lack of general theorizing about the organizational nature and implications of the structures jointly constructed by standards, certification, and accreditation. Partial organization sheds light upon a somewhat different picture than the previous literature on certification and accreditation has done. Therefore, we aim in this chapter to contribute new knowledge on the organization of standards, certification, and accreditation in general, and the construction of independence within this field in particular. By applying the partial organization framework, we try to show the usage and strength of this theoretical perspective.

In order to do so, we use one of our studies on certifiers and accreditors (Gustafsson, 2016) to illustrate empirically how certification and accreditation activities were organized over a period of forty years. With the help of the partial organization framework, we analyse how these firms organize for independence, with attention to the use of various elements of organizations. Where and why are they used and combined? What drives or stops additional organization? We demonstrate how membership proves to be the key element in securing independence. The chapter ends with a discussion about the complex system of organizations that are organized through various elements of organization. We argue that this highly organized system resembles a rational, authoritative Weberian bureaucracy; but instead of neutral clerks, the system we describe is populated by formal organizations. And unlike Weberian bureaucracy, the system of standards, certification, and accreditation lacks a central authority to govern and to which an overall responsibility could be ascribed for the decisions made by the organizations involved.

ORGANIZING FOR INDEPENDENCE IN THE CASE OF THE NEW APPROACH

One of the fundamental ideas of the European Union (EU) was and still is the free circulation of products and services. In 1985, the EU launched a framework to organize its Single Market in order to support and enhance the circulation of products, but also to enable organizations to work across borders. The framework was called The New Approach (Council Resolution 85/C/136/01). Its founding idea was that the rules used on the Single Market were to be primarily voluntary standards – that national public authorities would not issue rules that were often not calibrated among the member countries and often caused confusion and impeded trade. The obligatory requirements were to be found in Directives, but the Directives referred to standards. The EU decided to give the standardization organization, European Committee for Standardization (CEN), a mandate to issue standards with requirements and needs established by the Union, tailored for specific EU Directives issued by the Parliament and the Commission. The coupling of standards and Directives is called the *principle of presumption*, which means that standards and standardization bodies were ascribed a central role in the Union. The EU justified this way of regulating goods and organizations on the Single Market as a way of reducing technical and administrative barriers to trade among the Member States.

The coupling of standards to EU Directives is one way to construct a decided order and enhance the impact of standards. The EU also coupled standards to monitoring activities created specifically to support compliance with standards and called for certification. Certification is an auditing activity conducted by specific certification firms, with the purpose of confirming whether the audited organization complies with a specific standard – say, ISO 9001. If the certification auditor judges that the organization meets the criteria of the standard, a certificate is issued. The EU explicitly argued – and decided – that the monitoring of standard compliance should not be conducted by public authorities, but by private certification firms. This was referred to as 'an open system' (SOU 2006: 113) – a system open to every certification firm wanting to join the market for certifiers. The EU decided that competition among certification firms would be the best way of enhancing efficiency of the certifiers (COM 89 final – SYN 208, Resolution 90/C 10/01), and it was explicitly argued that the organization of certification should be lean, efficient, and 'non-bureaucratic'.

Here, rules are combined with monitoring, which is not an unusual combination; a number of public authorities work to monitor the implementation of public laws. However, contrary to the public-sector version, the standards are voluntary rather than mandatory (Brunsson & Jacobsson, 2000). The private sector also differs from the public sector in that neither the rules (standards), nor the monitoring (certification) are free of charge for the auditee. The organization being certified pays for both the standard and the certification service. And the certification industry is becoming a lucrative and expanding market (Galland, 2017). Here, the EU encountered problems regarding trust and independence: How does one know that the certification firm is really doing what it is supposed to do and is not working merely to maximize its profits, letting the commercial aspects of business overcome objective and neutral auditing with integrity? A critical difference between the construction of independence of (commercial) financial audits and of (commercial) certification is that for certifiers, there is a lack of strong professional guidance and support of the auditor's ideas about independence. There is no such professionalization in the certification system. Rather, another type of organization is being added to the certifying organization. The EU decided that the best way to secure independence among certifiers was to monitor them. This is where *accreditation* enters the scene. According to the New Approach, accreditation is a form of monitoring conducted by an accreditation organization organized as a public authority (EC 765/ 2008), although in other contexts, a nongovernmental organization (NGO) or even a for-profit company performs accreditation. In other words, accreditation constitutes meta-monitoring – a monitoring (accreditation) of the monitoring (certification).

Just like certification, accreditation is made with reference to standards. There is a specific standard for the accreditation of certifiers (the ISO/IEC 17021). In order for a certifier to be accredited, it must have structures that verify its independent work. For example, the certifier is required to identify and sanction deviations, thereby avoiding arbitrary assessment; to adhere to recommendations to avoid consultation services (or at least to organize consultation and training departments separately and staff these departments with employees who are not working with audits); to establish a committee for safeguarding impartiality; and to obey rules about time limits of contracts between an individual auditor and a customer firm – all in order to safeguard the independence of the certifier. When certifiers are accredited compliance with ISO/IEC 17021, therefore, their independence is supposed to be secured. Independence, in turn, is justified with reference to trust making in markets: If an organization's products and services are monitored in markets through independent auditing, then, that organization can be trusted.

Moreover, there is a specific standard for becoming an accreditor (the ISO/IEC 17011). When an accreditor is following ISO/IEC 17011, it is to be regarded as independent. In other words, both certifiers and accreditors are standardized, in the sense that they are monitoring others with reference to standards *and* complying with standards themselves. It seemed important for the EU to separate certification from accreditation through different standards, and one way of securing independence for certification and accreditation was to decide that certifiers not be allowed to accredit and that accreditors could not certify. Moreover, in order to secure the independence of the certifier and accreditor, they are not allowed to issue the standards they use; only the standardizers are allowed to develop these standards (EG 94/38, EG 765/2008).

But again, standards were not enough. The EU decided that in order to secure the independence of accreditors, more organization was needed. First, the ISO/IEC 17011 was coupled with a specific EU Directive (765/2008). Second, the EU decided that, contrary to the certifiers, accreditors should be closed rather than part of an 'open system'. The EU decided that each Member State had to choose only one accreditor and dub it 'The National Accreditation Body' (NAB), and that the NAB should have the status of a public authority. Also, the accreditor should not be for profit, and its monitoring activities should be non-commercial. (Auditors are paid for their work, however.) These decisions were justified as a way of securing independence for the accreditors. They, in turn, work to secure the independence of certification firms. The certification firms conduct audits of organizations in markets that would not be trustworthy in the eyes of buyers, consumers, business partners, investors, and others, if it were not for their certification.

The search and efforts to organize for independence do not stop with the organization of accreditation and the accreditation of certification, however. The EU also decided that the national accreditor must be a member of the European Accreditation (EA; EC 765/2008). The EA is a meta-organization that monitors the peer-review procedure; the EA members monitor each other through rigorous peer-review processes. The membership and the monitoring it connotes become meta-meta-monitoring, therefore – a monitoring of the accreditation of certification. Through membership in the EA, the monitoring and rules in the system are coupled: To become a proper member of the EA, the accreditor must prove its compliance with ISO/IEC 17011 (for accreditors), prove that the accredited organizations (the certifiers) comply with ISO 17021 (for certifiers), and prove that the certified organizations comply with whatever standard they are certified against (ISO 9001 or ISO 14001, for example). In that way, EA membership is supposed to stabilize and unify the system of accreditation, certification, and standards.

But in order for accreditation, certification, and standards to be used globally, yet more elements of organization were added – this time through another meta-organization. The International Accreditation Forum (IAF), the global equivalent to the EA, is a meta-organization, to which accreditors and regional meta-accreditation organizations all over the world, such as EA and the African Accreditation Cooperation, may apply for membership. The members perform monitoring on each other with reference to standards. One of the purposes of the IAF is to ensure that the monitoring performed by the various member accreditation organizations maintains a certain uniform standard around the globe. Critical in this context is the independence of the accreditors. A founding idea is that accreditations made by IAF members should be interchangeable; an accreditation made by an IAF member is valid all over the world; a certifier accredited by any IAF member should be able to perform certification audits in any country. This idea fits well with the IAF slogan 'Certified once – accepted everywhere'.

ESCALATING ORGANIZATION AND THE BIRTH OF A BUREAUCRACY

The empirical account illustrates how the search for independence resulted in the addition of elements to elements, driving more and more organization. As noted in the introduction, it is difficult for an organization merely to claim independence. Rather, a fundamental way of convincing others of its independence is for an organization to become dependent on another organization that endorses its independence. In our account of auditing organizations, the way of organizing for independence was illustrated by certifiers being monitored by an accreditor, which in turn was monitored by a meta-organization, and so on. In the context of certification and accreditation auditing within the EU, however, we also see the emergence of a highly but partially organized system of organizations and elements of organization that together contribute to the construction of the alleged independence of the auditing organizations involved.

In this section, we first discuss and differentiate among the elements, their specific combinations, and the escalating structures of adding more and more organization identified in our empirical account. We then direct our attention to the complex system of organizations and the large number of decisions on various elements of organization that tie these organizations together: How can it be characterized, and what are the research implications of these systems?

Dynamics of and among elements

The specific organization of standards, certification, and accreditation that we have illustrated in this chapter demonstrates the use of all elements of organization. Most notably, *rules* are the backbone of the entire system – standards are used as a measure to organize organizations. Standards are not mandatory, which makes them an element of organization in need of support. They are therefore coupled to official and coercive directives, providing them with a specific impact. Standards also work as a way of sorting *monitoring* activities: one standard for certification, another for accreditation. The monitoring activity is also tightly coupled to standards. Certification is only 'certification' and accreditation is only 'accreditation' when conducted with reference to specific standards. Moreover, there is a clear division of labour here, with organizations working independently with clearly specified but interrelated tasks.

The organizations involved in various monitoring activities, such as certifiers and accreditors, and one or several layers of memberships, are organized in a certain way; they are not merely individual organizations in the vast environment of organizations organizing for independence. Rather, they are carefully structured into what resembles a *hierarchy*. On the one hand, it is a decided order for decision making, following a clear division of labour. The certifier decides whether the auditee should become certified or not; the accreditor decides whether the certifier should be accredited or not; the European meta-organization, EA, decides whether the accreditor should become a member or not; and the global meta-organization, IAF, decides whether the accreditor can become a member or not. On the other hand, decisions are not coercive. Because certification and accreditation are monitoring activities tailored for standard compliance, and because standards are voluntary, a majority of certifications and accreditations are voluntary. Only occasionally are the decisions coercive. (In some industries, accreditation is mandatory.) The outcome of certification and accreditation could be understood as *sanctions*, just as sanctions and hierarchy are closely related – all of these decisions on approving or rejecting a certificate could be understood in terms of either a positive or negative sanction. In addition to rules, monitoring, sanctions, and hierarchy, we found the use of *membership*. Membership is used as a tool to dub organizations worthy and independent. Only organizations showing their independence by following specific rules and through careful monitoring may be granted membership. (It is never really clear, however, in what way independence is evaluated.)

Not only do we see the use of elements connecting organizations all over the world, but organization also seems to be escalating. There is a constant need for more organization: more rules, more monitoring, more membership, and more hierarchical levels are added over time. One explanation is that the standards used are partial, in the sense that they are not coupled to either the standardization organization or the organization adopting the standard. Standards need support both from other rules and from monitoring. But why does the monitoring require monitoring? An explanation can be found in the audit literature, as noted in the introduction: monitoring (such as audit) is a tool for gaining insight into the activities of formal organizations – social orders that people in general do not seem to trust. Monitoring is a way of gaining insight, securing whatever values are at stake. The need for insight is not fully satisfied through certification. Certification is conducted by a formal organization, and one would need, therefore, to gain insight about the certifier too. The same goes for the accreditor – a formal organization as well. The trust problem of needing to gain insight through monitoring is not solved, but is pushed forward to the next organization through the addition of more elements, resulting in the escalation of organization we have described.

The addition of more organization eventually comes to a halt, however. But why? We note that when adding the element of membership, escalation stops. We also note that membership is an element that was put to use *after* the establishing of monitoring and rules. Mandatory membership in the EA was decided in 2008, more than twenty years after establishment of the first structure of the New Approach, through which standards were coupled with directives and certification. At the global level, with the IAF as a unifying meta-organization, organizing for independence came to a halt. The hierarchy was complete and the system closed – ironically, because this way of organizing does not really comply with ideas about independence and the autonomy and sovereignty of formal organizations. Becoming a member in a meta-organization is a way of sacrificing some of an organization's own autonomy (Ahrne & Brunsson, 2008). Hence, membership should be the element that circumscribes the autonomy of its members to the greatest extent and thereby threatens the independence they are seeking. In other words, when constructing and organizing for independence for standards, certification, and accreditation, membership should be the least likely element to use. Nevertheless, the escalating structures of elements of organization stop when membership is used and the quest for independence seems to stop. Perhaps this occurs because members of the meta-organizations belong to the same category of organization; membership is granted for accreditors only. In that way, it becomes more important to team up with fellow accreditors than to show independence by resigning from membership. Thus, being part of the same meta-organization seems to enhance independence. The other members mirror the picture of a true accreditor. In other words, the auditing organization's independence in relation to the auditee is enhanced through dependencies on other, similar organizations.

A bureaucracy for and by organizations

The specific way of organizing standards, certification, and accreditation detailed in this chapter is described, on the one hand, as global and commercial, covers countries all over the world, and is based on ideas about free trade and competition. On the other hand, the ideas put forward about how this global set of organizations should work together are based on decisions about the way monitoring activities should be conducted, the careful organization – through decisions – of the coupling of rules (standards to directives), between rules and monitoring (standards to certification and accreditation), between rules and membership (standards as the basis for joining EA and IAF), between memberships (i.e., membership in EA as a prerequisite for membership in IAF). And this dimension of standards, certification, and accreditation shows a decided order resembling that of a Weberian rational authority. It is through organization – a widespread system of coupled decisions – that order is established. In the Weberian organization, decisions coupled to other decisions are also a significant feature of the rational authority that is characteristic of bureaucracy. There are no 'emergent orders', 'institutional fields', or 'hybrid governance'. What we see, rather, is organization – a decided and systematized order – division of labour, formalization, hierarchi-zation within organizations, and co-ordination among organizations.

(1) There is a clear division of labour – a clear distinction among standardization organizations, certifiers, and accreditors which relies upon the idea that each organization should perform one and only one specific task and that these tasks should not overlap. The standardizer cannot certify, the certifier is not allowed to accredit (at least not if it is supposed to be 'independent'), and the accreditor cannot issue standards. Given the division of labour, there is also a clear specialization process, fuelled by the independence ideal. The certifiers should only certify and the accreditors should only accredit. Neither should offer customers commercial consultancy services because, as the argument goes, such commercial activities could harm the objectivity and hence the independence of the audit process. This results in a specialization of tasks for the involved organizations – specified and made explicit in different standards.

(2) There is a formalization process – formalization in the Weberian sense of the term – by which practices are conducted through documentation, following specified procedures. Standards are becoming more detailed and more elaborate, the requirements lengthier and growing. And standards are covering more and more aspects of life; more and more organizations are falling under the demands of standards. From 2008 onwards, the EU has made recurrent efforts to the organization of standardization, certification, and accreditation, not least by making the accreditation organization a nationally appointed body. The standards are constantly updated, requiring more and more documentation, which, in turn, breeds the formalization of activities.

(3) There is a hierarchization process. When issuing Directive 765/ 2008 and demanding that Member States appoint only one accreditation organization per member country, the EU started a process that could be analysed as a way of centralizing the system.

There are fewer organizations conducting accreditation than certification; there are fewer meta-accreditation organizations than accreditation organizations; and there is only one meta-meta-accreditation organization at a global level, all of which can be illustrated as a pyramid with the IAF on top.

(4) There are coordination processes among organizations. The EU devotes sizable resources to ensuring that coordination, unification, and hierarchization exists among standardizers, certifiers, and accreditors. Therefore, the use of standards and the regulatory infrastructure supporting them (such as national legislation or EU directives) results in a decided order that distributes coordination: who gets to do what and who can decide over whom. By deciding on membership, the EU could organize all accreditation organizations into one meta-organization. Membership is also the element that could (with the help of rules and monitoring) enable a global reach for the standards, certification, and accreditation system through IAF.

There are, arguably, striking similarities between the organization of standards, certification, and accreditation and a formal organization characterized by a Weberian bureaucracy. But there are significant and interesting differences as well. The organization is partial; it is not a discernible entity. It has no address or name. One does not become a member of the bureaucracy organization, but a member of a specific meta-organization. And there is no monitoring that covers all the organizations involved; rather, there is partial monitoring based on specific decisions. There is no single rule that applies to all organizations involved (there is no constitution), and there are partial rules that apply to each separate organization, differentiating them from each other. Furthermore, in the Weberian case, neutral clerks must follow rules. In the standardization bureaucracy, formal organizations should follow standards. Unlike the Weberian bureaucracy, there is no central coordinator. (See Chapter 2.) There is no government, no head office, no sovereign, no clear principal, and therefore no clear agent (Gustafsson, 2016). The EU is the decision maker behind many of the structures, but the system of standards, certification, and accreditation grows beyond Europe and stretches globally, not least through memberships in the global meta-organization IAF. And even though we can identify a centralization of the system, following certification organizations to IAF, IAF is not a central coordinator. IAF is not authorized to make decisions that apply to neither accreditation nor certification organizations. IAF can make decisions only regarding membership, meaning also that the coordination is partial. This, in turn, means that there is no central function, position, or organization to which responsibility can be located – a central implication of partial organization. Generally, making a decision is a way of allocating responsibility; the decision maker is to be held responsible for the decision. (Or, one could escape responsibility by appearing to make no decisions; Brunsson 1990.) Because the complex organization of standards, certification, and accreditation is a decided order – based on decisions – responsibility is everywhere. There are many decision makers, but no one central decision maker – no king, CEO, or prime minister. This is also why we say that these systems *resemble* a hierarchy and that there is a hierarchization process: There is not an actual hierarchy because a traditional, Weberian hierarchy includes the clear allocation of responsibility. In the system we studied, responsibility is difficult to locate, because everyone and no one is responsible. One implication of partial organization, therefore, is that responsibility becomes diffused. Although the allocation of responsibility falls beyond the scope of this chapter, it should be a future research task.

In summary, we have analysed and discussed the use of elements of organization in a specific empirical sector: the EU-based framework for standards, certification, and accreditation. But the theorizing of this system could be generalized and understood as an organizational phenomenon, present in other areas in society. In other works, we have called this type of organization a macro-organization (Brunsson *et al.*, 2018) – a complete organization in the sense that all elements are used, but the structure is not a formal organization. Grothe Hammer (2017) refers to the phenomenon as an 'organization without actorhood', referring to one of the critical aspects noted in this chapter: The particular organizational phenomenon is lacking a name and an address. It is not an entity with the ability to make decisions applicable to all parts of it. Therefore, it is not a formal organization and therefore not an actor; it cannot act and has no agency.

We could also speak of an inflationary organizational bubble – the final stage of a hyper-organized society (Bromley & Meyer, 2015), wherein organizations rather than people are organized. It is indeed a substantiation of a society thriving not only on formal organizations, but also on the organization among them. It seems paradoxical that in order to ensure and secure independence for organizations, instead of becoming autonomous and sovereign, the organizations become dependent not only on each other, but also on the decided order surrounding them.

REFERENCES

Ahrne, G. & Brunsson, N. (2008) *Meta-Organizations*. Cheltenham: Edward Elgar.

Ahrne, G. & Brunsson, N. (2011) Organization outside Organizations: The Significance of Partial Organization. *Organization* 18(1): 83–104.

Bartley, T. (2007) Institutional Emergence in an Era of Globalization: The Rise of Transnational Private Regulation of Labor and Environmental Conditions. *American Journal of Sociology* 113 (2): 297–351.

Bartley, T. (2011) Certification as a Mode of Social Regulation. In D. Levi-Faur (ed.), *Handbook on the Politics of Regulation*. Cheltenham: Edward Elgar. 441–52.

Bernstein, S. & Cashore, B. (2007) Can Non-State Global Governance Be Legitimate? An Analytical Framework. *Regulation and Governance* 1 (4): 1–25.

Boiral, O. (2012) ISO Certificates as Organizational Degrees? Beyond the Rational Myths of the Certification Process. *Organization Studies* 33(5–6): 633–54.

Boiral, O. & Gendron, Y. (2011) Sustainable Development and Certification Practices: Lessons Learned and Prospects. *Business Strategy and the Environment* 20(5): 331–47.

Bromley, P. & Meyer, J. W. (2015) *Hyper-Organization: Global Organizational Expansion*. Oxford: Oxford University Press.

Brunsson, N. (1990) Deciding for Responsibility and Legitimation. Alternative Interpretations of Organizational Decision Making. *Accounting, Organization and Society* 15(1–2): 47–59.

Brunsson, N. & Jacobsson, B. (2000) *A World of Standards.* Oxford: Oxford University Press.

Brunsson, N., Gustafsson, I., & Tamm Hallström, K. (2018) Markets, Trust and the Construction of Macro-Organizations. In N. Brunsson & M. Jutterström (eds.), *Organizing and Re-Organizing Markets.* Oxford: Oxford University Press. 136–52.

Brunsson, N. & Sahlin-Andersson, K. (2000) Constructing Organizations: The Example of Public Sector Reform. *Organization studies* 21(4): 721–46.

Brunsson, N., Rasche, A., & Seidl, D. (2012) The Dynamics of Standardization: Three Perspectives on Standards in Organization Studies. *Organization Studies* 33(5–6): 613–32.

Council Resolution 85/C/136/01 of 7 May 1985 on a new approach to technical harmonization and standards.

COM 89 final – SYN 208, Resolution 90/C 10/01 A global approach to certification and testing.

Chapman, C. & Peecher, M. E. (2011) Worlds of Assurance. *Accounting, Organizations and Society* 36(4): 267–8.

EC and EG Directive 94/38 on information regarding technical standards and directives.

EG 2008/765 om krav på ackreditering och marknadskontroll i samband med saluföring av produkter och upphävande av förordning EE nr 339/93.

Fouilleux, E. & Loconto, A. (2016) Voluntary Standards, Certification, and Accreditation in the Global Organic Agriculture Field: A Tripartite Model of Techno-Politics. *Agriculture and Human Values* 34 (1): 1–14.

Galland, J.-P. (2017) Big Third-Party Certifiers and the Construction of Transnational Regulation. *The ANNALS of the American Academy of Political and Social Science* 670(March): 263–79.

Grothe Hammer, M. (2017) Organization without Actorhood. Exploring the First Degree of Organizationality. Unpublished manuscript.

Gustafsson, I. (2016) *Organisering av standarder, certifiering och ackreditering som en global styrregim.* Doctoral dissertation, School of Public Administration, University of Gothenburg.

Gustafsson, I. & Tamm Hallström, K. (2013) The Certification Paradox: Monitoring as a Solution and a Problem. In M. Reuter, F. Wijkström, & B. Kristensson Uggla (eds.), *Trust and Organizations. Confidence Across Borders.* New York: Palgrave. 91–109.

Gustafsson, I. & Tamm Hallström, K. (2018) Hyper-Organized Eco-Labels: An Organization Theory Perspective on the Implications of Tripartite Standards Regimes. *Food Policy* 75: 124–33.

Hatanaka, M. (2014) Standardized Food Governance? Reflections on the Potential and Limitations of Chemical-Free Shrimp. *Food Policy* 45: 138–45.

Hatanaka, M. & Busch, L. (2008) Third-Party Certification in the Global Agrifood System: An Objective or Socially Mediated Governance Mechanism? *Sociologica Ruralis* 48(1): 73–91.

Hatanaka, M., Konefal, J., & Constance, D. H. (2012) A Tripartite Standards Regime Analysis of the Contested Development of a Sustainable Agriculture Standard. *Agriculture and Human Values* 29(1): 65–78.

Humphrey, C. & Moizer, P. (1990) From Techniques to Ideologies: An Alternative Perspective on the Audit Function. *Critical Perspectives on Accounting* 1(3): 217–38.

Jamal, K. & Sunder S. (2011) Is Mandated Independence Necessary for Audit Quality? *Accounting, Organizations and Society* 36: 284–92.

Johansson, V. & Lindgren, L. (2013) *Uppdrag offentlig granskning*. Lund: Studentlitteratur.

Kouakou, D., Boiral, O., & Gendron, Y. (2013) ISO Auditing and the Construction of Trust in Auditor Independence. *Accounting, Auditing & Accountability Journal* 26(8): 1279–305.

Loconto, A. & Busch, L. (2010) Standards, Techno-Economic Networks and Playing Fields: Performing the Global Market Economy. *Review of International Political Economy*, 17(3): 507–36.

Marx, A. (2008) Limits to Non-State Market Regulation: A Qualitative Comparative Analysis of the International Sport Footwear Industry and the Fair Labor Association. *Regulation and Governance* 2(2): 253–73.

Marx, A. (2011) Global Governance and the Certification Revolution: Types, Trends and Challenges. In D. Levi-Faur (ed.), *Handbook on the Politics of Regulation*. Cheltenham: Edward Elgar. 590–603.

Meyer, J. W. (2010) World Society, Institutional Theories, and the Actor. *Annual Review of Sociology* 36: 1–20.

Meyer, J. W. & Jepperson, R. L. (2000) The 'Actors' of Modern Society: The Cultural Construction of Social Agency. *Sociological Theory* 18(1): 100–20.

Power, M. (1997) *The Audit Society: Rituals of verification*. Oxford: Oxford University Press.

Power, M. (2003) Auditing and the Production of Legitimacy. *Accounting, Organizations and Society* 28(4): 379–94.

Power, M. (2011) Assurance Worlds: Consumers, Experts and Independence. *Accounting, Organizations and Society* 36: 324–6.

Renard, M. C. & Loconto, A. (2013) Competing Logics in the Further Standardization of Fair Trade: ISEAL and the Símbolo de Pequeños Productores. *International Journal of Sociology of Agriculture & Food* 20(1): 51–68.

Shapiro, S. P. (1987) The Social Control of Impersonal Trust. *The American Journal of Sociology* 93(3): 623–58.

Sikka, P. & Willmott, H. (1995) *Accounting, Organization and Society* 20(6): 547–81.

SOU 2006:113 Öppna system för provning och kontroll – en utvärdering.

Tamm Hallström, K. & Gustafsson, I. (2014) Value-Neutralizing in Verification Markets: Organizing for Independence through Accreditation. In S. Alexius & K. Tamm Hallström (eds.), *Configuring Value Conflicts in Markets*. Cheltenham: Edward Elgar. 82–99.

Walgenbach, P. (2001) The Production of Distrust by Means of Producing Trust. *Organization Studies* 22(4): 693–714.

ACKNOWLEDGEMENT

We are grateful for the financial support from Handelsbankens for-skningsstiftelser (P2016–0017:1) and the Swedish Research Council (2017–01284) that made this research possible.

8 Queues: Tensions between Institution and Organization

Göran Ahrne, Daniel Castillo, and Lambros Roumbanis

How to stand in line is taken for granted; there are norms about queues and how they should be formed. The formation of queues is an institution: 'the archetypical waiting line assumes that it is leaderless or created and managed largely by the emergent norms of those in the queue' (Wexler, 2015: 166). But there are other forms of queues in which those in line do not need to be physically present; queuers' names and other documentations are all that is required for admission to a particular school or to obtain accommodations, for instance.

But queues outside organizations in which people literally stand behind each other for minutes, hours, or days require special prerequisites and have certain limitations. Research on queues has demonstrated that the institutionalized concept and its basic principles are changing. It seems that queues are becoming more and more organized. One aim of this chapter is an analysis of the interdependence between institution and organization. We investigate why and how queues are organized and the tensions that arise when a strong institution becomes the subject of combinations of partial organization.

Waiting in line is usually considered a time waster (Elster, 2009; cf. Hraba, 1985), whereas offering constant and unlimited access implies a waste of resources for organizations (Rafaeli *et al.*, 2005). Queues relieve pressure (Alexander *et al.*, 2012: 881). They are a form of buffering that organizations can use to protect their technical core from fluctuations in the environment (Thompson, 1961). But queues may also generate attention. Physical queues may paradoxically serve as a kind of marketing: queues become proof that the goods or services at the other end of the line must be worth waiting for. Perhaps that restaurant has a celebrated chef or that shop is having a sale. But it is also the case that manufacturers of new goods like Apple purposely deliver only small amounts of their products, thereby creating queues that generate attention (Wexler, 2015: 170).

A queue is an example of seriality. A serial structure consists of individuals held together in relation to a mutual external object, just as standing before and after each other in order of priority separates them. A queue can be understood as a 'negative principle of unity' (Sartre, 1976: 261). Many kinds of people with different backgrounds and resources may stand in the same line. But these qualities do not matter; their place in the queue is decisive:

> It matters a lot to me, in effect, that I have the tenth number rather than the twentieth. But I am tenth *through Others* in so far as they are Other than themselves, that is to say, in so far as the reason for their number does not lie in themselves.
>
> *(Sartre, 1976: 261)*

What makes Sartre's description of the line interesting is that it is a sociological analysis of the queue as an assembly that, in principle, merely presupposes a minimum of sociality. But as long as the queue is visible and people are actually standing before and after each other, it contains an embryo of change and collective action (cf. Ahrne, 1990).

The institution of queuing has strong legitimacy. Yet queues involve much latent tension between people standing in line because of their various needs and resources on the one hand, and between people standing in line and the organization from which they hope to obtain a service on the other. In this way a queue is a relatively fragile order.

In the rest of the chapter, we first investigate the queue as an institution and address why it may be insufficient despite its strong legitimacy. Then we illuminate the organizational elements used to organize queues. An analysis of the way queues can be organized provides useful suggestions for understanding the interdependence between institution and organization.

THE QUEUE AS AN INSTITUTION

Since the 1960s, social psychological and sociological research has shown that there are norms and attitudes concerning equality and fairness in the order of the queue (Mann, 1969; Schwartz, 1974; Larson 1987; Brady, 2002). In these early studies, queues were seen first and foremost as a self-regulating social system in which internalized norms govern the social order. Moral notions of justice are central to priority and the allocation of resources in queues (Schwartz, 1974; Kahneman, Knetsch, & Thaler, 1986; Elster, 2009; Ehn & Löfgren, 2010). Waiting one's turn is regarded as a virtue.

The fairness of queuing builds mainly on two principles: Anyone has the right to place oneself last in line, and only the time spent in the queue is decisive. Arrival at the queue is a central factor. One of the most important norms of the queue is the first-come–first-served principle, also called first-in–first-out (Larson, 1987; Alexander et al., 2012; Allon & Hanany, 2012).

One significant characteristic of a visible queue is its beginning and end, which allows a newcomer to know where to stand without cutting into the line. Ideally, the queue should move at a steady pace and preferably quickly. Queuers should not stand too close to or push and squeeze an adjacent person; nor should they leave too large a gap, which would create uncertainty about the end of the queue and increase the probability that someone may be tempted to sneak in.

Several studies show how attempts to break into the queue are regarded as unacceptable behaviour, causing anger and indignity (Mann, 1969). Attempts at jumping the queue go against democratic norms prescribing the principle of order of priority, based on social justice. In some contexts, however, there can be legitimate reasons for cutting into the line. Queuers lined up for train tickets, for instance, may allow others to cut in, to prevent them from missing their train (Allon & Hanany, 2012: 493).

Individuals in a queue may have a certain control over any attempts to cut into the line. But research on queues shows that only a small subset of people standing in a line is able to observe a deviation when one occurs (Allon & Hanany, 2012: 500). It may be difficult to maintain order if the queue is too long. Brady (2002) has shown that friendship may threaten the order in an extremely long queue: Holding a spot in the line for friends clearly threatens to subvert the first-come–first-served principle (Brady, 2002: 162).

If suspicion arises that the norms of priority are not being followed, there are few possibilities to intervene. It is up to everyone in the queue to do something – to say or call out something in the hope that others will follow. But leaving one's place in the line to suppress irregularities somewhere else in the queue may lead to quarrels and even to physical violence. If a queue is dissolved, its order of priority is lost, and who obtains access becomes strictly arbitrary – or a matter of physical strength.

One form of queuing that can create disorder in an institutional order is the so-called multiple queue, in which several service points exist in parallel, and the newcomers can decide which queue they consider most suitable (Elster, 2009). Multiple queues are most common in supermarkets, and the waiting time there cannot be guaranteed equal for every customer. The time spent in the queue depends on how fast the staff works and on how much time each customer requires (Rafaeli et al., 2005: 5). Few customers would choose the checkout line where the trollies are chock-full of groceries over lines where the customers are carrying a loaf of bread or a bunch of carrots. When a new checkout is opened, the advantage goes to the person who notices first: Seldom do those who leave other queues respect the previous order of priority.

The longer the wait, the more likely it is that the serial order is broken and queuers may start talking to each other about their situation and try to change it. Queues that stretch over days or even weeks are particularly susceptible to the queuers changing the forms of order. According to a survey of experiences in lines to buy tickets for the

1999 release of *Star Wars: The Phantom Menace,* such behaviour was common (Brady, 2002). The first-come–first-served principle was interpreted differently from line to line, and people banded together to create their own rules – especially towards the front of the lines. In many cases, it was decided that friends could keep each other's place in the queue, and people took turns standing in line. One group at the front of the line claimed the first sixty positions, because they had been waiting for sixty hours (Brady, 2002).

As an institution, the idea of how to form a queue is distinct, and it has strong legitimacy resting on commonly accepted values of equality and fairness. But the institution of queuing is narrow, and must be adjusted to accommodate certain situations. Waiting is easier when every queuer has a common notion about the correct way to stand in line. People who share this norm will not jostle and force their way to a more advantageous position; they maintain an idea of fairness. But if the line and the waiting time become too long, an institutional order may be insufficient.

ORGANIZATION TO STRENGTHEN THE INSTITUTION OF THE QUEUE

Rather than allowing the queuers to take over and create their own rules, it seems to be more and more common for organizations to intervene in the ordering of queues (Wexler, 2015). Even though queues in some contexts may have positive effects for the organizations, they can be inconvenient – if the premises are not large enough, for instance. Queues may also give rise to disorder and dissatisfaction, particularly if there are suspicions of unfairness in the queue. And because there is always the risk that people grow tired and leave the queue, lessening their business, organizations need to weigh the pros and cons of long queues.

But what organizational elements are used to organize queues? If the goal of the organization is to maintain or strengthen the queue as an institution, it can hardly create rules or make decisions about membership. The general norm regarding the decisive importance of the waiting time should suffice. And the norm that anyone should have the opportunity to stand in line is not compatible with a queue based on membership. Rather, the organization of queues is first of all about monitoring – various measures to control order and create trust in the arrangements.

One measure would be to mark and perhaps even protect certain areas for the queue – by showing where the queuers are expected to stand by installing ropes or fences, making it more difficult to cut into the line. Or the organization could employ guards to monitor the queuers and stop them from cutting into the line. But, in this form of partial organization, it is still about literally standing in line.

When queues are organized, they often change form; they become less obvious, and their structure becomes more abstract (Rafaeli *et al.*, 2005: 3) or even invisible (Zohar, Mandelbaum, & Shimkin, 2002). An example of a more abstract queue is the numerical queue (Rafaeli *et al.*, 2005: 5), which usually builds on a ticket system. In a numerical queue, the order is based on the first-come–first-served principle; upon arriving at the queue, each person receives a numbered ticket and can move about freely.

In a numerical queue, the organization monitors the queuing order by ensuring that anyone approaching the counter or checkout has the correct number. Because people do not have to stand in a line, the waiting time is more comfortable. It is usually possible to be seated or even to leave the premises for a while. This system may also allow the organization to estimate waiting times and thereby reduce uncertainty by informing people of the length of their waiting time (Liang, 2017: 5). This type of queue runs less risk of being transformed into a queue in which people band together to protest or make demands. But in most numerical queues, those waiting can still see each other, and are often able to see whose turn is next.

Through technological development, new more abstract and invisible forms of queues have been established. Not only is the transparency of the queue lost; the queuers may not even be visible. This development results in a total lack of control, creating a situation in which trust in the expert systems becomes essential (Giddens, 1991).

To create a certain level of trust and credibility, the organizers of telephone queues attempt to recreate some of the preconditions found in the physical queue. A voice may state that many people are currently calling. When callers end up in a telephone queue they are informed about the number of callers that will be responded to ahead of them. Ideally, the organizer regularly informs the caller about the progress of the queue and the caller's place in it. In this way, a virtual queue is created, evoking a feeling reminiscent of a traditional queue, in which queuers must be constantly present in order to guard their place in the queue.

In queues in which the waiting time can be counted in months or years, however, it is impossible to guard one's place at all times. Housing queues organized by private landlords or municipal authorities, for instance, may extend to several years. Several organizational elements are present in this type of queue, but they can still be based on the traditional norms of queues. Information from a municipal housing company expressively states: 'Longest time in the queue chooses first'. The company organizing the queue handles the monitoring, eased by the fact that the queue is digital. But other organizational elements have been added. Those who want to remain in the queue must register at regular intervals. Moreover, there are frequently rules for how a person at the front of the queue can choose among housing offers. And there are sanctions for those who do not follow the rules; they can lose several housing offers for some time. By using monitoring combined with rules, hierarchy, and sanctions, the organizers strive to maintain the basic queuing principle: Time in the queue is decisive.

The fact that a queue is organized with one or several organizational elements does not necessarily mean that the queue as an institution is replaced by organization; it may still exist as an idea both for those forming the queue and for the organizer. It would not be possible to organize a virtual queue – a telephone queue, for instance – without any idea of what constitutes a queue. In such cases, institution and organization reinforce each other.

ORGANIZATION TO BREAK THE MORAL ORDER OF THE QUEUE

In many cases, the aim of the queue's organizer is not only to secure its order but also to transform its basic principles and ideas of fairness. Instead of accepting the fact that place in the queue is decisive, the organizer may emphasize other circumstances, depending on who is queuing and why.

The fact that an organizer bypasses the order of priority and decides to give priority to certain people before others – selecting among those who are waiting – is definitely a break with traditional queuing norms. Some housing queues allow for the possibility of giving precedence to individuals who lack the opportunity of obtaining housing in any other way. It seems, then, that need may come before the priority principles of the queue. But this deviation occurs only in exceptional cases; it is not used for judging the needs for housing in general. One's place in the queue is still decisive in most cases, and the institution is still in place, albeit somewhat reduced.

Decisions do away with the order of priority in hospital emergency ward queues as well (Wexler, 2015: 169). This waiting room honours neither simple rules nor the traditional order of priority in queues. Here a hierarchical order is based on the organization's professional assessment of need. A patient with cardiac arrest or severe haemorrhage is received before a patient with a broken finger. But all decisions on priority are not equally self-evident, and may be questioned by others who are waiting their turn.

For a queue in which the first-come–first-served principle is strictly adhered to, there is no scope for decisions; there are no options. Decisions, however, can always be contested: 'Why was that person admitted before me?' The more people who receive special treatment in a queue or a waiting room, the greater the risk for decisions to be contested.

The cases of breaches with norms we have discussed so far have dealt with introducing hierarchy because of special needs; they have not dealt with the needs or interests of the organizers themselves. In many cases, however, when hierarchy is introduced, it is the organization's preferences, interests, and convenience that count.

In queues in front of clubs or exclusive restaurants, it is not unusual for a doorman to walk along the line choosing people to let in on the basis of various qualities: age, gender, physical attractiveness, or their acquaintanceship with the doorman. This is a hierarchical organization of the queue that gives special people authority to decide who will be admitted without any rules for the procedure.

Job queues arranged by day labour agencies provide another example of hierarchical organization of queues. For them, it is not position in the queue that counts, but the relationships and contacts with the dispatcher employed by the agency to make decisions about who gets which jobs among those present in the hiring hall: 'a dispatcher's discretion plays an important role ... insofar as it gives them capricious (yet patterned) control over the job-allocation queue, also known as the list' (Williams, 2009: 233).

Traditional norms may also be broken through the application of rules. A more and more common arrangement is to introduce differentiated queues, often involving differential pricing, whereby those who pay more may stand in a shorter queue or do not even have to stand in line at all. Such queues are called 'multi-level queues' or 'priority queues' (Alexander et al., 2012), and are common in airports, amusement parks, and tourist attractions. In accessing the Empire State Building, for example, customers are currently offered a fast track to its elevators and to security control (Sandel 2012: 19). When people are offered the opportunity of choosing between standing in line or paying a bit more to shorten the wait, 'money-rich and time-poor consumers will pay whereas time-rich and money-poor consumers will wait' (Alexander et al., 2012: 876).

Such rules are a challenge to the legitimacy of the queue. Studies of amusement parks show that multilevel queues were perceived to be unfair by those who did not pay extra, and they can have a negative impact on perceived satisfaction; seeing some people pass the line gives others a negative feeling about their visit to the park (Alexander *et al.*, 2012: 881). To avoid offending ordinary customers, some parks usher their premium guests through back doors and separate gates (Sandel, 2012: 19).

Researchers have noted a dilemma for the organizers, however; if priority queues were made invisible to other customers, the experience of standing in line was improved for those who did not pay to avoid the queues. Yet it means that the value of the priority was reduced, as these people could not observe the extent to which they actually saved time (Alexander *et al.*, 2012: 882).

In these latter examples of ways in which queues can be organized, there is little fairness left; instead it is the organization that uses its power to further its own interest in selecting the preferred customers from a larger number of people standing in a line. Such situations give rise to a clash between an institutional and an organized order, if people who are standing in line adhere to the principles of fairness inherent in the idea of a queue. When the organization of a queue goes against institutional norms rather than strengthening them, it loses legitimacy, often leading to dissatisfaction and anger; tension arises between organization and institution. When an organization decides the order in which people are admitted, little remains of the institution of the queue. The queue is no longer 'an emergent collective phenomenon', and the waiting line is no longer a line; it has morphed and is managed by those who run the organization (Wexler, 2015: 169).

Organization can be used to strengthen an institution, but an institution cannot take too much organization. With more and more organization, the institution is no longer taken for granted; decisions can be contested, and there is uncertainty about what to do and if there will be further changes. The institution is weakened and may even be dissolved. It is far from self-evident that access to an organization or its services and resources should even be in the form of a queue.

REFERENCES

Ahrne, G. (1990) *Agency and Organization. Towards an Organizational Theory of Society.* London: SAGE.

Alexander, M., MacLaren, A., O'Gorman, K., & White, C. (2012) Priority Queues: Where Social Justice and Equity Collide. *Tourism Management* 33: 875–84.

Allon, G. & Hanany, E. (2012) Cutting in Line: Social Norms in Queues. *Management Science* 58(3): 493–506.

Brady F. (2002) Lining up for Star-Wars Tickets: Some Ruminations on Ethics and Economics Based on an Internet Study of Behavior in Queues. *Journal of Business Ethics* 38(1): 157–65.

Ehn, B. & Löfgren, O. (2010) *The Secret World of Doing Nothing.* Berkeley: University of California Press.

Elster, J. (2009) Norms. In P. Bearman and P. Hedström (eds.), *The Oxford Handbook of Analytical Sociology.* New York: Oxford University Press. 195–217.

Giddens, A. (1991) *Modernity and Self-Identity.* Stanford: Stanford University Press.

Hraba, J. (1985) Consumer Shortages in Poland: Looking beyond the Queue into a World of Making Do. *The Sociological Quarterly* 26(3): 387–404.

Kahneman D., Knetsch, J., & Thaler, R. (1986) Fairness and the Assumptions of Economics. *The Journal of Business* 59(4): 285–300.

Larson, R. C. (1987) Perspectives on Queues: Social Justice and Psychology of Queueing. *Operations Research* 35(6): 895–905.

Liang, C-C. (2017) Enjoyable Queuing and Waiting Time. *Time & Society.* https://doi.org/10.1177/0961463X17702164.

Mann, L. (1969) Queue Culture: The Waiting Line as a Social System. *The American Journal of Sociology* 75(3): 340–54.

Rafaeli, A., Kedmi, E., Vashdi, D., & Barron, G. (2005) *Queues and Fairness. A Multiple Study Experimental Investigation* (manuscript). Faculty of Industrial Engineering and Management, Technion Israel Institute of Technology, Haifa: Israel.

Sandel, M. J. (2012) *What Money Can't Buy. The Moral Limits of Markets.* London: Allen Lane.

Sartre, J.-P. (1976) *Critique of Dialectical Reason.* Volume 1. London: Verso.

Schwartz, B. (1974) Waiting, Exchange, and Power: The Distribution of Time in Social Systems. *American Journal of Sociology* 79(4): 841–69.

Thompson, J. D. (1967) *Organizations in Action.* New York: McGraw-Hill.

Wexler, M. (2015) Re-thinking Queue Culture: The Commodification of Thick Time. *International Journal of Sociology and Social Policy* 35(3/4): 165–81.

Williams, D. (2009) Grounding the Regime of Precarious Employment: Homeless Day Laborers' Negotiations of the Job Queue. *Work and Occupations* 36(3): 209–46.

Zohar, E., Mandelbaum, A., & Shimkin, N. (2002) Adaptive Behavior of Impatient Customers in Tele-Queues: Theory and Empirical Support. *Management Science* 48(4): 566–83.

PART 3 Networks and Other Social Relationships

9 The Inter-Firm Network as Partial Organization?

Jörg Sydow

For more than three decades, research in the field of management and sociology has analysed the so-called network form of organization, not only in the field of public services, but also in business (Provan, Beyer, & Kruytbosch, 1980; Miles & Snow, 1986; Powell, 1990; Sydow, 1992; Jones, Hesterly, & Borgatti, 1997). Examples of inter-organizational networks are abundant, and can be found in almost any industry and region, or, in more theoretical terms, any 'organizational field' (DiMaggio & Powell, 1983). Three alliance systems dominate the global airline industry, and the biotech industry is prevalent in Silicon Valley, San Diego, and Boston. And the areas around Cambridge, England and Munich, Germany would have not developed without close collaborative relationships among start-ups, established pharmaceutical companies, and research institutes. The same is true for other science-based industries such as optics, robotics, smart materials, and environmental technologies. The production of cultural or creative goods depends upon the close collaboration not only of individuals, but also of organizations, as does the provision of human and industrial services. Although the actual spread of the network form of organization is difficult to establish, even within these extensively studied fields, the investigation of inter-firm networks or inter-organizational networks more generally has flourished over the decades – as documented by a significant number of literature reviews, for instance (e.g., Brass, Galaskiewicz, Greve, & Tsai, 2004; Provan, Fish, & Sydow, 2007; Majchrzak, Jarvenpaa, & Bagherzadeh, 2015).

The study of the quantitative spread and the specific quality of this organizational form is hampered, not least by the different names they are given: strategic alliances and networks; value-added, public-private, and cross-sectional partnerships; project and innovation networks; crisis and emergency-response networks; consortia for combining either research and development or standardization efforts; collaborative supply chains and global production networks; outsourcing and offshoring partnerships; regional clusters and industrial districts, among other terms (Sydow, Schüßler, & Müller-Seitz, 2016). Although the phenomenon indicated by these different names is not homogeneous, they all denote inter-organizational networks or, in the domain of business, inter-firm networks as a modern yet traditional form of economic governance that makes use of certain organizing principles (Sydow, 1992).

The study of inter-firm networks as an organizational form differs greatly from the study of social relations in general or, more precisely, from networks of social relations (including business relations) using social network analysis (SNA). SNA as a perspective or analytical tool (Wasserman & Faust, 1984; Hennig et al., 2012) allows the study of networks of relationships not only within, but also across and beyond organizations – in communities of practice, markets of exchange, or inter-firm networks, in all of which organizations may participate. Making increasing use of mainly quantitative network analyses, this network perspective is flagged as network theory (e.g., Borgatti & Halgin, 2011) and, more often than not, even adopts a relational ontology to understand network dynamics better (e.g., Emirbayer, 1997). Under no circumstances, however, should inter-firm networks as a form of governance of organizing economic activities be confounded with a network perspective, even if it follows a relational ontology that conceptualizes relations as unfolding processes rather than stable entities. In the end, nevertheless, a network perspective may well help to gain a deeper understanding of the network form of governance (Windeler, 2001).

Only a few years ago, Ahrne and Brunsson (2011) offered the concept of *partial organization* for analysing organized systems that, like standards or rankings of a different type, are not (complete) organizations. Partial organization, according to these authors, exhibits a 'decided order' – an order created by actors having made decisions about others, although not all of the five criteria of a formal organization are necessarily met: (1) decisions on *membership*, (2) decisions on *rules*, (3) decisions on how to *monitor members*, (4) decisions about positive and negative *sanctions*, and (5) decisions about *how to make decisions* (e.g., about hierarchy). (See Ahrne *et al.*, 2016; Ahrne and Brunsson, Chapter 1.) Even if only one of these five criteria is met, there is a case of partial organization. Importantly, the concept of partial organization not only allows for different degrees of organization, therefore, but also for the organizing of organizational environments, including markets and networks. It is notable, however, that partial organization refers to a lesser extent to a social system as an entity. Rather, based upon the works of German sociologist Niklas Luhmann (cf. Seidl & Becker, 2006), it provides a perspective on how systems are (partially) organized.

Given the widespread attention that Ahrne and Brunsson's concept of partial organization has already attracted, it seems that investigation of the insights that the concept has to offer is overdue. Further research may yield a deeper understanding of the governance form and the dynamics of inter-firm networks, which, at first glance at least, could be characterized as 'partially organized'. Looking at them as social systems or entities, one could even argue that inter-firm networks constitute *a partial organization of more or less complete organizations*. Under specific circumstances, as I argue at the end of this chapter, inter-firm networks could be considered, at least in some aspects, as being even *more organized than organizations*. What is more important, however, is the light that the partial organization perspective throws on inter-firm networks as a form of governance and the dynamics of this form.

The objective of this chapter, therefore, is to explore the potential of the concept in these respects, delineating differences and similarities and pointing to complementarities. Towards this end, I use the terminology characteristic of this field of study as the first step, to introduce inter-firm networks as a form of economic governance that needs to be created, reproduced, or transformed, with the help of network management practices, using several examples from various industries and regions. As a second step, I explore the insights that the partial organization perspective can provide into the process and the outcome of organizing inter-firm networks. Concluding, I summarize the major insights offered by the concept of partial organization, in order to deepen the understanding of inter-firm networks, which, together with other types of networks, constitute a 'society of networks' (Raab & Kenis, 2009).

INTER-FIRM NETWORKS: EMERGENT OR ENGINEERED?

Inter-firm networks such as those between airlines – and perhaps such other airline-related service providers as airport authorities, maintenance and repair, and logistics – are considered a form of economic governance either between or beyond the well-known dichotomy of market and hierarchy. (See, for instance, Williamson, 1991 and Powell, 1990, respectively.) No matter which of these governance perspectives is adopted, such networks are characterized by co-operation rather than competition among the network firms and by building and maintaining long-term rather than short-term relationships characterized by reciprocity and multiplexity. Although reciprocity refers to the norm of mutual obligations (allowing, for instance, for an exchange of knowledge that would not otherwise be possible), multiplexity points to the fact that most relationships in such arrangements are based on more than one type of exchange (e.g., technology or market-related knowledge). Typically, inter-firm networks – which, as in the case of the Star Alliance and the other two global alliance networks – may well include close competitors. They either evolve from former market-like exchange relationships via the quasi-internalization[1] of economic activities or they develop from hierarchical forms of governance (including, for example, corporate groups) via the quasi-externalization of such activities (Sydow, 1992; Sydow & Windeler, 1998). In the case of hierarchical governance, they are often driven by such strategies as focusing activities on the core competence of a firm and collaborating instead with the best providers of goods and services available.

Doz *et al.* (2000), investigating research and development consortia more closely, introduced the notion of 'engineered' networks, in order to differentiate this form of economic governance and its pattern of development from networks that have more or less unintentionally 'emerged' through social or economic exchange. Although the emergence of networks of relationships is emphasized primarily from a network perspective employing SNA, engineered networks correspond to an organizational form or mode of governance view of networks. In this respect, one could, in fact, follow the partial organization perspective and consider more or less engineered inter-firm networks as exhibiting a 'decided order', whereas emergent social networks may, by contrast, be considered the fabric of an 'institutionalized order'. Decided networks are indeed different from emergent or non-decided networks.

Other management scholars, in line with the belief that management can make a difference, emphasize this very aspect of intentional decision making by speaking of creating, designing, shaping, or leveraging networks of inter-organizational relationships (e.g., Lorenzoni & Baden-Fuller, 1995). Still others consider networks to be goal directed rather than serendipitous (Kilduff & Tsai, 2003; Provan *et al.*, 2007). Management and organization researchers tend, in fact, to conceive of inter-firm networks in this latter – decided – way as an outcome of intentional organizing, sometimes even overemphasizing the possibilities of engineering and design.

A more advanced understanding of organizing, based upon practice theories like structuration theory (Giddens, 1984), for example, would consider both 'engineered' and 'emergent' aspects of inter-firm networks, ask how and to what extent they interact, and investigate how the resulting patterns, including the reflexivity needed for engineering or designing them, have been 'institutionalized'. Institutionalized reflexivity means that organizational actors do not rely only on their own individual capacity and capability to monitor reflexively the conditions under which they act, the process of activities, and the outcome. Rather, the organization or, in this case, such inter-organizational arrangements as a special committee or even a network administrative organization, support these monitoring processes (Windeler, 2001). In turn, the extent to which such social systems are 'partially organized' by creating a decided order or, in my terms, being 'reflexively structured' (Sydow & Windeler, 1998; Windeler, 2001) will become an empirical question.

Dynamics of network governance

Consequently, inter-firm networks as a form of economic governance may be more or less reflexively structured and institutionalized – 'institutionalized' meaning not only taken for granted, but also stretching across time and space, no matter how the networks are governed precisely. Provan and Kenis (2008), in their typology which has proven extremely popular, distinguish three distinct forms of 'network governance': (1) lead-organization governance as in the case of so-called 'strategic networks' (Jarillo, 1988), (2) a shared form of network governance, and (3) governance by a dedicated network administrative organization. An example of a strategic network is a Japanese *keiretsu*, such as those strategically led by Mitsubishi and Toyota. The Toyota network in particular exhibits a relatively dense 'networked' structure because of a broad arrangement of organizing efforts directed at knowledge exchange and mutual learning between the lead firm and its first- and second-tier suppliers (Dyer & Nobeoka, 2000; Wilhelm, 2011; Aoki & Wilhelm, 2017). The Smart-house network in the Norfjord region of Norway provides an example of a network with a shared form of governance; it uses the Triple Helix Model and focuses on industry-directed innovation, health innovation, community innovation, and teaching and research, with the help of collaboration among firms, public-sector organizations, and universities (Sydow et al., 2016: 146–53). An example of a strategic network supported by a dedicated network administrative organization (NAO) is the Star Alliance, served by the Star Alliance Service

GmbH in Frankfurt, Germany. This NAO was originally established to connect the heterogeneous information systems of airlines and allow for seamless travelling, but has since adopted the broader mission of supporting the management and marketing of the alliance network (Sydow *et al.*, 2016: 67–74). Provan and Kenis (2008) consider shared governance as suitable only for networks with few organizational members, whereas lead-organization governance could be appropriate for larger numbers – particularly when supported by an NAO.

With regard to the dynamics of these systems, Provan and Kenis (2008: 246–7) argue that an inter-organizational network with a shared form of governance may well turn into either a network supported by an NAO, or even a strategic network characterized by lead-organization governance, especially if the number of network members becomes too large to handle in a participative mode of decision making and if the network is likely to dissociate into components. Such a dynamic development, possibly stimulated by further complexity, may require a lead organization to install an NAO. By contrast, Provan and Kenis consider a network change in the opposite direction, from a lead organization to shared network governance, to be highly unlikely. For once an inter-organizational network has been led by a 'hub firm' (Jarillo, 1988) or any other type of lead organization, other network members are unlikely to be ready to assume a (co-)leading role. The same is true for a network in which the coordination is supported by an NAO, as these types of organizations eventually tend to inertia, with the others relying on them. Although these propositions are plausible, it is possible to imagine different dynamics of network governance in settings such as crisis and emergency response (Berthod *et al.*, 2017).

Dynamics of network practices

Such dynamics, in inter-firm networks characterized by all three types of governance, are driven by decisions and actions of network management making use of a set of organizing practices that together contribute to the organizational character or 'organizationality' (Dobusch & Schoeneborn, 2015) of these systems. These practices include (1) selecting, reselecting, or deselecting network partners; (2) allocating or reallocating tasks, resources, and responsibilities among the network firms; (3) regulating collaboration within the network using formal contracts as much as informal rules; and (4) evaluating the cost, benefits, and risks within the collaboration, or simply the quality of the collaborative relationships, for either single network firms or the whole network (Sydow *et al.*, 2016). In accordance with the conception of organizing as 'reflexive structuration', network management practices – not least evaluation – are based upon institutionalized reflexivity that enables the creation of a decided order. At the same time and with regard to its institutionalization, the evaluation practice goes well beyond the reflexive monitoring of the conditions and consequences of inter-organizational interaction, because it is more organized.

In order to illustrate the relevance of these practices for network dynamics, consider again the case of Star Alliance. Not only are new members selected only after a thorough evaluation, using a list of eighty-five criteria; they are also continuously re-evaluated on safe travel, customer benefits and handling, frequent flyer accrual and redemption, branding and communication principles, and the consistent management of crisis and emergency, among other things. This not only highlights the network's extreme degree of organization, achieved with the help of selection and evaluation practices, but also the recursive interplay of these practices (Sydow *et al.*, 2016).

Network management, with the help of these and other practices, creates, reproduces, and eventually transforms inter-firm networks as a form of economic governance, giving rise to such systems and maintaining, changing, and eventually terminating them. At the same time, this form of economic governance, in this very process, enables and constrains network management as a practice (Provan *et al.*, 2007). The three forms of network governance are likely to vary, therefore, with regard to the degrees of reflexive structuring.

Although one would expect networks with a shared form of govern-ance, such as the regional Smart-house network, to be more of an emergent nature, lead-organization governance, as in the case of the Toyota network, is likely characterized more by formal contracts rather than informal contacts (Berends *et al.*, 2011). One reason is that lead organizations or hub firms tend to be larger and better resourced. Consider, for instance, manufacturers in the car industry, including Toyota, or general contractors such as HOCHTIEF in the global construction industry. These organizations are likely to exhibit greater capacity and capability for network management. But these organizations are also prone to export their often bureaucratic struc-tures and cultures into the network (Walker *et al.*, 1997). The third case, NAO governance, which is found not only in the global airline industry, but also in regional clusters or industrial districts, is also likely to reflect a higher degree of inter-organizational reflexivity. Otherwise, the network (or cluster) management would not have decided to create and maintain such an institution in the first place; and decisions are certainly an important – for some even *the* most important – ingredient in organizing (March & Simon, 1958; Brunsson, 1989; see also Apelt *et al.*, 2017).

INSIGHTS FROM A PARTIAL ORGANIZATION PERSPECTIVE

In their foundational article, Ahrne and Brunsson (2011) had already related the concept of partial organization to networks (and to institu-tions). This attempt was repeated more recently, when Ahrne *et al.* (2016) conceptualized not only networks, but also markets, standards, meta-organizations, and even families as being 'partially organized' systems, situated somehow *outside formal organizations*. Although formal organizations have long been dominated in a 'society of orga-nizations' (Perrow, 1991) and continue to be, I agree with Ahrne and Brunsson that the analysis of modern societies has, since Max Weber, made relatively little use of any concept of organization. In the mean-time, however, the classic form of formal organization seems to have lost some of its former relevance in a society which, for whatever reason, increasingly tends to favour individually based yet networked, virtual, and platform-based forms of organizing rather than big corporations (Davis, 2016) – even if big corporations are highly unlikely to disappear! In any case, this does not imply that theories of organization or concepts like that of a partial organization cannot contribute to a better understanding of society. On the contrary, the partial organization perspective promises to contribute exactly that, by addressing forms other than 'complete' forms of organizing – not only as an entity or outcome, but also as a process.

Insights with regard to outcome

Ahrne *et al.* (2016: 97) provide several examples of networks resulting from organizing efforts: hacker collectives, online communities, terrorist networks, and project networks (e.g., in the television industry). For comprehensible reasons, they do not treat these networks as opposites to organization. Rather, with reference to their foundational article, they emphasize that their concept of partial organization allows 'networks to be seen as social orders with varying degrees of *organization*'. (My emphasis, as the authors consider the singular to be important, referring to the abstract concept rather than to the actual practice of organized systems.) Although I agree about the usefulness of exploiting the conceptual understanding of organization for these network forms, the importance of which is definitely on the rise in modern society, the authors fail to include in their analysis the 'more organized', reflexively governed and 'decided' version of inter-firm networks.

Inter-firm networks, particularly when strategically orchestrated by a lead organization or hub firm such as Toyota – whether or not they are supported by an NAO, as in the case of the three airline alliance systems and the regional clusters – are typically characterized by a relatively high degree of 'institutionalized reflexivity' (Windeler, 2001). Institutionalization of reflexivity is considered constitutive for organizations (Giddens, 1984), but can also be achieved on the level of the entire inter-firm network, where the 'orchestrational work' (Bartelings *et al.*, 2017), supported by reflexivity, is performed inter-organizationally. This work can be done, for instance, with the support of trans-organizational procedures that help management staff to gather and store relevant knowledge that helps them to govern the network. In the words of Ahrne and Brunsson (2011), such institutionalized reflexivity, being a particular consequence of organizing, would allow them to *decide* 'better' about their social order.

Strategic and other types of networks, and, although to a significantly lesser extent, regional clusters have typically made decisions about (1) network membership, (2) network rules, (3) on how to monitor network members, (4) about positive and negative sanctions, and (5) about which decisions are binding. These decisions about what in Chapter 1 is called 'organizational elements' can be used by individuals or organizations 'to organize other individuals or organizations, even if they do not belong to the same organization'. These decisions are typically not reached via hierarchical fiat (Williamson, 1991), however, because they are not made within a single organization or a hierarchically coordinated collective of organizations (such as a corporate group). Rather, the decisions are reached either via consensus (as typical for a shared form of network governance) that may either have emerged or been engineered, or be de facto power based on the asymmetrical distribution of resources (as typical of lead-organization network governance), or on a mixture of both. What is more, inter-firm networks as social systems may not only be partial in the sense that one or more decisions about these domains has not been made (Type II, Figure 1). They may also be partial, in that decisions have been made in all of them, although not to the extent that one would expect in a formal organization (Type I, Figure 1).

Such inter-firm networks – or inter-organizational networks more generally (cf. Sydow *et al.*, 2016) – are, despite some hierarchical elements, rarely considered as hierarchies per se. Rather, as indicated previously, they are seen either as a *hybrid* form of

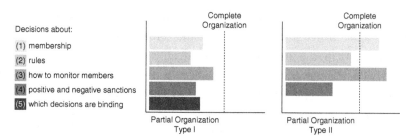

FIGURE I: Inter-firm networks: Two types of partiality

governance or as a form of organizing economic activities *beyond* market and hierarchy. Nevertheless, networks are more often than not confused with markets – obviously not with idealized markets as depicted in microeconomic textbooks, but with real markets, in particular business-to-business markets characterized by repeated transactions with more than one partner (such as industrial service networks), most often based on highly specific investments in building and maintaining the business relationships (Kleinaltenkamp *et al.*, 2005). Markets, according to Ahrne *et al.*, not least industrial markets, also exhibit some elements of partial organization and, as such, are an outcome of organizing: 'Just like formal organizations, markets are ordered not only by mutual adjustment and institutions, but also by organization' (2016: 97). Ahrne *et al.* provide several examples: decisions about the inclusion or exclusion of market members by licensing, the admission of products and services to a market only if they comply with certain standards, positive sanctions in the form of awards, and negative sanctions in the form of boycotts. Inter-firm networks, particularly if conceived of as a hybrid form of economic governance, indeed exhibit some characteristics of a 'domesticated market' (Arndt, 1979), which makes the distinction of these two forms of governance notoriously difficult.[2] For the networked firms to collaborate on a relatively long-term basis, producing and reproducing what is more often than not inter-organizational business relationships of the reciprocal and multiplex quality indicated previously. Close collaboration with lead customers or in-suppliers, however, does not mean that down-stream and upstream competition is eradicated entirely. Rather, in-suppliers continue to compete over their share of the pie (as, e.g., in the case of Toyota's dual-sourcing strategy) and, at least as impor-tant, out-suppliers seriously challenge them from time to time.

Insights with regard to process

This partial organization view of social systems is relevant for under-standing the development or *dynamics* of inter-firm networks (Majchrzak *et al.*, 2015), not only with regard to governance, but also to practices for handling or deciding about the tensions between com-petition and collaboration, for instance, which are characteristic of inter-firm networks. Such dynamics, which could result from either decisions in accordance with the decision makers' intentions or emer-ging from the unintended consequences of such decisions, can be defined as a change in state or form of the configuration of the actors in the network (organizations); the relationships among them (inter-organizational relations); and/or the network practices used to pro-duce, reproduce, or transform these relationships. In this respect, a practice from all four sets of network management practices – (1) selecting, (2) allocating, (3) regulating, and (4) evaluating – and any decision with regard to these sets of practices – can be a source of network dynamics, whether it was conceived of as change or as the reproduction of stability. In contrast to emphasizing the importance of decisions (as done from a partial organization perspective), a focus on practices (as informed by practice-based approaches like structuration theory) is more explicit not only about the duality of structure and agency (Giddens, 1984), but also about the need to produce and repro-duce an element of change and/or stability *continuously* in the face of tensions and contradictions.

Network dynamics, whether they result from isolated decisions or recurrent activities – i.e., practices – may well affect the entire net-work, by cumulating into a network-wide identity, for instance (Rometsch & Sydow, 2006). In most cases, however, such dynamics concern only dyads or a subset of relations (components) or practices, and would therefore have to be classified as 'confined change' (Halinen *et al.*, 1999), affecting only a subset of in-supplier relations. Moreover, such network dynamics may either produce or mitigate tensions and contradictions (Sydow & Windeler, 1998; Das & Teng, 2000; De Rond & Bouchikhi, 2004), which are also highlighted by a practice-based perspective on reflexive structuration. And, as in the case of somewhat routinized inter-organizational exchange, the dynamics may result not only from one or several of the network management practices introduced previously, but also from self-reinforcing processes (Masuch, 1985) triggered by the very practices on which they may also feed.

Furthermore, change processes may either be restricted to one level (e.g., the network) or reach across multiple levels of analysis (including the organization and/or the organizational field). Dyadic or network-level change may, for instance, be complemented by an organizational-level change in the capability of the buyer firm and be a restructuring of the field, because the in-supplier excluded from the network also dropped out of the market or field. Both effects may, however, result in additional tensions that have to be managed in the network, for instance, when dropping a long-standing relationship to a supplier has not been customary in the past and is not in line with the tradition of the particular form of collaboration (Hibbert & Huxham, 2010). Similar effects may result from a board decision in a holding company to disinvest from a subsidiary and thereby cut supplier relations. Obviously, the reverse path to change with a corporate group is also possible: acquiring a firm with redundant capabilities and thereby putting other group members under increased competitive pressure.

A partial organization perspective, because of its emphasis on bringing about a 'decided order' in other than completely organized systems, is likely to be more sensitive to the importance of such hierarchy-like processes as sources of change. Nevertheless, one should not forget that this perspective also sensitizes for decisions in markets that it considers partially organized. What is more, this perspective, not unlike the conceptualization of organizing inter-firm networks as 'reflexive structuration', emphasizes not only the need for change, but also for stability, conceiving of both as a duality rather than a dualism (Farjoun, 2010). Even the creation of novelty with regard to products and services, processes, modes, or systems, would be considered as arising from the tensions and contradictions between stability and change (cf. Fortwengel *et al.*, 2017).

With respect to this issue, the partial organization perspective would not differ greatly from other advanced (e.g., practice-based) conceptualizations of organization or organizing, although in contrast to Brunsson's (e.g., 1989) earlier work, it seems to place less emphasis on the tensions and contradictions arising in and to be managed with the reflexive structuring of (inter-)organizational relationships. At least Ahrne and Brunsson (see Chapter 1) emphasize that organization is only an attempt that, in the end, may not succeed in changing practice.

PARTIAL ORGANIZATION AS DECIDED ORDER?

Sympathetic as I am to the idea of using organization theory to understand more or less organized parts of society in general, and of applying the partial organization perspective to the study of inter-firm networks in particular, I would like to raise the level of reflexivity about this latter issue in some respects. First, conceptualizing organization, including partial organization, as mainly an outcome of decisions – as a 'decided order' – certainly helps to clarify the organizational character of social systems, including inter-firm networks, and to distinguish them from more emergent phenomena. On the other hand, at least from my perspective, the concept of partial organization places too great an emphasis on the 'engineering' aspect: the decision making and its outcome – the decided order. Consequently, too little emphasis is placed on the 'emergent' aspect – the institutionalized order – of organizational and inter-organizational structures. One significant reason for the relevance of emergent aspects of inter-organizational networks is the fact that their coordination cannot rely on hierarchical authority; one significant effect being that tensions and contradictions are likely to arise that are not easily dealt with successfully. Obviously, depending on the concrete type of inter-firm network and on the form of network governance, all the other four criteria of an organization (as entity) – decisions on membership, rules, how to monitor members, and decisions about sanctions – may well be met by inter-firm networks. Some of these criteria may even be met by formal but 'post-bureaucratic' organizations (Heckscher & Donnellon, 1994). However, the fifth element – decisions about how to make decisions – is not valid for inter-firm networks, to the extent that such decisions can actually rely on or promote hierarchical fiat. Although power differentials are certainly to be expected in most inter-firm networks, the less powerful, to some extent at least, 'have to' consent to the decisions and actions taken by the more powerful (lead) organizations.

As Ahrne and Brunsson (2011: 93) suggest, a partial organization such as an inter-firm network may indeed result from either lack of willingness or lack of ability among organizational actors to create and maintain a more complete organization. However, the limited possibilities to organize – reflexively structure inter-firm networks – may also stem from the subtle interaction of decided and emergent aspects in complex structuration processes, influencing not only the scope and pace, but also the non-linearity of change. In the face of self-reinforcing processes of one type or another (Masuch, 1985; Garud & Kumaraswamy, 2005; Sydow & Schreyögg, 2013), these structuration processes are – just as in formal organizations – likely to be only partially (!) under the control of the organizational actors. It is exactly this interplay of intentional design and unintentional emergence that has yet to be worked out by the partial organization proponents so far. (See, however, Garud et al., 2015.) Take again the example of the network of suppliers strategically led by Toyota. This strategic network is well known for the high level of trust and co-operation among its network members, paradoxically combined with a high level of competition and control. Such tensions and contradictions, especially if not managed extremely carefully, are likely to emerge behind the back of the organizational actors, to escalate and eventually trigger herding or any other type of self-reinforcing process, which is increasingly difficult to monitor or to control, not to mention to counter. In sharp contrast to any hierarchical arrangement, the network – although dependent upon the type of network governance – would not even allow the suppression of these tensions.

Focusing on the entity or system resulting from (partially) organizing, an inter-firm network may well be considered a *partial organization of more or less complete organizations* – the latter not really lacking boundaries, although in the face of cross-boundary collaboration, they may well be blurred (Schreyögg & Sydow, 2010). Considering inter-firm networks from this entity perspective as being 'partially organized' helps to emphasize that, as a form of economic governance, such systems are an outcome of decisions, or more precisely, from my perspective, organizing as 'reflexive structuration', allowing for both engineering and emergence, and particularly their subtle interplay. This is in relatively sharp contrast to social networks of relationships highlighted by a network perspective or network theory. But at least until now, the partial organization perspective provides little guidance for coping with process phenomena tied to time and temporality, including tensions and contradictions, in a way that enhances the efficiency, effectiveness, and innovativeness of an inter-firm network and the satisfaction of its organizational members or outside stakeholders.

In extreme cases, however, a particular inter-firm network, despite the constitutive lack of hierarchical authority, may, in sum, be even *more* organized than some formal organizations are, thus coming *closer* to a complete rather than a partial organization (of more or less complete organizations). Promising candidates for this extreme case are global airline alliances. With detailed rules on the one hand and complex consensus-building procedures on the other, they seem to have found effective substitutes for hierarchical fiat to govern inter-organizational relations.

REFERENCES

Ahrne, G. & Brunsson, N. (2011) Organization outside Organizations: The Significance of Partial Organization. *Organization* 18(1): 83–104.

Ahrne, G., Brunsson, N., & Seidl, D. (2016) Resurrecting Organizations by Going beyond Organizations. *European Management Journal* 34(2): 93–101.

Aoki, K. & Wilhelm, M. (2017) The Role of Ambidexterity in Managing Buyer-Supplier Relationships: The Toyota Case. *Organization Science* 28(6): 1080–97.

Apelt, M., Besio, C., Corsi, G., von Groddeck, V., Grothe-Hammer, M., & Tacke, V. (2017) Resurrecting Organization without Renouncing Society: A Response to Ahrne, Brunsson and Seidl. *European Management Journal* 35(1): 8–14.

Arndt, J. (1979) Toward a Concept of Domesticated Markets. *Journal of Marketing*, 43(4): 69–75.

Bartelings, J. A., Goedee, J., Raab, J., & Bijl, R. (2017) The Nature of Orchestrational Work. *Public Management Review* 19(3): 342–60.

Berends, H., van Burg, E., & van Raaij, E. M. (2011) Contacts and Contracts: Cross-Level Network Dynamics in the Development of an Aircraft Material. *Organization Science* 22: 940–60.

Berthod, O., Grothe-Hammer, M., Müller-Seitz, G., Raab, J., & Sydow, J. (2017) From High-Reliability Organizations to High-Reliability Networks: The Dynamics of Network Governance in the Face of Emergency. *Journal of Public Administration Theory* 27(2): 352–71.

Borgatti, S. P. & Halgin, D. S. (2011) On Network Theory. *Organization Science* 22 (5): 1168–81.

Brass, D. J., Galaskiewicz, J., Greve, H. R., & Tsai, W. (2004) Taking Stock of Networks and Organizations: A Multilevel Perspective. *Academy of Management Journal* 47: 795–817.

Brunsson, N. (1989) *The Organization of Hypocrisy: Talk, Decisions and Actions in Organizations*. Chichester: Wiley.

Das, T. K. & Teng, B.-S. (2000) Instabilities of Strategic Alliances: An Internal Tension Perspective. *Organization Science* 11(1): 77–101.

Davis, G. F. (2016) *The Vanishing American Corporation*. San Francisco: Berrett-Koehler.

De Rond, M. & Bouchikhi, H. (2004) On the Dialectics of Strategic Alliance. *Organization Science* 15(1): 56–69.

DiMaggio, P. J. & Powell, W. W. (1983) The Iron Cage Revisited: Institutional Isomorphism and Collective Rationality in Organizational Fields. *American Sociological Review* 48: 147–60.

Dobusch, L. & Schoeneborn, D. (2015) Fluidity, Identity, and Organizationality: The Communicative Constitution of Anonymous. *Journal of Management Studies* 52(8): 1005–35.

Doz, Y. L., Olk, P. M., & Ring, P. S. (2000) Formation Processes of R&D Consortia: Which Path to Take? Where Does It Lead? *Strategic Management Journal* 21(SI): 239–66.

Dyer, J. H. & Nobeoka, K. (2000) Creating and Managing a High-Performance Knowledge-Sharing Network: The Toyota Case. *Strategic Management Journal* 21(SI): 345–67.

Emirbayer, M. (1997) Manifesto for a Relational Sociology. *American Journal of Sociology* 103(2): 281–317.

Farjoun, M. (2010) Beyond Dualism: Stability and Change as a Duality. *Academy of Management Review* 35(2): 202–25.

Fortwengel, J., Schüßler, E., & Sydow, J. (2017) Studying Organizational Creativity as Process: Fluidity or duality? *Creativity and Innovation Management* 26 (1): 5–16.

Garud, R. & Kumaraswamy, A. (2005) Vicious and Virtuous Circles in the Management of Knowledge: The Case of Infosys Technologies. *MIS Quarterly* 29(1): 9–33.

Garud, R., Simpson, B., Langley, A., & Tsoukas, H. (2015) Introduction: How does novelty emerge. In R. Garud, B. Simpson, A. Langley, & H. Tsoukas (eds.), *The Emergence of Novelty in Organizations*. Oxford: Oxford University Press. 1–24.

Giddens, A. (1984) *The Constitution of Society*. Cambridge: Polity.

Halinen, A., Salmi, A., & Havila, V. (1999) From Dyadic Change to Changing Business Networks: An Analytical Framework. *Journal of Management Studies* 36(6): 779–94.

Heckscher C. & Donnellon, A. (1994) *The Post-bureaucratic Organization*. Thousand Oaks: SAGE.

Hennig, M., Brandese, U., Pfeffer, J., & Mergel, I. (2012) *Studying Social Networks*. Frankfurt: Campus.

Hibbert, P. & Huxham, C. (2010) The Past in Play: Tradition in the Structures of Collaboration. *Organization Studies* 31(5): 525–54.

Jarillo, J. C. (1988) On Strategic Networks. *Strategic Management Journal* 9(1): 31–41.

Jones, C., Hesterly, W. S., & Borgatti, S. P. (1997) General Theory of Network Governance: Exchange Conditions and Social Mechanisms. *Academy of Management Review* 22(4): 911–45.

Kilduff, M. & Tsai, W. (2003) *Social Networks and Organizations*. London: SAGE.

Kleinaltenkamp, M., Plinke, W., & Geiger, I. (eds.) (2015) *Business Relationship Marketing and Management – Mastering Business Markets*. Wiesbaden: Gabler.

Lorenzoni, G. & Baden-Fuller, C. (1995) Creating a Strategic Center to Manage a Web of Partners. *California Management Review* 37(3): 146–63.

Majchrzak, A., Jarvenpaa, S. L., & Bagherzadeh, M. (2015) A Review of Inter-Organizational Collaboration Dynamics. *Journal of Management* 41: 1338–60.

March, J. & Simon, H. (1958) *Organizations*. New York: Wiley.

Masuch, M. (1985) Vicious Circles in Organizations. *Administrative Science Quarterly* 29: 14–33.

Miles, R. E. & Snow, C. C. (1986) Organizations: New Concepts for New Forms. *California Management Review* 28(2): 62–73.

Perrow, C. (1991) A Society of Organizations. *Theory and Society* 20(6): 725–62.

Powell, W. W. (1990) Neither Market nor Hierarchy: Network Forms of Organization. *Research in Organizational Behavior* 12: 295–336.

Provan, K. G., Beyer, J. M., & Kruytbosch, C. (1980) Environmental Linkages and Power in Resource Dependence Relations between Organizations. *Administrative Science Quarterly* 25(6): 200–25.

Provan, K. G., Fish, A., & Sydow, J. (2007) Inter-Organizational Networks at the Network Level: a Review of the Empirical Literature on Whole Networks. *Journal of Management* 33(3): 479–516.

Provan, K. G. & Kenis, P. N. (2008) Modes of Network Governance: Structure, Management, and Effectiveness. *Journal of Public Administration Research and Theory* 18: 229–52.

Raab, J. & Kenis, P. (2009) Heading toward a Society of Networks: Empirical Developments and Theoretical Challenges. *Journal of Management Inquiry* 18(3): 198–210.

Rometsch, M. & Sydow, J. (2006) On Identities of Networks and Organizations – The Case of Franchising. In M. Kornberger & S. Gudergan (eds.), *Only Connect: Neat Words, Networks and Identities*. Copenhagen: Liber & Copenhagen Business School Press. 19–47.

Schreyögg, G. & Sydow, J. (2010) Organizing for Fluidity? On the Dilemmas of New Organizational Forms. *Organization Science* 21(6): 1251–62.

Schreyögg, G. & Sydow, J. (eds.) (2013) *Self-Reinforcing Processes in and among Organizations*. London: Palgrave Macmillan.

Seidl, D. & Becker, K. H. (eds.) (2006) *Niklas Luhmann and Organization Studies*. Copenhagen: Liber.

Sydow, J. (1992) *Strategische Netzwerke*. Wiesbaden: Gabler.

Sydow, J., Schüßler, E., & Müller-Seitz, G. (2016) *Managing Inter-Organizational Relations*. London: Palgrave Macmillan.

Sydow, J. & Windeler, A. (1998) Organizing and Evaluating Interfirm Networks: A Structurationist Perspective on Network Processes and Effectiveness. *Organization Science* 9(3): 265–84.

Walker, G., Kogut, B., & Shan, W. (1997) Social Capital, Structural Holes and the Formation of an Industry Network. *Organization Science* 8(2): 109–25.

Williamson, O. E. (1991) Comparative Economic Organization: The Analysis of Discrete Structural Alternatives. *Administrative Science Quarterly* 36(2): 269–96.

Wilhelm, M. (2011) Managing Coopetition through Horizontal Supply Chain Relations: Linking Dyadic and Network Levels of Analysis. *Journal of Operations Management* 29(7/8): 663–76.

Windeler, A. (2001) *Unternehmungsnetzwerke*. Wiesbaden: Westdeutscher Verlag.

NOTES

1. Whereas internalization would indicate the substitution of market by organization, quasi-internationalization would point to the substitution of market by network governance. For similar reasons, I prefer to speak of quasi-externalization rather than externalization (or outsourcing), as this term does not speak to the process of the emergence of an inter-firm network.

2. This is typical of hybrids and forms of governance, which, in reality, mix ideal types.

ACKNOWLEDGEMENT

I thank Michael Grothe-Hammer and Arnold Windeler for commenting on former versions of this chapter.

10 An Organized Network: World Economic Forum and the Partial Organizing of Global Agendas

Christina Garsten and Adrienne Sörbom

The motto of the world's largest global think tank – the World Economic Forum (WEF or Forum) – is 'Committed to improving the state of the world'. Many people have heard of this organization because of its renowned meeting held annually in the village of Davos, Switzerland, at which CEOs, top-level politicians, and heads of inter-governmental organizations (IGOs) congregate. Established as a Swiss foundation based in Geneva, it is active in global policymaking, but without a state-based mandate. It is difficult to assess if it is succeeding in its intent to improve and change the world, but it is reasonable to assume that it does have some form of leverage. This chapter analyses the specific order that the WEF creates around itself in the interest of establishing authority as a global policy actor (Garsten & Sörbom, 2018). WEF staff and participants at WEF activities would call this order a 'network'. We acknowledge the network aspects of the order, but argue that it is based primarily on organization; it is a partially decided order, hinging on the WEF's decisions. In this chapter, we answer the question of why this particular form was chosen over a regular organization, lacking the network aspects.

We are driven by a curiosity regarding global politics and contemporary problematics of government (Rose & Miller, 1992). In the literature on global politics, the WEF is mentioned as a key actor, but it has attracted relatively limited scholarly interest. What is especially lacking are studies based on primary sources such as interviews and ethnographic field work, through which an understanding of how the organization is able to be an actor in global policymaking is rendered possible (see, however, Pigman, 2006; Giesler & Veresiu, 2014). Researchers analysing global politics primarily focus on IGOs, such as the United Nations (UN) and the World Trade Organization (WTO), although there is a growing number of exceptions (e.g., Higgot, Underhill, & Bieler, 2000; Stone, 2008). As international relations scholar Diane Stone claims, public policy has 'been a prisoner of the word "state"' (Stone, 2008: 19). In order to understand national and global public policy, however, other types of organizations must be recognized as vital actors. This chapter adds to the growing literature on non-state actors in global policymaking by focusing especially on the WEF and its way of organizing to achieve authority in global policymaking. The WEF is a specific case in point because of its unique outreach. Not only does it attract a large number of high-profile political and economic leaders, which generates strong media coverage, but it has also created a vast number of working groups – internally termed 'communities' – in which well over 10,000 people are participating. They include heads of state, well-known artists; and high-ranking people from international organizations, churches, NGOs, and the world's largest corporations. In this sense the WEF is, in its own right, an actor in global governance, begging for scholarly attention to uncover what is happening in these communities and how it constructs authority in relation to other organizations. Moreover, we assume that in spite of its unique qualities, the WEF shares some organizational qualities with other think tanks and non-state governing bodies on global and national levels, especially regarding its way of achieving authority through the organization of its extensive network.

Authority is conceptualized here in line with James Coleman (1974), who stresses the ability to control the actions of others. Since the WEF cannot decide what other actors should do, it lacks the external decision-making capabilities that governments and IGOs may have. In turn, this entails a degree of uncertainty in regard to its authority. Essentially, it can control only the actions of its own employees. Moreover, as a Swiss-based foundation, it can rarely advertise the victories it may sometimes gain in global policymaking or diplomacy – two types of activities for which it has great interest but no mandate. As demonstrated in this chapter, however, the organization does achieve authority, mainly by establishing what we term a 'partially organized network' that extends the authority of the organization beyond the Swiss-based foundation. Employing the concept of partial organization, we show that the WEF draws upon three specific elements of organizing: membership, monitoring, and sanctioning. By making certain recurring participants into various forms of members in 'communities' that they both monitor and sanction, the Forum constructs an organized order around itself, which it can draw upon in the interest of setting global political agendas, in spite of its lack of external decision-making capabilities.

Empirically, this chapter builds on interview data with Geneva staff and participants at various WEF activities between 2011 and 2015. We conducted recorded interviews with WEF staff on three occasions at the headquarters in Geneva Switzerland. During this time, we met twice with Professor Klaus Schwab, founder and Chairman of the WEF Foundation. We also observed, in various invited and uninvited roles, WEF events in Cape Town, Davos, Dubai, and Istanbul, during which we conducted recorded interviews and had numerous spontaneous (and unrecorded) conversations in shuttles, networking areas, coffee shops, restaurants, and other locations. We also met with participants from these international events in follow-up events and meetings in Europe. Everyone mentioned in this chapter, with the exception of Chairman Schwab, has been given a fictitious name.

In the first part of this chapter we introduce the WEF, showing how its specific relationship to transnational corporations not only establishes it as an outsider in international relations, but also has significant consequences for what the organization can do and how it needs to structure its attempts to 'improve the state of the world', as its motto would have it. In the second part, we provide empirical evidence for the way the WEF constructs its activities, by describing two routes for accessing and creating resources and capital. In the final part, we discuss membership, monitoring, and sanctions as the organizational elements employed in these routes.

A NEW KID ON THE BLOCK

With few exceptions, the Westphalian international system was built on nation states. As Ruggie describes (2004), states constituted the international public, manifested in such organizations as the United Nations and the International Monetary Fund. In the latter part of the 1900s this domain did expand, however, to include not only IGOs, but also civil society organizations and transnational corporations, which together comprise the new public transnational domain (Ruggie, 2004). The WEF has established itself as an actor in this domain, even if in a somewhat different format than the IGOs.

The main difference between the WEF and IGOs relates to funding and mandates. The mandate of the UN, the prime example of an IGO, was based on the fifty founding nation states that wrote the initial charter. In 2011, when the newly created state of South Sudan joined, the UN could count 193 members. The member states are the funders that continuously mandate the UN to act, albeit with varying issues and enthusiasm. The WEF, on the other hand, is funded and mandated by corporations. Although initially established under the patronage of the European Commission and European Industrial Associations (Pigman, 2007: 8), it was re-formed into a non-profit Swiss-based foundation shortly after its inception in 1971. During the first few years, attendees at the Davos meetings funded the foundation with their fees, but in 1976, Professor Klaus Schwab instituted a reorganization that allowed corporations to become what the Forum termed 'members', paying the Foundation's costs through subscriptions (Pigman, 2007: 16). Almost forty years later, the organization was recognized by the Swiss state and gained formal status in Switzerland as an 'international institution' (World Economic Forum, 2017).

These two changes – allowing corporations to become funding members of the WEF and the Swiss government's recognition of the

WEF as an international organization – could make the organization appear to be an ordinary business association in the format of a meta-organization, representing its member organizations. Taking another look at the WEF, however, it becomes clear that it is not an association in which corporate funders have a say in decision making, in the way member organizations usually do. It is more correct to call them subscribers with restricted accessibility to the core of the organization. The famous Annual Meeting held in Davos in late January is not a meeting at which members gather to decide on the future direction of the organization; nor can the funders demand accountability for board decisions during the previous year. No such deliberations occur. The Davos event is an opportunity for those attending (funders and others) for doing business and politics, but it has little to do with what is commonly attributed to an 'annual meeting' of an association. Moreover, because the WEF has restricted the number of its funders to 1,000, 'membership' is open to a selected few accepted by the WEF. Taken together, this means that the WEF differs not only from international nongovernmental organizations but also international meta-organizations. The WEF is a Geneva-based foundation, funded by corporations and recognized by the Swiss state as an 'international institution' rather than a state-mandated international organization. The specific funding situation entails at least three key ramifications regarding what it can do and how it may act: It has limited decision-making possibilities, its funders may leave at will, and it depends upon other organizations for its authority.

First, then, compared to IGOs, the WEF is a corporate-funded organization with *limited decision-making scope*. A state has the right to decide about the people (citizens and others) who inhabit its territories and the organizations operating within its borders, and it can issue a mandate regarding its relationships with other states. Thus, IGOs working on the representative mandate of a nation state may be given the right to decision making on behalf of the state. Corporations, on the other hand, do not have this competence. The corporation exerts certain rights in relation to its employees and other corporations if it is a business combine, but it cannot decide for any-one outside itself (Ahrne & Brunsson, 2005). Fundamentally, then, an organization that is funded by corporations has no realm of decision making outside its own organization, unless a decision-making mandate has been explicitly delegated to it, and the WEF rarely receives this type of mandate.

Second, the WEF is an organization that *funders may leave at their discretion*. The funding relationship is renewed annually, and both WEF and the individual corporation can decide to terminate the relationship at any time. Again, comparing the WEF to an IGO makes this point evident. It is much easier for a business corporation to leave the WEF than for a nation state to leave the UN, for instance. Even though the UN is constantly described as being in crisis, and some countries have threatened to withhold their funding, only one state has ever attempted or threatened to leave the UN. WEF member corporations, on the other hand, do leave the WEF.

Third, and perhaps most important, because the WEF has no formal mandate to decide on issues with implications beyond its own full organization, it *relies on other organizations to achieve authority and pursue its agendas in other organizational contexts*. Thus, the WEF must build a form of organization that answers to these predicaments in order to reach outside and be significant to anyone but itself. This lack of capacity is a fundamental mechanism that helps to explain why the WEF has been formatted as a network. If the WEF aims to be something more than an overpriced meeting convener (which it has sometimes been accused of), it must rely upon others in order to utilize the ideas, concepts, solutions, and methods that spring from its activities. Towards this end, thousands of people that the WEF calls 'leaders' from 'all walks of life' are brought in to participate in its activities. These leaders are, in turn, encouraged to bring the ideas, projects, and deals back 'home' to employ in their everyday activities.

The authority of the WEF thus stems from its capability of relating strategically to other organizations. As long as people – 'the right people', according to the WEF – keep coming to its meetings and events, it will be able to mobilize them and achieve authority vis-à-vis other organizations. But it is an authority dependent on the active participation and support of 'the right people'. This authority does not exist in the form of a nation state-based mandate per se; it is established, maintained, and developed by the WEF itself. To be sure, the WEF may never have wanted another form of organization, as its current organization may have several advantages compared to organizations built on a state- or citizen-based mandate, but it is as correct to say that the restricted mandate efficiently precludes its organizational freedom.

CONSTRUCTING ROUTES FOR AUTHORITY

The ramifications of the WEF's funding situation are our starting point for understanding the partially organized network that the WEF has chosen to build. In the next two subsections we highlight two significant routes for the construction of authority: funding and the creation of communities.

Corporative funding

Financially, the WEF is built on its 1,000 funders, accepted into the organization because they are seen as 'companies that run the world economy forward'. For a corporation with global ambitions, WEF membership is a critical form of recognition that opens the door to global appreciation among the prime actors in their area of business. As our informants describe the situation, to be in Davos is to be seen as a global player and to see others. Participating funders use the meeting in Davos as a status arena. As one of our informants from a global consultancy corporation describes it: 'If you aren't there, you don't exist' (interview, Davos, January 2011).

Thus, corporations make good use of the money spent on the WEF. The Forum, on the other hand, needs both the financial and the social capital that business brings. Without corporate funding and the participation of top-level management, it would possibly not exist. At the same time, the WEF needs people from other spheres of activity in order to be the political animal it seeks to be. If only funders participated in its events, its political leverage would be significantly lower. Others, 'from all walks of life', need to join in, or it would merely be a corporate advocacy group. But each guest selected by the WEF means that subscribing corporations are able to send one fewer person. Thus, there is constant haggling at headquarters around who they would want to participate in Davos and other events.

Expert communities

The network-like organization that the WEF has created is based on what it terms 'communities'. It is through the organization of these communities that the WEF intentionally draws individuals into its circuit in different forms of constellations, thereby constructing authority beyond the foundation. Providing the communities with a degree of stability and predictability, mainly through the control of invitations and through monitoring and sanctioning of participants, the WEF can extend its own reach and capacity to act by 'borrowing' some of the agentic capacity of the community partakers. By so doing, the WEF may organize a position as intermediary that is valued by a large portion of its participants.

In the following quote, Paul Richardson, a top-level manager in Geneva, provides an example of how the WEF achieves authority in global governance without having the right to decide for others. The context is the UN's 2009 COP-15 climate change summit, held in Copenhagen, which, according to Richardson, was generally considered a failure. He tells the story of the key protagonists from the UN summit: Apart from then US President Barack Obama, they all met one week later in Davos, without the pressure of a particular diplomatic agenda.

> It was decompression. And our role? We, as organizers, pursue no particular agenda, but we provide space. And, after that meeting, Calderon suggested to move on with what later became the Cancun

Agreement. At the top level, there is an increasing demand for this kind of space. It works as decompression. Here, it is possible to say things that can't be said at top meetings.

(interview, Geneva, 8 September 2011)

What happened at the actual meeting in Davos, we do not know. The informant may have overstated the importance of the meeting, and we have not asked Prime Minister Calderon about where he got the idea for the UN agreement on climate change, the Cancun Protocol. But the words of the informant tell us how the Forum sees its own role. It is an intermediary in global politics, creating an arena for decision makers to meet and deliberate, and later picking up on the content from these deliberations in other organizational settings. In the understanding of WEF staff members, it is the communities that make this possible. Martin Lesoto, another senior manager in Geneva, describes communities as the key component for the WEF and the role it is able to play in global governance:

> So there is a lot of talk about building community. I believe that that is what the Forum fundamentally does and . . . why we are able to engage. The projects, the insights, even the events, those are all secondary. I mean events; actually, events are crucial for building community.
>
> *(interview, 19 September, 2012)*

Diana Gordon, another Forum manager, describes how the term 'community' within the Forum is both a group that is related to them and a group that is supposed to relate to stakeholders outside of the Forum:

> It's communities within the forum, but at large, in the sense that every community . . . I mean, it's really referring to the stakeholders of the organization, but with the understanding that each of these stakeholders represents a portion of society at large.
>
> *(interview, September 2012)*

These communities are more or less loosely organized groups of people, united around issues (Djelic & Quack, 2011); they include groups like the Foundation Members, The Network of Global Agenda Councils, Global Leadership Fellows, the Young Global Leaders, and the Global Shapers. But WEF communities established by the WEF around a specific issue, initiative, or project may exist without a name; they would meet a few times in Davos and other places, and then dissolve. By way of these loosely organized groups, the WEF taps into the expertise of others, thus insourcing part of its knowledge seeking by connecting other individuals and organizations. In so doing the WEF seeks and brings potentially valuable ideas and knowledge into its organizational core, where it is further elaborated upon and either translated into the WEF vocabulary or discarded. By the same token, it outsources the same ideas, relying on the funders and invitees for introducing ideas, perspectives, and solutions and elaborating upon them in settings outside the Forum. These double transfers channel resources into and out of the organization. In combination, they provide a basis for extending the capacity of WEF, while extending the potential influence of the other party.

CONSTRUCTING NETWORKS

The WEF thus draws upon the funding of corporations for its economic and social capital. In this capacity, it is the corporations that mandate the WEF to construct its high-status arena. But the mandate does not entail authority in Coleman's (1974) sense of the term, with the right to control the actions of others outside the organization. In the interest of being a global policy actor – not merely an arena – the WEF must therefore construct its own authority, primarily by drawing on the agentic capacities of others.

We argue that this construction is accomplished partly by making all funders and regular invitees into members of the WEF's partially organized network – members who it monitors to some extent and may sanction. We could write 'members' in quotation marks, because the funders who are termed 'members' by the Forum are members in name only. As Cassius Luck, high-level manager of the WEF, explained to us, 'Our members [the funders] are in a sense our subscribers; they are subscribing to an agenda that is not set by them' (interview, June 2015). By the same token, the invitees are described as 'members' only on an ad-hoc basis – when the WEF sees fit. This ad-hoc practice does not entail the right to return, even if the invitees would want to do so. Invitations are strictly the prerogative of WEF staff, and being on the list of invitations for one event is no guarantee of being invited to the next. Finally, the invitees do not pay member dues or appear on a member roster. Yet, as we demonstrate, invitees are treated like members in several ways, albeit with a degree of uncertainty regarding their status in the WEF. We therefore simply term them members of the WEF's partially organized network, comprising the environment that the WEF has established around itself, through which ideas may travel, basically from the WEF into the home organizations of invitees and funders and back again.

WEF employees refer to the construction of its environment as 'networking'. The emic term does capture part of what our analytical perspective suggests. A 'network' is based on non-organized contacts (Bommes & Tacke, 2005), and without this type of contact among participants, the WEF could not be influential. At times, these contacts form without any involvement from the WEF other than bringing people together; then the WEF has little or no knowledge of the networks that are unfolding. That would be the case for all contacts made in Davos nightlife at clubs, minglers, and parties. When doing fieldwork at WEF events, people have approached us on countless occasions, simply starting a conversation, not knowing who we are, and by no means encouraged by WEF to converse with us. They are merely as interested as we are in talking to others at the event, albeit for different reasons. And we have maintained contact with some of these people in various forms, just as they have maintained their business contacts or other contacts. Another version of the way networks unfold from WEF events is represented by the group of high-level officials from state authorities who consider themselves WEF community members, and who initiated a round of meetings with the intention of using what they had learnt in the meetings. This was not organized by the WEF, although they would have applauded the initiative had they heard about it (which they probably did). As Cassius Luck explained to us: 'We very much encourage ownership among our participants.'

Thus, invitees and funders are clearly networking, in an original sense of the term, creating non-decided structures linking persons and organizations, which is exactly what the WEF wants. Drawing on the key understanding of this volume – that organization should be defined as a *decided* order – we must at the same time acknowledge that apart from the hoped-for but spontaneous networking, a large part of the communities around the WEF are organized. They are based on concerted and decided activities, through which decided networks are created. Decisions are, of course, part of natural networks too. But these decisions are not taken in order to establish a network. In the order that WEF constructs around itself, the organizational elements of membership, monitoring, and sanctions are decisive.

WEF MEMBERSHIP: EMPIRICAL EXAMPLES

By turning funders and (some but not all) invitees into returning members, constituting the backbone of their partly organized environment, the Forum is able to construct an organization with authority. In the following part of the chapter, we present some empirical examples showing how the WEF constructs this partially organized network, drawing mainly on membership as an organizational element.

Selecting members

As Forum staff chronicle the process of constructing and developing the WEF's network, the stepping stone is finding people to invite. Finding exactly the right person for each panel, project, workshop, and mingler is therefore a main task at WEF headquarters. As Mustafa Wallah, senior manager, explained to us in Davos 2013, 'getting the exactly right moderator for a panel is pivotal to the success of the event'. Other staff informants have told us that some invitees have become great disappointments, if the moderator and other participants did not meet the standards. In practice this has meant that the original plan for the event – constructing a new community or partnership, for example – could not be completed. Thus, it is of great importance for both sides – the Forum employee and the invited persons – that the invitees perform well at meetings.

Using other colleagues for finding exactly the right person is the regular way to go about it. When we met Wallah's colleague, Diana Gordon, in Geneva, she explained their process of finding, for example, a moderator: They would choose from the pool of previous moderators. But, as she stressed, the Forum needs to 'freshen up the pool of moderators':

> Yes, we do try to use new moderators, but we would always try sort of smaller activities or smaller sessions first rather than the large sessions. But we choose ... we also work with a number of media leaders, but in particular those that are ready to push the envelope in terms of the format. So it's a real combination of word-of-mouth, through the networks, but then also research and looking for people.
>
> *(interview, September 2012)*

For everyone who is found interesting, there is a process of 'due diligence' undertaken, in order to ensure that the person and the organization is acceptable for the Forum – a time-consuming process. Finding a person who fits the Forum's mission and the task at hand is not always easy. Peter Berg works as a fellow within the Forum, spending a substantial portion of his working hours finding the right people for the groups he manages. He describes the process as a strange mix of complete freedom for him to find the right people, and a highly developed bureaucracy wherein layers of staff need to sign off before he is able to send an invitation to a person that he knew from the beginning 'for sure will be invited' (interview June 2015).

Becoming a member

One core group that the WEF organizes comprises the 1,500 experts invited to the United Arab Emirates every November for what is referred to internally as the 'brain trust meeting'. Issues are discussed at that meeting that may end up on the agenda of the coming year's Annual Meeting in Davos. The official term for this community is the Global Action Councils – GACs for short. On the WEF website they are presented as 'select, invitation-only groups on the key topics in the global arena. Each Council, comprised of 15–20 Members, serves as an advisory board to the Forum and other interested parties, such as governments and international organizations' (WEF 2015). Each Council of fifteen to twenty members 'serves as ... organizations'. In 2015 there were eighty-two such groups that participants are asked to join for three-year terms, during which time they are more or less given the right to return. As nothing is certain within the WEF, however, this right may be recalled or altered if someone is seen by the WEF as making an insufficient contribution.

Mathew Tong, an Oxford professor, is one of those who has acquired a more stable position. We met him at lunch in Dubai at the 2012 expert meeting, in the assigned 'networking area'. While trying to deal with the awkward international finger food, he described how he had been part of the brain trust summits for five years, and was somewhat of a veteran as far as 'brain trust meetings go'. With an ironic smile and playful tone, Tong told us that when he received his first invitation to Dubai, he had thought that the whole thing was a set-up – some kind of scam. So he phoned the Forum and asked them to e-mail him again. As it turned out, he enjoyed being part of WEF events. Not only because of the luxurious context (he said that he appreciated the hotel suite and the personal attendant), but also because of the real gains. Moreover, by participating over and over again, people aspire to qualify to 'the summits of summits': the WEF annual meeting in Davos. Tong says that he is certainly hoping that he will be invited, although that has not yet happened. With a half-smile, he claimed that he has a vague sense of why he keeps being invited to Dubai: 'I do have a small impact in Hong Kong. I am kind of big there', he says, adding 'but it's nothing of course'.

The above-mentioned Peter Berg is a member of another important WEF community: the Global Leadership Fellows (GLFs). In
a sense, although usually young, this group is even more exclusive
and has a more secure position within the organization than does the
GAC community, because it is based on the mere thirty new interns
that the WEF takes on annually to work for three years at Forum
headquarters in Geneva. They will have such administrative positions
as Senior Community Manager or Manager of Global Action Council
on this or that theme, and will commit a great deal of their many
working hours to arranging meetings such as the ones in Davos or
Dubai. At the same time, however, this group of fellows is constantly
monitored and evaluated. When we met Peter Berg, it became apparent that he was somewhat nervous about speaking with us, asking
such questions as 'Who has authorized our conversation?' Several
times he retreated, saying that he did not believe that he was allowed
to answer our questions. It was clear to us that he was worried that his
words would have negative repercussions for him.

Reporting journalists constitute another group that may be
invited to WEF events, and over time become a type of member that
may be monitored and sanctioned. In 2013, we participated at
the media dinner held annually in Davos for accredited media professionals. As mentioned in the welcome speech, the WEF holds this
dinner as a way of 'thanking attending media for the job that had been
put into reporting the event'. During the dinner it became clear that
the Forum had long relationships with some of the reporters. Beatrice
Kallis, a journalist from a major European media house, told us that
she had 'inherited her right to come and report from the annual meeting' from someone in her company and confessed that she wanted to
return. Therefore Kallis soon told us that she did not want her critical
views of the WEF to be known, as it was important for her job that she
could come back.

During dinner, a WEF employee came by to ask what Kallis had
reported from the event. Kallis later turned to us, saying that she saw
this as the Forum's way of checking that she had not made any

inaccurate statements – which she told us she had not. She explained how she had no intention of reporting anything that would appear critical of the Forum, as long as her journalistic principals were not compromised.

The decision for anyone to become a member of any type of WEF group lies primarily in the hands of Forum staff. For the individual wanting to become a regular participant, the WEF is making a critical choice, as it is endowing the participant with status. To be sure, some participants may have a stronger position than others. During the eight years of his US presidency, Barack Obama never honoured the WEF with his attendance. In such cases, the Forum can only invite and hope for a positive answer. In general, though, participants crave the attention of the Forum, hoping that they will become a WEF regular.

Accordingly, as some participants have whispered in our ears, they are afraid to tell us what they really think about the event and the Forum, because they want to return. These informants underscore what they consider the importance for one's career of becoming part of this network, meeting all these people they would otherwise never meet. And as our informants in the Geneva office claim, participants want to be able to write in their CVs that they are part of the network; they like to have the words 'World Economic Forum' related to them. 'You would not believe the effort we have to put in telling people that they can't come', Peter Berg tells us. 'Much more than saying that people can come.' And those contacting them range from heads of state to CEOs, journalists, and researchers – like ourselves.

Being allowed to come back

Crucial to returning, and thereby becoming an affiliated member, is to be seen as constructive and 'thinking outside the box', without being too radical. This is how Diana Gordon describes what, to her, constitutes a failure in finding the right person:

> CG: A: So, do you, like, regularly get disappointed? You take someone in and you think it's worthwhile and then they're not …

DG: Not regularly, but there are always people that we think, like, 'Okay, well that maybe served its purpose for that particular ... but it's not someone we would necessarily want to continue to engage with' ... They are brilliant, all of them, brilliant people. It's just that, you know, how available were they in the preparations? It's one aspect that we really have to take into consideration. And how willing were they to really understand what the mission and the vision of the Forum is, and not just bring their own idea to the table? How good are they, and not just ... obviously they are amazing thought leaders ... but how well are they able to articulate their ideas on a panel? All of these kinds of criteria have to come into play.

(interview, September 2012)

As Diana Gordon noted, a major point in being re-invited is to understand the 'mission and vision of the Forum', indicating that it is not enough to be 'brilliant'. 'They are brilliant, all of them', as Gordon told us. But the invitee will also have to fit the Forum's views about important content and format if they are to return.

Criticizing the Forum is fully possible for average participants if they express some level of trust in the organization. Expressing more fundamental criticism is difficult, but not impossible for someone who is either extremely famous (like Bono), or very young, like members of the Young Global Shapers group, whose role it is to be critical. In general, though, not complying with the basic ideas of the Forum means that the individuals and the organizations of their home base will be left out of the network and seen as inconsistent with the ethos of the Forum. What this ethos means in practice is transferred from WEF employees to participants during the planning of panels, seminars, and other events. For every session, there is an internal evaluation in combination with what is described as 'anecdotal' evaluations, through which response from other teams and colleagues are taken. In addition, there is a constant form of monitoring, whereby staff members discuss such issues as a moderator performance with colleagues and participants. As Diana Gordon described:

> To be honest, we do a lot during the event itself. We get a lot of – and we have a lot of – direct feedback and information. People are very willing to be open and share what their perspectives are . . . But again it's ad hoc. It's anecdotal. It's not a very thorough and consistent feedback, so that's where we need to get to. But we also rely on . . . our colleagues [to provide] feedback, the messages that they get from their constituents as well.
>
> *(interview, September 2012)*

Productive participants who are found to be compliant with WEF standards may be invited again. Recurring guests are highly valued internally, as they both make day-to-day life easier and serve as a prerequisite for the stability and longevity of the communities. Therefore, employees at the Geneva headquarters working with events, initiatives, and projects and so forth keep the participants that they invite under close supervision. They are seen as 'belonging to' a specific staff member, a relationship that can be a valuable asset internally. When moving from one position to another within the Forum, employees bring their contacts with them. And if Group X has found a new person to invite, Group Y cannot invite that person as well. Furthermore, there is a hierarchy in relation to these persons: The 'lower-level' invitation, given to people who do not relate closely enough to the event's core theme, will be superseded by invitations to those who do. As staff members explained, regulations about invitations are necessary because there is an inherent risk of overusing some people, making them prone to rejecting further invitations. Taken together, however, these rules illustrate how the participants at WEF activities become key assets in the organization's interest of organizing for authority in global governance. By finding and drawing upon these individuals (who are usually working on behalf of other organizations) and their interests in returning to the Forum, the WEF is able to construct authority beyond itself. In this interest, the organizational element of membership is pivotal.

A PARTIALLY ORGANIZED NETWORK

The WEF's motto, 'Committed to improving the state of the world', encapsulates the ambition and the situation of the organization. It aspires to be a positive force for the world at large, but cannot promise anything more than its commitment. Based on the mandate provided by its funding corporations, but lacking the authority of an international state-based organization, it must construct authority for itself as an actor in global governance. Group members from the vast and partially organized network render this authority – the possibility of affecting and shaping the actions of others (Coleman, 1990/1994: 66) – to the WEF in a mutual transaction through which the Forum can control actions of its participants as long as they are part of the WEF structure, at the same time as participants can use that authority for their individual gain, and to the benefit of the organizations they are part of outside the WEF. The participants, turned into members, are therefore the original authority bearers, but they vest this authority in the WEF. The WEF, on its behalf, confers status on the participants, thereby strengthening their capacities to perform in global markets and/or politics, while simultaneously furthering their personal interests.

Key to understanding the role that the WEF can play globally, both in relation to politics and business, is its peculiar form. It is neither a network nor an organization, but a combination of the two forms of order. As demonstrated in this chapter, the WEF has members only in a weak form. Neither funders nor guests can claim to be let in or have the right to return to the Forum. At its own discretion, the Forum decides these issues. The relationship to its funders and participants generally remains open for discussion.

Still, as the empirical examples of this chapter illustrate, the WEF maintains its on-going organizing effort by using membership in various formats, partly drawing on the advantages of organizing. Individuals are invited, and if they do well in the eyes of the Forum, they may become a recognized 'member of the community' if they wish to do so, although no membership fee has been paid and no papers are signed. In this sense, the entire arrangement gives the appearance of 'informality', as undecided, which is of utmost importance to the Forum. As Cassius Luck says, being an informal catalyst for change is their *raison d'être* (interview, June 2015). In spite of this informality, some invitees are given the status of recurrent WEF attendees and are treated as members of WEF groups. As such, they are continuously monitored and possibly sanctioned. If the contribution of individual attendees is appropriate, well performed, and valued as productive by WEF staff, they may become part of the decided network and allowed to return for subsequent meetings. To be sure, there are limits to the feasibility of the WEF disallowing some specific attendees. Some of them bring more social and economic capital than others. But we maintain that for the bulk of those who have been granted the level of recurrent participant, there is a strong impetus to follow the norms set by the Forum. If these members do not know what it takes to be productive in the WEF sense beforehand through belonging to the epistemic communities of global policymaking (Haas, 1992), participants who become network members learn from staff and other members about the requirements of being asked to return. In the same vein, monitoring and sanctioning is somewhat haphazard and anecdotal, as informants among staff tell us. Yet, this type of monitoring and sanctioning is built into the organization at all levels and in relation to all its groups.

Through these memberships, the WEF creates a partial organization in which ideas take shape and travel – from and between the Forum and its attendees and the organizations where they have their home-base. Accordingly, not only are ideas formulated at WEF meetings that may be translated and activated in other organizations with a stronger political mandate; the WEF is also orchestrating a social structure through which it diffuses these ideas. There are many advantages for the individuals taking part in this partial organization, as it may provide social, economic, and political capital. Presumably, this is why so many people aspire to be Forum members, even though the organized network is partly based on deception. The Forum decides on which invitees are to become members and treats them as such by monitoring and sanctioning them. This decision is not communicated verbally, however; nor does it entail the rights of membership common to associations. Both exit and voice (cf. Hirschman, 1970) are options that may be drawn upon by members should they not like to be organized. But there is an asymmetry in the relationship, as the Forum keeps its upper hand in deciding who will be allowed to return.

We maintain that this crossover form of order, mixing network and organization, is due both to the lack of a nation state-based mandate and the interest of appearing non-organized. The alternative could have been to form a meta-organization, having corporations as members in a stronger sense, but that would have been detrimental in at least two ways. Not only would that construct likely be viewed as a mouthpiece for corporate interests; it would also raise legitimacy issues in global politics, as corporations have an ambivalent position as political actors. A network, on the other hand, is almost harmless. A network is not an actor, it does not decide or even express viewpoints. It is, as the name of the WEF underscores, a forum, a meeting place for spontaneous activities. Additionally, the crossover form of organization is chosen because it keeps the centre of organization strong. Ordinary members, having the right to be part of governing the organization, would jeopardize Forum control of its affairs. As the organization stands now, governing capabilities are fully in the hands of the Forum's management thrust.

Along these lines, we submit that this particular form of organizing has been useful for the Forum in its attempts to improve the state of the world. By way of its particular form of memberships, creating a partial organization, it has been able to make room for itself in global governance. It composes itself into a more or less harmless arena, yet strives and claims to be of utter importance for the improvement of the condition of the world. In this way, it works partly under false pretences. Judging by the number of heads of state appearing at its meetings, this stance does not seem to hinder its goals. On the contrary, the character of a harmless network is what makes it useful; it comes with less liability than does participation within the framework of international, state-based organizations. It is, however, a strongly orchestrated and formatted character, shaped in the interest of the Forum continuously striving to bring its motto to life.

REFERENCES

Ahrne, G. & Brunsson, N. (2005) Organizations and Meta-Organizations. *Scandinavian Journal of Management* 21(2005): 429–49.

Ahrne, G. & Brunsson, N. (2011) Organization outside Organizations: The Significance of Partial Organization. *Organization* 18(1): 83–104.

Coleman, J. S. (1974) *Power and the Structure of Society*. New York: WW Norton.

Coleman, J. S. (1990/1994) *Foundations of Social Theory*. Cambridge, MA: Harvard University Press.

Djelic, M. & Quack, S. (2011) *Transnational Communities, Shaping Global Economic Governance*. Cambridge, MA: Cambridge University Press.

Garsten, C. & Sörbom, A. (2018) *Discreet Power: How the World Economic Forum Shapes Market Agendas*. Stanford: Stanford University Press.

Giesler, M. & Veresiu, E. (2014) Creating the Responsible Consumer: Moralistic Governance Regimes and Consumer Subjectivity. *Journal of Consumer Research* 41(3): 840–57.

Higgot, R., Underhill, G., & Bieler, A. (2000) *Non-State Actors and Authority in the Global System*. New York: Routledge.

Hirschman, A. O. (1970) *Exit, Voice and Loyalty: Responses to Decline in Firms, Organizations and States*. Cambridge, MA: Harvard University Press.

Jutterström, M. (2004) *Att påverka beslut – företag i EU: sregelsättande*. Stockholm: EFI, Ekonomiska Forskningsinstitutet vid Handelshögskolan I Stockholm.

Pigman, G. A. (2007) *The World Economic Forum: A Multi-Stakeholder Approach to Global Governance*. New York: Routledge.

Rasche, A., de Bakker, F., & Moon, J. (2013) Complete and Partial Organizing for Corporate Social Responsibility. *Journal of Business Ethics* 115: 651–63.

Rose, N. & Miller P. (1992) Political Power beyond the State: Problematics of Government. *The British Journal of Sociology* 43(2): 173–205.

Ruggie, G. (2004) Reconstituting the Global Domain: Issues, Actors, and Practices. *European Journal of International Relations* 10(4): 499–531.

Stone, D. (2008) Global Public Policy, Transnational Policy Communities, and their Networks. *The Policy Studies Journal* 36(1): 19–38.

Willets, P. (2011) *Non-Governmental Organizations in World Politics: The Construction of Global Governance*. New York: Routledge.

World Economic Forum (2015) Global Agenda Councils. Retrieved 25 May 2015 from http://globalsummitryproject.com.s197331.gridserver.com/archive/world_eco nomic_forum_meetings/www.weforum.org/communities.html.

World Economic Forum (2017) World Economic Forum Recognized by the Swiss Government as International Institution. Retrieved 28 February 2017 from https://widgets.weforum.org/history/2015.html.

11 Organizing Intimacy

Göran Ahrne

Common to all types of intimate relationships is closeness and strong emotions. Intimacy implies an interpersonal interpenetration, making communicative relationships denser; what one regards as relevant also becomes relevant for the other (Luhmann, 1986: 158). In most images of intimacy, love is a central component. But love contains a variety of emotions. The concept of love as used in ordinary language 'serves to hide and disguise the nature of human relationships' (Scheff, 2006: 112). Scheff makes a distinction between three components of love: attachment, attunement, and attraction. Attachment is a physical bond and a relatively stable emotion, whereas attunement and attraction are less stable. That love is a central concept denoting intimacy does not mean that intimate relationships are always loving and warm; they can contain other strong emotions, like fear, jealousy, and hate (Zelizer, 2005: 18).

Intimate relationships do not 'simply happen as the result of some instinctive process of mutual attractions' (Layder, 2004: 66). On the contrary, just as in all social relationships, it is relevant to ask how they are established and who is included, how those involved keep in touch with each other and know what they can expect from each other. In these respects, there are considerable differences between different types of intimate relationships. Despite strong emotions and a high density of communication, intimacy does not preclude organization. An investigation of the organization of intimacy can provide new insights about variations in the way organizational elements can be combined and with what consequences. Seeing relationships as intimate emphasizes certain similarities among them, but when one examines how they are established and organized, their differences are striking.

In this chapter I examine three intimate relationships – families, kinship, and friendship – in order to investigate combinations of organizational elements, and how varying combinations can be explained by the core component of love in each type of relationship.

But intimate relationships do not exist in a vacuum. To understand the organization of intimacy, it is necessary to look outside the relationship. States are important actors making decisions about rules for and the monitoring of families and kinship. But states in their turn depend on families; the connections between families and states have crucial consequences for the organization of states.

FAMILIES

Affiliation can be established in several ways within the same relationship. A nuclear family consists of the adult couple's relationship as well as the relationships between each parent and each child. In this section, I focus on the relationship between the adult partners, which can be understood as a romantic and erotic relationship based on love (cf. Blatterer, 2013).

In *Love as Passion: The Codification of Intimacy*, Niklas Luhmann (1986: 102) argues that love is a binary coded emotion; one is either in love or not in love. You are expected to be able to answer yes or no if you are asked if you love someone. This understanding of love is different from Anthony Giddens' theory of love in late modernity. According to this theory, love is a 'pure relationship', in which people do not make any decisions or plans for the future and no promises (Giddens, 1991, 1992). The relationship exists only as long as both partners feel that it provides 'enough satisfaction for each individual to stay within it' (Giddens, 1992: 58).

Giddens' theory has been heavily criticized (Jamieson, 1999; Lewis, 2002). A lasting love relationship involves more than the immediate satisfaction of each party. 'Love and care as expressed by a more practical doing and giving is as much the crux of their relationship, as a process of mutually discovering and enjoying each other'

(Jamieson, 1999: 485). But common financial and material resources over and above a continued relationship require a strong commitment.

Attraction is the main emotional component of a love relationship between adults. Its institutional logic 'is distinguished first by words; by each telling the other that one is in love with her/him' (Friedland *et al.*, 2014: 354). Attraction often grows stronger when expressed and talked about. All evidence shows that most long-lasting love relationships are organized, sooner or later, into some type of manifest relationship, when those who have decided to become a couple announce to the environment that they belong together and expect their friends and relatives to treat them as a couple. The discussion regarding same-sex marriages is evidence of the importance that people place on being recognized as a couple (Weeks *et al.*, 2001; Chauncey, 2004; Badgett, 2009).

Even if strong norms and ideas exist about how marriages shall be established and which marriage partners are preferred, a decision is required about exactly which individuals are going to form a new family. In this respect, families have always been partly organized through decisions about membership.

Decision making is a process, and the last step in this process is critical for expressing the commitment of the participants (Brunsson, 2007: 15). The literature on same-sex marriages provides evidence for the effects of a decision to become a couple – often through some type of ceremony, such as marriage. The would-be couple often declares this decision in the presence of other people. A woman describes the effects of such a ceremony, which was not a conventional marriage: 'I did feel differently afterwards. I don't know what did, I'll try and describe to you. It was like we had, sort of, it was nothing tangible, but it was like something had sort of passed between us that made us belong more really' (Smart, 2007: 70).

But the need to choose causes uncertainty, typical of decisions. Ann Swidler writes in *Talk of Love* that there is latent uncertainty in most love relations: if one's choice was the best option and if one should continue the relationship (2001: 201). And the more options there are, the greater is this uncertainty, rendering decisions increasingly complex. Eva Illouz demonstrates that it has become more difficult for people to make final decisions to establish a permanent relationship. A commitment phobia can be trigged by the experiences of having many opportunities for choice and a wide selection from which to choose, which also softens the intensity of the feelings: 'comparisons between different possible choices dampen strong emotions' (Illouz, 2012: 244).

For the past fifty years or so, the formation of families or more lasting love relationships has been dictated not only by existing institutions or laws (Lewis, 2001). Today a couple establishing a love relationship need not marry or even live together in order to become a couple – to have decided to be together in a way that changes their relationship and their relationship with relatives, friends, and state authorities.

Today's families come in many different guises, and they can be constituted and reconstituted in many ways; there are several models for establishing a family. How a family should look, then, should not be taken for granted; choices and decisions are required.

Those who want to establish a new family must make many decisions. Do they want to get married? Should they have a common surname, and if so, which one of their names or a third, completely different name? Do they want to live together? How should they handle their finances? The division of labour in a family is another urgent matter for decisions (Beck & Beck-Gernsheim, 1995; Roman & Peterson, 2011). Organization is required if the couple is to break with traditional gender norms. In an investigation concerning love and marriage, one interviewed woman says: 'Love and relationships must be organized if inequality between the sexes is not going to be reproduced in the name of love' (Adeniji, 2008: 84).

Many couples try to organize their life together. Family therapists advise couples to talk about their expectations of each other and to make common decisions about organizing their relationship, to avoid misunderstandings and disappointments. Rules are alternatives to norms. The woman who was quoted here as saying that love relations must be organized also told about how she and her partner struggled with the cleaning schedule that they had decided upon. Many contemporary families have rules for such activities as cleaning and cooking, or taking the children to nursery school.

Parents can decide about monitoring and sanctions for their children, but it is probably unusual for decisions about monitoring to be made in the relationship between the parents themselves. If they are living together, it is rather a matter of 'unobtrusive control' (Perrow, 1986: 128). Family life can contain several organizational elements, but an element of hierarchy is highly unlikely. That parents make decisions for their children is not an example of hierarchy; it is taken for granted.

The decision-making structure of families is imperfect. Family members often lack a clear notion of how to make common decisions or even when a decision has been made (Finch & Mason, 1993; Halleröd & Nyman, 2008). Many modern families can be understood as adhocracies – the opposite of bureaucracies. Decision making in adhocracies takes a great deal of time-consuming effort: 'people talk a lot in these structures' (Mintzberg, 1993: 277). It may be a democratic form of decision making, but it is exhausting and inefficient in the long run. Many adhocracies are slowly transformed: 'the organization simply selects the standard programs it does best and goes into business of doing them' (Mintzberg, 1993: 278). Many families run the risk of falling back into institutional norms requiring few decisions.

In the social science literature, families are generally regarded as institutions (Giddens & Sutton, 2017: 380; Young & Willmott, 1962). But a single family is not an institution; rather, it should be understood as an 'actualized relationship' (Morgan, 2011: 41). Families 'work with a mixture of social processes which combine the taken for granted and the actively shaped' (Finch, 2008: 722). In practice, 'actively shaped' often means organized.

The degree of organization varies from family to family, but it is unlikely that families are organized with all five elements. Regarding families as partially organized highlights their differences; families are not all cast in the same institutional mould. When members of a family make their own decisions, they can disobey traditions and norms and choose how to live together in their own way. But this decision leaves them open to having their decisions contested and criticized by relatives, neighbours, or authorities.

FRIENDSHIP

Relationships based on friendship differ from romantic love relationships. A person can be involved in many friendship relationships, and there are degrees of friendship. In fact, it is difficult to distinguish friendship from other similar relationships (Luhmann, 1986: 81). This does not imply that friendship is an open relationship that anyone can choose to join, however. Just like relationships of romantic love, friendship is a closed relationship (Weber, 1968: 43).

Friends have different expectations of each other than lovers do. They rarely talk with each other about their friendship, and promises are rarely made (Alberoni, 2016). Friendship relations have many similarities to networks. They are not actors in themselves, and they have no identity; they are 'silent' (Bommes & Tacke, 2005: 293). Friends are not and do not wish to be regarded as couples.

In the beginning, both friendship and love can be seen as emergent. But the trajectories of a love relationship and a friendship differ greatly. Most love relations evolve in one of two ways: Either the relationship is terminated or the lovers decide, sooner or later, to be together – to become a couple. This does not happen in friendship. That people do not make decisions or agreements about their friendship relations has been confirmed in surveys. In the answers to a question about how they know if certain people are their friends, respondents usually say that it is a feeling, something that they feel instinctively but nothing they can decide about (Ahrne, 2014).

There seems to be something about friendship that makes decisions about the relationship impossible or at least inconceivable, not compatible with the idea of friendship at all. Friendship is not so much about attraction or attachment, but rather attunement, which implies a 'dialectic of closeness and distance' (Scheff, 2006: 115). Friends are on the same wavelength; they do not have to explain things to each other. Friendship demands a kind of wordless understanding: 'that each can count on the other to understand what she or he says in just the way the person meant to say it' (Thomas, 2013: 32). Unlike erotic love, friendship is lost if it has to be explained or discussed, which is why it is impossible to decide about friendship. The recent idea of asking a Facebook user to be a friend goes against all the norms of friendship. Friendship is a delicate relationship that is upheld with as little organization as possible.

The absence of decisions and promises in friendship provides a certain freedom in comparison to romantic love. One does not have to choose between friends or have a best friend. One can have many friends and different friends for different occasions (Simmel, 1950: 326).

Friendship is confirmed through processes of reciprocity. It is by accepting and returning invitations that one demonstrates the wish to continue the relationship. Reciprocity cannot be decided in advance; it is not an explicit agreement to exchange something. The norm of reciprocity is related to gift giving (Mauss, 2002), but gift giving does not happen through explicit mutual agreement. Yet, there is an implicit expectation that the gift (or invitation or service) should be reciprocated. 'But the counter is not stipulated by time, quantity, or quality, the expectation of reciprocity is indefinite' (Sahlins, 1974: 194). Invitations need not be immediately returned, and one cannot take for granted that a gift will be promptly reciprocated. Even if gifts or invitations have been returned a number of times, indeterminacy remains (Gouldner, 1959).

Friendship requires repeated interaction in order to be maintained. In interviews about friendship, people are determined not to continue to call or invite people who do not call back or do not invite them in return (Ahrne, 2014). The lack of response is interpreted as a message that they are not interested in continuing the relationship. The absence of mutual decisions can explain what appear to be puzzling research results. In surveys on friendship there is usually a misfit: Many of the friends that a person mentions do not mention that person as a friend (Rubin, 1987: 17; Almaatouq et al., 2016).

Friends create their own customs and traditions, such as doing certain things on special occasions – meeting one day each month or once a year, for instance. Such emergent patterns of interaction relieve them of the trouble of making common decisions. Institutions such as birthday celebrations can also facilitate the continuation of the relationship. Birthday congratulations do not require an invitation or a mutual decision. Friends do not monitor each other, but they may sometimes hear gossip about each other. And there are no direct sanctions in friendship relations. We are rarely informed that someone does not want to continue a friendship with us. Unlike romantic relationships, in which explicit breakup speeches are the norm, friendships can usually be exited without explanation.

Sometimes it is not possible to avoid choosing among one's friends – making decisions concerning an activity that can accommodate only a limited number of participants: a book circle, a sports activity, or a dinner party, for instance. Decisions about which friends to ask and which friends not to ask can cause many complications that evoke jealousy and anger. Those who would have liked to join but were not asked may feel excluded, and the relationship can even be questioned.

A group of friends can be viewed as a network embedded in other social relations. Their relations are upheld on a regular basis without decisions when they meet at school or at work. This is why networks can be understood as parasites that 'live on the organizations that feed them' (Bommes & Tacke, 2005: 294). But if they lose their meeting place, organization is needed in order for them to be able to meet again on a regular basis. If the network comprises more than three or four individuals, it is difficult for the norm of reciprocity to maintain the network. One solution is to choose someone to be in charge of deciding and announcing when and where they will meet – for the group to submit to a hierarchy.

Friendship is the least organized of the intimate relationships analysed in this chapter. It is problematic to organize because, like a gift, it cannot bear much discussion. Friendship does not involve as strong a commitment as a romantic love or kinship relationship does. Neither are friendship relations expected to be as tight as love relationships, nor do they usually involve material resources.

KINSHIP

Affiliation is not a decision in kinship. Parents can decide to some extent if and when they want to have a child. But if we argue that kinship begins with the relationships between children and their grandparents (Zerubavel, 2012: 16), it is obvious that kinship relations are emergent. Kinship is a given for a newborn child (Spencer & Pahl, 2006: 41). It is a relationship that accompanies its entire life and is fundamental to the formation of its identity: 'you are a member and remain so whatever else happens in your life' (Finch, 1989: 234). Most other forms of affiliation 'can be revoked or withdrawn, either by your own action or those of others' (Finch, 1989: 234).

Kinship is a relationship with a name mutually known to its participants (often a common surname), and relatives are clearly distinguished from outsiders (Tilly, 2005: 44). There is also an order of succession in kinship structures: Children become parents and grandparents; there is a kinship career. Thus, a kinship structure can last for centuries; individual members die and are substituted with new members.

Because the original affiliation never ceases, kinship relations persist even without interaction. Kinship could be described as a kind of relational infrastructure; relations that are available and may be brought to the fore for various purposes, 'you know that you always *can* fall back on it' (Finch, 1989: 233).

To be related implies both rights and duties. Kinship has been described as a kind of insurance company 'into which one is enrolled at birth and from which one cannot unsubscribe' (Weiner, 2013: 100). At the same time, there is a mutual dependence among relatives; they have common resources, a reputation, and a status to defend (Weiner, 2013: 34–5). Relatives often check up on one another and rebuke one another.

Reciprocity is an essential element in kinship relations, but not in the same way as in friendship. Because the affiliation is given from the beginning, reciprocity has another character and function in kinship. There are other expectations of when and how gifts, services, help, or invitations should be reciprocated. It is a postponed reciprocity: 'an expectation that the giver will eventually get something back in some other time and place as yet unspecified, and possibly from a third party' (Finch, 1989: 165; Finch & Mason, 1993: 51).

Attachment is the most fundamental emotion in kinship. It is completely involuntary, and beginning in infancy, gives a physical sense of connection to the other relatives. Moreover, attachment is an emotion that can include people that one does not even like (Scheff, 2006: 112–13), which is not uncommon in a relationship like kinship.

During the 20th century in the social sciences, and perhaps particularly in sociology, there was a strong conviction that the importance of kinship would diminish with modernity, as achieved status replaced ascribed status. Research on kinship became a concern for social anthropologists and historians. But a considerable amount of research points to the continued importance of kinship relations for the care of children and old people (Heady & Kohli, 2010). With the increase of global migration, kinship relations are decisive for connections and protection (Tilly, 2005: 48). Kinship can also have continued political importance in the form of 'clan politics' (Schatz, 2004).

Ancestral ties are usually seen as natural bonds, with kinship extending beyond living relatives to deceased relatives of many generations ago (Zerubavel, 2012: 34). In such cases one often speaks of clans or tribes (James, 2006).

The strength of kinship ties is connected to their biological foundation – to the extent that kinship is often referred to as 'blood ties' (Zerubavel, 2012: 55). That biological kinship is taken for granted and cannot be decided may lead to a difference in ways of regarding direct descents and in-laws. Kinship that is the result of a decision does not hold the same quality or validity. The biological dimension of kinship 'makes us see adoptive parents as not the real parents, aunts and uncles by marriage as not real aunts and uncles, in-laws as not real relatives' (Rothman, 2000: 18; cf. Finch, 1989: 234).

But even though biological ties constitute the fundamentals of kinship relations, they cannot be totally conclusive. Biological kinship ties 'proliferate exponentially into ramifying networks of relatedness – they are simply *too* inclusive' (Robertson, 1991: 43). In practice, therefore, kinship relations are not merely natural, biological bonds; they are also social constructions (Zerubavel, 2012: 64). And kinship researchers must examine the roles of biological and social elements in the construction of kinship systems (Carsten, 2000: 29–33).

Biological ties may be understood as a raw material for decisions about specific kinship relations. Through its biological links, kinship acquires a natural imprint that provides legitimacy. Apart from distinguishing between the biological and the social, we must distinguish among the different ways of making social constructions. Broadly speaking, kinship is constructed culturally and institutionally, but specific kinship ties can also be decided. States constitute key decision makers regarding kinship. Most states have legislation on how kinship should be recognized, and these laws have implications for inheritance, for example. Religious organizations may also make decisions about kinship rules (Weiner, 2013: 201).

There is some 'degree of agency in how we identify ourselves genealogically' (Zerubavel, 2012: 77), and relatives can decide together how to describe their descent. By making choices among the possible ways of drawing their family trees, people try to influence their own identity and how others see them: 'pedigrees and family trees are therefore partly products of the choices we make about which ancestors to remember' (Zerubavel, 2012: 77). Decisions about kinship appear in many contexts: in business dynasties, in royal houses, or simply in families moving to a new city or a new country where they have no family.

Zerubavel (2012: 80–7) has distinguished a number of strategies for these decisions – rupturing the past through what he calls 'clipping', for example, the process of truncating the family tree, shortening the pedigree to exclude less desirable members. Another radical strategy is to change the family's surname. Or the relatives may decide on inclusion – by filling in genealogical holes, for example, or acknowledging the multilinear nature of the ancestral background and stretching the genealogical narratives back further.

Regarding other organizational elements, there is great variation historically between different forms of kinship. Kinship relations that may entail positions of power, like royal or noble houses, are probably more organized by rules and monitoring than other families are. There are rules about the way titles should be inherited – decisions that can be made within the family or by the state.

One example of kinship involving both hierarchy and sanctions is done through local clan councils that may consist of a political and judicial body of clan elders. It is not unusual in India for clan members to turn to such bodies to settle disputes. Not bound by requirements to provide due process, elders are typically more efficient than state courts. Their rulings are also enforced through powerful mechanisms of sanctions, from ostracism to economic marginalization (Weiner, 2013: 12).

But kinship-based social systems are no formal organizations: 'The loose, decentralized system of organization is a source of both strength and weakness for tribal societies' (Fukuyama, 2012: 77). One weakness may be that leadership is built on status rather than hierarchy. Even though kinship is not organized with all organizational elements, neither is it a naturally emergent formation. Rather, it is typically partially organized.

CITIZENSHIP AND STATES

So far, I have primarily discussed intimacy from the perspective of those involved in the relationships. But there are other actors engaged in the organization of intimate relationships. According to the United Nations Convention on the Rights of the Child, states have a responsibility for the welfare and rights of children. States make many decisions about rules for intimate relationships in which children are included; they can monitor and sanction relationships, and children can be taken away from their parents. But the connections among families, children, and states also affect the organization of states.

The word 'nation' indicates that birth is the original bond between individual people and a state (Robertson, 1991: 44). Most states have legal rules prescribing which newborn children can become their citizens. Laws about citizenship rest on two principles that can be combined in different ways. *Jus sanguinus* implies that one acquires at birth the citizenship of one's parents. *Jus solis* means that at birth one acquires the citizenship in the land where one is born (Heater, 1999: 80).

If the citizenship of a newborn child is carefully registered with date of birth and the names of the parents, the state does not make a decision. States have no alternative but to confirm the citizenship of those children who fulfil its rules. States have limited possibilities, in fact, to make decisions about their membership. Many states try to influence their citizens to have more or fewer children, depending on circumstances in the country, but once a child is born, they cannot decide whether the child is going to be recognized as a citizen or not.

When the modern concept of citizenship evolved during the 18th century, it was linked to the concept of a nation. In this way, the unfortunate idea arose that citizenship had something to do with a cultural and institutional affiliation such as common language or common religion (Heater, 2004: 94). But citizenship is foremost a question of political and social rights.

Even though most citizens in most states acquire their citizenship at birth, citizenship may also be acquired in a process by which states may choose whether to grant a certain person citizenship. The potential conflict between citizenship as a cultural community and citizenship as political and social rights can be triggered by the difference between ascribed citizenship and decided citizenship. A congenital citizenship is taken for granted according to the rules of the country, whereas a citizenship granted by a decision later in life may be contested.

Because states do not decide on their membership, they must be understood as partially organized. They have only a limited possibility of choosing which or how many citizens they want. On the whole, they cannot exclude or deport them. Rather, states may imprison citizens who are considered to have broken the law, or even, in some states, execute them.

Formal organizations are expected to be able to choose their members. In order for organizations to appear to be adequate actors, they are supposed to present the best possible set of members. A football team must choose its members well, and a university must be able to hire the best researchers and teachers and admit the best students. That is not the case for states; they must adjust to the citizens they get.

There is reluctance within the social sciences to regard states as organizations. Rather, they describe them as institutions. Perhaps this reluctance mirrors the fact that they are partially organized – that they cannot decide about their membership. In other respects, states are heavily organized: They have an abundance of rules, monitoring, sanctions, and detailed hierarchies. Decision making and organization are largely what states are engaged in, and decisions create huge differences among states.

INTIMATE RELATIONSHIPS AND PARTIAL ORGANIZATION

Intimacy is certainly not associated with organization. And one cannot argue that intimate relationships are formal organizations. But when one distinguishes among various organizational elements, some of them can be found in many intimate relationships. They can often be recognized as partially organized. And it is possible to gain a deeper understanding of the dynamics in relationships if they are perceived as partially organized rather than seeing them as institutions or networks.

In examining the appearance of organizational elements in intimate relationships, one can see considerable differences among them, not only in their degree of organization but also in the elements that are present – reflecting how a relationship has been established and changed. There is a connection between the elements that can appear in a relationship and the emotional content of that relationship. The relationship of a couple in a family is decided, but the relationships in friendship and kinship affiliation are not.

But there are also differences within the same type of relationship in how much and in which ways they are organized. Organization makes a difference. There is an element of membership in all families, for instance, but many families also have rules and sanctions. Kinship can be organized through several combinations of organizational elements other than membership.

But what does an investigation into the organization of intimacy contribute to the understanding of partial organization? One insight is the understanding that partial organization is far from a new social phenomenon. On the contrary, the use of some organizational elements in families and kinship has always been an essential part of these primordial relational forms. Even if much of what is known about marriage and kinship has been determined through cultural and local customs, there are usually options, and decisions must be made. It may be a decision about which of the cousins to marry, which ancestors to include in the family tree, or what sanctions should be imposed on relatives who have broken a rule.

A broadening of the analysis examining connections between states and intimate relationships demonstrates why states can use membership as an organizational element only to a limited extent. States are extremely organized in many respects, yet they are only partially organized. There is an interdependence between families and states; they presuppose each other. Families provide states with new citizens, and states decide about rules for families and for kinship, and they also monitor families – particularly the relationship between parents and children.

An investigation of organizational elements in intimate relationships also provides an awareness of the limits of organization. The appearance of certain organizational elements can, in some cases, completely change the character of a relationship. If the affiliation in kinship, friendship, or states were to be based on membership – decisions about each member – they would be transformed into something else. Therefore, they remain partially organized.

REFERENCES

Adeniji, A. (2008) *Inte den typ som gifter sig. Feministiska samtal om äktenskapsmotstånd*. Göteborg: Makadam förlag.

Ahrne, G. (2014) *Samhället mellan oss. Om vänskap, kärlek, relationer och organisationer*. Stockholm: Liber.

Alberoni, F. (2016) *Friendship*. Leiden: Brill.

Almaatouq, A., Radaelli, L., Pentland, A., & Shmueli, E. (2016) Are You Your Friends' Friend? Poor Perception of Friendship Ties Limits the Ability to Promote Behavioral Change. *PLoS ONE* 11(3): e0151588. https://doi.org/10.1371/journal.pone.0151588

Badgett, M. V. L. (2009) *When Gay People Get Married: What Happens When Societies Legalize Same-Sex Marriage*. New York: New York University Press.

Beck, U. & Beck-Gernsheim, E. (1995) *The Normal Chaos of Love*. Cambridge: Polity Press.

Blatterer, H. (2013) Friendship´s Freedom and Gendered Limits. *European Journal of Social Theory* 16(4): 435–56.

Bommes, M. & Tacke, V. (2005) Luhmann's Systems Theory and Network Theory. In D. Seidl & K. H. Becker (eds.), *Niklas Luhmann and Organization Studies*. Malmö: Liber. 282–304.

Brunsson, N. (2007) *The Consequences of Decision-Making*. Oxford: Oxford University Press.

Carsten, J. (2000) Introduction: Cultures of Relatedness. In J. Carsten (ed.), *Cultures of Relatedness. New Approaches to the Study of Kinship*. Cambridge: Cambridge University Press. 1–36.

Chauncey, G. (2004) *Why Marriage? The History Shaping Today's Debate over Gay Equality*. New York: Basic Books.

Finch, J. (1989) *Family Obligations and Social Change*. Cambridge: Polity Press.

Finch, J. (2008) Naming Names: Kinship, Individuality and Personal Names. *Sociology* 42(4): 709–25.

Finch, J. & Mason, J. (1993) *Negotiating Family Responsibilities*. London: Routledge.

Friedland, R., Mohr, J. W., Roose, H., & Gardinali, P. (2014) The Institutional Logic of Love: Measuring Intimate Life. *Theory and Society* 43(3/4): 333–70.

Fukuyama, F. (2012) *The Origins of Political Order. From Prehuman Times to the French Revolution*. New York: Farrar, Straus and Giroux.

Giddens, A. (1991) *Modernity and Self-Identity. Self and Society in the Late Modern Age*. Cambridge: Polity Press.

Giddens, A. (1992) *The Transformation of Intimacy. Sexuality, Love & Eroticism in Modern Societies*. Cambridge: Polity Press.

Giddens, A. & Sutton, P. W. (2017) *Sociology*. 8th edition. Cambridge: Polity Press.

Gouldner, A. W. (1959) *For Sociology. Renewal and Critique in Sociology Today*. Harmondsworth: Penguin Books.

Halleröd, B. & Nyman, C. (2008) Dela rätt är inte lätt. In A. Grönlund & B. Halleröd (eds.), *Jämställdhetens pris*. Umeå: Boréa. 175–93.

Heady, P. & Kohli, M. (2010) Introduction: Towards a Political Economy of Kinship and Welfare. In P. Heady & M. Kohli (eds.), *Family, Kinship and State in Contemporary Europe*. Frankfurt: Campus Verlag. 15–30.

Heater, D. (1999) *What Is Citizenship?* Cambridge: Polity Press.

Heater, D. (2004) *A Brief History of Citizenship*. Edinburgh: Edinburgh University Press.

Illouz, E. (2012) *Why Love Hurts*. Cambridge: Polity Press.

James, P. (2006) *Globalism, Nationalism, Tribalism. Bringing Theory Back In*. London: SAGE.

Jamieson, L. (1999) Intimacy Transformed? A Critical Look at the 'Pure Relationship'. *Sociology* 33(3): 477–94.

Layder, D. (2004) *Emotion in Social Life. The Lost Heart of Society*. London: SAGE.

Lewis, J. (2001) *The End of Marriage*. Cheltenham: Edward Elgar.

Luhmann, N. (1986) *Love as Passion. The Codification of Intimacy*. Cambridge: Polity Press.

Mauss, M. (2002) *The Gift: The Form and Reason for Exchange in Archaic Societies*. London: Routledge.

Mintzberg, H. (1993) *Structure in Fives. Designing Effective Organizations*. Englewood Cliffs: Prentice-Hall.

Morgan, D. H. J. (2011) *Rethinking Family Practices*. Basingstoke: Palgrave.

Robertson, F. (1991) *Beyond the Family. The Social Organization of Human Reproduction*. Cambridge: Polity Press.

Roman, C. & Peterson, H. (2011) *Familjer i tiden. Förhandling, kön och gränslöst arbete*. Umeå: Boréa.

Rothman, B. K. (2000) *Recreating Motherhood*. New Brunswick: Rutgers University Press.

Rubin, L. B. (1985) *Just Friends. The Role of Friendship in Our Lives*. New York: Harper & Row.

Sahlins, M. (1974) *Stone Age Economics*. London: Tavistock Publications.

Schatz, E. (2004) *Modern Clan Politics. The Power of 'Blood' in Kazakhstan and Beyond*. Seattle: University of Washington Press.

Scheff, T. (2006) *Goffman Unbound. A New Paradigm for Social Science*. Boulder: Paradigm Publishers.

Smart, C. (2007) *Personal Life. New Directions in Sociological Thinking*. Cambridge: Polity Press.

Spencer, L. & Pahl, R. (2006) *Rethinking Friendship. Hidden Solidarities Today*. Princeton: Princeton University Press.

Swidler, A. (2001) *Talk of Love. How Culture Matters*. Chicago: Chicago University Press.

Thomas, L. (2013) The Character of Friendship. In D. Calouri (ed.), *Thinking about Friendship. Historical and Contemporary Philosophical Perspectives*. Basingstoke: Palgrave Macmillan. 30–44.

Tilly, C. (2005) *Trust and Rule*. Cambridge: Cambridge University Press.

Weber, M. (1968) *Economy and Society*. Volume 1. Berkeley: University of California Press.

Weeks, J., Brian, H., & Donovan, C. (2001) *Same Sex Intimacies. Families of Choice and Other Life Experiments*. London: Routledge.

Weiner, M. S. (2013) *The Rule of the Clan. What an Ancient Form of Social Organization Reveals about the Future of Individualism*. New York: Farrar, Straus and Giroux.

Young, M. & Willmott, P. (1962) *Family and Kinship in East London*. Harmondsworth: Penguin Books.

Zelizer, V. A. (2005) *The Purchase of Intimacy*. Princeton: Princeton University Press.

Zerubavel, E. (2012) *Ancestors and Relatives. Genealogy, Identity, and Community*. Oxford: Oxford University Press.

12 How Is 'Organized Crime' Organized?

Göran Ahrne and Amir Rostami

Two questions in organized crime research create concern: What is organized crime, and how should it be conceptualized and defined? (Finckenauer, 2005; von Lampe, 2008; 2018). Organized crime has become an umbrella label for various forms of criminal collaborations. This issue is problematic because the analyses of individual cases and individual conceptualizations do not capture the coexistence of a whole spectrum of criminal relationships or the social interactions among them. The consequences of the conceptual confusion are not merely semantic, but also involve legal and policy implications for our understanding of the nature of criminal organizing (Levi, 1998; Rostami, 2016b).

There have been more than 200 attempts to delimit the concept of organized crime (von Lampe, 2018; 2016), many of which are based on the framework of a formal organization. Conklin (2010) argues, for example, that organized crime is characterized by a division of labour, coordination of activities through rules and codes, and an allocation of tasks in order to achieve certain goals. Other definitions emphasize the existence of a hierarchical structure and a restricted membership. But the term 'network' is used to denote some forms of organized crime – forms often regarded as more recent (Holmes, 2016: 5–8).

In this chapter, we explore the usefulness of applying the idea of partial organization as one way of mitigating the confusion surrounding the notion of organized crime. Our point of departure is that it is not a question of whether criminal collectivities are organized or not; rather, it is a question of how and to what extent they are organized. Which organizational elements are used, and in what combinations in different types of criminal endeavours?

WHAT IS 'ORGANIZED'?

Even though the central obstacle to the development of a useful conceptualization of organized crime has been the notion of 'organized' rather than that of 'crime' (Finckenauer, 2005; Gottschalk, 2009), we believe that in order to analyse variations in all that can be contained within the concept of organized crime, we must also discuss what the concept of crime itself actually means in this context.

The term 'organized crime' seems to imply organizations in which the members meet on a regular basis to plan and perform criminal acts. But according to recent research, most of the crimes committed by members are not performed with other members. Criminal collaborations are mainly outside the framework of the organization, and sometimes even involve members of rival gangs. More than 80 per cent of gang co-offending in Hells Angels in Sweden, for example, occurs with non-gang members (Rostami & Mondani, 2017). Even in the case of street gangs, most criminal collaborations are with non-members, outside the territorial boundaries of the gang (Rostami et al., 2017; Rostami, Leinfelt, & Holgersson, 2012). Much evidence suggests that even mafia-style criminal collaborations frequently occur with people other than the core members (Lurigio, 2012). Actual collaborative criminal acts are commonly organized in the form of temporary criminal projects – projects that may be viewed as a way of dealing with extraordinary tasks within or between organizations (Bakker, 2010). One clear form of a criminal project is a bank robbery, which can be described as temporary organization with clearly defined time frames and goals.

Instead of understanding organized crime as the corporations or workshops of the criminal world, it is probably more accurate to see them as equivalents to professional organizations, trade unions, or perhaps guilds. Their mission is to protect and watch the professional interests of their members, providing them with a collective identity and strength. The main motive is to obtain protection, inclusion, and safety in a hostile environment. For the collective protection of members, violence serves as a central function. Physical violence is the basic means of power, both internally and externally.

If we understand collectivities that are usually regarded as organizers of crime as efforts to create solidarity and a collective strength for groups of criminals, we get other possibilities for understanding why they are established and the extent to which and how they are organized. Preconditions for solidarity and safety depend on the environment in which they exist, if there are other sources of loyalty and strength, and how participants are recruited.

In this chapter, we examine three types of collectivities that are often seen as examples of organized crime: outlaw motorcycle gangs (OMCs), street gangs, and mafias. Our analysis departs from the five organizational elements: membership, rules, monitoring, sanctions and hierarchy. (See Chapter 1.) When we examine the occurrence of organizational elements, we find substantial differences among these three cases of organized crime. In the OMCs we have studied, all organizational elements are well developed. In street gangs, on the other hand, the appearance of organizational elements varies among the gangs, and they rarely have more than a few elements at any one time. Moreover, there are few organizational elements in mafias, and the combinations of elements that may exist are not the same as in street gangs. In the analysis of street gangs and mafias, we discuss obstacles to and problems with organization and decision making, but also look for functional equivalents of organizational elements. Finally, we discuss the implications of our comparative analysis for the concept of organized crime.

We focus our analysis on cases appearing in Sweden during the past twenty years, but we also refer to international studies of similar groups. The empirical data from Sweden is based on several sources: (1) forty-two interviews conducted between 2008 and 2016 with members of organized crime groups in Sweden, such as gang leaders, gang members, and other key actors, and (2) approximately 730 police document files, such as intelligence documents, police protocols, and court judgments relating to organized crime in Sweden. (See Rostami, 2016a; Rostami *et al.*, 2017.)

OUTLAW MOTORCYCLE GANGS

In the collective imagination and in the understanding of many policy-makers, affiliation in criminal organizations is usually seen as membership expressed in visible organizations with symbols of identification and of the claiming of power (Brå, 2015). This situation is typical of OMCs – male bikers organized around the passion of motorcycles in clubs with a clear law-breaking agenda (Quinn, 2001; Quinn & Forsyth, 2009; Quinn & Shane Koch, 2003). The big four OMCs are Hells Angels Motorcycle Club (Hells Angels); Bandidos Motorcycle Club, also known as Bandidos Nation (Bandidos); American Outlaws Association (Outlaws); and Pagan's Motorcycle Club (Pagans). These are the largest OMCs as measured by membership and international expansion (Barker, 2014; NGIC, 2015). Hells Angels, for example, has more than 450 chapters in 56 countries (Hells Angels Motorcycle Corporation, 2017). Several OMCs have existed for more than fifty years.

OMC membership is based on local authorization at the chapter or charter level and on a contract between the organization and the member. In the case of the Hells Angels, every new membership must be reported to and registered by the Hells Angels Motorcycle Corporation in California, USA. Becoming a member is a long, involved process. Members must undergo an initiation period as candidates – hangarounds, and later, if accepted at that level, as probationaries or prospects – before they can possibly receive full membership, which is usually decided by unanimous vote among members (Barker, 2014; Lauchs, Bain, & Bell, 2015).

Accepted members are subjected to an initiation ceremony, in which they receive their patches; membership status is communicated through the type of patch that the member is allowed to wear on the back and front of his jacket. Because membership in an OMC constitutes a lifelong commitment to the club, its identity, and its lifestyle, candidates are socialized gradually as they renounce their private attachments and prove their loyalty to the organization.

It is up to the organization to decide who can leave without consequences. Members leaving the organization without authorization are labelled as being 'out in bad standing', and any other member may punish that person with fines or violence (Polismyndigheten 2010, 2015). Leaving the organization as 'left in good standing', on the other hand, means that the former member may maintain contact with the organization (Hells Angels MC 2005; Polismyndigheten 2010, 2015).

OMCs have a military-like hierarchy, with each chapter usually having elected officers for such designated roles as president, vice-president, treasurer, road captain, and sergeant-at-arms (Lauchs *et al.*, 2015). The president is the chapter leader, elected by chapter members. In many chapters, a vice-president serves as the president's deputy. Members vote democratically on major decisions, and in case of disagreement, the president casts the deciding vote. Meetings are held weekly at the chapter level and regularly at the national, continental, and international level, depending on the organization. At these meetings, comprehensive guidelines, bylaws, and strategic decisions are taken. The secretary takes meeting minutes, maintains member lists, records motions and election results, and distributes this information to the membership (Bandidos, 2015; Hells Angels MC, 2010; Rikskriminalpolisen, 2012). The treasurer is responsible for the chapter budget, the collection of membership fees, and payment of bills. These organizations are highly bureaucratized, with extensive written documentation. OMCs typically have rules based on the original Hells Angels' guide. One respondent described Hells Angels' rules:

> Hells Angels has a black book that X and three other members have written that constitutes the World Rules. Bandidos have their Bible. Each country has its rules [bylaws]. But every country tries to take as much as possible from World Rules, but adjusts it.
>
> *(Bandidos, 2015)*

There are strict rules for meeting procedures at the local, national, continental, and international levels that are binding on all chapters (Lauchs *et al.*, 2015). Each chapter must hold a club meeting once a week and an annual general meeting in the first quarter of each year (Bandidos, 2015). Rules for interpersonal behaviour are detailed. No form of violent behaviour towards other members is allowed, and there are rules against the spreading of false rumours about members. Actual criminal activities, however, are not decided by the organization. Any criminal activity conducted by members or candidates is on their own accord, as long as it does not impact the brand of the organization.

Sex-related crimes and domestic crimes are prohibited, because they erode the image of the organizations. In some chapters, specific types of narcotic abuse are also prohibited. An elected sergeant-at-arms monitors and sanctions members, enforcing internal chapter rules and taking responsibility for carrying out the punishment. Sergeants-at-arms from different chapters meet regularly to discuss security issues in the organization (Rikskriminalpolisen, 2012).

OMCs require strict attendance. Every candidate must 'attend Bandidos MC events in their home region and country and be prepared to support the Bandidos Nation at all times' (Bandidos, 2015: 42). The control culture is internalized so that every member can control every other member. In cases in which it is not possible to observe members directly – when a member is incarcerated, for example – the organization assures that the member receive financial support through a defence fund – to which all members are obliged to contribute financially, keeping him under the influence of the organization. Incarcerated members receive continuous visits from prospects as a way of providing emotional support. The goal of these measures is to maintain self-control within the organization and reduce the risk of incarcerated members collaborating with authorities or members of other gangs (Bandidos, 2015; Rikskriminalpolisen, 2012; Rostami *et al.*, 2017). Members can be rewarded with a higher rank in the organization, but the more common rewards are medals – primarily patches for various distinctions. In Bandidos, for example, a special patch, *vida miembro* (life member), is given to members who have undertaken an extraordinary effort for the Club, with the condition 'that he has served a minimum of 15 years in the Club and been an officer in the Club for 7 years and been nominated by another Life Member or National President' (Bandidos, 2015: 29). If members fail by breaking the guidelines of the club, they are punished with a fine or become subject to violence (Bandidos, 2015; Rikskriminalpolisen, 2012; Rostami *et al.*, 2017).

The cases of OMCs that we have analysed are established, formal organizations with what appears to outsiders to be a surprisingly well-developed organization. They have a long history with organized international contacts, and they have their own premises. OMCs stand out as ideal-typical for the concept of organized crime. When compared with street gangs or mafias, in fact, they appear unique.

STREET GANGS

A street gang is a more diffuse phenomenon than an OMC, and more difficult to identify. The population of street gangs is consistently in flux. A street gang, although usually comprised only of males, can be defined as 'any durable, street-oriented youth group whose own identity includes involvement in illegal activity' (Klein, Weerman, & Thornberry, 2006: 414). 'Durable' in this definition means that the gang exists for at least several months, but there is great variation in the stability and structure of street gangs. Many new gangs dissolve after a short time, and few gangs have a lifespan of more than ten years. The number of members is rarely greater than fifty. We can find gangs with explicit insignias and membership similar to the OMCs, but there are also those with an unclear role differentiation and constantly changing membership (Prowse, 2013).

Members of street gangs often see themselves as the antithesis of both commercialized motorcycle gangs and relative-based mafias. Gang members regard themselves as equals. But there are differences in this respect among street gangs. A couple of the most well-known gangs in Sweden seem to try to imitate the organization of OMCs for more than a short period, but with little success.

The most obvious similarity in organizational elements between OMCs and street gangs is membership. It is also because of decisions about membership that one can talk about street gangs as organized and something other than a network of friends. Membership has two functions:

(1) The selection process and decisions about membership create a boundary between gang members and non-members, and everyone – both members and non-members – know who belongs to a certain gang. Members often have common marks such as tattoos or special clothing.
(2) A decision about membership transforms friendship into another type of bond; membership gives a stronger commitment to the gang as a whole. (See also Chapter 13.)

In many street gangs, members compare their bonds with kinship bonds. There is a notion among the members that the gang is a territorial family, a substitute to the biological one, with conceptions about brotherhood and fatherhood as central narrative, and in which other relationships outside of the gang become secondary. But this is an ideal that is rarely realized.

Becoming a member of a street gang is not a long-lasting and rule-governed a process as in an OMC. Street gang members are generally recruited from existing friendship circles: childhood and neighbourhood friends, schoolmates, or former cellmates (Prowse, 2013). An active member usually sanctions a new member's entry into the gang, and the one who introduces the new member has full responsibility for the newcomer. One common criterion for membership is previous experience of co-offending with or having served time with an active member. There is often a membership procedure.

But many street gangs have problems growing beyond a rudimentary stage, and most of them are relatively short-lived: Membership is variable, and the solidarity is non-lasting. One explanation for the problems in establishing a strong membership in most street gangs is their local embeddedness. Members of a street gang have a common cultural and territorial affiliation; the connection with the local community is tight. Consequently, gang members share their everyday lives with non-members such as friends and relatives, which blurs the boundaries of the gang (Barkman & Palmkvist, 2011). When members have close relations with non-members, loyalty to the gang is threatened, and the gang's cohesion and solidarity is challenged.

The origin of street gangs in friendship circles also has an impact on the possibility of introducing other organizational elements. It seems, in fact, that it is primarily the member's pre-existing roles in friendship circles that influence his positions in the gang. Most street gangs fail to make decisions about hierarchy (Decker & Pyrooz, 2015; Thrasher, 1927). Much of the decision making and division of labour rests on some form of 'adhocracy' and the status of some members.

Only a few of the most prominent street gangs in Sweden seem to have a hierarchy. These structures are not written in detail, but have been recounted in interviews with gang members and in police intelligence reports (Rostami et al., 2017). Moreover, their hierarchies are unstable. When the Werewolf Legion was founded in Stockholm – as a prison gang in the beginning – the hierarchy consisted of a president and a vice-president. Because of internal conflict, however, the members removed the president, and a council governed by three 'generals' replaced the gang's leadership. Each general had subordinates called 'captains' (team leaders), who in turn ruled over the so-called soldiers (regular members) and other associates (Rostami et al., 2017).

In most street gangs, there is nothing that comes close to the strict rules found in OMCs. There are no rules for meetings, for example. The gang rarely has its own premises. Instead they meet in streets, squares, pubs, and member's homes.

The Werewolf Legion, which is unusually organized for a street gang, has ten general, written rules that are more like a 'code of ethics' outlining a set of principles about the relations between the gang and its members (Rostami *et al.*, 2017). In other street gangs in Sweden, such as the Angereds Tigrar in Gothenburg, the Örnligan and WYG in Stockholm, and M- and F-falangen in Malmö, nothing comes close to a set of decided rules (e.g., Barkman & Palmkvist, 2011).

There are no decisions about ways to monitor or sanction members in most street gangs, either. Each member makes a commitment to the group by being present and available to the others. Members demonstrate their loyalty by being visible in the 'street life' and being with other members. Loyalty is measured in time and resources devoted to the gang. Absence and failure to be visible may lead to repudiation, and expulsion from the gang is coupled with both economic and physical punishment (Rostami *et al.*, 2017).

Street gangs are more similar to networks than they are to such formal organizations as OMCs. But in contrast to networks, they have a decided membership, which makes the street gang much more visible than a network. In this sense, a street gang is organized. But in most street gangs, there are few or no other organizational elements. Its collective resources are sensitive to the composition of individual members, making the organization both time-bounded and transient. The fact that the original friendship ties among members and between members and non-members has a negative impact on the possibilities for more organization constitutes a vicious circle. Because of its short life span, a street gang cannot develop into an organization that is able to break these original ties.

MAFIAS

If we assume that the aim of criminal organizing is to build loyalty, strength, and thereby protection in a hostile environment among criminals sharing the same threats and uncertainty, OMCs and street gangs share the same predicament. They try to do this in similar ways, although OMCs are much more successful at it than street gangs are; most street gangs fail, or succeed only for short periods.

For mafias, the situation is quite the reverse. Mafias have their origins within kinship; affiliation is emergent and not decided; it is given and taken for granted through kinship bonds. A mafia can emerge within a collectivity that already offers what OMCs and street gangs try to accomplish through membership; the mafia's kinship offers strong cohesion and loyalty that provide strength and protection.

Kinship and family relations in an environment dominated by other ethnic groups tend to create especially strong bonds of solidarity, and the mafia becomes a 'closed and self-sufficient world opposing the larger one containing it' (Paoli, 2003: 18). This helps to create closer ties and camaraderie among families, even as it prevents infiltration from law enforcement (Lurigio, 2012).

Decisions about mafia membership are the exception. In a developed mafia – as in Italy – those who are directly involved in criminality may form a distinct group separate from other relatives (Paoli, 2003: 19). But this group is almost exclusively recruited from families belonging to the traditional kinship structure. Only rarely do individuals come from outside the original narrow circle of families, because outsiders cannot be expected to identify with the strong values inherent in the traditional subculture (Paoli, 2003: 92).

Through gift institutions (Mauss, 2002) and principles of generalized reciprocity (services and material) (see also Chapter 11), kinship relations are reproduced and an interdependence is established between groups of the community. Members of a mafia family are expected to help each other when requested and to maintain principles of honesty in their interactions with each other (Paoli, 2003: 81).

The Syriac mafia in Sweden, for example, rests on three components: family ties, ethno-religious identity, and Church affiliation (Rostami *et al.*, 2017). Their activities and relationships extend far deeper and are much broader than crime. Most of the relatives are not involved in criminal activities. The Syriac/Assyrian community in Sweden has created a largely paperless financial system, whereby relatives borrow from each other and make arrangements for payment of debts through mediation (Södertälje Tingsrätt, 2012). This system presents opportunities for parasitizing on such social fields in the community as finance, politics, and culture, including the municipality and public authorities (Rostami et al., 2017). Through embedded kinship relations, those who are participating in criminal activities gain access to various forms of capital, including violence and cultural and economic capital, creating influence and an ability to act in multiple fields in the community (Rostami et al., 2017).

In kinship, any type of decided hierarchy is unusual. (See Chapter 11.) Rather, influence and power are based on status, and age is the strongest source of status. Occasionally, young members possessing a valuable resource, such as a political position, means of violence, or language skills can gain considerable power, as can women who play a key instrumental role in establishing legal companies. But the process by which power is balanced and negotiated among families within the larger kinship group is not based on rules. Yet there is a rudimentary form of hierarchy, because leading positions are rotated among families to maintain a balance of power.

Because a mafia consists of a web of relationships with many layers of collaborations, there is a need for moderating disagreements on several levels, for preventing disorder and upholding control. Both in the Italian context and in the USA, superordinate bodies of co-ordination have been established to reduce internal competition and violence, resolve disputes, and plan and implement common actions (Paoli, 2003: 4). Similar structures have been detected within the Syriac mafia. There is a council of elders, in which leaders from each family meet to resolve common problems and disputes, frequently with the participation of a representative of the Church. They can also make decisions about sanctions.

OMCs have their own premises and rules for holding meetings, in which members are obliged to be present. In street gangs, members see each other and hold meetings in various places in the local environment, and it is important for members to maintain their visibility.

In the Syriac mafia, religious and cultural traditions serve the same functions.

The Church is used as a platform for a variety of events, such as wedding parties, New Year's celebrations, baptisms, and concerts involving large community gatherings (Södertälje Tingsrätt, 2012). Visibility can be achieved by attending ceremonies, such as Sunday mass, weddings, funerals, and cultural feasts, all of which become critical loyalty markers. These events serve several functions. Not only do they provide opportunities for meeting spontaneously and keeping in touch with each other; they also offer occasions for political mobilization and business activities – for selling smuggled alcohol, meat, or other illegally acquired goods. These events depend on a broad range of services and suppliers who provide wedding cakes, party clothes, photographic services, music, and flowers. They provide a high financial and commodity turnover for small businesses, which is why their owners must stay on good terms with the leading families, in order to be part of this entertainment industry (Finansinspektionen, 2014; Södertälje Tingsrätt, 2012). In addition, as regards wedding parties and other targeting events such as funerals and sports club events, there is a tradition among certain guests of giving cash gifts to the host – often large cash gifts that make it possible to keep revenues off the books (Södertälje Tingsrätt, 2013). Through ceremonial visibility and donations, affiliates not only show their loyalty to and affection for the system, thereby enabling them to gain access to the economic system of the criminal activities; it also reinforces interdependence among actors within the community.

THE DIVERSITY OF ORGANIZED CRIME

When we use a more precise and differentiated concept about what constitutes an organization, we see considerable differences between the three forms of organized crime that we have examined. They differ not only in the amount of their organization, but also in the ways in which they are organized.

A few multinational outlaw motorcycle gangs have gradually been able to form strong formal bureaucratized organizations containing all the organizational elements. But in the world of organized crime they are rare. The two other cases of organized crime that we have examined have not been organized nearly as much. One obstacle for the organization of street gangs is their local embeddedness and limited duration, which loosen the boundaries of the gang. Street gang members have competing loyalties with old friends and relatives, and there is a lack of internal rules.

For a mafia, the situation is quite the opposite. Because its embeddedness in kinship relationships provides cohesion and protection, it need not rely on organization. Through its strong kinship ties, a mafia has access to several functional equivalents to the organizational elements one can find in OMCs. Instead of rules, there are traditions and customs; instead of hierarchy, there are levels of status. Such institutionally grounded cohesion is often stronger and more long lasting than the cohesion that occurs within an organization.

Variation among the three cases is so obvious and significant that one could ask if it is possible to classify them within the same category. Can they be meaningfully identified as organized crime? Yet, all three are somewhat organized. When we examine the occurrence of various organizational elements, we can see that being organized can imply a number of combinations of organizational elements. One lesson at least can be drawn: It is not enough to state that something is organized or not. It is just as important to determine how: in which ways and how much. Instead of being content with asking if a criminal configuration is organized, it is necessary to go through all organizational elements to examine if they are applied – and if not, to look for functional equivalents.

Nor can we see the three cases as different models for organized crime; the variation within each category is too broad, and there is considerable overlap between them. The variation is particularly obvious in street gangs, and some street gangs are, in fact, seen as networks. There are variations in the degree of organization, even among established outlaw motorcycle gangs. There is also a substantial variation in how mafias are constructed in different parts of the world, and the occurrence of organization in mafias changes over time.

Moreover, in the ecology of organized crime, there are also symbiotic relationships among differently organized collectivises – between mafias and street gangs, for instance.

There is an abundance of phenomena under the concept of organized crime that we have not discussed. We assume that prison gangs, corruption networks, organized financial crimes, and even violent extremism manifest similar complexity and variation in their organization (for a study of the partial organization of networked corruption see Yu, Kang, & Rhodes, 2018). But most cases of organized crime are dynamic and must be understood as fluid processes, often shifting shape with individuals moving between them.

There is not a ready set of models from which criminals can choose if they want to organize. Criminal organizing happens in a process involving much contingency. How criminal groups evolve depends on their opportunity structure, such as the presence or absence of allies and enemies – the capacity of the state to provide services and to enforce the rule of law. Configurations of organized crime are rarely stable, and how they are organized depends on their stage of development.

The question, then, is thus: why is the common practice in organized crime research and criminal policy to grasp criminal relationships within the framework of formal organizations? One explanation is that it is easier to examine and think of organizations in which there are documented decisions about such elements as membership, rules, and hierarchy. It is a more difficult task to examine less organized and more fluid collectivities. To get a more differentiated picture, more knowledge would be required, but it is difficult to obtain – particularly in criminal environments.

A wide range of societal problems is assessed and labelled as organized crime, despite uncertainty as to where its boundaries should be drawn. When the legal definitions of these boundaries are over-stretched and the term 'organized crime' is used as a tool to stir the emotions of a target audience, the result may be a general inflation in the severity of penalties and an erosion of civil rights and personal integrity (Flyghed, 2002). This is particularly troubling, given the tendency to frame law-breaking acts committed by underprivileged groups as organized crime. White-collar crime, sometimes labelled financial crime, committed by groups with a higher social status, often fall outside the framing of organized crime, despite being highly organized.

To be able to grasp the dynamics among various forms and stages of organized crime, it is necessary to employ a more differen-tiated concept of organization, which can help us to identify the emergent and decided elements that give rise to the forms of criminal collaborations that we want to describe. When examining different combinations of organizational elements, we will be able to distin-guish between different degrees of organization, while at the same time including more configurations of collective crime as more or less organized. A more mixed understanding of variations in the organiza-tion of organized crime can support the work of discovering and pre-venting illegal activities and be of importance to lawmakers and courts.

REFERENCES

Bakker, R. M. (2010) Taking Stock of Temporary Organizational Forms: A Systematic Review and Research Agenda. *International Journal of Management Reviews* 12(4): 466–86.

Bandidos. (2015) *The Bible of the Bandidos Motorcycle Club Europe: The Basic Rules of the Bandidos MC Europe.*

Barker, T. (2014) *Outlaw Motorcycle Gangs as Organized Crime Groups.* Heidelberg: Springer.

Barkman, T. & Palmkvist, J. (2011) *Maffiakrig.* Stockholm: Albert Bonniers Förlag.

Brå. (2015) *Organised Crime.* Retrieved 19 January 2016 from www.bra.se/bra/bra-in-english/home/crime-and-statistics/organised-crime.html.

Conklin, J. E. (2010) *Criminology.* Englewood Cliffs: Prentice-Hall.

Decker, S. H. & Pyrooz, D. C. (2015) *The Handbook of Gangs*. New York: John Wiley & Sons.

Finansinspektionen. (2014) Återkallelse av tillstånd: 13–399.

Finckenauer, J. O. (2005) Problems of Definition: What Is Organized Crime? *Trends in Organized Crime* 8(3): 63–83.

Flyghed, J. (2002) Normalising the Exceptional: The Case of Political Violence. *Policing and Society* 13(1): 23–41.

Gottschalk, P. (2009) *Policing Organized Crime: Intelligence Strategy Implementation*. CRC Press.

Hells Angels Motorcycle Corporation. (2005) Hells Angels Bylaws Sweden.

Hells Angels Motorcycle Corporation. (2010) Bylaws.

Hells Angels Motorcycle Corporation. (2017) Charters Worldwide. *Hells-Angels.Com*. Retrieved 27 April 2017 from http://affa.hells-angels.com/charters.

Holmes, L. (2016) *Advanced Introduction to Organised Crime*. Cheltenham: Edward Elgar Publishing.

Klein, M. W., Weerman, F. M., & Thornberry, T. P. (2006) Street Gang Violence in Europe. *European Journal of Criminology* 3(4): 413–37.

von Lampe, K. (2008) Organised Crime in Europe: Conceptions and Realities. *Policing: A Journal of Policy and Practice* 2(1): 7–17.

von Lampe, K. (2016) *Organized Crime: Analyzing Illegal Activities, Criminal Structures, and Extra-Legal Governance*. London: SAGE.

von Lampe, K. (2018) Definitions of Organized Crime. Retrieved 8 February 2018 from www.organized-crime.de/organizedcrimedefinitions.htm.

Lauchs, M., Bain, A., & Bell, P. (2015) *Outlaw Motorcycle Gangs*. Basingstoke: Palgrave.

Levi, M. (1998) Perspectives on 'Organised Crime': An Overview. *The Howard Journal of Crime and Justice* 37(4): 335–45.

Lurigio, A. J. (2012) Mafia Myths and Mythologies in *Encyclopaedia of Transnational Crime & Justice*. Thousand Oaks: SAGE.

Mauss, M. (2002) *The Gift: The Form and Reason for Exchange in Archaic Societies*. London: Routledge.

NGIC. (2015) *2015 National Gang Report*. Washington, DC: National Gang Intelligence Center.

Paoli, L. (2003) *Mafia Brotherhoods: Organized Crime, Italian Style*. Oxford: Oxford University Press.

Polismyndigheten. (2010) *Förundersökningsprotokoll*. Göteborg: Polismyndigheten i Västra Götaland.

Polismyndigheten. (2015) *Rapport Bandidos MC*. Stockholm: Nationella operativa avdelningen.

Prowse, C. E. (2013) *Defining Street Gangs in the 21st Century: Fluid, Mobile, and Transnational Networks*. New York: Springer.

Quinn, J. F. (2001) Angels, Bandidos, Outlaws, and Pagans: The Evolution of Organized Crime among the Big Four 1% Motorcycle Clubs. *Deviant Behavior* 22(4): 379–99.

Quinn, J. F. & Forsyth, C. J. (2009) Leathers and Rolexs: The Symbolism and Values of the Motorcycle Club. *Deviant Behavior* 30(3): 235–65.

Quinn, J. F. & Shane Koch, D. (2003) The Nature of Criminality within One-Percent Motorcycle Clubs. *Deviant Behavior* 24(3): 281–305.

Rikskriminalpolisen. (2012) *Rapport: Hells Angels MC och Red and White Crew*. Stockholm.

Rostami, A. (2016a) *Criminal Organizing: Studies in the Sociology of Organized Crime*. PhD dissertation. Stockholm Studies in Sociology New Series 62, Stockholm University.

Rostami, A. (2016b) Policing Gangs and Organized Crime – Experiences from Conceptual Confusion and Its Consequences from Two Swedish Case Studies. In C. L. Maxson and F.-A. Esbensen (eds.), *Gang Transitions and Transformations in an International Context*. New York: Springer. 279–89.

Rostami, A., Leinfelt, F., & Holgersson, S. (2012) An Exploratory Analysis of Swedish Street Gangs: Applying the Maxson and Klein Typology to a Swedish Gang Dataset. *Journal of Contemporary Criminal Justice* 28(4): 426–45.

Rostami, A. & Mondani, H. (2017) Organizing on Two Wheels: Uncovering the Organizational Patterns of Hells Angels MC in Sweden. *Trends in Organized Crime*. Retrieved 24 May 2017 from http://link.springer.com/10.1007/s12117-017-9310-y.

Rostami, A., Mondani, H., Liljeros, F., & Edling, C. (2017) Criminal Organizing Applying the Theory of Partial Organization to Four Cases of Organized Crime. *Trends in Organized Crime*. Retrieved 1 July 2017 from http://link.springer.com/10.1007/s12117-017-9315-6.

Södertälje Tingsrätt. (2012) Mål Nr: B2781-10.

Södertälje Tingsrätt. (2013) Mål Nr: B182-12.

Thrasher, F. M. (1927) *The Gang: A Study of 1,313 Gangs in Chicago*. Chicago: University of Chicago Press.

Yu, K.-H., Kang, S.-D., & Rhodes, C. (2018) The Partial Organization of Networked Corruption. *Business & Society* https://doi.org/10.1177/0007650318775024.

13 Brotherhood as an Organized Social Relationship

Mikaela Sundberg

The word 'brotherhood' is often casually referred to in relation to such settings as secret societies, fraternities, the military, and outlaw bikers. Fellow soldiers are considered 'brothers in arms', and members of Hells Angels Motorcycle Club or other outlaw biker clubs refer to each other as 'brothers'. As a social relationship however, brotherhood has been explored only fragmentarily in the research literature, and it remains unclear how it can be conceptualized.

Brotherhood is perhaps most frequently mentioned in the literature on outlaw bikers (e.g., Wolf, 1991; Hopper & Moore, 1983; Schouten & McAlexander, 1995), but more as an empirical term than an analytical concept. Wolf (1991), for example, describes the interpersonal relationships within the outlaw club, the Rebels, as characterized by love and unconditional loyalty. As one member of the Rebels put it, 'Brotherhood is love to the members of the club ... You know there's going to be a brother there to give you a hand when you need it ... There's going to be a brother there to talk to when you need someone to talk to' (Wolf, 1991: 96). Because loyalty, love, and the importance of talking are traditionally emphasized as characteristics of friendship as well (e.g., Ahrne, 2014: 55, 66; Collins, 2004: 84), the conflation of brotherhood and (strong) friendship in some of the literature is unsurprising. (See, e.g., Grundvall, 2005; Kiesling, 2005.) Yet if only these characteristics are emphasized, brotherhood becomes undistinguishable from friendship. Although these two social relationships clearly share similarities in their substantive content, crucial differences must also be noted. Brotherhood is a collective relationship with a group of people, not merely a relationship with specific individuals. More specifically, brotherhood exists in groups with strong collective solidarity and 'we-feeling'. It is related, therefore, to a form of mechanical solidarity, resulting from intense group belonging and homogeneous beliefs and sentiments common to all the members of the group, rather than an ethos of individualism and ties that link individuals with crisscrossing loyalties (Durkheim [1902] 2013: xxviii, xxix, 101). But is collective solidarity sufficient to distinguish and define the relationship and maintain it over time?

The aim of this chapter is to advance the conceptualization of brotherhood as a social relationship, in part through a comparison with friendship. I argue that we can distinguish the specificity of brotherhood by comparing these relationships more closely and by paying particular attention to the ways in which they differ with respect to decision making. A fundamental difference between brotherhood and friendship is that friendship cannot be decided upon, whereas brotherhood seems to be connected to membership, thereby making it relatively less 'free floating'. More specifically, I suggest that brotherly relationships form *within* existing organizations, but in some cases extend beyond the organization to include former members. Although organizations are crucial for breeding fraternal relationships, brotherhood can be understood as a partially organized social relationship based on membership and supported and facilitated by rules. What are the consequences of brotherhood being decided upon rather than being spontaneous?

To discuss these matters, I draw examples from three settings in which there is a strong rhetorical emphasis on brotherhood: outlaw biker clubs, the armed forces, and Catholic monasteries. Both women and men engage in the military and in monastic life, but whereas the military represents a mixed-gender organization, women and men are separated in monasteries. I investigate the relationship from a gender-neutral perspective, which differs from previous research in which the masculine character of brotherhood is commonly emphasized. For example, research on occupational environments like firefighting or leisure time activities like football sometimes relate brotherhood to homosociality (e.g., Cockburn, 1991; Lindgren, 1999; Fundberg, 2003; Olofsson, 2013). In this context, homosociality refers to the strengthening of male cohesion for power relative to women. Focusing on homosociality therefore neglects the internal dynamics among 'brothers', while reducing brotherhood to a male phenomenon. This perspective is anticipated, of course, given the etymology of the term. Any metaphor of kinship implies assumptions about gender relations (Clawson, 1989: 258), but does this mean that sisterhood differs entirely from brotherhood? Despite the fact that concrete brotherhood/sisterhood relationships often seem to remain exclusively male *or* female, it does not follow that their social form differs. For terminological simplicity, however, I stick with the notion of brotherhood exclusively.

MATERIAL AND METHOD

I use different sources of material to illustrate the overall idea, rather than presenting an in-depth empirical analysis. Regarding the military, I rely on material collected during an ethnographic study of the organization of everyday life at French Foreign Legion regiments. (See Sundberg, 2015: 13–19 for details.) This study included observations at and around four regiments, sixty-three interviews with various members of staff, and document analysis. I also use material from an on-going study of social relations within and the organization of French Cistercian monasteries, including interviews, observations, and document analysis. For this chapter, I draw primarily from the interview material, comprising interviews with four monks and one former monk from three monasteries, and with nine nuns from two monastic communities for nuns. There are, in fact, two branches of Cistercians – Cistercians of the Common Observance and Cistercians of the Strict Observance – but for the purposes of this chapter, they are relatively homogeneous, and I make no distinction. Regarding the outlaw biker clubs, I have no primary data, but rely upon previous research, primarily from the USA and Canada, documentary writing on Hells Angels in Sweden (Wierup and Larsson, 2007), and one autobiography of a former member of Hells Angels in Sweden (Wierup and Olsson,

2012). Inspired by partial organization terminology, I have coded these two Swedish books, and present relevant aspects of this coding here. The literary sources have obvious shortcomings concerning reliability and validity, and may well include exaggerations and dramatizations of events. However, by drawing upon accounts of Micke, a former member, and those of other previous members, in *Helvetet inifrån* (*The Hell from Inside*) Wierup and Olsson (2012) provide a glimpse into the fate of excluded members – one of the more negative aspects of brotherly cohesion that provides a valuable counterweight to the more positive accounts of current members as reported in previous biker research.

THE ROLE OF MEMBERSHIP AS THE BASIS FOR BROTHERHOOD

Friendship is a spontaneous and voluntary relationship between two individuals or a group of people who choose for themselves with whom they will become friends. Although friends are often shared, all of my friends are not friends with one another, and there is no expectation that they should be. Brotherly relationships are not relationships between separate individuals, however; it is not up to the individual to consider someone a brother or not a brother. Brotherhood is a collectivist and exclusive relationship, in which a decision concerning membership determines who is and is not a brother. In certain organizations, then, becoming a member means, by definition, becoming a brother or sister. Yet monastic orders, military organizations, and sometimes outlaw biker clubs often include thousands of members, active at various locations. Is every member of the organization a brother or sister then? In principle, yes. But in everyday life, brotherly relational practices are concentrated in the sub-units of the organization (i.e., the outlaw biker chapter, the platoon/company/regiment, or the monastic community). These practices are considered in greater detail in the section on expectations, but first I discuss entry into the relationship and its scope, both within and outside of the organization.

Entering brotherhood

Given the interest in distinguishing between friendship and brotherhood, one significant question relating to entrance into an organization is: 'What is the importance of personal relationships or friendship with existing members for a presumptive member to become a member?' Recruitment into the Foreign Legion, like into the armed forces in general, occurs through professionalized machineries, followed by education in military academies or conforming instruction programmes. It is certainly possible that recruits know each other in advance, and that this relationship has played a role in their pursuit of a military career (cf. Sundberg, 2015: 50ff.), but from an organizational viewpoint it is irrelevant for the recruitment process. The individual relationships between members and outsiders do not influence the decision on whether to accept these outsiders as members. In other words, friendship plays no role in military membership.

Although outlaw biker clubs, especially Hells Angels, draw inspiration from the armed forces regarding terminology for positions in the club (e.g., officer, sergeant-in-arms), recruitment into outlaw biker clubs differs significantly from military recruitment; membership in outlaw biker clubs is stepwise. Candidates (or strikers, as they are sometimes called) advance from hangarounds to prospects to – eventually – full members. (See also Chapter 12.) Presumptive members, and especially full members, are expected to get to know one another and interact with all other members in order to encourage the formation of universal friendship, at the expense of subgroups (Wolf, 1991: 101f.). Consequently, social interactions among prospects and full members play a significant role in recruitment decisions. The final decision on whether someone will be accepted as a member occurs through voting among full members. Once a prospective member has been included, it is no longer up to individual members to decide upon the nature of their relationship with the new member. The vote decides who counts as a brother and who does not.

Membership in Catholic orders is also stepwise, but entails a much longer process. (See, e.g., OCSO, 2014a.) First, the candidate makes short visits to the monastery of choice. If the candidate has a sincere desire to enter the community, and if the community agrees with the request to continue with the process, s/he moves into an observership stage inside the community that lasts for a couple of months and is guided by a novice director. Together with the novice director, the candidate decides whether to continue to postulancy (which lasts about six to nine months) and then to the novitiate (about two years). The novice receives more formal instruction, dresses in a religious habit, and officially becomes a member of the order. If seen as suitable for community life, the novice is admitted to profession of temporary vows as a temporary professed junior, and after three to nine years, the junior may petition to make final vows and become solemnly professed. These two last steps are dependent upon a vote among the professed members of the community.

In this entrance process, the novitiate is the longest and most important formative step, and Cistercian novices' interactions with one another and with permanent members play a role in 'recruitment' into monasteries. One nun, who had previously been responsible for the integration and education of novices, explained what she considered the principal signs of whether a novice would be able to stay in the monastery, using one novice as specific example:

> For me, it is especially the young one's behaviour, the young one during work. How she, when she, when several of us work, for example in the dairy, it is a common work, and I saw quickly during work that she couldn't stay because she did not reveal herself, didn't know how to integrate in the group; she was all the time quarrelling. Well one still has to live together, that is still a minimum. So it was especially that I saw how she was living the fraternal relations.

In addition to praying and reading, Cistercians place great emphasis on manual labour and producing goods for sale. Typical monastic products include biscuits, fruitcakes, comfiture, honey, chocolate, or liqueur. The quote suggests that interpersonal relations with other members, specifically during work, play a critical role in being accepted as a monastic member. Outside of working duties, however, presumptive members (postulants and novices) are restricted mainly to contact with the novice directors and the abbot or abbess. Unlike in outlaw biker clubs, novices are sequestered from too much contact with professed, full members. (See also Bianco, 1992: 186.)

Exiting brotherhood

Brotherhood relationships may sometimes extend beyond the cessation of membership in a formal organization. Being an ex-member is sociologically different from being a non-member who has never belonged (Ebaugh, 1988: 169ff.), and exit from the organization may be irrelevant from a brotherly viewpoint. The French Foreign Legion shares with other elite corps the basic structure of the notion of 'once a legionnaire, always a legionnaire', reminiscent of the US Marines' motto: *Semper fidelis* (Always faithful). Strong identification with one's former role in the armed forces is common (e.g., Jolly, 1996; Higate, 2000). Outside the Legion as an organization, membership in one of the Legion's many veteran associations is a concrete manifestation of long-term identification, but also a way of being recognized as a former member. Former members who served at different times or in different regiments also form 'old boys' networks', as one former member called it, outside organized veterans' associations, supposedly because they have something in common. Ties among former members draw upon a conception of the Legion as an imagined community, including present and former members. In fact, there are many examples of former members establishing contacts with other former members whom they never knew during service. For instance, former members may join a local, annual celebration of the Battle of Camarón – the most important military tradition of the Legion – among Legion veteran associations outside of France. They also establish Facebook groups with former members, sometimes also with present members of similar geographic background (e.g.,

Scandinavian). Such ties are largely impersonal, as they are primarily based on former membership rather than any form of personal acquaintance. They may therefore be considered as expressions of Legion brotherhood.

Other brotherly relationships presuppose continued membership. A nun is certainly not a nun after having left monastic life behind her. Although she continues to be a 'sister' for the remaining nuns in the most general Christian meaning, she is not a sister of the community in practice. Former members of Hells Angels are no longer referred to as brothers, and how remaining brothers should relate to the former member is dictated by rules, as discussed in the next section.

In summary, there is a short and long-range brotherhood. In the short-range, more bounded forms of brotherhood, the relationship ends when one leaves the organization. In the long-range forms of brotherhood, the relationship continues after organizational membership has ceased, even if brotherhood presupposed membership in the organization in the first place. In addition to veterans of armed forces units, similar forms of brotherly relationships beyond organizational boundaries are likely to be found among alumni networks of former students – especially from boarding schools or elite schools. From the point of view of partial organization, the long-range form is an example of a relationship based on membership as the principal organizational element and of organization outside organizations.

EXPECTATIONS AND THE CONTENT OF A BROTHERLY RELATIONSHIP

As mentioned in the introduction, part of the reason for conflating brotherhood and friendship has to do with similarities between love and loyalty; another has to do with egalitarianism. Status differences and inequalities are threats to friendship (see, e.g., Ahrne, 2014), and although the examples of brotherhood I discuss all occur within organizations characterized by strict ranking systems, the *brotherly* relationship is, in principle, flat. This conflict is explicitly articulated in monasteries. Many monastic responsibilities are organized vertically, and certain positions are more powerful than others. For religious reasons however, brotherly egalitarianism is a more profound feature than is the rank of the member. As one monk related to me:

> Even if [the abbot] is called 'abba', father ... he is, above all himself, brother, and under the authority of the rule and one sole Father who is for us our God ... What is at the top in our human life is not the top of everything, but he is also under one other authority. Thus the intention, one could say, of fraternal life, it is ... if one is given authority it's in the *service* of that fraternity, but it is the power to precisely ... pass *beyond* different determinants. Of age, culture, education, and that all those elements that ... constitute our life are not the primary, but ... that one is free to call a doyen, who's 90 years old, with 60, 70 years of monastic life, one can go to him and call him brother and ask him for advice or for a favour.

Regardless of social differences between monastic members determined by their position in the community and such other traditional stratification markers as age and education, their brotherly relationship means that they should all be considered equals. This form of collective of equals differs greatly from a dyad of friends in its *universality*, *duty*, and *decided expectations*.

Because brotherly relationships are *universal*, relationships between members are based upon their mutual membership in their organization – not upon personal ties, as is friendship. Any expectations about the way a brother should relate to a brother applies to all brothers. One local Swedish Hells Angels chapter had the following written rule: 'If a civilian hits your brother, you should hit him without asking why. Your brother is not always right, but he is always your brother. *It is one for all and all for one*' (Wierup and Larsson 2007: 45, emphasis added). The view that an attack on a member is an attack on the club is a sign of the universalism that is inherent in brotherhood. Every member is seen as a part of the club, and to let down a member is to let down the club. In many monasteries there are forgiveness rituals in front of the community, at which individual members apologize for having spoken harshly to another member, for example. These rituals are also exhibiting that violation of an individual member is a stain on the *community*, whereas friends are accountable only relative to one another – not to some other entity. In the Legion, as an armed forces unit, cohesion relative to an external enemy is obviously essential, but to unite against other external threats in everyday life also forms part of what is expected of members. One famous expression, *À moi la Légion!* (Come to me Legion!), refers to the notion that if a member is in need of help outside his camp, he can cry out these words and any other member nearby will (should) come to his rescue. (See also, Hallo, [1994] 2007: 93.)

Reciprocity is a fundamental aspect of friendship and networking (e.g., Ahrne 2014: 111ff.), because it is a voluntary give-and-take practice that is crucial for maintaining the relationship. In contrast, brotherhood comprises a *duty* to help. Brothers in biker clubs are always obliged to lend a hand to brothers in need (Wolf 1991: 77, 83; see also, e.g., Hopper and Moore 1983: 62; cf. Clawson 1989: 256, 262 on Freemasonry), and even be willing to risk everything for the brothers, particularly if a member is threatened. (See also, Wolf 1991: 97f.) Monastic members also emphasize service to their brothers, but their services usually consist of such simple gestures as handing a brother a towel to dry the dishes or passing a tray during communal meals. These services, although explicitly expected (cf. Grün [2004] 2005: 84–5), are not particularly demanding – quite different, in fact, from the demands on a biker to be 'willing to risk everything' to help a fellow biker.

The explicit expectation on legionnaires and bikers to stand up for one another suggests that it is a decided expectation – either that it is a rule or has a rule-like character. There are explicit formulations in the Legion, for example, proclaiming universal member solidarity. The second point in the code of honour for legionnaires states, in fact, that 'every legionnaire is your brother in arms whatever his nationality, his race or his religion might be. You show to him the same close solidarity that links the members of the same family' (cf. Clawson 1989: 255 on Freemasonry). Through the notion of 'brothers *in arms*', the importance of solidarity in relation to external (violent) threat is suggested. Expectations for interpersonal relationships among members are also expressed through the phrase 'camaraderie [is] your strength', in the third point of the code. In addition to expressions and mottos, there are other ways of encouraging solidarity. As one official Legion PowerPoint presentation stated, 'Everything does not go by itself, solidarity is not spontaneous, it passes through examples and it is sometimes imposed.' To force friends into acts of solidarity is contradictive, or at least counterproductive, but organizations can initiate their decided forms of solidarity. The Legion charges small but mandatory fees to the *Foyer d'entraide de la Légion étrangère* (FELE, The Foreign Legion Home Help), from which veterans may apply for monetary assistance, and to the association for one's membership category (non-commissioned officer or enlisted). Solidarity is a 'constraint', as one senior non-commissioned officer put it.

Another sign that universal solidarity in the Legion is decided rather than spontaneously developed is that legionnaires express doubts about trust and loyalty in everyday life. One sergeant cited an expression that he had heard from colleagues and that he believed to be accurate: 'All the legionnaires are comrades, but we still lock up our belongings.' This quote reflects cynicism and awareness of the mismatch between actions and prescriptive rhetoric concerning the way in which 'all legionnaires' should relate to one another. Universal solidarity is prescribed, but like any decision, it is not necessarily practiced or believed in. One junior enlisted member was exceptionally clear regarding this point when explaining the difference between reciprocity among personal 'buddies' and the lack of 'cohesion' among everyone else:

> Of course you have your individual buddies, and you will help each other out every once in a while. But if I look at the history of what

> I have seen, and I, like, put together everything to an overall result,
> I would say there is no cohesion; there is no camaraderie; there is
> just every man for himself.

I do not know how representative these quotes are of the overall view
on trust and cohesion in the Legion. Yet they represent examples of
members openly articulating to an outsider their questions about the
strength, and indeed the existence, of brotherly, comradely relationships. On the basis of previous literature on outlaw biker clubs, such
utterances from their members appear unlikely. In biking clubs,
demands for help and services are strong and explicit, and to disregard
complying with them may lead to sanctions, as I discuss in the next
section. Thus, despite similarities in expectations, the consequences
differ.

Ex-legionnaires provide evidence for an extension of brotherhood across organizational borders through stories about recent
ex-legionnaires being informed about and offered jobs from other
previous members. Former members have offered contacts in
private security to more recent ex-members or provided intern-
ships in their companies. It is possible that these practices correspond to expectations of solidarity outside of the Legion that
cannot be conceived of as decided. In many ways, these former
members constitute a network, but it should be noted that the
network originates in previous membership.

FRIENDSHIP AS A THREAT

Tensions between different forms of relationships exist in every organizational setting, and there is always potential conflict involved
when members become friends. Friendship may conflict with organizational expectations on impartiality and confidentiality relative to
other members. Because brotherhood involves efforts to uphold an
equal and universal love among all brothers, particularistic friendships threaten brotherhood. Although it is clear that certain organizational problems arise when legionnaires relate to each other as friends

(see, e.g., Sundberg, 2015: 124–5, 154), the conflicts between brotherhood and friendship are more salient in outlaw biker clubs and monasteries, perhaps because the very existence of brotherhood is more apparent there.

Monks and nuns spontaneously admit that they 'like' some of their fellow members more than others, and that they get better along with some than with others, but there is also emphasis on the fact that these factors should not affect the brotherly relationship. As one monk related to me, one 'cannot smile at one brother' and not another. One should not treat individual members differently, and small cliques are especially problematic. As one monk said: 'There shouldn't be just small groups ... No. One has to assure everyone ... an equal love – brotherly.'

Monastic members sometimes stress how friendship is beautiful or positive in principle, but it is evident that it is considered problematic in practice. Only friendship between individual members that 'enriches the community' or is 'for the community' is acceptable. It is difficult to imagine Alberoni's (2016) view of friendship: born out of a collective, but also formed against this collective. In practice, friendship seems to be considered a threat that encourages the friends to turn away from the collective. As one nun said: 'It should not be that I hide with those it goes well with.' She also proclaimed: 'You can't just stick with those you like. If I would like to do that, I would leave. To welcome someone like a sister isn't friendship; it is not spontaneous. It is with the sisters I don't get along with so well that monastic life plays out.' This nun's account makes two significant points: the difference between brotherhood and friendship and the fact that community is primordial. First, whereas friendship is likely to start from an initial appreciation of someone (one 'likes' the person) and to develop into a closer relationship on that basis (in combination with other components; see Ahrne, Chapter 11), the order is reversed in monastic brotherhood. One is first a brother or a sister, which implies an obligation to love. Members are *prescribed* to accept and love every other member *because* they are members. The prescription to love has a spiritual basis in Christian charity and should ultimately include every human being; but in practice, the request to love is most important when applied to other monastic members. Second, and related to the first point, is the fact that community and the brotherly bonds it should maintain are primordial. There is an effort to accept members that one is not attracted to at first and with whom one does not get along well, rather than avoiding them or attempting to deepen or establish personal relationships with more appreciated members.

Few members have questioned the social situation in monasteries, but one monk mentioned a former member who had left the monastery after completing his time as a novice. According to the monk, the novice said that 'it's not true relations' inside the monastery and that 'one has too much distance'. The everyday interaction between monastic members is usually limited. Unlike outlaw biker clubs, in which there is always supposed to be a brother to talk with when one needs it, it is preferable that monastic members avoid talk, in order to preserve a constant dialogue with God. Legitimate conversations concern working tasks, community discussions, and discussions on spiritual progress with a director or confessor. (See, e.g., OCSO, 2014b.) Although monks are allowed to ask any other monk for advice, nuns are expected to turn only to their superior if they need to discuss something (spiritual or practical).

Brotherly relationships are expected to be homogeneous, but homogeneity can differ in different brotherly relationships. Whereas relationships between monastic members (should) remain distant, biking club culture promotes intense socializing. Forming individual friendships, side by side with brotherly relationships, would therefore appear as an ideal in some sense, but in fact, friendship can be problematic in a biker club as well. A personal relationship between individual members can never compensate for a failure to perform one's role as a brother (cf. Alberoni, 2016). Friendly ties are key when a person joins a biker club, but once inside the club, the relationship with to the individual as a member, rather than as a friend, must be primordial. Consider the following story about the expulsion of a member of Hells

Angels (Michel), which the narrator tells from the perspective of a former Hells Angels member, Svempa:

> Svempa was the one who once had engaged Michel, but by this time he also thought that Michel had used all his trust. 'The patch had turned him into an idiot, he built castles in the air and acted like an idiot. There was no doubt that he should be thrown out.' [said Svempa]
>
> *(Wierup and Olsson, 2012: 199)*

Once a member's bad reputation has been established, there is a risk that he will be thrown out – and by violent methods. (See also Chapter 12.) Expulsion from Hells Angels as an organization sometimes works according to the same principle as expulsion from a network, in the sense that the member and brother is frozen out, and a 'used trust' between people may, of course, also affect their friendship. In other cases of expulsion, friendship and brotherhood conflict with each other. Some remaining members may consider expulsion of the friend/member, and thus the cessation of membership, as the correct measure, but be less willing to accept the reality that the friendship is also over. Former member Micke felt grief over one expulsion: 'The insight that him and Ebba [Micke's girlfriend] would have to pretend that the former friends did not exist made Micke feel bad' (Wierup and Olsson, 2012: 259). Neither members nor their partners are allowed to be in contact with former members who have left in 'bad standing'. (See, e.g., Wierup and Olsson, 2012: 205, 281.) Former member Svempa relates his expulsion from his own perspective: 'I realized it was over, I just had to adhere to what was decided. Is that brotherhood?' (Wierup and Olsson, 2012: 205). Svempa questioned how 'the brothers' could turn their back on him, and Micke also started to doubt 'all beautiful words about brotherhood' after 'those bonds of loyalty and friendship that the old members had formed successively had been torn down and broken' (Wierup and Olsson, 2012: 261).

Yet the answer to the perceived conflict of values lies in precisely the (theoretical) conception of brotherhood that this chapter has intended to present: Whereas friendship is a spontaneous relationship between individuals, brotherhood is a decided relationship based on a collectivist bond. If one no longer belongs to that collective, one is no longer a brother, and does not deserve to be treated as one. There is no contradiction in the fact that brothers turn their backs on previous members; rather, it is a logical consequence of the priority of the collective relative to the individual. The form that an individual member's relationship with previous members should take has been decided upon, and 'bad standing' therefore differs from reputations. Brotherly relationships justify sacrifice of personal relationships to meet collective demands, and this point is clearest with regard to expulsion from outlaw biker clubs. Perhaps unexpectedly, given the etymology of the term, brotherhood implies substitutability. Individual brotherly or sisterly relationships can break down, and new brothers replace the old, reaffirming the essential role of membership.

TRADING PERSONAL RELATIONSHIPS FOR DECIDED IMPERSONAL LOVE

In this chapter, I define brotherhood as a specific social relationship, in contrast to previous research in which brotherhood is conflated with friendship. Unlike friendship, brotherhood requires a decision to become member in an organization in which membership implies brotherhood. Because brotherhood is based on membership, it does not depend on reciprocity to continue. There are expectations for universal loyalty, however, and it is generally a duty to help and perform requested services. This universal demand is related to what are ideally the egalitarian brother-to-brother relationships. Because brotherhood presupposes a strong collectivist priority, competition with personal relationships is inherent, but may remain latent until conflicts between the relationships become clear, as in the case of outlaw bikers exiting in 'bad standing'. Yet a reason for signalling resemblance between brotherhood and friendship could be considered an example of organizational hypocrisy (cf. Brunsson, 2006), as it probably appears more attractive to presumptive members than the substitutability inherent in brotherhood.

In addition to the common characteristics discussed in this chapter, the salience and strength of brotherhood varies across empirical settings, specifically as it concerns the role of membership in the formal organization, its rules, and sanctions. Brotherhood may be limited to organizational members, but in the longer range, organizational membership at some earlier point is enough to count one as a brother. Brotherly relationships may also differ in the way expectations about loyalty relate to negative sanctions for lack of compliance. Brotherhood in the French Foreign Legion, and probably military organizations in general, represents a combination of extended range and rules that are unattached to sanctions. Legionnaire brotherhood presupposes entrance into the French Foreign Legion, but allows exit. At least in peacetime, the emphasis on brotherhood appears more rhetorical than practical. Outlaw biker clubs represent a different combination because they presuppose continued membership and conflicts with friendship if someone leaves a club in 'bad standing'. In both these examples of brotherhood, there is emphasis on uniting towards a common, external 'enemy'. There is, however, an important difference. Whereas former members of the armed forces are assumed to be on the 'same side' as present members, at least in wartime, the boundary between present and former members of outlaw biker clubs is stricter. This is not the case only if they have left in 'bad standing' or joined a competing biker club, but also because outlaw biker clubs are composed of *outlaws*, and thus in conflict with the rest of society. Cohesion is, in a sense, the only defence they have, which may be why the stress on loyalty is so strong and the *talk* of brotherhood so important, regardless of whether it exists in practice (cf. Brunsson 2006). A final aspect concerns differences in what the homogenous relationships between brothers should look like. Outlaw biker clubs and monasteries appear to be opposites here. Outlaw biker clubs proclaim equally intense interaction among members, whereas interaction among members of Catholic monasteries should be equally distant and cool. Despite the explicit emphasis on love, relationships remain impersonal. Perhaps it is easier to maintain similar relationships among all members, and maintain brotherhood, when restrictions limit members from forming closer, personal relationships more explicitly.

REFERENCES

Ahrne, G. (2014) *Samhället mellan oss. Om vänskap, kärlek, relationer och organisationer.* Malmö: Liber.

Alberoni, F. (2016) *Friendship.* Leiden: Brill.

Bianco, F. (1998) *Voices of Silence. Lives of the Trappists Today.* Anchor Books.

Brunsson, N. (2006) *The Organization of Hypocrisy. Talk, Decisions and Actions in Organizations.* Malmö: Liber.

Clawson, M. A. (1989) *Constructing Brotherhood: Class, Gender, and Fraternalism.* Princeton: Princeton University Press.

Cockburn, C. (1991) *In the Way of Women.* London: Macmillan.

Collins, R. (2004) *Interaction Ritual Chains.* Princeton: Princeton University Press.

Durkheim, E. ([1902] 2013) *The Division of Labour in Society.* 2nd edition. S. Lukes, ed. Basingstoke: Palgrave Macmillan.

Ebaugh, H. R. (1988) *Becoming an Ex. The Process of Role Exit.* Chicago: University of Chicago Press.

Fundberg, J. (2003) *Kom igen, gubbar! Om pojkfotboll och maskulinitet.* Stockholm: Carlssons.

Grundvall, S. (2005) *Gemenskap, manlighet och marginalitet. En studie av en västsvensk bikerklubb.* Gothenburg: Gothenburg University, Department of Social Work.

Grün, A. ([2004] 2005) *Saint Benoît. Un message pour aujourd'hui.* Paris: Desclée de Brouwer.

Higate, P. R. (2000) Ex-Servicemen on the Road: Travel and Homelessness, *Sociological Review* 48(3): 331–46.

Hopper, C. B. & Moore J. (1982) Hell on Wheels: The Outlaw Motorcycle Gangs. *Journal of American Culture* 6(summer): 58–64.

Jolly, R. (1996) *Changing Step: From Military to Civilian Life: People in Transition.* London: Brassey's.

Kiesling, S. F. (2005) Homosocial Desire in Men's Talk: Balancing and Re-Creating Cultural Discourses of Masculinity. *Language in Society* 34(5): 695–726.

Lindgren, G. (1996) Broderskapets logik. *Kvinnovetenskaplig tidskrift* 1: 4–14.

OCSO: Order of Cistercians of the Strict Observance (2014a) Steps to Becoming a Monk or Nun. Retrieved 24 September 2014 from www.trappists.org/becoming-trappist/steps-becoming-monk-or-nun.

OCSO: Order of Cistercians of the Strict Observance (2014b) Monastic Discipline – Lifestyle. Retrieved 23 September 2014 from www.trappists.org/newcomers/ monastic-discipline/lifestyle.

Olofsson, J. (2013) 'The Profession of Firefighting Is about Teamwork, It Is about Trusting Each Other': Masculine Enactments and Generational Discrepancies within the Swedish Fire Service. *Culture, Society & Masculinity* 5(1): 75–88.

Schouten, J. W. & McAlexander, J. H. (1995) Subcultures of Consumption: An Ethnography of the New Bikers. *Journal of Consumer Research* 22(1): 43–61.

Sundberg, M. (2015) *A Sociology of the Total Organization: Atomistic Unity in the French Foreign Legion*. Farnham: Ashgate.

Wierup, L. & Larsson, M. (2007) *Svensk maffia. En kartläggning av de kriminella gängen*. Norstedts.

Wierup, L. & Olsson, D. (2012) *Helvetet inifrån. Femton år i Sveriges största brottsorganisation*. Reporto.

Wolf, D. R. (1991) *The Rebels: A Brotherhood of Outlaw Bikers*. Toronto: University of Toronto Press.

PART 4 Social Movements and Collective Action

14 The Dilemma of Organization in Social Movement Initiatives

Mikko Laamanen, Sanne Bor, and Frank den Hond

Social movement initiatives are distinct from *social movement organizations* (Zald & Ash, 1966; McCarthy & Zald, 1977); participants in social movement initiatives do not want to emulate the decided social order that is typically found in social movement organizations and, more generally, in formal organizations. These initiatives are collective action groups that experiment with *horizontal*, non-hierarchical forms of organizing. We present a case study of such a social movement initiative, illustrating the persistent, ever-present dilemma of organization inherent in horizontal organizing. We see the organizational question not as whether organization affects social movement initiatives, but as how their participants attempt to organize in ways that are reflective of their ideals (cf. de Bakker, den Hond, & Laamanen, 2017; den Hond, de Bakker, & Smith, 2015). With a focus on the production of organization, we develop our argument about the tensions between horizontal organizing versus bureaucracy (i.e., the introduction of hierarchy and rules), and horizontal organizing versus oligarchy (i.e., the usurpation of social order by a few). These tensions are central issues in the emergent theorization of partial organization (cf. Chapter 17).

Our empirical analysis centres on *timebanking*. A timebank is a group of people that maintains a local complementary currency system and engages in social movement activity by challenging the prevailing hegemony, not only in its political and economic dimensions, but also in its associated cultural dimension (Eskelinen, 2014; Laamanen, Wahlen, & Campana, 2015; North, 2014). In banking time rather than the national currency, timebankers create alternative, non-monetary currency systems seeking to transform markets and social interaction. Many timebanking initiatives eschew formal organization. Central to their projects of showing how an alternative to the current hegemony can be viable is the concept of horizontal organizing or, in short, horizontality: 'the continuous process of challenging the centralization of power to attain as much equality as possible between actors' (Maeckelbergh, 2011: 2). Yet, the experience of timebankers is that it is well-nigh impossible to rely solely on the emergent social order in their organizing. For this reason, timebanking is a particularly illuminating case for exploring the challenges of organizing a community that attempts to meet the mundane needs of its membership, while practicing horizontality and aiming to change society in political, economic, and cultural terms.

The question we focus on in this chapter, therefore, is: *How have the participants in a timebank attempted to resolve the dilemma of needing, but not wanting to have, a decided social order?* Our analysis draws on the experiences of participants active in organizing a timebank in Finland. Through them, we are able to illustrate how their community has struggled with horizontality. Their explicit wish to organize without creating a bureaucracy, while simultaneously resisting oligarchization, and their continuing struggle to do so, provides an opportunity to expand upon earlier studies of organizing in social movement initiatives (e.g., Blee, 2012; Dobusch & Schoeneborn 2015; Freeman, 1972; Sutherland, Land, & Böhm, 2014). In this chapter, we explore how they sought to navigate between decided and emergent social order.

THE INSTABILITY OF ORGANIZATION

Several ideas that challenge traditional assumptions of organization have emerged in organization theory over the past few years (Böhm, 2006; den Hond *et al.*, 2015; Parker *et al.*, 2014). This research commonly points to the myopia related to understanding organization as a constituted formality, as a way of organizing that is presumably politically neutral and functionally efficient (if not also morally superior; du Gay & Vikkelsø, 2016). By pointing out and exploring the possibility of alternative organization (Parker *et al.*, 2014), it criticizes the idea that social organization seems always already formed, pre-determined and given (Böhm, 2006: 5). Partial organization theory represents a possible way of adding to this literature by problematizing the choices that are inherent in and behind any decision to modify social order.

Formal organizations, the topic of study for the classical writers of organization theory, are characterized by extensive decision making on five elements of organization: membership, hierarchy, rules, monitoring, and sanction. (See Chapter 1.) For two reasons, however, social order in organizations cannot be characterized solely by or understood as decided social order. First, social order in organizations is not only decided, but also simultaneously emergent; emergent social order stems from the relationships (networks) among members and from their shared beliefs, identity, and behavioural patterns (institutions). Second, people in organized settings (organizations, collectives) may forgo the possibility of decision making on one or more of the elements of organization and rely instead on emergent sources of social order for coordination and collaboration. We understand partial organization to be descriptive of the temporary and evolving pattern or mixture of emergent and decided sources of social order (Bor & den Hond, 2015) in settings in which people collaborate to accomplish some common purpose.

As a legacy from the classical writers, traditional views of organizing have rested on assumptions of unity, unequivocality, and goal specificity, to which Herbert Simon added the prime importance of decision making. By contrast, partial organization theory does not need to depend on these assumptions if it problematizes decision making and takes seriously the possibility of relying on emergent social order as a means of coordinating collaboration. Although in an overall sense, *some* decision making – and therefore a decided social order – seems necessary for organization to happen or to be meaningful, the necessity of specific instances of decision making can always be challenged. A decision or proposal for a specific form or element of decided social order can be rejected, other decisions considered and preferred, or no decision made (a non-decision; Bachrach & Baratz, 1963). Whereas one can imagine some (collaborative) social setting in which social order does not depend on decision making (Berger & Luckmann, 1967: 70 ff.), we cannot imagine any instance of organization in which there is no emergent social order. In this sense, *organizing* – rather than *organization* – needs to be understood as decision making in order to affect the prevailing social order, an intervention in the then-present mixture of emergent and decided sources of social order. Organization is thus inherently unstable not only because changing conditions in the environment demand decision making, but also because the relationships between organizational participants evolve over time, as do their shared beliefs, identity, and behavioural patterns. Emergent social order evolves for various reasons: in reflexive response to the prevailing social order, in reaction to decision making that seeks to affect it, and autonomously (cf. Tsoukas & Chia, 2002).

Resisting decided social order

The participants of many contemporary social movement initiatives attempt to practice horizontality: a form of organization that is democratic and inclusive in participation and that eschews authority, leadership, and structure among the characteristics of formal organization. Proponents of horizontality shun Weberian legal-rational and traditional authority, as embodied in hierarchy and, by extension, in the other elements of organization. Their preferred social order is prefigurative (Boggs, 1978), inasmuch as they attempt to show the promise of their horizontal ideal in present action. Indeed, their modus operandi is to expose the possibility of another societal order. Activists and activist groups are pivotal in 'turning a critical lens on what *is* and imagining what *can be*' (Blee, 2012: Acknowledgements; emphasis in original), in relation to organizing and decision making, for example (Maeckelbergh, 2011; Teivainen, 2016; Yates, 2015). Thus, in terms of partial organization, they may refuse to distinguish between members and non-members, to privilege some participants with the right to instruct other participants, and to constrain individual responsibility and choice through rules and through systems of monitoring and sanctioning.

However, horizontal organizing and avoidance of decided social order may not prevent the emergence of a social order in which a few participants establish hegemonic power over the many. Nor does it resolve the challenge of maintaining an open, participatory style of decision making and coordination (Clemens & Minkoff, 2004). The instability of organization in social movement initiatives can thus lead to two types of outcomes. There may be an accumulation of decision making, such that they eventually come to resemble bureaucracies (*bureaucratization*, e.g., Graeber, 2015), or there may be an accumulation of authority, and eventually the usurpation of social order by a minority of participants (*oligarchization*, cf. Leach, 2005; Michels, 1965; Tolbert & Hiatt, 2009; Zald & Ash, 1966).

The participants in social movement initiatives explore the possibility of resisting both bureaucratization and oligarchization. If they wish to remain horizontal, they must stay clear of two tendencies. First, they need to resist the *tendency to rely increasingly on decision making* as the main source of social order in their initiative, if they do not want to end up mimicking the characteristics and rigidities of a bureaucratic organization (cf., Ahrne & Brunsson, 2011; Reedy, 2014). Second, they must resist a *tendency towards the institutionalization* of social practices and relationships that confirm differences in status and that may eventually result in oligarchy. In recognition of the risks of both bureaucratization and oligarchization, extensive experimentation with horizontal organization has taken place (Graeber, 2013; den Hond *et al.*, 2015; Reinecke, 2018). Horizontal, prefigurative organization does not represent a clear-cut model of organization, but rather an *ideologically informed experiment*. Being ideological, it effectively leaves the organizational question unanswered beyond the rejection of a decided social order and a handful of general guidelines, such as how to achieve consent within a group.

THE HELSINKI TIMEBANK

In this section, we analyse the organizing of *Stadin Aikapankki* (STAP: Helsinki Timebank). Our analysis draws on data that we collected as part of an on-going larger-scale ethnographic investigation on how local communities build alternative economies. The data utilized here include semi-structured interviews conducted between March and May 2015, archival materials (internal documents, some available through the Internet), the timebank's electronic workspace, and field notes from participant observation and informal conversations. We interviewed eleven participants in what STAP members refer to as the 'core group'. Some interviewees have been active in STAP, others joined later, and some interviewees had recently ceased active participation in the core group. The first author took field notes between March 2015 (when he joined STAP and became involved in the work of the core group) and October 2016. The lived experience of being an outsider to the community with the intention of becoming an insider proved valuable in understanding the interviewees' accounts of their experiences in STAP. Given the close connectedness of the core group of individuals, we dealt with issues of respondent privacy (Clark, 2006) by assuring full anonymity to the interviewees.

We first introduce STAP as partially organized. We then highlight two episodes in which the organizational question became prominent, and finally present its outcomes or, rather, how the organizational question remained unresolved.

STAP as partially organized

Our empirical case of STAP is a local alternative currency community operating in metropolitan Helsinki, Finland, since 2009. Its currency is the *tovi*: a play on words. (The Finnish word 'tovi' translates as 'a while', or 'a moment'.) One tovi has the value of one hour of work: Sellers receive one tovi as a credit for every hour of work they render to other members of the community (the buyers of the sellers' services), and in turn, sellers become buyers when they spend their credit on services from other community members. The exchange rests on *generalized* reciprocity: Community members are not required to 'buy' services from the people to whom they previously 'sold' their service; rather, they are expected to offer and exchange services actively with anyone in the community.

There were two types of motivations for the creation of STAP. On the one hand, it was an attempt to increase the wellbeing of its individual participants, the community of participants, and ultimately the greater common good of the city. On the other hand, it was an attempt to develop and experiment with a variety of alternative social, economic, and environmental practices to the dominant capitalist framework (Alhojärvi *et al.*, 2015; Laamanen *et al.*, 2015). In combination, they show how STAP is a truly prefigurative social movement initiative aimed at developing a communal culture for a socially and ecologically just local economy, in which every person has equal value and opportunity to participate.

STAP adheres to two principles: stigmergy and adhocracy. *Stigmergy* relates to the organizing of work, whereas *adhocracy* stands for a decision making mechanism. Stigmergy is the collectively negotiated, distributed action of independent actors (Elliott, 2006). In STAP, this translates into work being distributed through self-organization as members sign up for and execute tasks when they observe that tasks need to be done. The core group's online electronic workspace and e-mail list are means by which members facilitate stigmergy. Adhocracy is the flexible and situational organizing for decision making, to allow for maximum participation and minimum specification of authority. Adhocracy is practiced most pronouncedly in the membership meetings, in which those members present have the power to pass decisions. The distribution of work through stigmergy is subject to adhocratic decision making, for example, to prevent the accumulation of power and to allow everyone to join decision making processes at any time they participate in the group. On this basis, STAP has prevented itself from becoming an organization in the traditional meaning of the word. STAP deliberately chose not to register as an association, which, in the Finnish context, would have implied an obligation to define and assign organizational roles, tasks, and responsibilities. STAP members saw these implications as the imposition of hierarchy that would be incompatible with the principles of stigmergy and adhocracy.

In some ways, however, STAP did introduce organizational elements, albeit minimally. Participants must be registered as members to be able to exchange services in the timebank. Yet, STAP has made it easy for new members to join; anybody can participate by registering through its website. An administrator, a core group member who is entrusted with the task, processes new membership applications. In the process, the administrator checks only the completeness of the information provided. Becoming a member, then, is a straightforward process: a routine administrative operation rather than a decision on individual applications. This process is not without its problems, as a former administrator elaborates:

> As our member register has over 3,500 names, I'm not sure if most of these [members] even remember that they ever became members. I sometimes get requests for account openings from people with existing accounts . . . The personal details are generally not checked [when an account is opened] . . . Should I open an account, if Donald Duck registers as a member and gives Duckburg as the address? Technically, it [registering as a member] does not require more than a name, address, and e-mail.

The exchange of services among STAP members is subject to the acceptance of a shared set of norms and rules. Some rules relate to the overall administering and functioning of STAP, such as the build-up of a community fund through a levy on all transactions. The community fund is used mainly to reimburse members for services delivered to the collective. Others are essentially norms: shared expectations of appropriate behaviour within the community.

Monitoring and sanctioning are delegated to members rather than being centralized and enabled through transparency. STAP was founded in October 2009, and by October 2017, more than 14,200 transactions with a value of a little over 34,000 tovi had been administered on an online platform. Exchanges are facilitated through the distribution to STAP members of monthly listings of offerings and requests. To increase transparency and trust and to ensure that members' debits are under the allowed maximum of 50 tovi, every member has full access to all other community members' details and to all the exchanges registered on the online platform.

As tovi are not convertible to monetary currencies, amassing tovi is not economically rational. Nevertheless, some members maintain accounts with substantial surplus balances (+200 tovi), which they justify in membership meetings as not having any needs but a great willingness to help (and perhaps anxiety for receiving help, cf. Papaoikonomou & Valor, 2016). If a member has a deficit of more than 50 tovi, a core group member is mandated to contact this member and offer support to start providing services in the community. In extreme cases, the community can decide to reset the overdrawn account to zero, drawing on the community fund.

Sanctioning rarely happens. Members are advised to resolve between themselves any disagreement about the timeliness or the quality of service delivery. If members are unable to resolve the disagreement, an appointed team may mediate. Such mediation is participatory and conciliatory:

> Conciliation has been used very little ... I don't see that this is a sanctioning mechanism [but] meant for people to find a common solution ... We [the conciliators] do not take a stance on what is right and what is wrong, we let the people talk to one another ... We don't take a stance on who is lying and who is not ... We have rules for exchange; they are beginning to be quite exhaustive ... I'm that kind of a bureaucrat that some intervention process has to be created ... I don't know how this could work without rules.

The membership meeting, the supreme decision making body of the collective, has effectively relegated operational discretion to specific individuals in their role of administrator or as members of the core group. They do not acquire the right to command others, however, because STAP has no hierarchy. Yet, the regular administration of tasks by specific individuals offers them the possibility of wielding tacit forms of power (cf. Breton *et al.*, 2012). In the spring of 2010, an e-mail list and an electronic workspace were created for a core group of people who participate more actively than regular members in the administration of STAP. The group is in charge of initiating and maintaining such activities as accepting new members; creating the newsletter; organizing membership meetings, exchange markets, and community events; and promoting the timebank to potential members. At its largest, the core group had around 40 members; the current core group consists of 21 people. In principle, every member of STAP can step forward and become part of the core group, but relatively few have done so.

All STAP members receive an invitation to participate in meetings, but in practice, often only a handful of people attend. Decision making during the membership meeting is noteworthy, because decision making power has always been adhocratic. Decisions are relative only to and limited to a specific meeting, with the possibility that the next meeting overrules a previous decision. Adhocracy renders decision making non-representative:

> Neither our meetings nor the core group has ever been representative in any way. Or rather, not representative of the entire membership or legitimized by anyone in particular. We have not chosen any representatives. People [represent] themselves.

There are few recurring items on the agenda of the membership meetings. The agenda is distributed just before the meeting and often amended during the meeting. Over the few past years, the agenda has included such topics as participation in events and collaborations with external entities, including the City of Helsinki and other solidarity/alternative economy groups. One core group member expressed her mounting discontent about the way membership meetings are run and with their composition, as 'random samples' of the most 'random people' of the collective's membership are typically present:

> We should have a long-term perspective on thinking about how to deal with the global responsibility strategy of the City of Helsinki [in which timebanking is mentioned as a key development area]. Then along comes the membership meeting, where we spend an hour on [issues such as] logging in to the [online] platform, baking cakes for the next meeting, and such ... There are those who have strong opinions on whichever random issue. There's someone who thinks that we need to start purging members, whatever. It can be anything. There is no continuity.

Thus, in spite of its members not wanting STAP to be an organization, various elements of decided social order are present. Membership was introduced early on, albeit in a weak form. The creation of the core group can be seen as the introduction of some form of authority. But otherwise, there has been little, if any, decision making on rules, monitoring, and sanctions. Among these elements of organization, only membership was fully accepted; other elements remained controversial and were occasionally contested or just ignored.

At the same time, the *lack* of decided social order remained equally controversial. Although in theory stigmergy should reduce the need for decided social order within STAP, in practice it has remained problematic and contested. A member of the core group concludes:

> Stigmergy is not written down anywhere ... To some extent I think that this is part of [one central actor's] ideological background ... A way to do things organically, to grow and develop in a common learning process ... I think, however, that it will be a thousand years

Table 1 *STAP Development Timeline*

October 2009	The predecessor to STAP is founded with a membership of five individuals
Spring 2010	First membership meeting; formation of the core group
May 2010	Formation of STAP
From 2011 onwards	Increasing public exposure of the initiative
November 2011	Mapping of STAP values
2012	Rapid increase of membership
March 2013	Discussion: 'Why do we need STAP?'
May 2013	Introduction of ABC
June 2013	Tax investigation
September 2013	Tax instruction draft and STAP statement
November 2013	Ruling on taxation in timebanks
February 2014	Meeting to discuss organizational form
June 2014	STAP reaches out to the City of Helsinki
2015	Reintroduction of the monthly meetings
May 2016	Seminar: 'Let's Save the Timebanks'

[until true stigmergy is realized]. Maybe I am a bit impatient, but I want to do things here and now.

In what follows, we illustrate how STAP struggled with organizational form and authority; how on the one hand it perceived a need for decided order, while on the other hand attempting to keep it at arm's length.

ORGANIZATIONAL DYNAMICS IN STAP

Of particular interest for partial organization in this local social movement initiative is the formation of authority and the maintenance of horizontality, which relate to 'situations and patterns or interactions between organizers and the organized that give rise to more or less organization' (Ahrne & Brunsson, 2011: 95). The impetus for collective contemplations on organizing emerged from two highly salient issues: an internal issue, relating to the growth of the initiative in terms of membership; and the other external, relating to the prospect of having to comply with rulings of the Finnish tax authorities. Table 1 offers a timeline of major events in the history of STAP. It serves as a background to the subsequent discussion.

Membership, growth, and rules

In its early days, STAP was a 'rather unorganized activity', and equality and inclusiveness were central to its horizontal operating practice. As one member elaborated:

> When they founded the timebank, it had four housewives as members who decided amongst themselves to exchange [the equivalent of] tovi for babysitting for each other ... back then adhocracy probably worked quite well. It would have been stupid to set up an administrative body or an association or something else.

In accordance with the practice of horizontality, articulated as stigmergy and adhocracy, administrative tasks were to be distributed among the individuals who signed up to perform them. As STAP membership grew exponentially, however, from the initial group of a handful of acquaintances and friends in late 2009 to around 3,300 in 2017, this model exhibited its limits. It was in the face of a growing membership base that it was agreed at the 2010 membership meeting to create an e-mail list for the core group of people who did most of the coordination of the tasks associated with operating the timebank. This model worked for some time with the core group, but coordination became an issue again in late 2012, when STAP observed its strongest growth in membership.

Certain problems can be identified, as the following quote illustrates: 'In practice, work got done because there was a particular core group, albeit vaguely formed and compositionally mutable' (Membership meeting minutes, 2 February 2014). Indeed, there were no appointed roles or responsibilities beyond those assumed by the core group. In practice, routine work fell onto this small group of individuals, particularly one of the founding members. Limiting

action to spontaneous enrolment created *de facto* barriers to participation by those members who wanted to become more active. Active
members had more knowledge about what was going on, what was
needed, and what had been done, and they had the contacts required to
administer the timebank effectively. This situation led to an increasing separation between the core group and the rank-and-file members,
whose marginalization was further enhanced as new members found
it difficult to integrate into STAP. Many new members were less
ideologically motivated than the initiators were and had less intuitive
understanding of STAP's practice of horizontality.

With the increase in membership and a growing heterogeneity
in members' motivations to participate, discussions began on ways of
explicating the norms and practices of horizontality to new members,
ways of aligning new members' values and identities with those of
STAP, and ways of developing mechanisms for socializing new members into the network. The membership meeting agreed on the articulation and publication of the values and practices that underlie STAP's
identity.

In 2013, STAP created a document entitled the ABC. It
outlined the identity and purpose of the community in its key
practices and values, a tovi etiquette for exchanges and interactions,
and STAP's ways of working and decision making. Introduction of
the ABC followed a perceived need to explicate the community's
values, such as horizontality, solidarity, and inclusion, as rooted in
the alternative economy movement. Formulating the ABC was
a demanding process. Core group members recounted intense, heavily debated discussions on content. Two factions had formed, their
division cutting through both the core group and the regular membership. One faction emphasized the ideological outlining of STAP
and regularly referred to the way the collective is embedded in the
solidarity economy convictions of the founding members. The other
faction was more pragmatic and attentive to the actual trading
practices and to how trading in in the community may be stimulated and facilitated.

Ultimately, the ABC serves to inform prospective members about STAP's goals, how the timebank works, and the norms and rules it adheres to. (Although written in the imperative, tovi etiquette is seen merely as suggesting correct behaviours.) Supporting the familiarization processes of new members and opening access to administrative work in the core group was aimed at removing any significant hindrances to participation. Upon joining STAP, new members are requested to read the ABC. Nevertheless, as one core member said, 'We don't seem to do a good job of introducing people to the ways of working in the timebank.' Thus, STAP was in a situation in which the membership meeting became the *de facto* introductory event, and the community's rules lost some of their significance. As one member illustrated:

> [Membership meetings] always start with the basics, as there is always someone there to ask how to use the timebank ... knowing nothing and then there are those who have been there the whole time ... [the meetings] go through the same issues every time and that begins to frustrate people.

Thus, as the membership of STAP increased, members began to realize that their way of coordinating tasks and responsibilities had its limits. This was resolved, first, through the creation of the e-mail list and electronic workspace for members who wanted to take responsibility for coordination and administration. But even within this core group, there were significant differences in the activity levels of its participants. As membership began to increase significantly, there was a decrease among new members in the awareness of and identification with the timebank's practices. The ABC and the tovi etiquette it contains is an effort to make explicit the norms that underlie the practices of the timebank: rules, but not rules that are backed up with monitoring and sanctions. A second consequence of growth was that authority became concentrated within a relatively small group of people, not because they sought to dominate the timebank, but because of the scale and speed of growth, and, as Breton *et al.* (2012)

describe, the participants that do assume such responsibilities tend to become entrenched as leaders and distinct from other participants.

Expectation of compliance

The second major episode actualizing STAP organizing came from external sources. In the years of substantial growth between 2010 and 2013, STAP received extensive media coverage in the Finnish mainstream media. The community was included in various processes, such as the City of Helsinki's development of a strategy of global responsibility. Consequently, political interest and discussion around initiatives in the alternative economy were in high gear.

In spite of the positive press and political appraisal of its initiative, the community eventually came under investigation by the Finnish tax authorities as part of their shadow-economy prevention. The Finnish tax authorities released a report outlining work in the community entitled 'Timebanking in Finland' in June 2013 and, consequently, asked for a response from STAP. Much of the input of active members was aimed at attempts to counter the possible adverse effects of a pending tax decision, particularly if it were hostile to the activities in the community. The activities also revealed tensions in the way administrative work in the community was being conducted.

> When the tax authorities came to us for an official statement, it would not have happened through spontaneous *churning* [i.e., adhocratic decision making]. Then we had to work in a very structured way to formulate our stance. If I had done it by myself, it would have been quite different. I would have addressed each section [each tax authorities' argument]. 'The tax authorities thinks this; I answer thus' … But [our statement] became vague. It was a compromise, and at 10 past 4, with a deadline at 15 past 4 on the [same] day, people started to debate on foundational things. At this point I said, 'Not now. Now we finish this paper.' It can be that sometimes we need a tougher

[authority/structure], and sometimes a more creative and spontaneous movement.

In November 2013, the tax authorities made a decision on the taxation of voluntary work by natural persons. The tax authorities' decision was a severe blow to the community, as it departed significantly from the June report and the suggestions made by STAP in its response to the report. The decision caused confusion among the community's participants. Where tax liability relates only to professional work performed in the community, many participants decided to stop engaging in exchanges, in order to avoid any adverse tax consequences. The effects of the tax authorities' decision and the community's work in taking a stance took their toll on participation. As one core member said:

> Now I feel that with all this effort around tax, activity has collapsed, faded away. Part of the community is afraid of any tax consequences. I don't know if it's also some kind of combat fatigue. For my part, maybe it's just that. Not sure if a new rise is coming after this slump. It's slumped all right; for instance, when [a core group member] gets excited and sends a message to the core, it's very few that react to these nowadays.

As a result, there was a significant decline in new membership applications and exchanges. Frustration mounted within the core group as their attempts to influence official decisions turned out to have been in vain. The tax decision effectively paralysed active participation in both the core group and in STAP more generally, but it also revitalized the conflict around ways of organizing.

Non-decision on a new constitution

The intense periods of work on community rules and dealing with the tax issue led to the build-up of tensions within the core group. As one founding member said:

> I did a lot of lobby work for our proposal to the tax authorities. But what happened was a shock to all of us. We were disappointed and

frustrated, and this started to affect people. The end of 2013 was a hostile period, with more or less open conflict ... There was some debate on the STAP list, and I know that people in smaller groups were talking behind each other's backs ... I was given feedback on what I had done wrong, what I should not have done, and that sort [of thing] ... My answer was that we should think about this organizational stuff, and in February 2014 we had this meeting [on organizational form]. I remember it being a little traumatic.

This founding member's experience convinced her to step down from active membership in the core group. The mainstay of the critique that emerged was that an implicit authority had developed over the years around the founding members, whose functions, responsibilities, and ownership of the timebank had effectively made them indispensable in decision making. This situation was not without its problems. As one core member explains, those who participated in the discussions with the tax authorities had self-selected (e.g., they had the time and energy to engage in this work), but lacked legitimacy and a mandate from the community, which the authorities expected them to have.

To address this authority issue, a membership meeting in February 2014 focused on the question of organizational form. The pros and cons of two opposing structural alternatives – adhocracy and hierarchy – were extensively discussed: What would they imply for such topics as decision making, members' responsibilities, and STAP values? The members at the meeting also discussed gender imbalances between a male-led structure and a fluid community, in which the main responsibility for work fell onto the female membership. Yet, the conflict between the two alternatives is less than obvious, given that ease of decision making was considered a positive feature of both, for instance.

No decision could be arrived at during the meeting, and organizational discussions withered soon after. The minutes of the February 2014 meeting state that the 'organizing matrix' was shared on the community website for the membership to comment on and continue work with. Sharing the matrix with the membership was aimed at generating an inclusive conversation. Only one comment has since been posted on the thread, however; it critiqued the preoccupation with form in favour of a model with a function-driven (role-based) approach to organizing (i.e., bureaucracy). Thus, lack of clarity around the organizational form continued, as did the conflicts between proponents of more rules and a constitution and those preferring to work in a strictly horizontal manner.

In the face of all this disagreement and non-decision, two noteworthy interventions occurred in May 2014: A coordinator role was created, and the core members were explicitly asked if they would be willing to continue in their roles.

The first intervention was the creation of a coordinator role. This decision was a compromise, intended to maintain a fluid, light hierarchical structure and to help get things done.

> It was May [2014], if I remember correctly, in a membership
> meeting that we decided that, according to the organizing
> discussion, we would need a coordinator. An appointed coordinator.
> The only person who was willing was [the current coordinator] ...
> But this is the thing. In this work, you would need a strong person
> [laughs] to be an initiative-taking coordinator ... I feel that [the
> current coordinator] had done really valuable practical work ... [but]
> they have not become a power-wielding coordinator.

The intention of the second intervention, asking core members if they wanted to remain, was initiated in order to support active participation in the core group by letting the core members decide if they still wanted to contribute. About half of them decided not to continue, and the group was reduced to twenty members. A founding member recollects:

> All of last spring, I did nothing; nor did anyone else. And so that
> conversation [on organizing] was just discarded. And then I gave
> justification [for my non-involvement], as I had to finish my

dissertation, but also to see what would happen if I retreated. Whether someone takes that space ... I said to [another founding member] in one message: 'What if we both just quit? Would it not be inclusive when we would say, hey, if you complain that we use too much power, use it yourselves? Now, take it and occupy it, like that.' And I must have written on the list a message that I would be taking to the sidelines, and hope that somebody else would take [centre stage].

In order to maintain the community despite these various conflicts, there have recently been several attempts at member activation, such as reintroduction of regular membership meetings and attempts to build collaboration with the City of Helsinki (particularly through a seminar held in 2016). Thus, attempts were made to rebuild the community internally, while continuing to turn a blind eye to the question of organization and to mobilizing external actors to legitimize timebanking as a pro-social activity.

THE INSTABILITY OF PARTIAL ORGANIZATION

This chapter highlights a setting in which organization in the form of decision making under hierarchy, rules, monitoring, and sanctioning is unwanted. It expands recent conceptual discussion on partial organizing in social movement initiatives (de Bakker *et al.*, 2017) by demonstrating empirically why organization is or is not introduced, and why and how it remains partial. By asking how these timebank members attempted to practice horizontality, we set out to examine the way they produced organization at the intersection of their ideological avowal to horizontality in prefiguring an inclusive social order of the economy, on the one hand, and their struggle to resist bureaucratic and oligarchic tendencies in their organizing, on the other hand. We have illustrated their decision not to make decisions and their inability to do without a decided social order. Their organizing was incremental, triggered by both internal (growth in membership) and external (intervention by the tax authorities) events.

STAP exhibits several characteristics of partial organization. On the preceding pages, we have particularly dealt with the ways in which expectations for both stigmergy/adhocracy and authority emerged and occasionally resulted in decision making. The case of STAP demonstrates the activation of some elements of organization, such as establishing the core group, creating the ABC, and defining the position of coordinator. Other elements of organization were plainly rejected, particularly by those members whose approval seemed to count most. Thus, elements of decided order remained contested; the vesting of authority in specific individuals was not permanent and a hierarchy was not introduced. The ABC is a clear example of the introduction of organization – of decided social order – into the emergent social order. Membership growth and the resulting lack of familiarity with the workings of STAP among new members made it necessary to guide the behaviour of members, which led to the creation of rules in the form of stated values and a code of conduct.

Tensions in the community remained, as some active members criticized the few individuals who did most of the work, saying that they wielded too much power. Yet the criticizing members were unwilling to assume responsibility. Interventions to introduce more decided social order faltered and no decision on organizational form was made. The two factions that wanted different degrees of organization began to challenge each other, a pattern not uncommon in social movement initiatives (Sutherland et al., 2014). In many groups, there is a small number of participants that assume group-level responsibilities, thereby generating distinction for themselves and dependency in others. Yet, their central position in leading and decision making render them targets of criticism (Breton et al., 2012). If the criticism is dismissed, suppressed, or ignored, groups may evolve towards oligarchy. Freeman (1972) warned against the 'tyranny of structurelessness', whereby nobody is responsible or accountable, and those with central positions can gain a great deal of tacit power.

Sutherland and his co-authors (2014) suggest that the tendency to oligarchization, stemming from differences in knowledge and capability among participants, inequalities in gender structures, or collaboration in cliques, is neither insurmountable nor inevitable. Continuous reflective practices and willingness to learn would be key factors in fostering a more equal and collective authority. When roles of collective responsibility are rotated among participants, for example, and when participants are stimulated to develop and exercise their skills in collective responsibility, they may evolve towards a mode of organizing that is closer to their ideal of horizontality (cf. Sutherland et al., 2014). Such reflective practices were not enacted in STAP. Nevertheless, our interviews and observations suggest that at least the members of the core group were aware of the authority issues at stake, but they were unable to agree on how to move forward. Although its horizontality was not without problems, STAP did not develop into either a bureaucracy or an oligarchy. Its members are expected to steer, manage, and undertake activities collectively, yet the core group, while open to all members, was seen as a selective group that, due to their engagement, wielded a tacit, privileged form of power.

We highlighted the critical juncture in the practicing of stigmergy and adhocracy at STAP, when those who came to wield power become subjects of criticism, and rank-and-file participants experienced the flipside of this situation. Horizontality may produce marginalization for ordinary members and render it difficult for new members to participate. As one participant commented:

> Every timebanker joining [STAP] feels like an outsider for a very long time. In fact, most timebankers feel more or less like outsiders, because there is a very small group of people that have done a lot and maintained intensive involvement ... [they were] insiders enough to do something.

The idea of horizontality sustains the current unstructured situation at STAP. The conflict for participants is that adhocratic decision making is manifestly open to everyone and can be influenced by any participant, yet the ultimate approval for decisions and courses of action is sought from a few individuals. Problematically, this form of authority alienated some active members, who then left the core group. Others voiced their concerns and suggested an organization between decided and emergent order.

In conclusion, we are advancing the argument that the partial organization in many local social movement initiatives is ridden with tension. As we have demonstrated with the case of STAP, these tensions were created by a need for organizing and a principled resistance to the establishment of social order through organizational elements.

REFERENCES

Ahrne, G. & Brunsson, N. (2011) Organization outside Organization: The Significance of Partial Organization. *Organization* 18(1): 83–104.

Alhojärvi, T., Ryynänen, S., Toivakainen, N., & van der Wekken, R. (2015) Solidaarisuustalous. In M. Jalonen & T. Silvasti (eds.), *Talouden uudet muodot*. Helsinki: Into. 210–30.

Bachrach, P. & Baratz, M. S. (1963) Decisions and Nondecisions: An Analytical Framework. *American Political Science Review* 57(3): 632–42.

Berger, P. L. & Luckmann, T. (1967) *The Social Construction of Reality: A Treatise in the Sociology of Knowledge*. New York: Doubleday.

Blee, K. M. (2012) *Democracy in the Making. How Activist Groups Form*. Oxford: Oxford University Press.

Boggs, C. (1978) Marxism, Prefigurative Communism, and the Problem of Workers' Control. *Radical America* 11/12(1): 99–122.

Böhm, S. (2006) *Repositioning Organization Theory*. Basingstoke: Palgrave Macmillan.

Bor, S. & den Hond, F. (2015) *Social Order & Organisational Dynamics*. Working paper. Presented at the 4th European Theory Development Workshop, Cardiff, 24–25 June 2015.

Breton, E., Jeppesen, S., Kruzynski, A., & Sarrasin, R. (2012) Prefigurative Self-Governance and Self-Organization: The Influence of Antiauthoritarian (Pro) Feminist, Radical Queer, and Antiracist Networks in Quebec. In A. Choudry, J. Hanley, & E. Shragge (eds.), *Organize! Building from the Local for Global Justice*. Oakland: PM Press. 156–73.

Clark, A. (2006) *Anonymising Research Data* (NCRM Working Paper 07/06). Southampton, UK: National Centre for Research Methods. Retrieved 9 June 2015 from http://eprints.ncrm.ac.uk/480/.

Clemens, E. S. & Minkoff, D. C. (2004) Beyond the Iron Law: Rethinking the Place of Organizations in Social Movement Research. In D. A. Snow, S. A. Soule, & H. Kriesi (eds.), *The Blackwell Companion to Social Movements*. Malden: Blackwell. 155–70.

de Bakker, F., den Hond, F., & Laamanen, M. (2017) Social Movements: Organizations and Organizing. In C. Roggeband & B. Klandermans (eds.), *Handbook of Social Movements across Disciplines*. Cham: Springer. 203–31.

den Hond, F., de Bakker, F. G. A., & Smith, N. (2015) Social Movements and Organizational Analysis. In M. Diani & D. della Porta (eds.), *The Oxford Handbook of Social Movements*. Oxford: Oxford University Press. 291–305.

Dobusch, L. & Schoeneborn, D. (2015) Fluidity, Identity, and Organizationality: The Communicative Constitution of Anonymous. *Journal of Management Studies* 52(8): 1005–35.

du Gay, P. & Vikkelsø, S. (2016) *For Formal Organization: The Past in the Present and Future of Organization Theory*. Oxford: Oxford University Press.

Elliott, M. (2006) Stigmergic Collaboration: The Evolution of Group Work. *M/C Journal* 9(2). Retrieved 26 December 2017 from http://journal.media-culture.org.au/0605/03-elliott.php/.

Eskelinen, T. (2014) *Aikapankkien yhteiskunnalliset vaikutukset ja verotus*. Helsinki: Vasemmistofoorumi.

Freeman, J. (1972) The Tyranny of Structurelessness. *Berkeley Journal of Sociology* 17: 151–65.

Graeber, D. R. (2013) *The Democracy Project. A History. A Crisis. A Movement*. London: Penguin.

Graeber, D. R. (2015) *The Utopia of Rules. On Technology, Stupidity, and the Secret Joys of Bureaucracy*. Brooklyn: Melville House.

Laamanen, M., Wahlen, S., & Campana, M. (2015) Mobilising Collaborative Consumption Lifestyles: A Comparative Frame Analysis of Time Banking. *International Journal of Consumer Studies* 39(5): 459–67.

Leach, D. K. (2005) The Iron Law of What Again? Conceptualizing Oligarchy across Organizational Forms. *Sociological Theory* 23(3): 312–37.

Maeckelbergh, M. (2011) Doing Is Believing: Prefiguration as Strategic Practice in the Alterglobalization Movement. *Social Movement Studies: Journal of Social, Cultural and Political Protest* 10(1): 1–20.

McCarthy, J. D. & Zald, M. N. (1977) Resource Mobilization and Social Movements: A Partial Theory. *American Journal of Sociology* 82(6): 1212–41.

Michels, R. (1965 [1911]) *Political Parties: A Sociological Study of the Oligarchical Tendencies of Modern Democracy*. New York: Free Press.

North, P. (2014) Complementary Currencies. In M. Parker, G. Cheney, V. Fournier, & C. Land (eds.), *The Routledge Companion to Alternative Organization*. London: Routledge. 182–94.

Papaoikonomou, E. & Valor, C. (2016) Exploring Commitment in Peer-to-Peer Exchanges: The Case of Timebanks. *Journal of Marketing Management* 32 (13–14): 1333–58.

Parker, M., Cheney, G., Fournier, V., & Land, C. (2014) Imagining Alternatives. In M. Parker, G. Cheney, V. Fournier, & C. Land (eds.), *The Routledge Companion to Alternative Organization*. London: Routledge. 31–41.

Reedy, P. (2014) Impossible Organizations: Anarchism and Organizational Praxis. *ephemera: theory & politics in organization* 14(4): 639–58.

Reinecke, J. (2018) Social Movements and Prefigurative Organizing: Confronting entrenched inequalities in Occupy London. *Organization Studies* 39(9), 1299–321.

Sutherland, N., Land, C., & Böhm, S. (2014) Anti-Leaders(hip) in Social Movement Organizations: The Case of Autonomous Grassroots Groups. *Organization* 21 (6): 759–81.

Teivainen, T. (2016) Occupy Representation and Democratise Prefiguration: Speaking for Others in Global Justice Movements. *Capital & Class* 40(1): 19–36.

Tolbert, P. S. & Hiatt, S. R. (2009) On Organizations and Oligarchies. Michels in the Twenty-First Century. In P. S. Adler (ed.), *The Oxford Handbook of Sociology and Organization Studies: Classical Foundations*. Oxford: Oxford University Press. 174–99.

Tsoukas, H. & Chia, R. (2002) On Organizational Becoming: Rethinking Organizational Change. *Organization Science* 13(5): 567–82.

Yates, L. (2015) Rethinking Prefiguration: Alternatives, Micropolitics and Goals in Social Movements. *Social Movement Studies: Journal of Social, Cultural and Political Protest* 14(1): 1–21.

Zald, M. N. & Ash, R. (1966) Social Movement Organizations: Growth, Decay and Change. *Social Forces* 44(3): 327–41.

15 Alternating between Partial and Complete Organization: The Case of Anonymous

Dennis Schoeneborn and Leonhard Dobusch

The notion of 'partial organization', as introduced by Ahrne and Brunsson (2011), has contributed to organization theory in various significant ways: First, the concept has widened the focus of organizational scholarship to a study of a heterogeneous landscape of rudimentary organizational phenomena – beyond formal and conventional exemplars of organization. Second, by specifying five constitutive elements of 'complete' organization (membership, hierarchies, rules, monitoring, and sanction mechanisms), the notion of partial organization offers a taxonomy that allows for the examination of social formations regarding their degree of 'organizationality' (Dobusch & Schoeneborn, 2015; Schoeneborn, Kuhn & Kärreman, in press). Last but not least, the notion of partial organization provides organizational scholarship with a new programmatic agenda (cf. Ahrne, Brunsson, & Seidl, 2016): Instead of being solely concerned with the study of organizations as a specific empirical phenomenon, the idea here is to see the concept of organization as a theoretical lens through which scholars can study various social formations *as* organization (e.g., social movements, Haug, 2013; terrorist networks, Schoeneborn & Scherer, 2012; or families and intimate relations, Chapter 11).

These merits notwithstanding, in this chapter we develop the argument that the notion of partial organization needs to be further developed: Thus far, the concept has been employed primarily as either (1) an analytical tool to distinguish between decided orders on the one hand, and other forms of order such as networks and institutions on the other (see Chapter 1), or (2) an analytical means of assessing whether certain social formations exhibit characteristics of a decided order, and thus can be seen as either 'complete' or 'partial' organizations. At the same time, the underlying assumption in most of these works seems to be that a state of 'completeness' or 'partialness' would usually be durable. Therefore, recent works call for further research into the dynamics of the way a social formation can reach 'organizationality' to a greater or lesser degree (Dobusch & Schoeneborn, 2015) – that is, by moving from a state of partialness to completeness and vice-versa (cf. Chapters 1 and 2; Ahrne, Brunsson, & Seidl, 2016; Rasche, de Bakker, & Moon, 2013). In response to this call, we argue that a processual and dynamic theory of partial organization is needed that would allow us to understand in greater depth how and the extent to which decided orders are able to add and subtract organizational elements. This, in turn, raises questions of how the various elements of organization are interconnected, what is the 'glue' that holds them together, and how sticky is this glue, anyway?

In what follows, we advance the argument that theoretical perspectives which focus on such communicative events as the key constitutive elements of organization (e.g., Bencherki & Cooren, 2011; Blaschke, Schoeneborn, & Seidl, 2012; McPhee & Zaug, 2009) can serve as a useful explanatory lens for studying the dynamic inter-relations and 'stickiness' of the different organizational elements of decided orders. We illustrate our theoretical considerations by presenting selected results from our empirical investigations of the case of the hacker collective, Anonymous (cf. Dobusch & Schoeneborn, 2015).[1] Our main finding of studying the Anonymous case is that longer periods of 'partialness' alternate with temporary punctuations, during which the social collective accomplishes a 'completion' of its organizationality. In this chapter, we demonstrate how our analysis of this case can inform previous theorizations of partial organization (Ahrne & Brunsson, 2011; Ahrne, Brunsson, & Seidl, 2016; Apelt et al., 2017) and contribute to the development of a processual theory of partial organization.

A COMMUNICATION-CENTRED PERSPECTIVE ON HOW
THE ELEMENTS OF (PARTIAL) ORGANIZATION
INTERRELATE

To tackle the question of how different organizational elements of decided orders interrelate dynamically, we suggest turning to a theoretical stream that has gained increasing attention in organizational scholarship over the past two decades: the *communication as constitutive of organization* (CCO) perspective (Ashcraft, Kuhn, & Cooren, 2009; Brummans *et al.*, 2014; Schoeneborn & Vásquez, 2017; Schoeneborn *et al.*, 2014). This choice is based on two main reasons. First, we argue that the CCO perspective exhibits a natural fit in this context. Similar to Ahrne and Brunsson's notion of partial organization (2011), CCO scholarship is offering a 'low-threshold' theory of what can be an organization (Schoeneborn & Vásquez, 2017). Seen from a CCO viewpoint, rudimentary forms of organization and organizing can emerge spontaneously in various social settings. The organizationality of a social formation is established as soon as communication events occur on behalf of a collective of actors – the organization – and recursively relate to each other in a networked form (cf. Bencherki & Cooren, 2011; Blaschke *et al.*, 2012; Dobusch & Schoeneborn, 2015). In the same context, some works in CCO scholarship (e.g., Schoeneborn, 2011) focus on decisional communication as the specific type of communicative events with the capacity to constitute and form organizations (in the tradition of March & Simon, 1993; or Luhmann, 2018). This theoretical focus, in turn, exhibits compatibilities with Ahrne and Brunsson's (2011) minimum definition of organization as a 'decided order'. Second, the CCO perspective allows us to understand organizations as 'ongoing and precarious accomplishments' that need to be continuously enacted and re-enacted in communication events (Cooren *et al.*, 2011: 1150). Thus, CCO scholarship can provide theories of partial organization with a processual understanding of how the various organizational elements interrelate and jointly constitute organizational phenomena.

In the following, we briefly sketch how this particular interplay is theorized in CCO scholarship.

The Four Flows model by McPhee and Zaug (2009) suggests that four specific processes or 'flows' of communication jointly constitute organization: *membership negotiation* (i.e. interactions that clarify the inclusion and exclusion of individuals and establish an organizational boundary), *self-structuring* (self-reflexive interactions aimed at the design and control of organizational processes), *activity coordination* (interactions in which organizational members or groups dynamically adapt to situational circumstances), and *institutional positioning* (interactions that shape an organization's relationship to its environment, e.g., to customers, suppliers, competitors, or other stakeholders). However, organizations are assumed to emerge only when all four flows co-occur (Browning *et al.*, 2009). As Schoeneborn (2011) has argued, the four flows can ultimately be boiled down to decisional communication in the sense of Luhmann (2018). In that regard, if compared to Ahrne and Brunsson's framework (2011), the model by McPhee and Zaug (2009) represents a different way of specifying and distinguishing the very elements that constitute organization as a decided order. Strikingly, however, McPhee and Zaug (2009) understand all these constitutive elements as flows, and thus as inherently processual in character. For instance, the element of membership is seen here as recurrent processes of negotiation, which individuals are authorized to partake of or not in the organizational endeavour.

Importantly, McPhee and Zaug's Four Flows model (2009) tends to decentralize the role of the individual human actor in constituting the organizational endeavour – which is similar, in this respect, to other CCO approaches, such as Luhmann's (2018) or Taylor & Van Every's (2000). Again, this feature becomes particularly relevant when considering the flow of membership negotiation. What matters for the constitution and perpetuation of organization is not the specific individual member as such, but rather a sequence of communication events that explicitly or implicitly draw a boundary between the inclusion and exclusion of members. Recent works from CCO scholarship propose, along the same line of thinking, to replace the individual-centric category of 'membership' with the activity-centric notion of 'contributorship' (Bencherki & Snack, 2016; see also Chapter 4). In this way, the Four Flows model (McPhee & Zaug, 2009) offers a useful vocabulary for developing further the idea of partial organization towards a processual understanding, because it emphasizes an organization's need to reinstate continuously its very constitutive elements (or 'flows', in their terminology). Yet the question remains *how* organizations actually ensure this continuous co-occurrence of the four flows that constitute their existence.

This question, in turn, can be answered by drawing on Bencherki and Cooren's (2011) theoretical considerations. Their article shares with larger CCO scholarship the assumption that the constitution of organizations proceeds in and through communicative events (defined as distinct incidents of meaning negotiation via talk and/or text that occur in a specific spatio-temporal context; see also Blaschke *et al.*, 2012; Vásquez & Cooren, 2013). The authors argue that various and scattered communicative events are held together in what they call a 'possessive' constitutive relationship. This relationship, in turn, is driven by the interplay of two alternating dynamics: attribution and appropriation. *Attribution* links communication events with 'the organization' as a common reference point or social address. Such attributions typically occur in speech acts, but are independent from whether the author of an attributive claim is a member or non-member of the organization. For instance, attributions can involve speech acts by individuals claiming to have the authority to execute actions on behalf of an organizational actor (e.g., Columbus proclaiming Cuba to be Spanish territory in the name of the Spanish Crown; see the example given by Taylor & Cooren, 1997: 428–9). Alternatively, they can involve speech acts by third parties that ascribe a perceived action to an organizational actor (e.g., news media reports that initially attributed the Madrid bombings in 2004 to the Basque separatist terrorist organization ETA, even if the attacks later turned out to have been executed by single perpetrators sympathizing with jihadism; cf. Corman & Schiefelbein, 2008).

Appropriation, in turn, works in the opposite direction. Over time, through the aggregation of attributions of communication events towards an organizational address, the organizational address begins to develop a life of its own in the sense of 'possessing' the very communication events that constitute its existence in the first place. The dynamic of appropriation requires that a boundary is drawn between what is included in the organizational endeavour and what is not. One empirical example would be an organization that retrospectively claims an action as having been executed on its behalf, such as the (so-called) Islamic State's (IS) retrospective announcement that it was responsible for shooting down Russian Metrojet Flight 9268 over the Sinai peninsula in 2015 in revenge for Russian air strikes in Syria. These extreme examples of organization allow us to highlight the core dynamics of Bencherki and Cooren's model (2011) in a pronounced form. It is valid to assume, however, that such attribution-appropriation dynamics also occur continuously in more conventional organizational settings (e.g., business firms or state bureaucracies), where they do not depend on spectacular communicative events, but are stabilized through contractual relations, for example. In turn, the possessive capacity of organizations increases the likelihood that new and consecutive communication events are executed and are attributed to the organizational address. In this regard, Bencherki and Cooren's (2011) conceptualizations imply a self-reinforcing cycle (cf. Sydow, Schreyögg, & Koch, 2009) of an attributive movement from communicative events and actions *towards* the organizational address and, *au retour*, an appropriating movement from the organizational address towards communicative events (cf. Figure 1). Whereas Bencherki and Cooren (2011) decsribe with their model the communicative constitution of organizations more generally, we believe that the model can be particularly useful in explaining the interconnection among the various organizational elements of decided orders (Ahrne, Brunsson, & Seidl, 2016), as we elaborate in a next step.

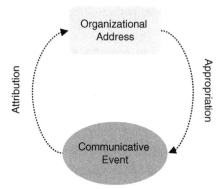

FIGURE 1: Attribution–appropriation dynamics in the communicative constitution of organization (our own visualization, based on Bencherki & Cooren, 2011)

EMPIRICAL ILLUSTRATION: THE CASE OF ANONYMOUS

In the following, we illustrate our theoretical considerations by drawing on selected insights from our larger empirical research project on the 'hacktivist' (i.e., hacker and activist) collective, Anonymous (see Dobusch and Schoeneborn, 2015, for a more detailed description of the study's findings). Anonymous is an organized group of hackers where 'members' conceal their personal identity from both external observers and other self-declared members. Various such groups that attribute their actions to Anonymous as a social address engage in collective actions of a political and non-political nature, such as taking down or infiltrating websites or participating in street protests. Anonymous is part of a larger community of online activists propagating free software, access to knowledge, and Internet freedom more generally (cf. Coleman, 2013).

In this chapter, we argue that Anonymous can be seen as a form of 'decided order', in the sense that Ahrne and Brunsson (2011) use the term, as hackers engage in interconnected, collaborative episodes of organizing and decision making on behalf of Anonymous as a collective entity. Each hacker operation (e.g., a distributed denial of service attack in order to temporarily shut down a website) comprises a number of interconnected events of 'decisional communication' (in the sense of Luhmann, 2019; or Seidl, 2005). Via pertinent online communication channels (e.g., Twitter and Facebook accounts or such collaborative web-authoring tools as etherpads), hackers coordinate themselves and reach such collective decisions as who to attack, when to attack their target, and how to attack it. Although each hacker operation comprises a series of collectively made decisions, the question remains whether these dispersed episodes are ever cross-connected, thus collectively forming a 'decided order' in the sense of a larger organizational endeavour (cf. the question of 'scaling up' from local interactions to organizational entities or actors, as discussed by Blaschke *et al.*, 2012; Cooren & Fairhurst, 2009). We argue that such cross-connectivity among hacker operations is at least ensured by sharing the same signifier – Anonymous – as a joint organizational address and reference point. Another indication that the various operations form a joint organizational endeavour is that we can empirically observe efforts of boundary maintenance in this case – that is, debates among hackers over which hacker operation should be seen as part of Anonymous and which should not (cf. Dobusch & Schoeneborn, 2015).

In this sense, while Anonymous can be seen as a decided order, we argue that it should also be considered as partial organization, especially in that it lacks decision making on formal membership or on formal, written rules. In the Anonymous case, anyone can simply contribute to the organizational endeavour by announcing and executing hacker operations on its behalf – and without subscribing to any formal rules or attaining individual membership status beforehand. Rather, membership is performatively accomplished by self-attributing one's communicative actions to Anonymous, in conjunction with third-party observers abstaining from challenging or even corroborating these attributions. These features allow Anonymous to operate in a decentralized, fluid, and flexible way (cf. Coleman, 2014), while rendering Anonymous' identity and boundary highly precarious: If anyone can speak on behalf of Anonymous, who *cannot* speak on behalf of Anonymous, after all?

To tackle this puzzle, in our research project on the Anonymous case, we have studied in detail especially those hacker operations that had given rise to extensive public contestations and negotiations on whether these operations were executed on behalf of Anonymous as an organizational actor. In the context of our theoretical considerations, one of those contested episodes – the so-called *OpFacebook* hacker operation – is particularly relevant (cf. Dobusch & Schoeneborn, 2015). In August 2011, a group claiming to be part of Anonymous declared war on Facebook, announcing via a newly established Twitter account called @OpFacebook that an upcoming takedown of the social media networking site would occur on 5 November 2011. The announcement had been prepared collaboratively through PiratePad, a public online tool for anonymous collaborative writing. The announcement triggered debates and caused confusion among external observers (e.g., among news media and online bloggers), especially with regard to the authenticity of the planned hacker operation and its links to Anonymous. Assessments ranged from doubtful statements (e.g., in a news post on CNet.com: 'Is Anonymous unanimous on Facebook plot?') to confirmatory statements (e.g., by PCMag.com: 'If a few people get together in the name of Anonymous and decide to hack Facebook on November 5, Anonymous is behind the planned Facebook hack'). In turn, other groups, attributing their communicative acts to Anonymous, initially renounced the authenticity of Operation Facebook via a post on the pertinent Twitter account, *AnonOps*: 'TO PRESS: [...] #OpFacebook is just ANOTHER FAKE'. Some backpedalling on the same channel followed this message: '#OpFacebook is being organised by some Anons. This does not necessarily mean that all of #Anonymous agrees with it.' So for several weeks, both outside observers and self-declared members of Anonymous were uncertain if the communicative acts of the OpFacebook operations could be rightfully attributed to Anonymous as an organizational actor.

This public debate was ultimately settled with a publicly staged performance. On 4 November 2011 – just one day before the planned attack on Facebook – the individual identity of the alleged originator of OpFacebook was exposed publicly in yet another open letter, published again via the Twitter account, @AnonOps:

> One skiddy queer chap named Anthony [last name redacted] from the USA in Ohio decided to take it upon himself to have some lulz with creating an imaginary opfacebook and pawning it off as a legit anon op. Despite us telling this mate several times we did not support his op, he continued to push his agenda for lulz. This op is phony but he continues to say it's an anon op.

This announcement declared the end of Operation Facebook as an 'official' Anonymous operation. The hackers that used the AnonOps account evidently accomplished this form of closure by relatively harsh sanctioning mechanisms, in that they revealed the hacker Anthony's full name and personal contact information. With this public sanctioning, they managed to indicate retrospectively a clear (hierarchical) distinction between those 'members' who have the authority to establish such a sanction mechanism and a 'non-member', who is excluded by being de-anonymized. More specifically, the hacker pseudonyms used to announce and organize OpFacebook were delegitimized by revealing the individual identity behind them, and their respective communicative acts were thereby retroactively disattributed from Anonymous.

In hacker jargon, this practice is also known as 'doxing': compiling documents and personal information that allow for the exposing of another hacker's identity (cf. Coleman, 2014: 418). In the OpFacebook episode, the practice of doxing served as an effective means of proving that those hackers who revealed the other hacker's actual identity were more skilful, and thus need to be seen as the 'real' (members of) Anonymous. This is also shown by the fact that after the public exposure of the hacker named Anthony, the debates about the connection between the OpFacebook episode and Anonymous were finally settled and did not continue.

TOWARD A PROCESSUAL UNDERSTANDING OF PARTIAL ORGANIZATION

In this final section, we re-describe the Anonymous case and the OpFacebook episode by drawing on the theoretical terminology we have introduced earlier. We believe that the Anonymous case is particularly useful as a basis for advancing the notion of partial organization toward a processual and event-based understanding: On the one hand, in principle, Anonymous leaves the boundary open on who can partake in and contribute to the organizing activities, and thus can be seen as partial organization, at minimum in the membership dimension. On the other hand, the OpFacebook episode and Anthony's public exposure and exclusion shows that Anonymous seems to have the capacity to add certain organizational elements at least situationally, thus leading to a temporary 'completion' of an otherwise partial organization. In other words, at least for the duration of the event, the social collective, Anonymous, acts as if it were a full-fledged organization. In that sense, certain social collectives such as Anonymous demonstrate the ability to alternate between a continuous state of 'partialness' on the one hand and a situationally mobilized state of 'completeness' on the other hand. Importantly, this completeness is accomplished only through a certain communicative event, as the OpFacebook episode illustrates.

Going beyond our initial study on the Anonymous case (Dobusch & Schoeneborn, 2015), we interpret the staged performance of the doxing practice in the OpFacebook episode as a communicative event wherein all five organizational elements fall into place – in a 'cascade' or 'domino' effect. More specifically, through the performative act of (1) *sanctioning* one individual hacker (i.e., publicly naming and shaming the initiator of OpFacebook), hackers operating in the name of Anonymous convincingly demonstrated the collective's ability to (2) *monitor* its contributors (given that it was the precondition for the sanctioning in the first place). Furthermore, (3) the practice of sanctioning involved the showcasing of implicit *rules* about appropriate acts on behalf of Anonymous (at least in the sense of a case-by-case precedence), (4) the showcasing of *hierarchies* (i.e., in the sense that some hackers evidently are skilled enough to 'hack other hackers'), and (5) the showcasing of a *membership* category (i.e., at least in the sense of a distinction between inclusion and exclusion). In other words, through the communicative event of doxing an individual hacker, Anonymous publicly 'celebrated' a decision that convincingly demonstrated the social collective's ability to mobilize all five elements of complete organization, at least situationally.

Coming back to our initial question about the glue that holds the five organizational elements together, in the Anonymous case it seems that this stickiness is accomplished through a temporal simultaneity and a choreographed and staged performance in a particular communicative event. In the OpFacebook episode, it is the public exposure of one individual hacker that brings all five elements to the fore simultaneously, even if those elements were mobilized only in preparation for the staged performance and do not necessarily represent durable capabilities of the social collective. In that sense, we argue that theories of the performativity of speech acts (cf. Gond *et al.*, 2016) can provide the theory of partial organization with an event-based explanation of how the five elements of organization can be set into interrelation (in line with larger considerations on a communicative constitution of partial organization; see Dobusch & Schoeneborn, 2015; Schoeneborn & Scherer, 2012). Declarative speech acts such as public sanctioning or excommunication, for instance (cf. Cooren, 2004: 386), allow for showcasing organizationality by performing various organizational elements and capabilities simultaneously.

We further believe that the dynamics between the various organizational elements of partial and complete organization (Ahrne & Brunsson, 2011) can be better understood by drawing on the idea that the communicative constitution of organizations occurs through alternating dynamics of attribution and appropriation (see Bencherki & Cooren, 2011). In the OpFacebook episode, we can perceive public debates in which organizing activities (e.g., the planned takedown of

Facebook) rather than individual actors get attributed to Anonymous as organizational address. Yet the fluid and partial character of the organizational endeavour can be overburdened by too many of such attributions, in that these contributions create ambiguities about which activities count as part of Anonymous and which do not. In the OpFacebook episode, such attributions led, at some point, to the opposite movement of disappropriation (e.g., the public exposure and exclusion of an individual actor to disappropriate the activities initiated by this actor). Strikingly, however, this disappropriation focused primarily on the membership dimension, through re-attributing the hacker practices that were initially undertaken on behalf of Anonymous to yet another type of social address: the individual hacker who was exposed and excluded.

In summary, the idea of a communicative constitution of (partial and complete) organization, and especially the idea of attribution/appropriation dynamics, allows us to understand the interplay of the elements of partial organization as alternations between moments of being partial and fluid (that allows for multiple and polyphonic attributions) on the one hand; and occasional moments of being complete (in which a movement of disappropriation settles the polyphony and reinstates a boundary) on the other hand.

Taken together, our chapter contributes to theories of partial organization in two main ways: First, we directly respond to earlier calls for a processual view on partial organization (see Ahrne, Brunsson, & Seidl, 2016; Rasche, de Bakker, & Moon, 2013; Rasche & Seidl, Chapter 2). More specifically, by applying a communication-centred understanding to the phenomenon of organization (e.g., Ashcraft, Kuhn, & Cooren, 2009; Bencherki & Cooren, 2011; McPhee & Zaug, 2009), we add to the further development of theories of partial organization by demonstrating that the elements of organization are not given, but need to be instantiated again and again in processual form through visible organizational practices attributed to an organizational address. In the same context, we present the argument that certain organizational phenomena (such as Anonymous) appear to be able to alternate between a state of partialness and completeness in back-and-forth movements.

For future research on partial organizational phenomena, this perspective implies focusing empirical research specifically on speech acts that establish such attributive or (dis)appropriating links to and from an organizational address (see Bencherki & Cooren, 2011). Furthermore, with our study of the Anonymous case, we believe that we have identified a pattern of alternations between a continuous partial character and situational completion that is likely to apply to a particular sub-species of partial organization as well: those that remain partial in the membership dimension (e.g., other social movement-like organizations, such as Wikipedia: Puranam, Alexy, & Reitzig, 2014; or al Qaeda: Comas, Shrivastava, & Martin, 2015). Further research is needed to validate whether this identified process pattern can be traced in this form for other exemplars of this sub-type.

REFERENCES

Ahrne, G. & Brunsson, N. (2011) Organization outside Organizations: The Significance of Partial Organization. *Organization* 18: 83–104.

Ahrne, G., Brunsson, N., & Seidl, D. (2016) Resurrecting Organization by Going beyond Organizations. *European Management Journal* 34(2): 93–101.

Apelt, M., Besio, C., Corsi, G., von Groddeck, V., Grothe-Hammer, M., & Tacke, V. (2017) Resurrecting Organization without Renouncing Society: A Response to Ahrne, Brunsson and Seidl. *European Management Journal* 35(1): 8–14.

Ashcraft, K. L., Kuhn, T. R., & Cooren, F. (2009) Constitutional Amendments: 'Materializing' Organizational Communication. *Academy of Management Annals* 3: 1–64.

Bencherki, N. & Cooren, F. (2011) Having to Be: The Possessive Constitution of Organization. *Human Relations* 64: 1579–607.

Bencherki, N. & Snack, J. P. (2016) Contributorship and Partial Inclusion: A Communicative Perspective. *Management Communication Quarterly* 30 (3): 279–304.

Blaschke, S., Schoeneborn, D., & Seidl, D. (2012) Organizations as Networks of Communication Episodes: Turning the Network Perspective Inside Out. *Organization Studies* 33(7): 879–906.

Browning, L. D., Greene, R.W., Sitkin, S. B., Sutcliffe, K.M., & Obstfeld, D. (2009) Constitutive Complexity. In L. L. Putnam & A. M. Nicotera (eds.), *Building*

Theories of Organization: The Constitutive Role of Communication. New York: Routledge. 89–116.

Brummans, B., Cooren, F., Robichaud, D., & Taylor, J. R. (2014) Approaches in Research on the Communicative Constitution of Organizations. In L. L. Putnam & D. Mumby (eds.), *SAGE Handbook of Organizational Communication.* 3rd edition. Thousand Oaks: SAGE. 173–94.

Coleman, G. (2013) *Coding Freedom: The Ethics and Aesthetics of Hacking.* Princeton: Princeton University Press.

Coleman, G. (2014) *Hacker, Hoaxer, Whistleblower, Spy: The Many Faces of Anonymous.* New York: Verso.

Comas, J., Shrivastava, P., & Martin, E. C. (2015) Terrorism as Formal Organization, Network, and Social Movement. *Journal of Management Inquiry* 24(1): 47–60.

Cooren, F. (2004) Textual Agency: How Texts Do Things in Organizational Settings. *Organization* 11(3): 373–93.

Cooren, F. & Fairhurst, G. T. (2009) Dislocation and Stabilization: How to Scale up From Interactions to Organization. In L. L. Putnam & A. M. Nicotera (eds.), *Building Theories of Organization: The Constitutive Role of Communication.* New York: Routledge. 117–52.

Cooren, F., Kuhn, T., Cornelissen, J. P., & Clark, T. (2011) Communication, Organizing and Organization: An Overview and Introduction to the Special Issue. *Organization Studies* 32(9): 1149–70.

Corman, S. R. & Schiefelbein, J. S. (2008) Communication and Media Strategy in the Islamist War of Ideas. In S. R. Corman, A. Threthewey, & H. R. Goodall Jr. (eds.), *Weapons of Mass Persuasion: Strategic Communication to Combat Violent Terrorism.* New York: Lang. 69–96.

Dobusch, L. & Schoeneborn, D. (2015) Fluidity, Identity, and Organizationality: The Communicative Constitution of Anonymous. *Journal of Management Studies* 52(8): 1005–35.

Gond, J. P., Cabantous, L., Harding, N., & Learmonth, M. (2016) What Do We Mean by Performativity in Organizational and Management Theory? The Uses and Abuses of Performativity. *International Journal of Management Reviews* 18(4): 440–63.

Haug, C. (2013) Organizing Spaces: Meeting Arenas as a Social Movement Infrastructure between Organization, Network, and Institution. *Organization Studies* 34(5–6): 705–32.

Luhmann, N. (2018) *Organization and Decision.* Cambridge: Cambridge University Press.

McPhee, R. D. & Zaug, P. (2009) The Communicative Constitution of Organizations: A Framework for Explanation. In L. L. Putnam & A. M. Nicotera (eds.), *Building*

Theories of Organization: The Constitutive Role of Communication. New York: Routledge. 21–47.

Puranam, P., Alexy, O., & Reitzig, M. (2014) What's 'New' about New Forms of Organizing? *Academy of Management Review* 39(2): 162–80.

Rasche, A., De Bakker, F. G., & Moon, J. (2013) Complete and Partial Organizing for Corporate Social Responsibility. *Journal of Business Ethics* 115(4): 651–63.

Schoeneborn, D. (2011) Organization as Communication: A Luhmannian Perspective. *Management Communication Quarterly* 25(4): 663–89.

Schoeneborn, D., Blaschke, S., Cooren, F., McPhee, R. D., Seidl, D., & Taylor, J. R. (2014) The Three Schools of CCO Thinking: Interactive Dialogue and Systematic Comparison. *Management Communication Quarterly* 28(2): 285–316.

Schoeneborn, D., Kuhn, T. R., & Kärreman, D. (in press). The communicative constitution of organization, organizing, and organizationality. Organization Studies.

Schoeneborn, D. & Scherer, A. G. (2012) Clandestine Organizations, al Qaeda, and the Paradox of (In)visibility: A Response to Stohl and Stohl. *Organization Studies* 33(7): 963–71.

Schoeneborn, D. & Vásquez, C. (2017) Communicative Constitution of Organizations. In C. R. Scott , L. Lewis, J.R. Barker, J. Keyton, T. Kuhn & P.K. Turner (eds.), *International Encyclopedia of Organizational Communication.* Hoboken: Wiley. 367–86.

Seidl, D. (2005) Organization and Interaction. In D. Seidl & K. H. Becker (eds.), *Niklas Luhmann and Organization Studies.* Copenhagen: Copenhagen Business School Press. 145–70.

Sydow, J., Schreyögg, G., & Koch, J. (2009) Organizational Path Dependence: Opening the Black Box. *Academy of Management Review* 34(4): 689–709.

Taylor, J. R. & Cooren, F. (1997) What Makes Communication 'Organizational'? How the Many Voices of a Collectivity Become the One Voice of an Organization. *Journal of Pragmatics* 27: 409–38.

Taylor, J. R. & Van Every, E. (2000) *The Emergent Organization: Communication as Its Site and Surface.* Mahwah: Erlbaum.

Vásquez, C. & Cooren, F. (2013) Spacing Practices: The Communicative Configuration of Organizing through Space-Times. *Communication Theory* 23: 25–47.

NOTE

1. In this chapter, we draw on data excerpts from a larger empirical study on the Anonymous case (published as Dobusch & Schoeneborn, 2015) and discuss its implications for theories of partial organization.

16 Collective Action through Social Media: Possibilities and Challenges of Partial Organizing

Noomi Weinryb, Cecilia Gullberg, and Jaakko Turunen

On 31 August 2015, a group of fifteen Swedish friends opened a new Facebook page called *Vi gör vad vi kan* ('We do what we can'). Its message[1] was open to anyone who read it, and tens of thousands of people responded:

> We collect clothes, toiletries and other items for refugees who arrive to the Greek island of Lesbos. On 17 September our first truckload will be sent – and a few of us will travel there to help out, human to human, to distribute the supplies that you and others have contributed. What you can do:
>
> Donate money
>
> All the money we collect will be used for transportation and to buy items that are better to buy on location, such as food, water, and baby formula. The easiest way is to *swisha* [bank transfer through mobile phone] what you want to contribute to [mobile phone number]. It is also possible to give directly to a bank account [personal bank account number].
>
> Donate supplies
>
> What can you do without? People on the run need clothes, shoes, caps, diapers and baby clothes, toys, hygiene articles. NOTE! The items sent have to be in good condition, and clean and dry to avoid the risk of rot during transport.

This chapter tells the story of how, in just over a week, a small group of activists could raise SEK 9 million (approx. EUR 900,000) via Facebook – money that was deposited into a private bank account – and how they met the ensuing challenges involved in allocating the funds and packing and distributing the tonnes of clothes and other items collected.

The advent of social media has radically changed the possibilities for individuals to organize on a mass scale (Bennett & Segerberg, 2012; Bennett & Segerberg, 2013; Gerbaudo, 2016). Yet social media also creates a number of challenges for communicating and legitimating organizational decisions. Of central importance is the openness of Web 2.0, the decided order that constitutes an organization (Ahrne & Brunsson, 2011; Macnamara & Zerfass, 2012; Luhmann, 2013), and the power structure introduced by technology (Treem & Leonardi, 2013; Kaun & Uldam, 2017).

In this chapter, we explore how the notion of partial organizing can develop our understanding of mass action coordinated through social media, and how the technology of social media affords a specific type of partialness. More specifically, we explore the organizational consequences of the technological affordances of the social media platform and how they enable power segmentation (Kaun & Uldam, 2017) – albeit not necessarily a legitimate hierarchical authority (Weber, 1947; Weber, 1978) – to those who hold the administrative reins of communication. This, in turn, creates challenges for auditability and accountability (Power, 1997; Jang, 2005). Our study indicates that tensions between a perceived possibility of interactivity and power exertion that is not perceived as legitimate can be exacerbated when large-scale collective action is coordinated primarily thorough social media.

This chapter reports on a qualitative case study of 'We do what we can', hereafter referred to as *We Do*. The study spans the period from 31 August 2015 to 21 September 2016, covering the emergence and development of *We Do* for just over a year. The main part of our qualitative data set comprises 350 pages (yet with some overlapping, due to technical constraints) in PDF format of detailed conversations among activists and founders on the official Facebook page of *We Do*, conversations visible to all participants. In addition, we have studied the homepage of *We Do*. The Facebook-based data is a form of qualitative web archiving (Brügger, 2011; Lomborg, 2012) that captures the chronological development of the page. Conversations on the Facebook page of *We Do* include multiple participants, and interaction builds on not only the initial message, but also subsequent reactions. Our qualitative approach centres on the meaning of this content creation and interaction. Because all Facebook quotes used in this chapter are undated and are anonymized and translated from Swedish to English by the authors, the commentators cannot be traced by a direct online search. Our analysis is focused on organizing, rather than any specifics related to any individual activist.

Now, using broad strokes, we chronicle the story of *We Do*. Then we focus our analysis on the partial organizing activities that constituted the initiative, and draw out the specificities that organizing through the platform of Facebook may entail.

THE STORY OF WE DO

In 2015, the European Union received an unprecedented number of refugees when the number of first-time asylum applications reached over 1.2 million (Eurostat 44/2016, 2016). During the summer and autumn of 2015, most of the refugees arrived on the Greek islands, having ventured over the sea from Turkey (UNCHR, 2015). On 2 September, a three-year-old boy named Alan Kurdi drowned and was washed ashore in Turkey, rendering a visual image to the suffering of the migrants. The image circulated widely in the media. *We Do* emerged to give a voice to frustrated Swedes who wanted to engage in an action that would help the refugees.

The story of *We Do* begins when one of the founders visited Lesbos on holiday in July 2015 and ended up volunteering to help refugees on the island. She raised SEK 35,000 (approx. EUR 3,500) among her friends and relatives, and with this money she rented a bus and brought food and water to the incoming refugees. Swedish media began to write about the initiative. In August 2015, this founder gathered fourteen other women, friends, and friends of friends, and launched an initiative 'to do something, anything, to avoid having to feel so powerless' in relation to the tragedy of the refugees on the Mediterranean shores. This core group consisted of lay people who were not experienced in professional aid and healthcare work. In fact, at the time of our study, most of the founders worked in the fields of culture and public communication.

We Do was launched on 1 September 2015. The group opened a page on Facebook, created a homepage, and gained wide exposure in the media. A private person's bank account was used as the deposit site for meeting the goal of raising SEK 500,000 (approx. EUR 50,000).

On 1 September 2015, SEK 10,000 (approx. EUR 1,000) was raised. On 2 September, the image of the drowned boy Alan Kurdi began to circulate in traditional and social media. Even though *We Do* did not use the picture directly, many others did, and in a mass attempt to somehow alleviate the pain that is evoked by the drowned boy, many individuals began to refer to the hashtag #*Vi gör vad vi kan*. By the end of the second day of *We Do*, there was SEK 831,485 (approx. EUR 83,150) in the bank account. On 3 September, the amount grew to SEK 5 million (approx. EUR 500,000), and on 4 September to SEK 6.3 million (approx. EUR 630,000). During these early days, the founders received a great deal of attention from television, radio, and print media. By 9 September, the amount raised had reached SEK 9 million (approx. EUR 900,000).

But *We Do* did not only want to raise funds; the goal was also to gather a variety of items for refugees. Between 10 and 14 September, clothes, shoes, and toiletries, corresponding to 5,204 moving boxes or 14 truckloads, were gathered in Stockholm. Many local volunteers joined together, sorting and packing the goods at theatres and at the Stockholm Half Marathon. Furthermore, companies began to sponsor the effort with food and transport. On 17 September, the first group from *We Do* left for Lesbos; it comprised the founders plus such volunteering professionals as medics, security staff, humanitarian workers, and interpreters. Upon arrival on Lesbos, *We Do* used some of the funds to rent buses and help refugees move across the island. The search for partner organizations on Lesbos resulted in collaboration with *Médecins du Monde* (Doctors of the World).

Back in Sweden, October 2015 began with a gathering of local Swedish volunteers sorting, packing, and sealing the 2,500 boxes of clothes collected in September. This effort took place in a borrowed warehouse in the city of Enköping, located an hour from Stockholm, and was framed as a grand event. On 5 October, an airline sponsored a plane with 2.5 tonnes of supplies, and a new team of volunteers was sent to Lesbos. Two days later, the first truck, carrying 7 tonnes of supplies, arrived on Lesbos; a company had sponsored both the truck and the driver. There were more donated items in the warehouse in Enköping than could be received and accommodated on Lesbos, however. So on 21 October, collaboration was initiated with the aid organization Hiwa, which was working with refugees in a permanent refugee camp in Iraqi Kurdistan, where *We Do* was sending a truckload of clothes and other necessities.

The next episode on Lesbos was of a smaller scale than the first one had been. At the end of October 2015, *We Do* sent a volunteer nurse and physician to Lesbos. On 7 November, a final sorting session took place in Enköping. The day after, a truckload of winter clothes was sent to Lesbos, and ten days later one more truck was sent. At this point, 4,000 boxes of donated items had been sent to the island. On 19 November, a new collaboration was announced: *We Do* would start funding Clowns Without Borders to work in the refugee camps on Lesbos. Three days later, another cooperation with an established organization was announced – this time the International Rescue Committee (IRC) – to work with the distribution of clothes and other supplies that had been sent to the island. There was still a plethora of donated items in Sweden that were not suitable to be sent to Lesbos in the wintertime: summer clothes and light shoes, for example. On 27 November, *We Do* announced that items that were not 'suitable for people on the run' would be donated to Human Bridge, a humanitarian organization that specializes in medical supplies. The donated items were to be sold and the surplus to be given to those in need. In December, an additional collaboration was announced with Starfish – a local Lesbos initiative whose mandate was to help refugees on the island. Another truckload of supplies was also sent to Hiwa in Iraqi Kurdistan. In mid-December, *We Do* proudly announced that 7,457 boxes – a pile higher than the highest Swedish mountain, Kebnekaise – had reached those in need.

We Do ended 2015 by transforming itself into a registered fundraising foundation,[2] placing it under the control of the County Administrative Board. This organizational format permits the collection of funds, but allows only those persons forming the board of the foundation to be considered members in the partial-organization sense of the word. In addition, the scope of the activities of the new organization is significantly wider than the call that was quoted at the outset of this chapter. The following notice was published on the *We Do* Facebook page on 22 December 2015:

> The Fundraising Foundation's purpose is to provide support and assistance to people in need who are, or have been, on the run from war-torn areas, natural disasters or other circumstances that caused the flight. The Foundation can also work so that these people integrate into the society where they arrive, that the people can return to the place they fled from or maintain contact with friends and relatives who remain there.

In January 2016, *We Do* decided to fund two more organizations helping refugees on Lesbos: Pikpa and Lighthouse Relief. It also helped another initiative – Refugee Council at the Border – to send a truckload of supplies to Lesbos.

At the end of January 2016, *We Do* began to engage in refugee aid within Sweden, and in February 2016 it collected and distributed warm winter clothing to asylum seekers there. The distribution of clothes was again accomplished in cooperation with Human Bridge. A new campaign was launched to collect money for winter clothes, but only SEK 8,500 (approx. EUR 850) was raised – enough to buy an additional forty-five jackets.

On 20 March 2016, the EU concluded an agreement with Turkey that would prevent refugees from crossing over to the Greek islands.

In April 2016, refugees began to be deported from Lesbos to Turkey, and Pikpa, a partner organization in Lesbos, was threatened with closure. As the political context changed in Europe, the activities of *We Do* moved to the Greek mainland. At the end of April 2016, the collaboration with Doctors of the World Greece resulted in *We Do* funding a mobile medical clinic with the name of *We Do* printed on it.

In the summer of 2016, additional funding was donated to buy 4,100 pairs of flip-flops and slippers for refugees on Lesbos, and water coolers for camps on the island. At that point, *We Do* was funding food and water in eleven refugee camps in other parts of Greece, distributed with the help of a local volunteer who was also a refugee. Selected as one of four Swedish initiatives, *We Do* participated in the UN Summit for Refugees and Migrants in New York in September 2016. At the time of writing, there is still activity on the *We Do* Facebook page, but it is the data generated through September 2016 that we have analysed.

THE PARTIAL ORGANIZING OF WE DO

Focusing on Facebook interactions, we now embark on an analysis of *We Do*, discussing how different organizational elements interplay in its creation as a Facebook initiative and its eventual development into a fundraising foundation. We begin by analysing the lack of membership and hierarchy and move on to a discussion of the issues of rules, monitoring, and sanctions.

Who are we, and what is our role?

Although fifteen friends – the *core* – initiated *We Do*, it began as an open, inclusive, and seemingly egalitarian initiative. The message posted on Facebook was broad, and anyone who wanted to contribute was welcome to join. *We Do* made no specific decision on membership. As the name stipulates, we can all make a difference together, as long as 'we do what we can'. The initial message, combined with the name of the initiative, indicates that there was no apparent hierarchy in place; there were no decisions on who was in charge, everyone was entitled to identify with, help, realize, and perhaps also participate in developing, the budding initiative. In its first days, the core of *We Do* began to distinguish between its role and that of the online activists, by articulating the difference between 'we' and 'you': '*We* are shocked. A SHOCK OF HAPPINESS. At the moment *you* have helped *us* to collect an unbelievable SEK 3,621,000 (approx. EUR 362,100) for refugees on Lesbos!' (Emphasis added.) This we–you distinction is significant, because it indicates how the idea of *We Do* as an inclusive and egalitarian initiative was challenged from the beginning.

The same division between those who organized the initiative and those who donated money could be seen during the next few days, just that the sum had skyrocketed: 'While you slept, the money gathered is up to 6,327,436 crowns [approx. EUR 632,744]! It rarely feels more justified than now to say GOOD MORNING!' 'Fantastic you – you have now collected 9,016,707 crowns [approx. EUR 901,671] for refugees on Lesbos!'

These posts help us to understand that the division of labour was clear to the core members: *We* collect money; *you* donate and sleep. The posts received happy replies from the activists, typically cheering the core and the fact that the fundraising had advanced so well. A typical comment was: 'You are fantastic!'

In the early days of the initiative, *We Do* served as an enabler for the individual who made comments like 'Thanks for giving me the opportunity to do something.' Comments such as 'Makes me so happy' and 'Thank you for letting me help' celebrated the joint achievements. These comments were often followed by more general jubilations about compassion: 'There is hope for compassion.' Or more obvious collective praise was used, such as 'Well done Sweden; this gives hope for humankind.'

In the egalitarian invitation to *We Do*, anyone is welcome, as long as they are willing to do what they can. *We Do* is understood to be acting vicariously for those who want to engage. Together, the activists and the core work to spread 'the good', and in this way to counteract 'the evil' in this world. As the ingenious name says: by engaging in

We Do, they are doing what they can, becoming a part of the fluid 'we'. This is the virtue and benefit of the initiative according to many activists. They may not all be able to travel to Greece and help those in need directly, but by being included in this floating 'we', they are gratified by the possibility of altruistic engagement. Yet the core continued to distinguish between 'we' and 'you'.

The fuzzy membership status of the activists is relevant for the way in which they relate to and participate in *We Do*. Activists appear to understand themselves either as members of an organization, accepting its authority, being in a sense the 'you' in relation to the power that seems to be situated in the core, or they describe themselves as a part of a wider 'we' that spans the activists and core alike. In their usage of this broad sense of 'we', each activist feels entitled and empowered to be not merely a member, but a spokesperson and potential leader of the initiative.

The distinction between 'we' and 'you' reflects a segmentation of roles, and implicitly of power, yet it was initially seen by activists as benevolent, as it constituted an opportunity for them to do good. Some commentators questioned the clear differentiation between the core and the activists, however, attempting to blur the we–you distinction. Initially, this was not done as a form of criticism in the face of power segmentation, but rather in line with the inclusiveness of the initial message. The initiative is larger than the core and the activists; it spans 'us all', but it is not about portraying the activists as being in servitude to the core. Soon after the core started distinguishing itself from the activists, the following reply was addressed to the core: 'You are fantastic! You and the Swedish people, that is!!!' There was also an explicit coupling of Facebook activists and the core, pointing to inclusiveness, egalitarianism, and shared experience as the centre of the interactive initiative: 'You make/we make a difference.'

Power of technology rather than legitimate authority

Despite expressions of egalitarianism, from the outset there has been not only a verbal, but also a technical power asymmetry in *We Do*. As

initiators, the core incorporates administrative rights on its homepage, on its Facebook page, and on its image-based Instagram account.
This means that the core can use the collective voice of *We Do* when
communicating with and to Facebook activists. Meanwhile, activists
communicate with their personal Facebook accounts using real or
false names, but in both cases representing individual voices in their
comments. In contrast, the core primarily communicates with activists through its official name – *We Do* – and rarely reverts to the
personal name of the commentator. The activists can go to the homepage of *We Do*, see who the core founders are, and read interviews with
some of the founders in mainstream media; but it remains largely
unclear who actually sits behind the screen and communicates with
the activists. *We Do* frequently uses the expression 'we promise',
signalling that the people behind its name are in charge. But the
difference between activists interacting in an egalitarian manner
with personal Facebook accounts and the impersonal communication
of the core under the name *We Do* exacerbates the power segmentation of the initiative, essentially pointing to a covert, and not necessarily legitimate, power centre. On two levels, then, there is
opaqueness: Who is in charge? And who are 'we'? As to the first
question, the power segmentation between the core and the activists
is unclear, and is not constituted by any decisions. And as for
the second question, the covert communication of the core enhances
the power asymmetry between the individual activists and the seemingly impersonal core.

By controlling the constituting communicative tools of *We Do*,
the core can thus exercise power over the organizing efforts. This does
not necessarily equal legitimate authority, however. It is not legiti-
mated by a decision (hierarchy); nor is it based on claims of expertise or
the like. Instead, it is a consequence afforded by the technical properties of the platform; technology renders the core a power base, which is
sometimes overt and sometimes obscured. Although the power asymmetry is initially interpreted by activists as benign, enabling
a vicarious altruism, it soon becomes clear that the power afforded

to the core by the technical platform also entails repressive elements: As administrators, the core can exclude posts and people from communicating; yet it is not clear to the activists which posts have been deleted and which activists have been blocked. The obscured power centre of the core thus blurs the not necessarily legitimate, albeit existing, power structure of the initiative. The power rendered to the core by the platform enables the core to create a sense of blending with and simultaneously distinguishing themselves from the activists on Facebook. This is why the blurred notions of 'we' and 'you' become central components of *We Do*.

The very distinctiveness of the *We Do* initiative – to gather such a large amount of funds and goods in a short time – was dependent on the activists' mass engagement. It is especially in this situation that the core is to act vicariously on behalf of the activists, ensuring that the donations are distributed to those in need and that the funds are well spent. Yet, it is also with regard to the forms of activism that are sanctioned by the core that the power segmentation becomes most overt. There are, for example, more and less attractive ways to participate. The predominant type of engagement in *We Do* relates to donations of money or goods. This concerns by far the largest group of activists, but at least at the time of the study, many of the activists wanted to travel to Lesbos as well; they wanted to make a difference in a more tangible manner by meeting the refugees as they arrived in Europe. They wanted to be part of the 'we' group. The core explicitly stated, however, that only a small number of select professionals were eligible to volunteer for *We Do* in Lesbos. Although able to implement this decision, the core was repeatedly nudged by the activists to expand its volunteering offers beyond Sweden.

In responding to activist demands to volunteer in Greece, the core justified its restrictive decision by arguing a lack of expertise. According to the core, *We Do* – with its self-described group of lay people – lacked the expertise to guarantee the safety of lay volunteers sent to Greece. This was not the first time that *We Do* has referred to its lack of expertise and to the necessity of consulting other, more knowledgeable persons; it frequently refers to its local partners and its contacts in Greece as key sources of expertise in the decision-making process for allocating funds and donated items. *We Do* appears to draw more on expertise from other small help initiatives than from established ones, which could be seen as a way of justifying the decision making of the lay core, as activists frequently picture *We Do* as a good counterweight to such large organizations as the Red Cross. In late September 2015, however, *We Do* launched its first official cooperation with Doctors of the World, which was chosen because 'They have helped us with the analysis of needs, and will be able to receive medical material that we have obtained from sponsors.' In late October, *We Do* engaged two medical experts who were sent to Lesbos to help refugees and to provide the core with information. Both local and expert knowledge, therefore, form arguments used to justify the decisions of the core.

The power of the core is not unlimited, however. It is easier to prevent the activists from doing something (like volunteering for *We Do* in Greece) than to make them do something (like engaging in additional packing and sorting of donated goods in Sweden). After initial large-scale interest in such volunteering in Sweden, *We Do* found it difficult to obtain enough volunteers for the final packing round in Enköping in early November. In an attempt to redeem the engagement, famous Swedish entertainers were engaged to amuse volunteers on the journey from Stockholm to Enköping. The core also advertised the packing event as an opportunity to 'FEEL that you make a difference', trying to emphasize the benefits of this type of engagement for the 'you' group. Yet, the core seemed painfully aware that neither entertainment nor good causes were sufficient to make these less-rewarding tasks attractive to the activists, and many activists wanted to experience a deeper and different type of engagement, as part of the 'we' rather than the 'you'.

There are other limits to the power rendered the core by the technological affordances. The name 'We do what we can' was, in practice, available for anyone to use. In fact, the name invited that development, given the unclear notion of 'we'. One activist expressed anger at seeing an initiative called 'We do what we can' selling donated items in a park in Gothenburg, and *We Do* answered on Facebook that it had no such activities outside of Stockholm. The spread of non-sanctioned freelance initiatives quickly became a burden, discussed and debated by activists on Facebook, and *We Do* expressed its explicit distance from such operations. The other way to solve this issue was to create a copyrighted logotype, which the core quickly accomplished. Nevertheless, there have been reports of at least one fraudulent initiative with a similar, albeit not identical name. *We Do* is hardly able to control any of the copycats, whether frauds or not.

Rules and their (re)interpretation by 'we' and 'you'

Activists continued to interpret and reinterpret the growing number of Facebook communications from the core, especially communications about its rules and restrictions. The activists identifying as the 'you' readily shared, quoted, and defended the information provided by the core, thereby lending legitimacy to the power exercised. Activists who felt entitled to inclusion in the broader notion of 'we' reinterpreted the rules, however, sometimes by attempting to provide concrete examples of more abstract rules, and sometimes by directly questioning the legitimacy of the rules established by the core.

Interpretations ranged from the necessity of including certain items, like toys and feeding bottles, to suggestions for expanding *We Do* into many parts of Greece. And why not to other parts of Europe and the Middle East? Comments highlighting the terrible situation in Hungary and on other Greek islands were among the first suggestions, but more practical advice was also presented: renting buses to transport refugees from the coast to the camp on Lesbos, for example. Although these interpretations and suggestions proliferated, *We Do* had barely had time to collect and sort most of the donated goods, much less to have moved any substantial portion of the donated items to Lesbos or to allocate the funds it had gathered. In essence, the main achievement, regardless of the suggestions for expansion proliferating on Facebook, was gathering goods and funds, rather than actually beginning to distribute the donations on a large scale.

One outcome of all of these Facebook interactions is that the territorial focus on Stockholm quickly vanished, and some of the activists established their own *We Do* collection points around Sweden aimed at maximizing the amount of collected goods to be sent to Stockholm at a later date. Facing this development, the core of *We Do* made a major change in the original, relatively open invitation for engagement. A new rule was established: Only individuals are allowed to bring donations to Stockholm. Privately arranged trucks transporting goods from individuals who participate in sub-collections in other parts of Sweden are not welcome.

As time passed, the core articulated other restrictions limiting the type of goods that *We Do* would accept. These specifications may be seen as the core's reaction to the activists' broad interpretation of what could be included in the collection. Requests for 'hygiene articles', for example, triggered responses varying from sun protection lotions to soap, necessitating a more precise definition of 'hygiene articles', and a further development by which the founders sometimes gave preferred status to corporate donors. After a short time, *We Do* primarily asked for travel-sized hygiene items.

The escalating interaction among activists and the amount of gathered goods, coupled with the growing self-reflexivity of the core regarding the difficulty of handling the large amount of donated items, triggered a process of refocusing the initiative away from the activists and towards corporate donors. Already by the beginning of the second week of collection, *We Do* began to discourage donations of goods from individuals, encouraging activists to donate elsewhere, and justifying that decision with the practical explanation that new goods are easier to transport. The way in which the rules have developed reflects the evolving focus of *We Do* away from enabling activists to help and towards more instrumental logistical concerns.

Yet, the interaction between the core and the Facebook activists who viewed themselves as part of the broader sense of 'we' not only resulted in limitations, but also seemed to diffuse new ideas that fed into the core's decisions on resource allocation. As *We Do* was flooded with donations, for example, some donations were redirected to refugees in Iraqi Kurdistan, thus overstepping the set limits of the initial call, which was focused on Lesbos. The eventual cooperation with Hiwa and deliveries sent to Kurdistan can be seen as a response to the common activist request to 'think bigger than Lesbos'.

This tendency to push for an expansion of the scope of *We Do* and demand immediate action seems to be inherent in the mode of Facebook communication, by which almost every new post suggests something different. One interpretation of the core's exertion of power is that it is a tool to handle the logistical hurdle implied by the seemingly exponential growth of suggestions – the response to which is the introduction of rules to deter and exclude. Unable to orchestrate a certain type of action, *We Do* increasingly used Facebook to limit and block action. This was first done by limiting the scope of activities to private individuals in Stockholm, then by largely excluding private individuals in favour of corporate donators. These restrictions effectively pushed the activists who were not already identified as the 'you' of the initiative to assume this more passive membership role in the face of power – not necessarily legitimate, but tangible, power – as exercised by the core.

This negative sanctioning has disappointed many activists, both those who have identified as the 'you' and those who have viewed themselves as the 'we'. The engagement of the 'you' activists has been limited because they have not been able to follow the swiftly changing rules and their on-going interpretations in the Facebook conversations. They have unintentionally done the wrong thing, but still express a desire to participate and engage. But those who have felt entitled to produce their own interpretations of the rules – the 'we' activists – express both disappointment and anger. Rejection ultimately means that they are not part of the 'we'. Even though the restrictions on goods may seem like a simple procedure, it results in many activists reflecting on the fact that their efforts to engage were not well received, or even not received at all, provoking hurt and anger. How can *We Do* help them in their altruistic strivings if they are not allowed to donate the goods they have gathered?

If we are you, then those in charge should be monitored!

As the resources of *We Do* grew, the activists began to realize the power that the core had acquired. Despite the core initially being interpreted as benign and altruistic, it remained unclear how its actions were audited and accounted for. This situation became increasingly problematic, and coupled with the anger sparked by the rejection of activists' donations and the desire to volunteer in a more meaningful manner than packing and sorting goods, demands for monitoring began to be raised against the core, pointing to a growing distinction between the core and the Facebook activists, both 'you' and 'we'. Suggestions and criticism began to undermine the idea that the core was the group most fit to distribute the gathered goods and funds by virtue of being lay people, just like the activists. The core was gradually being challenged; many of the suggestions were accompanied by expertise – informing the core about issues like the types of feminine hygiene products that would be most suitable for women from specific countries. In these discussions, activists acknowledged the power possessed by the core, given the affordances of the technical platform, but they also questioned the legitimacy of the authority of the core. Especially those who viewed everyone's engagement as being equally part of the wider sense of 'we' found the power and ambivalent expertise of the core questionable. Activists expressed demands that the core and the initiative as a whole should be audited like any other non-profit organization: adhering to certain standards, such as the distribution of goods and funds in the best possible way, being accountable and transparent in its decisions, and adhering to demands for monitoring.

Discussions on monitoring and the lack of monitoring occurred more and more frequently as *We Do* raised funds to a level of SEK 9 million (approx. EUR 900,000). Discussions began to appear in Facebook threads, in which activists – both donors and potential donors – began to question how the donations, especially the money, were being used and monitored. There was fierce interaction between activists who criticized and activists who defended the core. The defenders of *We Do* often used words like 'confidence', 'trust', and 'good judgement', downplaying the need for monitoring. These activists can be interpreted as the 'you'; they have accepted the power of the core and may have viewed it as legitimate from the beginning.

Activists on both sides tend to raise constant comparisons to established non-profits. Their hopes for *We Do* revolve around its differing from those established organizations, which are too slow, not being in place where they should in Lesbos, and where donated funds are swindled through unnecessary administration. *We Do* stands out as showing 'genuine engagement' rather than 'having a steering committee with golden trousers'. Facebook activists also note that 'the Red Cross and Save the Children are truly big actors, which we know. What we also know is that these organizations do not work on non-profit grounds.' The core encourages this reasoning to some extent, building on the idea that this initiative is the one that will be 'there' on Lesbos and do 'what they can', which implicitly seems to 'do what is needed'.

We Do moved away from the ethos of its name of doing some-thing, when mentioning the need for 'long-term and strategic plan-ning' rather than 'rushing to decisions'. This approach was immediately met by demands for instant action: 'Help is needed now!' – something that *We Do* outlined only four days earlier as a motivation for the lack of any established monitoring routines of its operations. In a contradictory manner, the 'we' activists who criti-cized *We Do* simultaneously demanded more accounts for priorities and use of funding, thereby encouraging both immediate action and time-consuming administrative procedures. This juxtaposition of money and the possibility for 'genuine', non-profit action is a central aspect of the emergence of *We Do*, and something that marks the gradual transition from being a Facebook initiative preoccupied with material donations and with an unclear membership, to becoming a fundraising foundation focused on the allocation of funds.

In fact, it seems as if the power base of the core, rendered by the specificities of the technology, eventually becomes incompatible with the lack of monitoring. Although power seems to be possible to exercise through Facebook without having legitimate hierarchical authority, it is difficult to adhere to demands for monitoring without introducing an elaborate organizational structure. These challenges pertain especially to the impossibility of adhering systematically to accountability demands without having formal auditing practices in place. Even though the core attempts to offer ad hoc solutions on Facebook to requests for auditability and accountability by posting numbers and pictures of its activities, it soon opts for the simplicity of a readymade organizational structure by registering as a fundraising foundation. By doing so, however, it takes the final step in completely excluding the activists. As the selected organizational format is legally memberless, the only members allowed are the board members of the foundation. The multiple understandings of roles in the fuzzy collective 'we' thus proceed via an increased separation of functions, and finally end up with the core completely excluding both the 'we' and the 'you' activists. Yet, the core fulfils the demands for auditability and accountability by adhering to the legislative procedures of the fundraising foundation. In addition, the organizational format renders legitimacy to the authority of the core members in their role as board members.

There is now a hierarchy and a clear membership. The core has also created bylaws for the foundation that enable more degrees of freedom in the allocation of funding. However, the new organizational form excludes activists from influencing the foundation's activities. The large-scale engagement of *We Do* in Facebook activity and new fundraising drives soon waned. Although SEK 9 million (approx. EUR

900,000) was raised in an extremely short time in the 2015 autumn frenzy of the *We Do* Facebook initiative, a similar fundraising call in early 2016 by the *We Do* foundation resulted in a meagre SEK 8,500 (approx. EUR 850).

LARGE SCALE BUT SHORT TERM: THE POSSIBILITIES AND CHALLENGES OF PARTIAL ORGANIZING THROUGH SOCIAL MEDIA

The gradual change of *We Do* from an open and egalitarian social media initiative into the specific format of a fundraising foundation may appear puzzling at first glance. However, the moves taken to limit donations to corporations, to restrict access to activism by recruiting professional volunteers, to grow a network of established partner organizations, and eventually to recede to the monitoring practices of a fundraising foundation were all attempts by the core to handle an initiative that had unexpectedly grown exponentially. The commitment and interpretations of a seemingly ever-growing number of activists enabled *We Do*'s continued growth, but also created unmanageable demands. This development may be a key feature of mass engagement through social media, and we suggest that it is strongly related to the possibilities and challenges of partial organizing.

In the case of *We Do*, the technological affordances of the social media platform – the existence of power without legitimate authority, coupled with the undefined status of activists – all made *We Do* particularly receptive and malleable to the particularities of partial organizing through social media. As the core attempted to introduce elements of organizing, such as rules and sanctions, these moves were undercut by a lack of legitimate hierarchical authority (Weber, 1978). The unclear membership was central to the initiative and motivated activists to demand the establishment of monitoring practices while simultaneously cherishing *We Do*, precisely because it lacked elaborate (and costly) administrative structures. This indicates that predominant rationalized ideas about what it means to be an organization (Meyer & Bromley, 2013; Bromley & Meyer, 2014) influenced *We Do*. But equally important were the technological affordances (Treem & Leonardi, 2013; Kaun & Uldam, 2017) of the platform in the development of the initiative. It is through the unorganized character of the initial call to engagement that large-scale social action was enabled, as its very openness rendered it accessible and attractive. Such an open initiative generates demands for monitoring among those engaged, however. This openness coupled with the mass engagement seems to make it even more important to understand and monitor the ways in which the initiative developed. Yet, those very demands resulted in the implementation of a decided order that essentially limited the very engagement that made the large-scale initiative possible in the first place.

The interactive nature of Web 2.0 provides ample opportunities for organizers to communicate and entice activism on a large scale (Macnamara & Zerfass, 2012). As previous research has shown, social media may enable collective action – or rather, connective action – through personalized action frames (Bennett & Segerberg, 2012; Bennett & Segerberg, 2013). The digital enthusiasm that follows is often not sustainable, however, and its evanescence is almost inevitable (Gerbaudo, 2016). Our chapter demonstrates how the very partialness that large-scale organizing through social media entails can provide an explanation for this evanescence.

Social media invites interaction and introduces an element of face-to-face communication to organizational decisions, especially as personal social media accounts are often used. It becomes difficult to ascertain which decisions belong to the organizational initiative and which emerge from the activists' interpretations of those decisions and their own will to communicate their ideas about what should be done. Social media also makes it possible to engage continuously in further interpretations, reinterpretations, and misinterpretations of decisions communicated by the Facebook page administrators, destabilizing the durability and consistency of those decisions. Even though this can happen in all decision-making processes, the written polyphony of large-scale social media interactions makes it especially difficult to infer the context, meaning, and direction of communicated decisions, which may complicate, and perhaps even hamper, the long-term organizing efforts of a social media initiative.

Our case demonstrates that the polyphonic conversations on social media are only one of the components influencing engagement. In addition, we want to emphasize that the power base afforded to those holding administrative rights of the Facebook account where action is coordinated is also central to the development of the *We Do* initiative (Kaun & Uldam, 2017). Despite the multiple concurrent threads of communication on Facebook, the technical power base rendered to those in charge of the communication tools can enable them to delineate the role of activists, and eventually limit and exclude activists altogether – but not without cost. Our case demonstrates how power can be exercised on social media without hierarchy or any other form of legitimate authority (Weber, 1978), as a power segmentation enables decision making by those who hold the reins of the communication. In turn, even though membership may be initially ambiguous and unclear, this issue may be articulated more clearly with time, as roles are assigned and delimited through the power accorded the administrators by the technical platform. Yet, as this power structure becomes more pronounced over time, it may be overtly and sometimes aggressively repudiated in online conversations unless it is somehow perceived to be legitimate. The interactive monitoring afforded by the platform, possibly aggressive but not necessarily substantial, can address such criticism to a limited extent. As monitoring demands are reinforced by larger societal and global trends promoting auditability and accountability (Power, 1994; Power, 1997; Jang, 2005), it may become impossible for those in positions without legitimate power to sustain their position without incorporating standardized practices of monitoring (Brunsson & Jacobsson, 2000). In this process, they may be forced to legitimize their own power, and in establishing themselves in a hierarchical position, they may risk the very basis of the large-scale social media engagement they have facilitated, and the partialness of the social media initiative is replaced by a more complete organizational form (Ahrne & Brunsson, 2011).

The development described in this chapter may be potentially idiosyncratic for the case of *We Do*, but we argue that it may also be taken as an example for understanding the very partialness that is a central component of fast and large-scale organizing through social media. The undecided order of a social media initiative may hold sufficient power to initiate it, but it may become too strenuous to manage in the long run without authority derived from a legitimate organizational hierarchy (Weber, 1978). Such authority may be difficult to achieve precisely because of the opaqueness of the membership status of the activists, and the lack of means to fulfil monitoring demands legitimately. As our chapter has demonstrated, it seems, therefore, that despite the power and communication structures enabled by social media platforms, bureaucratic ideals on how to organize and how to legitimize that organizing in the long run are sustained on social media as well. As Weber wrote more than a century ago:

> When those subject to bureaucratic control seek to escape the influence of the existing bureaucratic apparatus, this is normally possible only by creating an organization of their own which is equally subject to the process of bureaucratization.
>
> *(Weber, 1947: 38)*

REFERENCES

Ahrne, G. & Brunsson, N. (2011) Organization outside Organizations: The Significance of Partial Organization. *Organization* 18(1): 83–104.

Bennett, W. L. & Segerberg, A. (2012) The Logic of Connective Action: Digital Media and the Personalization of Contentious Politics. *Information, Communication & Society* 15(5): 739–68.

Bennett, W. L. & Segerberg, A. (2013) *The Logic of Connective Action: Digital Media and the Personalization of Contentious Politics*. New York: Cambridge University Press.

Bromley, P. & Meyer, J. W. (2014) 'They Are All Organizations' – the Cultural Roots of Blurring between the Nonprofit, Business, and Government Sectors. *Administration & Society* 49(7): 939–66.

Brunsson, N. & Jacobsson, B. (2000) *A World of Standards*. Oxford: Oxford University Press.

Brügger, N. (2011) Web Archiving – between Past, Present, and Future. In R. Burnett, M. Consalvo, & C. Ess (eds.), *The Handbook of Internet Studies.* Chichester: Wiley-Blackwell. 24–42.

Gerbaudo, P. (2016) Constructing Public Space| Rousing the Facebook Crowd: Digital Enthusiasm and Emotional Contagion in the 2011 Protests in Egypt and Spain. *International Journal of Communication* 10(2016): 254–73.

Jang, Y. S. (2005) The Expansion of Modern Accounting as a Global and Institutional Practice. *International Journal of Comparative Sociology* 46(4): 297–326.

Kaun, A. & Uldam, J. (2017) 'Volunteering Is Like Any Other Business': Civic Participation and Social Media. *New Media & Society.* (prepublished 17 September 2017) DOI:10.1177/1461444817731920.

Lomborg, S. (2012) Researching Communicative Practice: Web Archiving in Qualitative Social Media Research. *Journal of Technology in Human Services* 30(3–4): 219–31.

Luhmann, N. (2013) *Theory of Society.* Stanford: Stanford University Press.

Macnamara, J. & Zerfass, A. (2012) Social Media Communication in Organizations: The Challenges of Balancing Openness, Strategy, and Management. *International Journal of Strategic Communication* 6(4): 287–308.

Meyer, J. W. & Bromley P. (2013) The Worldwide Expansion of 'Organization'. *Sociological Theory* 31(4): 366–89.

Power, M. (1994) The Audit Society. In P. Miller & A. Hopwood (eds.), *Accounting as Social and Institutional Practice.* Cambridge: Cambridge University Press. 299–316.

Power, M. (1997) *The Audit Society: Rituals of Verification.* Oxford: Oxford University Press.

Treem, J. W. & Leonardi, P. M. (2013) Social Media Use in Organizations: Exploring the Affordances of Visibility, Editability, Persistence, and Association. *Annals of the International Communication Association* 36(1): 143–89.

Weber, M. (1947) *From Max Weber: Essays in Sociology.* New York: Oxford University Press.

Weber, M. (1978) *Economy and Society: An Outline of Interpretive Sociology.* Berkely: University of California Press.

NOTES

1. All quotes are translations from Swedish.
2. In Swedish: *insamlingsstiftelse.*

PART 5 The Partial Organization of Formal Organizations

17 Partial De-Organizing for Innovation and Strategic Renewal? A Study of an Industrial Innovation Programme

Frank den Hond, Kati Järvi, and Liisa Välikangas

The idea of partial organization has not been fully explored. Relatively little attention has been paid to 'organization *within* organizations' or to the possibility of partial *de*-organization. We explore this possibility in the context of business firms for which innovation and strategic renewal are imperatives, and we propose that a partial de-organizing lens may help to understand how, and how successfully, companies seek to innovate and strategically renew themselves by suspending one or more of the elements of corporate organizing through partial de-organization.

The idea of partial organization has gained some traction by promising to offer analytical tools for the study of uncertainty, complexity, and unpredictability in social life. It revives classical ideas about organization (e.g., March & Simon, 1993), but it also extends such cognitively flavoured proposals by viewing organization as both 'a socially defined set of rules' that have the purpose of 'stabilizing an ever-mutating reality by making human behavior more predictable' and as 'an outcome, a pattern, emerging from the reflective application of the very same rules in local contexts over time' (Tsoukas & Chia, 2002: 570). Yet, the idea of partial organization has not yet been brought to full fruition; it needs to be amended to leverage its promise fully. We do so by emphasizing its relevance for 'organization *within* organizations', and then by exploring the possibility of partial de-organization: first conceptually, in this section, second with a specification in the area of innovation, in the next section, and then empirically, through a case study of an industrial company that initiated a series of projects to renew itself through partial de-organization. We conclude with a discussion of some implications of our exploration.

Partial organization has been used predominantly to argue for the presence of 'organization outside organizations'. The idea is that organizations – including business firms, government authorities, meta-organizations, NGOs, and private interest groups – introduce one or several elements of organization to reduce or bring under managerial control the chaos, complexity, unpredictability, and uncertainty in their environments. Empirical and conceptual examples are in the organization of markets, in standard setting and the issuing of certification and prizes, in the organization of value chains and networks, and in various instances of collaboration between organizations. This extra-organizational orientation of the idea of partial organization fits linguistically well with the word 'partial': Beginning with the status of being *non*-organized, in which social order is emergent, the decision to introduce one or more elements of organization renders some environment partially organized.

Yet, we propose that a move in the opposite direction is also possible. We argue that organizations are partially organized, in the sense that emergent sources of social order remain relevant, in addition to decision making, and, furthermore, that they may seek to become less organized, by deciding to abrogate, abolish, or suspend, temporarily or permanently and for the entirety or for parts of their organizations, one or more elements of organization. Such partial de-organization of organizations is a relatively neglected area of interest. But if we can speak of the partial de-organization of organizations, then a question arises: What remains after the suspension, abrogation, or abolishment of some element of organization?

Although organization is appropriately related to and associated with decision making, the social order in organizations – as specific entities – is not wholly and fully dependent on it. Social order in organizations has both decided and emergent sources. Social order is the relatively stable, regular, and predictable pattern of co-operative behaviour, such as exists in organizations (Elster, 1989). It can be premised on decision making, and decision making is therefore a decided source of social order in organizations. However, social order may also emerge as people build relationships (networks) and develop common understandings and behavioural patterns (institutions); it has emergent sources (Ahrne & Brunsson, 2011). We argue that emergent sources of social order are relevant for their effect on the stability of extant social order in organizations and for the way they foster or constrain organizational action and outcomes.

Five examples spring to mind. (1) People are *members* of an organization and are therefore in a formal relationship to other members. Yet informal relationships – such as those based on sympathy, friendship, animosity, or shared interests – are often at least as important as formal relationships. (2) People often do what their bosses tell them to do: *Hierarchy* matters. But occasionally or frequently they decide for themselves or engage in a task after consultation or in concert with colleagues that are not their bosses; and sometimes they simply ignore orders. (3) *Rules* have a strange status in organizations; they can be statutory, yet they are not always followed, either by their letter or in their spirit. Furthermore, rules are often distant from what people actually do, or why they do it, and may be invoked only in the case of uncertainty or conflict. Or, rules are opportunistically used by 'office rats' to get their own way. Moreover, people in organizations develop shared behavioural patterns and expectations about how things are done here, which may divert significantly from what is written down and agreed upon as a rule. (4) People in organizations are not only *monitored* officially – in terms of the productivity, efficiency, or quality of their task accomplishment – they also monitor each other using official and informal criteria. Gossip is but one manifestation, as is the rare compliment that one receives from a colleague for a job well done. As much as a compliment is a reward, gossip may give rise to social sanction, when its object becomes socially tainted or excluded, for example. (5) In other words, *sanctioning* and *rewarding* in organizations are not only in recognition of one's performance according to the criteria used for official monitoring; they are also social phenomena that help sustain or disrupt social order in organizations.

This list of examples is not comprehensive, and need not be. We are certain that anyone who has been a member of an organization can attest to the presence and relevance of emergent sources of social order, as co-existing with, complementing, and sometimes substituting for decision making as a decided source of social order. The organization of organizations is a result of interaction between decided and emergent sources of social order. Social order in organizations is never stable, as its emergent sources pop up and die out on a continuing basis. People develop new relationships and sever old ones, and shared behavioural patterns and expectations develop over time. Decision making in organizations is therefore not only in relation to changes in their environments, but also in relation to the evolving social order within them. Managers make decisions to counter the development of social order when they deem undesirable the direction it is taking. Such decision making within organizations – design decisions (Barberio *et al.*, 2018) as opposed to routine decisions that follow from standard operating procedures, or such mundane decisions as having a cup of coffee – serves to counter, control, and conduce the chaos, complexity, unpredictability, and uncertainty in their internal environment. Yet, these decisions may not only command obeisance, but, inevitably, they also provoke unintended and unanticipated changes in the prevailing emergent social order. Resistance to change is but one example.

Many types of organizations, ranging from business firms and corporations, through state bureaucracies, to autonomous social movement groups (see Chapter 14) struggle with the question of how to organize. The model of complete, formal organization – a social order that is fully premised on decision making – is criticized from various angles. Instrumental and functional arguments emphasize its inefficiencies and/or inefficacies in goal accomplishment and its difficulties in adapting to changing circumstances, whereas political-ideological arguments point out its oppressive, alienating, and undemocratic character. Our focus in this chapter is in line with instrumental and functional arguments.

Many business firms and corporations seek to overcome the limitations of complete, formal organization through (partial) de-organizing, for example, because they believe that when they reduce the burden of decided social order, their workers can be more creative, while maintaining or even increasing their sense of commitment to and responsibility for the organization. Such de-organizing can be quite radical, but even in the cases of Zappos and other so-called holacracies, there is decided social order. Partial de-organizing may apply to a subset of the organization's members, and for a limited amount of their working time (e.g., Google's well-known but now abandoned policy of giving employees 20 per cent of their working time to pursue their own projects). In our empirical case, it was for a small selection of employees from different parts of the company who had never met, for varying amounts of their working time during an eight-month period, and with an explicit task that was outside their regular work responsibilities. But before delving into the empirical section, we first need to articulate how the idea of partial (de-)organization speaks to the difficulties that many firms face when they want to innovate or strategically renew themselves.

INNOVATION AND THE ORGANIZING PARADOX

In the context of business firms, innovation relates to doing things in a different way, and strategic renewal relates to doing different things. The difference between innovation and strategic renewal is relative and gradual. Innovation is typically used to refer to the introduction of new products or processes. In a narrow sense, it is considered the next step after invention, whereas, in a broader sense, it is seen as including the organizational ramifications of various types of innovation (Henderson & Clark, 1990) and new ways of thinking (Volberda, van den Bosch, & Mihalache, 2014). Strategic renewal is typically understood to be more fundamental and concerned with a change in a company's strategic orientation and purpose. It may relate, for example, to choices of market, business model, and value proposition, ways of working and culture, or change of organizational structure. Our use of the terms reflects, more than anything else, the difficulty of clearly separating 'doing things in a different way' from 'doing different things'; we use the word 'innovation' as a shorthand for both.

Management writers tend to agree on two things when discussing innovation. First, innovation is critical for organizational competitiveness. It is often cherished and lauded in executive speeches, in fact. Second, firms face many barriers in the pursuit of innovation, and therefore find it notoriously difficult to accomplish innovation. Some scholars have observed that companies force their innovation programmes and capabilities to adopt the prevailing decision-making processes, risk tolerances, timeframes, perspectives, and best practices that inhabit the rest of the organization (Philips, 2011). Others have argued that the very processes and structures that were responsible for the success of established companies prevent them from developing breakthroughs to create future success (Davila & Epstein, 2014).

This innovation paradox is well known; successful innovation requires management, yet management processes and practices must not kill budding innovation. The innovation paradox has had various formulations: the inability to do things differently (Farson & Keyes, 2003), the tendency for exploitation to drive out exploration (Benner & Tushman, 2003), and the tension between induced strategy and autonomous action in internal venturing (Burgelman, 1983). Many companies that were once celebrated as success stories fell into an innovation trap (Välikangas & Gibbert, 2005).

Why do organizations have such a difficult time with something that ought to be their core capability? There are multiple laundry lists of assumed reasons for an organization's failure to innovate. Dougherty and Hardy (1996) point to the difficulties of connecting innovation with routine operations, the lack of resources that can be or are targeted at innovation, insufficient collaborative structures and processes that would coordinate innovative ideas, and lack of an actionable strategy that would value innovation over the current way of doing business. Others speak of such operational issues as budgeting and strategic planning, which make the inclusion of more serendipitous innovation difficult, or of the 'bureaucratic process that grinds execution to a halt' (Hansen & Birkinshaw, 2007: 9). Company structures and processes that are fine-tuned to serve existing businesses and to create stability and reliability thereby suppress change and drive out exploration (Beck, Bru, & Woywode, 2008; Benner & Tushman, 2003). Efficiency requirements dictate no slack resources, even if slack could support innovative behaviours (Bourgeois, 1981). Burgelman (1983, 1991) notes that some autonomous action always exists within an organization, but also that it must accomplish strategic forcing in order to be able to change the management-driven induced strategy. Similarly, Garud, Tuertscher, and Van De Ven (2013: 796) suggest that managerial processes 'are likely to constrain the natural emergence and flow of innovation processes'. Top management's cognitive capability can be entrenched (Prahalad & Bettis, 1986) so deeply that it fails to embrace change and to recognize the importance of disruptive and outlier business models (Välikangas & Gibbert, 2016). Innovation involves emotions, and fear may prevent people from articulating the need for change (Vuori & Huy, 2015). Organizations may simply be complacent and lack motivation for innovation (Tushman & Nadler, 1986). Whereas some scholars thus argue that management pays too little attention to innovation, others make the exact opposite argument: 'The innovation paradox is that the more your firm pays attention to innovation, the less likely it will be to be successful at innovation' (Phillips, 2008).

This controversy may suggest that the issue is not so much *whether* management attends to innovation, but *how* it does so. Davila and Epstein (2014) suggest that the same factors that once lifted a company to great heights eventually work towards its fall once the market situation changes. It is a tough call. Dougherty and Hardy (1996: 1133) find that 'where individual innovation projects were successful, they depended on the efforts of particular individuals to use their organizational positions . . . to further and protect innovation efforts; they did not result from an organization-wide commitment to innovation'. Therefore, when innovation succeeds against all organizational odds, it is often because of the efforts of some individuals rather than the result of organizational support. Innovation happens despite organization, not thanks to it.

It may be well justified, therefore, to suggest that mature companies need to reverse some of the organizing from complete to partial if they want to make room for innovation. Research on ambidextrous organizations suggests that companies may enhance their capability to explore and exploit simultaneously, by temporarily or structurally separating exploration and exploitation activities (Simsek et al., 2009), or by allowing employees to allocate time to projects of their own interest. The challenge is to create a space in which participants can liberate themselves from management control and its related hierarchical mode of organizing. Others advise more holistic change, which would require a revolution in organizational approaches to innovation, including drastic changes in corporate culture, leadership style, strategy, incentives, and management systems (Davila & Epstein, 2014; Farson & Keyes, 2003). This would 'enable and encourage individuals to make their own judgments about how to divide their time between conflicting demands [for exploration and exploitation]' (Gibson & Birkinshaw, 2004: 210). Following these authors, we can conclude that the innovation challenge is often conceptualized in terms of organizational design and management. Building on this conceptualization, we argue that underneath the innovation paradox is an organizing paradox, as a desire for managerial control competes with the acknowledgement of a need to reduce it (Contino & den Hond, 2009).

We offer an original perspective to innovation by addressing the innovation paradox through the underlying organizing paradox; we approach it from ideas about partial de-organization and the possibility of reversing organization through decision making. We report on our study of a mature industrial company – characterized by highly formal management and organizational structures – that partially de-organized to create a space within the organization to foster innovation and strategic renewal. Our theoretical interest is in understanding whether and how such a partially de-organized space can foster innovation and contribute to strategic renewal.

The Groundbreakers programme

We conducted a qualitative case study of a globally operating industrial firm that has sought to create space for innovation and strategic renewal in response to continuously declining demand due to digitalization and related trends. In the mid-2000s, the company found itself in a prolonged struggle for survival. After massive reorganization, the company had to move on. Its top management team developed the view that the company's future success was in exploring new business areas for growth and innovation opportunities. By 2011, the top management team had successfully saved the company, but lack of expertise in areas beyond the company's traditional businesses hampered its ambitions for growth. Companies often replace the top management team in such situations (Tripsas, 2009), but this company chose differently: It established an internal development programme for strategic renewal, baptized 'Groundbreakers'.

We characterize the programme as the company's effort to de-organize partially within the otherwise complete organization. The purpose of the programme and the tasks of its participants was to help the CEO and his top management team with their daunting challenge of 'questioning old ways of doing this and finding new and different solutions to satisfy customers, shareholders, and employees', as the company-internal advertisement of the programme announced. Employees from varying backgrounds (e.g., gender, geography, expertise, and hierarchical position) were selected to work in project teams on critical challenges to the company. They were relatively autonomous from the rest of the company but in collaboration with top management. Their mission was to break out of the ordinary and to propose radically new solutions for a pre-defined problem, challenge, or opportunity. A participant captures the spirit of top management's expectations for the project teams:

> the CEO ... more or less said ... 'I want you now to go out and explore; I want you to challenge what is already existing in the company' ... and he said, 'I don't want an evolution. I want the revolution.'

The fifth edition of the Groundbreakers programme was on-going while the second author was collecting data (July 2015 to October 2016). Each of the five editions included two to four projects, in which four to participants worked in cross-functional, cross-hierarchical teams (Table 1). The projects lasted for eight months, and concluded with the presentation of their proposal to the company's top management. Each project team had a sponsor, who was often the head of the division for which the project was most relevant. The team members had no prior working experience with each other or the sponsor and no parti-cular expertise in the subject matter of their project. The company believed this setup increased chances of the team developing novel solutions for their challenge.

We interviewed thirty-eight participants across all projects and eight top managers, including some sponsors.

Authority versus autonomy

After carefully reading and discussing the interview transcripts, we realized that a central theme was how project teams dealt with the relationship or tension between top management's authority (with hierarchy; Ahrne & Brunsson, 2011) and the opposite condition of autonomy, which was given to the teams to enhance their ability to develop and propose viable new solutions.

Table 1 *Projects and Number of Interviewees per Edition of the Programme*

Groundbreaker Edition	Topics of the Projects	Number of Participants	Number of Participants Interviewed
I	1. Global Responsibility I	12	6
	2. Innovation I		
II	3. Internal Reorganization	14	5
	4. New Market Area		
	5. Supply Chain Improvement		
III	6. Differentiation	14	7
	7. Global Responsibility II		
	8. Food Preservation		
IV	9. Getting a Grip on Time	16	11
	10. Innovation II		
	11. Product Management		
	12. Hidden Value in Supply Chain		
V	13. Industrial Digitalization	16	9
	14. Insight-Driven Innovation		
	15. Leading Edge Supply Chain Service		
	16. Key Account Management		
Total		**72**	**38**

Autonomy in a job or a task reflects the extent to which the agents are able to decide for themselves *what* needs to be done, *when* it needs to be done, and *how* it is to be done (Morgeson & Humphrey, 2006). We found that not all project teams were equally successful in establishing their autonomy from top management; they tended to struggle or to take some time to establish their autonomy. This tendency related, on the one hand, to (group) psychological processes; and on the other hand, to attitude and willingness on the part of the top management team.

Regarding the group psychology of the project teams, it is relevant to consider their composition. Having been granted autonomy, but coming from different backgrounds and never having met, team members needed to sort out how they would work together. 'None of the four of us were given the role of a leader. It was explicitly brought up that we need to discuss the leadership issue by ourselves. At any point, none of us was a clear leader of the team.' For another project team member, it 'was a little bit strange and difficult for me in the beginning – not strange, maybe difficult – working in the team when the roles were not pre-defined'.

They also needed to relate to their sponsor and the top management team. One project team member referred to her team's sponsor as a 'kind of god, godfather'. They had to bridge the social distance to top managers; it took them time to learn to frankly speak to power. For example,

> All of a sudden you're exposed to the [top management team]. Of course you get nervous ... maybe the second time or the third, we were a bit braver.

For some project team members, this transition felt like a personal accomplishment. 'Having kind of pushed through that discomfort of having to come up with things on your own also made me grow more in a way.' Likewise: 'Close interaction with the whole group, [with the] leadership team, including the CEO, made you realize, actually, that they were just normal, normal people ... that gave me a lot of confidence.'

At the same time, some project teams acknowledged that the success of their work depended as much on their being free to explore and develop as it did on their keeping in touch and involving the sponsor and the top management team. One team 'scheduled a meeting with ... our CEO, and it was very good to feel from [him]'.

Yet, sponsors and the top management team did not always agree with the ideas that project teams developed.

> If [the project team] meets up with the sponsor, the sponsor may sometimes agree, sometimes disagree. The [project team] must figure out [if they] should listen to the sponsor and align with the sponsor. Or should they rather follow their own beliefs and so forth?

Several project teams were able to accomplish a balanced rapport with their sponsors and the top management team. Some sponsors, however, found it difficult to relinquish their authority; they exerted a strong influence on their project team, on the focus of their teams' projects, and on the actual content of the final proposals. Whereas in several projects 'even the sponsor doesn't seem to have an idea about the aim of the project', in other projects, it happened that the sponsor 'set the expectations very, very clear. It was crystal clear what he wanted.'

STRIKING A BALANCE

Autonomy is a condition for project teams to develop novel ideas, but one that is not easily established. Simultaneously, several project teams, sponsors, and members of the top management team were aware of a need for the emerging ideas to be grounded in the company's corporate context. These considerations made us realize that autonomy may be related to the innovativeness of the final proposal and to the question of whether the final proposal is implemented. We used the following expectations as heuristics to unravel how partial de-organization can be related to innovation and strategic renewal.

- A **high** level of project team autonomy vis-à-vis the team's sponsor and the top management team is **beneficial** to the innovativeness of the project proposal but **decreases** the likelihood that it will be implemented.
- A **high** level of project team autonomy vis-à-vis the team's sponsor and the top management team, when **balanced** with considerations for the company's context, is **beneficial** to the innovativeness of the project proposal and **increases** the likelihood that it will be implemented.

- A **low** level of project team autonomy vis-à-vis the team's sponsor and the top management team is **detrimental** to the innovativeness of the project proposal but **increases** the likelihood that it will be implemented.

Autonomy, Innovativeness, and Implementation in the Projects. For each project, we examined carefully the level of autonomy that the team was able to establish, the level of innovativeness of the final proposal, and whether or how the proposal was implemented. Table 2 summarizes our findings.

Autonomy. We looked for interview quotes that would indicate how autonomous the various project teams were vis-à-vis the top managers comprising the teams' sponsors. Obviously, we sought to corroborate our classification of a specific project team based on what appeared to be the shared view of its participants. Over time, it can be noted that the 'what needs to be done' part of autonomy became increasingly specified. Whereas the projects in the first edition were formulated vaguely – 'how we could become a global leader in innovation by 2020' (Project 2) – later projects were more specific. Project 16 offers an extreme example of a highly specific project objective; it stipulated, with imperatives:

> Propose a key account management process (activities) for [the division] and for cross-divisional customers. Based on benchmarks and research, define the following: What is a key account; what should the key-account management process look like; what is the key account manager's role and responsibility? Define the governance, collaboration, and reporting structures needed to maximize customer centricity and sales result.

As indicated in Table 2, some project teams were relatively autonomous, others much less so, and yet others seemed to have been able to strike a balance. For the sake of brevity, we explain how we decided on our classification by presenting illustrative examples rather than discussing all projects extensively.

We classified teams as high on autonomy when they positioned themselves as independent from their sponsor or the top management

Table 2 *Summary of Findings*

Ground breaker edition	Project	Autonomy (vis-à-vis TMT/ sponsor)	Innovativeness (newness) *	Innovativeness (conceptual-specific)	Implementation (what?)	Implementation (when?)	Autonomy→ Innovativeness **	Autonomy→ Implementation **
I	1	high	new to the organization, *not* adapted to the setting	specific (radically new ideas)	nothing	never	+	+
II	3	high	new to the organization and adapted to the setting	largely conceptual, but with some specific elements	the least radical parts of the proposal	adopted for further development	+	+/−
II	5	high	new to the organization and adapted to the setting	specific, best practice	parts of the proposal	immediately	+	−
V	14	high	new to the organization and adapted to the setting	largely conceptual, but with some specific best practice elements	N/A	N/A	+	N/A
V	15	high	improving practices already established in the organization	specific (project description in highly operational terms)	parts of the proposal	−	−	+/−

Table 2 (cont.)

Ground breaker edition	Project	Autonomy (vis-a-vis TMT/ sponsor)	Innovativeness (newness) *	Innovativeness (conceptual-specific)	Implementation (what?)	Implementation (when?)	Autonomy→ Innovativeness **	Autonomy→ Implementation **
I	2	balanced	new to the organization, *not* adapted to the setting	specific (mixture of off the shelf and radically new ideas)	parts of the proposal	implemented later	+	+/–
II	4	balanced ***	new to the organization, *not* adapted to the setting	specific (market study for new business segments)	nothing	never	–	–
III	6	relatively high, aware of need of support	new to the organization and adapted to the setting	N/A (no materials on the proposal itself, only talk about)	proposal	immediately	+	+
III	7	balanced	new to the organization and adapted to the setting	highly conceptual	parts of the proposal	adopted for further development	+	+/–
III	8	balanced ***	adapting a model already established in the company	specific (market study for novel product ideas)	nothing	never	–	–
IV	9	balanced	new to the organization and adapted to the setting	conceptual idea with operationalization	proposal	immediately	+	+
IV	10	balanced ***	new to the organization and adapted to the setting	largely conceptual, but with some specific elements	parts of the proposal	adopted for further development	+	+/–

Table 2 (cont.)

Groundbreaker edition	Project	Autonomy (vis-à-vis TMT/ sponsor)	Innovativeness (newness) *	Innovativeness (conceptual-specific)	Implementation (what?)	Implementation (when?)	Autonomy→ Innovativeness **	Autonomy→ Implementation **
V	16	balanced	new to the organization and adapted to the setting	specific (project description in highly operational terms)	parts of the proposal	immediately	+	+
IV	11	low (not allowed by sponsor)	new to the organization, *not* adapted to the setting	specific (standard global practice, best practice)	proposal	immediately	+	+
IV	12	low (initially high, but sponsor blocked the team's intended solution)	adapting practices already established in the company	specific	N/A	N/A	+	N/A
V	13	low (sponsor very directive)	some ideas new to the organization without adaptation + list of on-going pilots	conceptual (the strategy part), highlighting existing internal best practices and identifying potential new pilots	N/A	N/A	+	N/A

* *Note*: inspired by Volberda *et al.* (2014).

** *Note*: + = case confirms expectation; +/– = case somewhat confirms expectation; – = case does not confirm expectation.

*** *Note*: in these projects, the divisional innovation manager had strong influence over the project.

team, or even if they resisted attempts to influence the direction of their project. In Project 1, for example, the team appeared to have established a high level of autonomy. As one participant explicitly stated, 'We were not afraid to really defend our standpoints' and 'I think that we all had the guts to fight for what we believed in.' Project 5 is particularly noteworthy; the team seemed to have consciously decided whether or not to follow advice from the sponsor, given their mission to change things. 'Some things [i.e., suggestions by the sponsor] we took on board ... But some of the things we did not take on board ... Because we, we knew that we were there to change things.'

Other project teams scored high on autonomy but also seemed to have sensed that they could not accomplish a revolution without support from top management. Project 7 was able to develop a balanced approach:

> We actually had very frequent contact with the sponsors since the start of the project ... At every module, basically once a month, we had to report to the sponsor. But in between the modules, every two weeks we would have a meeting with our sponsor to see his response to our initial prototyping and presentation ... And he gave, suggested, very good feedback ... he thinks that we are on several key spots, but he also added several key spots that we have missed in doing our interviews, and which is very helpful to our project to move forward.

Finally, some teams were unable or unwilling to ascertain their independence. A major reason for rating these projects as low on autonomy was that the sponsor did not leave much space for the teams to take initiative, using them as instruments for advancing pre-established ideas. The sponsor for Project 11, for example, was adamant that product management had to be implemented. This sponsor also told us explicitly how he tried to influence the project team to come up with the proposal that he wanted:

If I come and say to everybody all the time what they shall do . . .
they feel pretty useless . . . If you help them and let them try out and
just push them a little bit and left it [to] them [to] find it themselves,
then they invented it themselves. So it's very simple.

Innovativeness. Volberda *et al.* (2014) present an interesting classification for assessing levels of innovativeness. They distinguish among
innovations that are *new to the world, new to the organization and
adapted to the setting,* and *new to the organization without adaptation.* We modified their classification to the contingencies of the
various projects, in order to qualify the project teams' level of innovativeness. We were surprised to find that none of the project teams were
able to develop ideas that we could rate as *new to the world.* The idea
was, after all, that they would develop ideas to 'revolutionize' the
company. Arguably, the project team members' lack of experience
and specialized knowledge goaded them into orienting themselves
first and foremost on ideas and innovations by best practice companies, forerunners, or leaders in industries unrelated the company's.
Consequently, project teams were able to develop ideas *new to the
organization* (or perhaps even new to the industry), either *adapted to
the setting* or *without adaptation.*

Various project teams *adapted* their new ideas *to the setting,*
meaning that considerable thought had to be given to make the idea
appropriate to the company. Other teams presented their ideas as
readily implementable without much need for adaptation to context
(i.e., off the shelf, *new to the organization without adaptation*). For
example, Project 11 on product management resulted in a 'step by step
process [on] how [the company] should go forward when they want to
implement product management'.

When coding for innovativeness of the project proposals, we
realized that a second dimension was relevant, too. Some proposals
were highly abstract, offering conceptual ideas. Other proposals were
pragmatic or had highly specific recommendations, comprising lists of
precise and actionable items. Again, Project 11 offers an illustration of

a team that adapted and elaborated its conceptual ideas to fit the context of the company.

Implementation. As the project teams were supposed to identify options to revolutionize the company, it is of interest to examine whether (elements of) the proposals were implemented. We therefore looked for information in the interviews that allowed us to estimate first, whether a project's proposal was implemented (*for the most part, parts of the proposal,* or *not at all*), and second, the delay between the presentation of the proposal and the timing of implementation (*immediately after the presentation, with some delay,* or *not at all*). Given that our interviews with participants in the first few editions were retrospective, that most participants went back to their original jobs after completion of their project, and that interviews for the last edition were conducted while the projects were still on-going, there was no consistently clear indication of implementation across all projects.

We believe that the results of our coding (Table 2) offer some support for our expectations regarding the relationships between autonomy and innovativeness and between autonomy and implementation.

FROM AUTONOMY TO INNOVATIVENESS

We found that thirteen projects confirm the expectation that high (low) autonomy increases (decreases) the likelihood of innovative project outcomes. Project 11, for example, which was rated low in autonomy and low on innovativeness, proposed the implementation of a set of standardized best practice solutions that were readily available off the shelf and that the top management could easily embrace. We also rated Project 13 as low on autonomy. This team worked on industrial digitalization, under the guidance of an extremely directive sponsor. The team struggled for a long time with what 'industrial digitalization' could actually mean. As one project team member said in the second interview: 'the whole group didn't have a clue what this digitalization was, and what it's not', and in the first interview, early in the project, 'even the sponsor doesn't seem to have an idea about the aim of the project'. Apparently, the team settled on a broad understanding that any use of information technology to help increase efficiency would count as industrial digitalization. In our interpretation, lack of understanding about the core concept of the project prevented the team from moving beyond a proposal for a listing of on-going and potential pilots plus an estimate of their possible benefits.

Projects 3, 5, 7, and 9 are examples of projects that we rated high or balanced on autonomy and that developed innovative ideas; we discuss these projects in the next section in relation to implementation.

Projects 4, 8, and 15 apparently contradicted our expectation of an association between a high level of autonomy and a high level of innovativeness. We discuss Projects 4 and 8 in the next section. Project 15 was high on autonomy but did not propose particularly innovative ideas. We explain this apparent contradiction by pointing out that this team was required to develop proposals on 'leading-edge supply chain services' for a specific lead customer, but it was not allowed to contact this customer. Team members started their project by exploring best practices in other companies that could inspire their proposal. The team also interviewed workers at the company, however, which made them realize that improvement of established working practices was needed, and that work-level contact with the customer would reveal opportunities for improvement. This proposal and their organizing of work-level contacts with the customer went against its mandate:

> You sent us out on a quest to find new shiny things. What we found was something else. When we talked to our customers, [they say] we are rated average in Finland. We are not exceeding their expectations, because their expectations are for us to get the basics right. For example, deliveries on time.
>
> *(Project 15 presentation notes)*

Because this team operated autonomously, it was able to challenge the assumption underlying their initial assignment, namely that the company needed 'new shiny things'; they proposed, instead, to improve and optimize established practices on the shop floor, which was then adopted for further development.

FROM AUTONOMY TO IMPLEMENTATION

Projects 1, 6, 9, 11, and 16 confirm our expectations. Project 11 (low autonomy) was discussed previously; there is no surprise that the proposal was immediately implemented. Project 9 (balanced autonomy) was mandated to 'get a grip on time', to discover whether and how time management could benefit the company. There were 'huge discussions' with the project sponsor,

> because he was pushing something that he called lead-time management as a management philosophy or a concept and, I was saying that, you know, there is no such thing as lead-time management. It is not an established management concept. But he said, okay, define it, tell me what lead-time management is.

The team was therefore motivated to find an equivalent to the just-in-time approach from the automotive industry that would be meaningful to the company. Its members developed a concept that, according to the project sponsor, 'acted as a catalyst to start the biggest process development programme in ... product history, ever'. Project 1 (high autonomy) was about leadership in global responsibility. Its proposal had two elements: the formulation of a new company purpose, formulated in collaboration with Project 2, and a number of relatively radical ideas, such as 'collaboration with [a renewable energy company in a developing country] to utilize the land around windmills for farming' and 'establishing a co-operative with locals in [China]'. Whereas the formulation of purpose may have inspired future projects and the company in a broader sense, the other ideas were quickly forgotten.

Project 3 and 15 (high autonomy) and Projects 2, 7, and 10 (balanced autonomy) somewhat confirm our expectations in the sense that *parts* of the proposal were implemented or taken up for further development. The team in Project 3 developed a toolbox for leadership, focusing on motivational issues and internal communication. Some elements in the toolbox were elements of standard human resource (HR) management practices; others were radically new ideas. Some of the HR elements were adopted for further development by the HR function, whereas the more radical elements were disregarded.

Among Projects 2, 7, and 10, Project 7 offers a nice illustration. The team set out to develop a proposal on 'how to make global responsibility an integral part of our company's culture' at all levels of the company. After extensive interviewing, they concluded that the company was willing but neither able nor ready to strengthen a global responsibility strategy. They formulated their proposal as a need for the company to internally and externally align its strategy, structure, processes, people, and environment, and offered suggestions for further development. Although their proposal was highly abstract, some of their suggestions were adopted for further development.

Projects 5, 4, and 8 ran contradictory to our expectations. Project 5 looks like an outlier case that disconfirms expectations, as the team was highly autonomous, whereas elements of the proposal were immediately implemented. The project was about improving logistics, and the team studied examples of firms with the most complex logistical systems imaginable as sources of ideas. Their work was received with criticism, however. Two examples of intermediate feedback are: 'This is hopeless; this is complete crap', and 'Yes, this is better than last time, but still not executable.' At some point, the team realized that best practices from other companies were of little value, as supply chain logistics is done 'on the ground'. Finally, resisting the interdiction to talk to the lead customer, they organized a one-day workshop to break through established practices in supply-chain management, and

> immediately, these two people [one from our company, the other
> from the lead customer] who haven't even spoken in ten years, start
> to say that 'Hey, why don't we do that that way then? Why can't you
> give me that where I can do this, and then you can have it six days
> early?' They'll say 'Okay, let's do that.' And that's sort of
> one million euros saved, for a year.

The immediate implementation of Project 5 was of those parts of the
proposal that immediately and substantially paid off. In this way,
Project 5 is similar to Project 15 (and Project 12, not discussed here).
These teams came to realize that big innovation is not always the
most appropriate solution, and decided that small innovation through
adaptation of working practices may be a better way forward.

Projects 4 and 8 (and 10) stand out for a different reason. We
classified these cases as balanced in terms of autonomy between the
sponsor and the top management team. Nevertheless, the proposals
from Projects 4 and 8 were not especially innovative; nor did they
make it through to implementation. Both projects were in the same
division, and the innovation manager was able to develop significant
influence over the two projects. She was hired when the second
edition of Groundbreakers (Project 4) had just started, and left the
company when the fourth edition (Project 10) was underway. During
this time, she managed to gain significant influence over these
projects and resist their implementation, presumably because the
ideas were not hers and the manager did not agree with the team
approach.

PARTIAL ORGANIZATION THEORY AND STRATEGIC MANAGEMENT

From the information presented here, we conclude that, in general
terms, our proposals regarding the balance between autonomy, innovativeness, and implementation are validated. We now discuss some
limitations to our study, and then explore theoretical and managerial
implications.

By no means do we wish to give the impression that our analysis has statistical validity, not only because of the small number of projects, but also because the projects cannot be treated as independent cases. After all, top management chose the projects' themes and goals, formulating them with their experiences from previous editions in mind, and some sponsors were involved in multiple editions of the programme. Nevertheless, we believe that our study does offer valuable insights for partial organization theory. If decision making is central to organization, then partial de-organizing is not merely about deciding to eliminate elements of organizing. Our cases suggest that what matters is primarily about *how*, exactly, de-organizing is done, and that learning can result from experience.

Our study contributes to partial organization theory. First, it shows that elements of organization *can* be suspended, at least to some extent and temporarily. If partial organization theory is an invitation to analyse the gradual introduction of organization in unorganized settings through decision making, then our chapter suggests that partial de-organization is not only a logical, but also an empirically valid complement to partial organization. Second, it turned out that suspending hierarchy was the hinge towards partial de-organizing. We can think of theoretical reasons why this would be the case: Hierarchy may be considered a first-order decision, as it defines who has the authority to make decisions, including decisions on other elements of organization. We leave it for future research, however, to confirm or disconfirm and to elaborate upon the question of whether hierarchy is critical in partial de-organizing. Third, our study offers evidence that partial de-organization may have consequences for innovation. We believe that we offer support for the idea that an organization paradox underlies the innovation paradox, and that suspension of hierarchy increases autonomy, which in turn creates conditions favourable for innovation.

Yet, *exactly how* can partial de-organization create conditions favourable to innovation? Revisiting our cases, we suggest that there are three ways through which enhanced autonomy helps to develop novel, innovative ideas: recombination of knowledge, allowing for serendipity, and breaking organizational routines.

The nature of innovation as recombination of existing knowledge has been well recognized (Galunic & Rodan, 1998). Because the team members had different bodies of expertise and experience, they were well positioned to recombine and complement each other's emerging insights. As one team member described: 'We all did our research on our sites and then came together again and looked at the big picture, and eventually all sorts of new ideas emerged.' In addition to sharing their views, the teams learned from outside:

> And that was really, I mean that was the best part of the programme, I would say, to actually be allowed to spend time to learn from other companies. Very, very helpful. Why is Google so innovative? Why is Lego so innovative? And then we really started to see the pattern and also what differentiates them.

The second observation is that partial de-organizing allowed for serendipity, which is a significant aspect of innovation (Garud et al., 2013; de Rond, 2014). We heard comments such as 'we were learning on the fly', making 'novice mistakes', the 'hallelujah moment' in defining a project, and acknowledging the existence of less structure in opening up for serendipity. One comment credited 'not knowing' with being a serendipity enabler: 'You know nothing, and you simply have to learn and then try to do your best to come up with something.' The comment that 'we saw things that [more experienced people] would have never challenged' points to the absence of cognitive bias that may have contributed to openness for occasional serendipitous insight. Likewise, leaving one's office was supportive of developing new and unexpected insight: 'I think, if you want to be creative, you have to leave your office.' This may imply down-to-earth work:

> I think that the epiphany point came to us when we realized that this is not something fancy, this is not rocket science. This is something you need to stick your hand into, sweat a little bit, get

> your hands dirty, and make sure that you really work with the
> warehouse workers and, uh, and figure out how to best load a truck.

Finally, partial de-organizing may have invited and allowed team members to break organizational routines and thereby contribute to innovation. As we noted earlier, the literature extensively discusses routines as constraints on innovation (Dougherty & Hardy, 1996; Hansen & Birkinshaw, 2007). Therefore, making space for new behaviours may be important. Yet, working differently can be politically challenging: 'Others did not like us meddling in their area.' In some areas, like customer relationships, the teams acknowledged the need to proceed more carefully.

> Because if you are suddenly stepping into ... one of the bigger
> accounts, there is a current structure around that customer. So, you
> also need to work closely with that team so that they do not feel sort
> of excluded, so you need to take them on board, uh, in this journey.

The emphasis in many conversations was again on the outside view in supporting different ways of thinking and doing: '[They] are excellent but they have been working on the area for twenty to thirty years and cannot look from outside the box as someone external can.' New tools were designed to support the breaking of organizational routines. The friction inside the team as people learned to collaborate was perhaps fruitful. And finally, the breaking of routines was by no means easy: 'We had to use some cunning to be able to turn things around.'

Implications for strategic management

In terms of strategic management, our analysis suggests that de-organizing may help to solve the organization paradox at least partially, by making space for emergent elements that are recognized as important for innovation. Reducing structural constraints by partially de-organizing does not seem to address the necessary strategic sense-making of the organization's environment, however (Rouleau & Balogun, 2011). During the analysis, we wondered about the lack of radical innovations. Even if some teams had come up with something *new to the world*, the ideas would probably have remained largely unimplemented, particularly if they were not adapted to the company context. This requirement to connect to the corporate strategic context is well known in the literature; it requires both the formulation of workable, attractive options and political activities to convince top management to accommodate them in corporate strategy (Burgelman, 1983).

Partial de-organizing works against imperatives of political connectivity and strategic sensemaking, even if some teams did better than others in communicating their ideas and making them strategically relevant. In other words, although decided social order comes with a certain established way of making strategic sense of activities, team members from de-organized spaces do not share the same received assumptions, precisely because the social order in their team is largely emergent. Therefore, the teams face the uphill challenge of providing context to their innovation, such that top management, inhabiting a decided social order, understand their strategic significance. Emergent social order did seem to benefit from latent sensemaking, in that some of the proposals found their way to implementation as part of later projects. Thus, later project proposals may have provided the necessary strategic and structural context for the implementation of earlier developed, orphan ideas.

In conclusion, a high level of autonomy may be required for innovation teams to create ideas that depart from the structural and strategic context of the company, and this may make it difficult for top management to relate to them. In order to increase the chances that their ideas are implemented, project teams need to balance their autonomy with an appreciation of the firm's strategic and structural context. The odds may be increased when they get beyond awe or fear and learn to communicate with top management and to connect in strategic terms to the company's business environment.

REFERENCES

Ahrne, G., Aspers, P., & Brunsson, N. (2015) The Organization of Markets. *Organization Studies* 36(1): 7–27.

Ahrne, G. & Brunsson, N. (2011) Organization outside Organizations: The Significance of Partial Organization. *Organization* 18(1): 83–104.

Barberio, V., Höllerer, M. A., Meyer, R. E., & Jancsary, D. (2018) Organizational Boundaries in Fluid Forms of Production: The Case of Apache Open-source Software. In L. Ringel, P. Hiller, & C. Zietsma (eds.), *Research in the Sociology of Organizations. Toward Permeable Boundaries of Organizations?*, vol. 57. Bingley, UK: Emerald. 139–68.

Beck, N., Bru, J., & Woywode M. (2008) Momentum or Deceleration? Theoretical and Methodological Reflections on the Analysis of Organizational Change. *Academy of Management Journal* 51(3): 413–35.

Benner, M. J. & Tushman, M. L. (2003) Exploitation, Exploration, and Process Management: The Productivity Dilemma Revisited. *Academy of Management Review* 28(2): 238–56.

Bourgeois, L. J. (1981) On the Measurement of Organizational Slack. *Academy of Management Review* 6(1): 29–39.

Brunsson, N., Rasche, A., & Seidl, D. (2012) The Dynamics of Standardization: Three Perspectives on Standards in Organization Studies. *Organization Studies* 33(5–6): 613–32.

Burgelman, R. A. (1983) A Process Model of Internal Corporate Venturing in the Diversified Major Firm. *Administrative Science Quarterly* 28(2): 223–44.

Burgelman, R. A. (1991) Intraorganizational Ecology of Strategy Making and Organizational Adaptation: Theory and Field Research. *Organization Science* 2(3): 239–62.

Contino, C. & den Hond, F. (2009) Sense and Sensibility in Managerial Advice. In A. F. Buono (ed.), *Emerging Trends and Issues in Management Consulting: Consulting as a Janus-Faced Reality*. Volume 9. Greenwich: Information Age Publishing. 207–38.

Davila, T. & Epstein, M. (2014) *The Innovation Paradox*. San Francisco: Berrett-Koehler Publishers.

de Rond, M. (2014) The Structure of Serendipity. *Culture and Organization* 20(5): 342–58.

Dougherty, D. & Hardy, C. (1996) Sustained Product Innovation in Large, Mature Organizations: Overcoming Innovation-to-Organization Problems. *Academy of Management Journal* 39(5): 1120–53.

Elster, J. (1989) *The Cement of Society. A Survey of Social Order.* Cambridge: Cambridge University Press.

Farson, R. & Keyes, R. (2003) *The Innovation Paradox: The Success of Failure, the Failure of Success.* New York: Free Press.

Galunic, D. C. & Rodan, S. (1998) Resource Recombinations in the Firm: Knowledge Structures and the Potential for Schumpeterian Innovation. *Strategic Management Journal* 19(12): 1193–201.

Garud, R., Tuertscher, P., & Van De Ven, A. H. (2013) Perspectives on Innovation Processes. *Academy of Management Annals* 7(1): 775–819.

Gibson, C. B. & Birkinshaw, J. (2004) The Antecedents, Consequences, and Mediating Role of Organizational Ambidexterity. *Academy of Management Journal* 47(2): 209–26.

Hansen, M. & Birkinshaw, J. (2007) The Innovation Value Chain. *Harvard Business Review* 85(6): 121–30.

Henderson, R. M. & Clark, K. B. (1990) Architectural Innovation: The Reconfiguration of Existing Product Technologies and the Failure of Established Firms. *Administrative Science Quarterly* 35(1): 9–30.

March, J. G. & Simon, H. A. (1993 [1958]) *Organizations.* 2nd edition. Cambridge: Blackwell.

Morgeson, F. P. & Humphrey, S. E. (2006) The Work Design Questionnaire (WDQ): Developing and Validating a Comprehensive Measure for Assessing Job Design and the Nature of Work. *Journal of Applied Psychology* 91(6): 1321–39.

Phillips, J. (2008) The Innovation Paradox. Retrieved 1 November 2016 from http://innovateonpurpose.blogspot.fi/2008/10/innovation-paradox.html.

Prahalad, C. K. & Bettis, R. A. (1986) The Dominant Logic. A New Linkage between Diversity and Performance. *Strategic Management Journal* 7(6): 485–501.

Rouleau, L. & Balogun, J. (2011) Middle Managers, Strategic Sensemaking, and Discursive Competence. *Journal of Management Studies* 48(5): 953–83.

Simsek, Z., Heavey, C., Veiga, J. F., & Souder, D. (2009) A Typology for Aligning Organizational Ambidexterity's Conceptualizations, Antecedents, and Outcomes. *Journal of Management Studies* 46(5): 864–94.

Tripsas, M. (2009) Technology, Identity, and Inertia through the Lens of 'The Digital Photography Company'. *Organization Science* 20(2): 441–60.

Tsoukas, H. & Chia, R. (2002) On Organizational Becoming: Rethinking Organizational Change. *Organization Science* 13(5): 567–82.

Tushman, M. & Nadler, D. (1986) Organizing for Innovation. *California Management Review* 28(3): 74–92.

Välikangas, L. & Gibbert, M. (2005) Boundary-Setting Strategies for Escaping Innovation Traps. *Sloan Management Review* 15 April 2005.

Välikangas, L. & Gibbert, M. (2016) *Strategic Innovation: The Definitive Guide to Outlier Strategies*. Harlow: Pearson FT Press.

Volberda, H. W., van den Bosch, F. A. J., & Mihalache, O. R. (2014) Advancing Management Innovation: Synthesizing Processes, Levels of Analysis, and Change Agents. *Organization Studies* 35(9): 1245–64.

Vuori, T. O. & Huy, Q. N. (2015) Distributed Attention and Shared Emotions in the Innovation Process: How Nokia Lost the Smartphone Battle. *Administrative Science Quarterly* DOI:2010.1177/0001839215606951.

ACKNOWLEDGMENT

We thank Nadia Söderling for her assistance in the empirical analysis.

18 The Partial Organization of International Relations: International Organizations as Meta-Organizations

Göran Ahrne, Nils Brunsson, and Dieter Kerwer

Since the end of the Cold War, international governmental organizations (IGOs) have become ubiquitous in world politics. In order to cope, scholars have begun to conceptualize IGOs as organizations – as autonomous entities with the capacity to act independently (Ellis, 2010; Koch, 2009; Ness & Brechin, 1988). This approach is in contrast to the perception of IGOs merely as arenas or design features of international regimes, in which the representatives of member states act, but the organization itself does not. Yet, of the several thousand IGOs presently in existence, most are comparatively weak organizations – much less powerful actors than states or multinational corporations. Indeed, even such large IGOs as the United Nations (UN) are frequently criticized for not acting swiftly and forcefully when needed in international crises.

In order to understand IGOs as organizations, scholars have primarily resorted to two theoretical approaches. According to *principal–agent theory*, IGOs must be considered actors that pursue their own interests; it is not merely states that create IGOs and delegate certain tasks to their secretariat actors (Abbott & Snidal, 1998; Hawkins, Lake, & Tierney, 2006). It is the autonomy of a secretariat that forces a state into the role of a principal monitoring agent. An alternative approach to IGOs, *bureaucratic organization theory*, has specified the sources of autonomy (Barnett & Finnemore, 1999, 2004; Weaver, 2008; Biermann & Siebenhüner, 2009; Trondal 2010). An IGO's influence rests upon bureaucratic authority – on the specific expertise of its employees and their adherence to general norms and decision-making procedures (Barnett & Finnemore, 2004: 20–29). This theory has also proposed an explanation for the reason secretariats tend to deviate from their mandate. Deviations are not mere expressions of self-interested strategies of bureaucratic resource maximization, but are better seen as 'mission creep' – as an effort to obtain better control of the organization's environment by slowly expanding its mandate (Barnett & Finnemore, 2004: 9). In short, both these theoretical perspectives suggest that IGOs, by virtue of their large secretariats, become much more significant actors on the international stage than hitherto recognized.

We share with these approaches the underlying conviction that understanding IGOs as organizations is a fruitful perspective. It suggests that scholars draw on the rich stock of theories that has been developed in organization studies over the past sixty years or so, as they attempt to understand international organizations. The application of traditional theories of organizations to IGOs can be partly misleading, however. In accordance with these theories, both principal–agent theory and bureaucratic organization theory are based on the assumption that members of the IGOs are individuals – typically employees of the secretariats. The organizations are understood as consisting of their secretariats, whereas the member states loom in the environment, not really considered part of the organization. Although the control and actions of secretariats are highly relevant issues in the relatively few IGOs that have large secretariats, studies of secretariats provide only partial answers to the broader issue to be discussed in this chapter: the relevance and power of IGOs in general – both those with and without secretariats.

We need to go beyond the standard assumption in organization theory that the members of organizations are individuals and acknowledge that IGOs are not organizations with individual membership, but associations of states, which are, in themselves, organized actors. As such, IGOs are 'meta-organizations' – organizations with other organizations as their members.

A large variety of organizations belongs to this type. Although meta-organizations are associations, their members may be other types of organizations such as firms, states, or even associations. National associations of firms, unions, or sport clubs provide examples of meta-organizations. Many national meta-organizations are, in turn, members of international meta-organizations: international sports associations such as Fédération Internationale de Football Association (FIFA), and international business associations such as Association des Constructeurs Européens d'Automobiles (ACEA) and the International Egg Commission (IEC). Meta-organization theory points to several crucial differences between organizations with individuals as their members and organizations with other organizations as their members (Ahrne & Brunsson, 2005, 2008).

At the core of meta-organizations we find a real paradox: Meta-organizations are autonomous actors with autonomous actors as their members. This paradox has numerous ramifications for the way meta-organizations such as IGOs are established, how their decisions are made, which organizational elements they can use, and how they can influence their members and the wider environment.

In contemporary Western societies, organizations, including states, typically pose as social actors – as independent and sovereign entities with self-interested goals, commanding independent resources and having clear boundaries (Meyer et al., 1997; Brunsson & Sahlin-Andersson, 2000; Drori, Meyer, & Hwang, 2006). Any deviation from this image can be interpreted as an anomaly, or at least as a weakness of the organization.

Actorhood becomes a challenge in meta-organizations. If organizations have to pose as autonomous actors and if meta-organizations are autonomous, how can organizations that are members of another organization also be autonomous actors? Members of individual-based organizations or of meta-organizations must regularly relinquish some autonomy, allowing the organization or meta-organization to make decisions affecting what the members can and should do. There is a considerable difference between individuals as members and organizations as members, however. The lack of autonomy that an individual experiences in organizations is problematic, particularly for people with organizational positions that provide almost no freedom to make their own decisions, as in some manufacturing industries; or in cultures in which people are expected to demonstrate a high degree of actorhood, as in many contemporary Western societies (Meyer & Jepperson, 2000). For an organization lacking autonomy, however, the situation is more serious – even a mortal threat. Organizations are precarious social constructions in which some degree of autonomy is a constitutive aspect: It is difficult to convince people that something is an organization if it cannot make some decisions on its own; rather it would, at best, be considered a department of another organization. (See Drori et al., 2006: 14–17.)

If a member organization has no autonomy vis-à-vis a meta-organization, it becomes irrelevant for its own members. A meta-organization is also expected to have autonomous decision-making power, however, and becomes irrelevant without a minimal degree of autonomy. Both the members and the meta-organization are victims of the paradox that the members must be autonomous actors, although belonging to an autonomous organization; and the meta-organization must be an autonomous actor, even though its members are autonomous. In practice, this paradox makes the meta-organization and its members compete for autonomy, leading to severe and intricate problems of actorhood.

In subsequent sections, we point to some peculiarities of IGOs and demonstrate how they can be explained, combining theories about meta-organizations and partial organization. We first discuss the ways in which IGOs tend to be weak actors. We want to show that the IGOs' weaknesses are due not to specific design flaws, but are inherent in their construction as meta-organizations, rendering organization difficult. IGOs have decision-making problems in general and decisions about rules, monitoring, and sanctions in particular. They also have problems reforming themselves in order to become stronger. Yet IGOs have strengths that are seldom acknowledged by the other approaches in which IGOs are viewed as organizations. They use membership to gain power. They are easily established and have an expansive dynamic that allows them to compensate for some of their weaknesses over time. In conclusion, we highlight how our approach sheds new light on IGOs and their paradox.

THE CHALLENGE OF ACTORHOOD: WEAKNESSES OF INTERNATIONAL GOVERNMENTAL ORGANIZATIONS

Seeing IGOs as organizations suggests that IGOs are, in fact, powerful actors. Yet, most IGOs have problems living up to the image of a strong actor: They are not autonomous enough, they have problems organizing collective action, and they have fewer resources at their disposal than their members have. Their character as meta-organizations can explain their weaknesses. In the next section, we explain in greater detail some of the problems of decision making, of deploying organizational elements, and of organizational reform.

Problems of Decision Making

Organizations are social systems constructed and run by decision making (March & Simon, 1958/1993; Luhmann, 2000). One crucial way in which organizations allow for collective decisions to be made is through *delegation*. In organizations, members, owners, or other principals often delegate decision-making competencies to a professional management. By doing so, they greatly enhance the decision-making capacity of organizations.

In meta-organizations, it is difficult and therefore uncommon to delegate key decisions to top management with a great deal of leeway, because it would imply a threat against the autonomy of the meta-organization's members and their leaders. Thus, the authority of the meta-organization's managers is limited, and rarely do they have far-reaching decision-making power (Ahrne & Brunsson, 2008: 114–16). For meta-organizations, visible management is a problem, as it enhances the visibility of the members' loss of autonomy and provides a focal point for resistance.

We suggest, therefore, that powerful secretariats in IGOs are the exception rather than the rule. And indeed, their employees are called secretaries rather than executives and their offices are called secretariats rather than headquarters. Leaders of IGOs are typically less well known and have less status and power than the presidents or prime ministers of their members, and they have difficulty exaggerating their importance in a way that is typical of the leaders of firms and states.

Delegation difficulties lead to peculiar decision-making problems in meta-organizations. Because there is little delegation to top management, crucial decisions are made by members, via negotiations and voting. But using the majority principle in voting is difficult, because the minority must relinquish much of its autonomy. This is true even for an advanced IGO such as the European Union (EU). (See Finke *et al.*, 2012.) Furthermore, it is not obvious what constitutes a majority among organizations. A simple majority rule with one vote per member, which is an institutionalized principle in individual-based associations (Warren, 2001), does not have the same legitimacy in a meta-organization, where the possible variety among members is greater. In IGOs, one can ask, for instance, whether states with more members of their own or states that contribute more resources should have more votes. Any principle for defining a majority can be questioned – a fact that undermines the authority of majority decisions.

As in other meta-organizations, it is common among IGOs that decisions can be made only by consensus, giving each member the right to veto each decision. But this principle is also problematic: It guarantees autonomy for the members, but virtually no autonomy for the meta-organization.

Decision-making problems can be avoided, of course, by avoiding decisions. The zone in which decisions are made by the meta-organization can be reduced in order to minimize the damaging effect on member autonomy. But there is a price to be exacted: the relevance of the meta-organization.

Finding a balance in meta-organizations between member autonomy and organization autonomy is a challenging task, accomplished by carefully choosing the more exact content of decisions. Decisions vary in their effect on member autonomy. Decisions concerning tasks of the meta-organization's employees (if there are any) are the least threatening decisions. What the employees do is somewhat distant from the members. With the help of principal–agent theory and in other ways, they can blame the employees and their lack of control over them. So, paradoxically, adding a large secretariat to an IGO may be a way of rescuing both member autonomy and IGO autonomy. This could explain why member states have continually blamed the European Commission or the management of the International Monetary Fund (IMF) for certain activities, yet have failed to undertake any serious effort to reform them.

Decisions need not concern actions. They may concern talk: what the meta-organization says or what each member says. One would usually expect decisions about talk to be more easily made than decisions about actions are, because they do not require resources or actions from the members – only statements. A situation in which it is easier to make decisions about what to say than what to do tends to produce more talk than action. Meta-organizations may become highly competent in deciding on resolutions that look good but imply little action. Hypocrisy becomes a tempting option when the organization encounters conflicting demands: compensating the lack of action in line with a certain interest by producing talk and decisions that support that interest. Or hypocrisy becomes the result of internal conflict: The organization satisfies members with diverging interests by acting in accordance with the interest of some members and making statements in accordance with the interest of others (Brunsson, 2007). Hypocrisy is a widespread phenomenon in several international meta-organizations, such as the World Bank and the World Trade Organization (WTO) (Lipson, 2007; Weaver, 2008).

The partial organization of IGOs

The decisions of IGOs are primarily addressed at their members. IGOs manage to coordinate action to the extent that members comply with and implement decisions made on behalf of all their members. But being an actor is easier for individual-based organizations than for meta-organizations. Organizations can resort to organizational elements that increase the likelihood of decision making being consequential and the likelihood of achieving coordinated action: membership, rules, monitoring, sanctions, and hierarchy. (See Chapter 1.) Although meta-organizations are basically constructed in the same way as other organizations, in practice they often encounter difficulties in deploying these elements (Berkowitz & Dumez, 2015). It is this characteristic of the meta-organization that creates the same difficulties in IGOs.

The meta-organization's setting of rules for what members shall do creates a challenge to member autonomy. But the avoidance of binding rules can reduce the challenge. It is common for meta-organizations to formulate standards – non-binding rules. Standards are less threatening than binding rules because the decision is split into two components: the organization's setting of the standard and the member's decision to comply (Brunsson & Jacobsson, 2000). Standards are common in IGOs, where they are often called 'recommendations', 'best practices', 'guidelines', or 'benchmarks'; in International Relations (IR) research they are often referred to as 'soft law' (Mörth, 2004). Standards are often the only way of reaching decisions about rules. In the domains in which the EU has no formal competencies – labour market policy, for example – it does not refrain from decision making, but adopts voluntary best practice standards instead. (See Heidenreich &

Zeitlin, 2010; Borrás & Jacobsson, 2004.) Similar techniques have been employed in other IGOs (Schäfer, 2006).

Decisions about the effective monitoring of members are also difficult to make and enforce in meta-organizations, because members do not want to demonstrate that the meta-organization or its members are not fully complying with various rules. Monitoring needs attractive labels or arguments such as peer reviews and the search for best practice – concepts often used in the EU in relation to monitoring.

A meta-organization's ability to sanction members effectively is severely curtailed. The fact that both a meta-organization and its members are organizations affects the balance of resources between them. Because most of the members have existed as organizations long before the meta-organization was established, they generally have more resources at their disposal than the meta-organization has (although there may be wide differences in available resources among members). As a result, the typical meta-organization is relatively poor, controlling fewer resources than most of its members. Because states command most of the resources and because large states are extremely resourceful organizations, it must be expected that an IGO cannot command the resources necessary for a positive and forceful incentive.

Meta-organizations face similar difficulties using negative sanctions, because few members would accept those sanctions. An illustration was provided by the Kyoto Protocol. Its binding emission targets called for hefty fines to member states that failed to meet them. Yet, when Canada faced the prospects of paying a large fine, it simply reneged on its obligations by exiting from the Kyoto protocol (*The Globe and Mail*, 2011). More importantly, the ultimate negative sanction – the IGO excluding a recalcitrant member – is seldom a realistic option. Meta-organizations depend on their members to a much larger extent than individual-based organizations do, because the members are not as exchangeable as they are in most individual-based organizations. IGOs face the same challenges: Expelling members is likely to have negative repercussions for the IGO itself. What would have happened to the European Monetary Union if Germany or France had been expelled for having violated the Maastricht criteria for several consecutive years? How would the character of the UN change if it were to expel states with a serious record of human rights violations?

Organizational elements cannot be considered in isolation in meta-organizations; their combination and their combination with decision-making procedures are key factors. Using one element may require the avoidance of other elements or certain forms of decision making. IGOs can seldom make majority decisions on binding rules, for example, compliance with which is monitored and sanctioned. It is easier to make decisions about binding rules that are not monitored or sanctioned, especially if those decisions can be made by consensus. As a member of the International Whaling Commission, Japan is obliged to abandon the hunting of whales. Nevertheless, Japan continues to hunt whales for 'scientific purposes', and although international non-governmental organizations (INGOs) have continuously questioned this practice, the International Whaling Commission has turned a blind eye.

In summary, the difficulties of using organizational elements in meta-organizations help to explain why IGOs have problems influencing and coordinating their members, and therefore have problems achieving coordinated organizational action. Furthermore, when extensive resources are needed for action, meta-organizations are at a disadvantage, because most of the resources required belong to their members and may be difficult or time consuming to mobilize. Members may exploit their organization's dependence on their resources to influence meta-organization decisions. The UN Security Council is a well-known example of an organization that is highly dependent on the resources of member states. Although it can authorize measures to preserve or restore peace, it cannot implement them. Rather, the Security Council must rely upon the willingness of its members to commit troops. After Iraq attacked Kuwait in 1990, for example, the council adopted several resolutions condemning the aggression and authorizing countermeasures. But it took a coalition of states to end the Iraqi occupation of Kuwait.

Members of meta-organizations often have a much better chance of providing strong actorhood. That is true for IGOs in which the members are powerful states. There is often a risk that one or a few member states will act on their own rather than contributing to IGO actions. A good example is the EU's difficulty in developing a common foreign policy in order to have a more marked influence on world politics and to defend Europe's interests vis-à-vis powerful states.

The actorhood problem is particularly obvious in handling situations of crisis or conflicts in which quick decisions are required. Decision-making opportunities are limited, as it may be difficult to arrange meetings for member representatives on short notice. And decision making is a protracted and often tedious procedure (Codding & Rutkowski, 1982), with complicated negotiations among representatives, some of which may also act as 'veto players', waiting until the last minute to declare their final position (Tsebelis, 2002). This weakness can be observed in many IGOs. The resolution of the European debt crisis from 2009 is a good example of the difficulty IGOs face in responding to a crisis; crisis resolution required many meetings over several years, yet yielded extremely slow progress, even though there was constant pressure from financial markets to act swiftly.

Problems of Reform

In recent years, many IGOs have been subject to reforms: Well-known examples are the UN Security Council, the North Atlantic Treaty Organization (NATO), the WTO, the IMF, the EU, and the World Bank. (See, e.g., Hurd, 2008; Lindley-French, 2007; Weaver, 2008.) The overwhelming impression is that these reforms have been partial successes at best. Unsuccessful reforms have often given rise to yet other attempts. IGOs appear to be highly resistant to planned change.

They may undergo a great deal of change, yet not be easily changeable because of their problems in organizing.

Organizational reforms are common phenomena in most large organizations, and their implementation is often problematic. But in comparison with individual-based organizations, meta-organizations appear to be peculiar organizations, ineffective and even flawed, and in need of reforms. Because of the weaknesses described here, however, they have great difficulty deciding upon and implementing radical planned changes, including changes aimed at reducing the weaknesses.

Some demands for reform originate in the meta-organization's position in its environment. In order to interact forcefully with other organizations, not least those with individual membership, a strong actorhood of the meta-organization is often required and is sometimes expected by external parties, creating grounds for claims for reform. For IGOs, a case in point is the EU (Kerwer, 2013). One key catalyst of the EU's Common Foreign and Security Policy has been demands by the USA and others for the EU to strengthen its capacity to contribute to peacekeeping. On other occasions, external parties have not appreciated forceful actions from IGOs, and they may try to stir up reforms intended to increase the autonomy of members. Although some EU members, such as France and Germany, opposed the invasion of Iraq in 2003, the USA sought to weaken the EU by specifically appealing to the new member states of Central and Eastern Europe, such as Poland, to join the war effort in exchange for military co-operation. By doing so, the USA may also have hoped to make future attempts of the EU foreign policy framework more difficult (Hill & Smith, 2011).

The weaknesses of IGOs not only produce demands for these types of reform, but also make reforms difficult to accomplish. IGOs have problems deciding on the specific content of reforms because they do not agree on the direction that the organization should take: towards more or less actorhood. And weak actorhood presents a difficulty for implementing reforms. With decision-making problems, a weak leadership, and lack of sanctions at their disposal,

IGOs can be expected to have difficulties in implementation. A striking feature of IGO reforms is the number of times they have failed – as demonstrated in the case of the World Bank, for instance (Weaver, 2008).

In recent years, IGOs have also been confronted with demands for reforms for more democracy. Here the situation is even worse: There seems to be a general lack of solutions. The constitution, as a compound of two types of autonomous actors, suggests that IGOs, by definition, reduce the autonomy of member states, and that demands for democratizing IGOs are therefore legitimate. Restrictions of national autonomy by the IGO easily appear to be in conflict with the fundamental norm of democratic self-determination – when the WTO has denounced its members' social and environmental regulation as mere informal barriers to trade, for example. Calls for democracy can arise among member states, but also among *members* of member states. Citizens of democratic states fear that their citizenship is jeopardized by IGOs (Usherwood & Nick, 2013).

The meta-organization perspective suggests why demands for democratizing IGOs are so difficult to satisfy. The crucial defining element of democracy is the representatives' accountability to their constituencies (Keohane, Macedo, & Moravcsik, 2009). Increasing the democratic legitimacy of IGOs through representation, however, places the IGO in a dilemma, because, as previously mentioned, there are no satisfactory voting rules. Using the principle of one vote per member renders the influence of citizens in small states disproportionately large. Conversely, if voting rules are aimed at a more faithful representation of the population of its member states, they are likely to undermine democracy within their smaller member states, as they risk being outvoted by larger states.

The alternative strategy of strengthening democracy in IGOs through horizontal control (see Dryzek, 2006; Steffek, 2010) is also problematic. Demands for increasing horizontal control have triggered a wide-ranging discussion on how IGOs could become more transparent and accountable to international nongovernmental organizations and a wider global public sphere. IGOs that need to be responsive to the demands of the INGOs in their environment, however, will find it more difficult to respond to demands from their members whenever these demands differ. Thus, increasing horizontal democratic accountability is likely to undermine vertical accountability to its members.

Overall, there are no clear-cut solutions for increasing democracy in IGOs or other meta-organizations. Democratic ideas that have been conceived with reference to individual-based organizations do not seem to be able to constitute stable forms of *meta-democracy*.

THE STRENGTHS OF INTERNATIONAL GOVERNMENTAL ORGANIZATIONS: THE SALIENCE OF MEMBERSHIP

So far we have explained why most IGOs are usually weak actors by referring to their decision-making problems in general, and their organizational decision-making problems in particular. If efficient actorhood were the only way for IGOs to exert influence, however, it would be impossible to explain their salience. We must look for something other than actorhood in order to explain the strengths of IGOs. The fact that meta-organizations tend to be weak actors that have difficulty acting on their environment in a strong and coherent way does not necessarily mean that they have little influence on that environment. Bureaucratic organization theory points to more subtle mechanisms that have been exploited by a few large IGO secretariats – influence through their specialist expertise, for example. By contrast, we suggest other sources of influence – sources available to meta-organizations, whether they have built large secretariats of experts or not. Although meta-organizations have problems using many of the organizational elements of hierarchy, rules, monitoring, and sanctions, they face less of a challenge with the element of membership. Much of the strength of a meta-organization comes from its ability to decide who can become a member, and this type of decision is a major instrument for influencing its environment. The strengths of IGOs can be understood in relation to their creation, their expansion, and their long-term influence on their members.

Establishing International Organizations

In the field of IR, the establishment of IGOs has been seen as a task requiring substantial effort. According to principal–agent theory, states create international organizations only under specific circumstances (Abbott & Snidal, 1998), delegating tasks to a new international organization only if its benefits outweigh the costs of creating it. These costs are not only the resources required in establishing a secretariat, but also the political cost of reduced sovereignty. Furthermore, states must overcome the problems of monitoring secretariats, which are likely to behave as self-interested agents (Hawkins et al., 2006). A major hypothesis results from this perspective: Creating an international organization is a tedious process, and one that is likely to remain a rare event. Creating the UN's relatively large number of international organizations after World War II appears to have been a heroic effort, mostly on the part of the USA, and is unlikely to be repeated.

Given this perspective, it is difficult to explain the rapid expansion of international organizations over the past 50 years. Between 1981 and 1992 alone, the Union of International Associations reported a dramatic increase in the number of IGOs: from 1039 to 1690 (Shanks et al., 1996: 596). There are several recent examples of quick organizing, as an effect of the financial crisis of 2009: the creation of the new G20, the upgrading of the Financial Stability Forum to the Financial Stability Board, and the creation of the European Banking Authority. The BRICS, the group of 'emerging economies' comprising Brazil, Russia, India, China, and South Africa, are about to turn their regular annual meetings into a formal international organization. A little-noted example of a regional IGO is the Arctic Council, founded in 1996 – an organization in which member states bordering on the Arctic commit themselves to sustainable development. The expansion of INGOs has been even more impressive, expanding from approximately 200 in 1900 to approximately 4,000 in 1980, and reaching some 7,600 by 2010 (Boli & Thomas, 1999: 13). Roughly 90 per cent of these INGOs are meta-organizations (Ahrne & Brunsson, 2008: 21). The rapid expansion of both IGOs and INGOs is easier to understand from our perspective than from any of the alternative theories.

It is relatively easy to create an organization with other organizations as its members. Establishing a meta-organization requires few resources compared to the resources controlled by the member organizations; the constituting members merely need to pool a tiny fraction of their resources. Initially, the administration of the meta-organization is often conducted by people already employed by some of the members. Most meta-organizations can be expected to produce inexpensive decisions, and talk rather than engaging in costly actions.

Organizations have little incentive to resist membership in a meta-organization once the creation of one has been suggested. The low cost is one factor for the ease with which organizations agree to membership. In addition, given the relatively small number of members – five to ten members are often enough to start a meta-organization – there are ample opportunities for the potential member to exert influence. Furthermore, meta-organizations seldom begin with a programme that seems to be a severe threat to the autonomy of its members.

For IGOs, to avoid using the concept of organization sometimes reduces the fear of producing the image of lost autonomy for its member states. Other labels are created: 'committees' (e.g., the Basel Committee on Banking Supervision), 'public-private partnerships' (e.g., the Roll Back Malaria Partnership), 'forums' (e.g., World Forum on Energy Regulation), 'task forces' (e.g., the Financial Action Task Force on Money Laundering), or 'initiatives' (e.g., the Global Methane Initiative). Upon closer scrutiny, however, such forms of co-operation often turn out to be meta-organizations or turn into meta-organizations over time.

For a state to remain outside an IGO under creation would deny it the influence that membership provides. Even states that had been against the initiative to establish an IGO may choose to join, in order to prevent the organization from making certain decisions or even to obstruct its activities. An organization that can recruit both its supporters and its opponents as members is an easy organization to form.

Enlarging International Organizations

It is no surprise that IR scholars have developed a keen interest in enlargement in recent years, given that after the end of the Cold War, Western IGOs such as the EU and NATO have decided to accept a number of formerly socialist states (e.g., Schimmelfennig, 2003). Yet, enlargement has usually been analysed merely as a minor challenge facing the organization.

Conventional organization theory suggests that the recruiting of new members is a crucial albeit relatively routine task for most organizations. Meta-organization theory, by contrast, suggests that recruitment into meta-organizations is not merely a routine task to uphold the operational capabilities of an organization. Rather, it is one of the most important strategies available to meta-organizations if they are to exert any influence. Meta-organizations tend to have greater influence on candidates than on members because, although they cannot easily sanction members, they can strongly influence candidates through their conditions of access. A static approach to analysing power and membership is therefore misleading. The current membership is the result of past power: the power of turning what was the meta-organization's environment into organization through membership. And existing power is the power to make that transformation happen now and in the future. Power is also related to the degree to which the organization is able to make would-be members adapt to its demands. From this perspective, it becomes clear why the EU and NATO sought to gain control over Eastern Europe through enlargement in the 1990s.

Its gate-keeping power is enhanced if an organization has monopoly status, which is more typical of meta-organizations than it is of most kinds of individual-based organizations; there is typically only one meta-organization within a certain sphere of activity. This characteristic of a monopoly is inherent in the mission to be the representative of special issues or themes, whether specified by geographical region or by task. Becoming a member of a meta-organization is attractive, because it can facilitate interaction with all the relevant organizations in that domain or because it provides an organization with the opportunity to gain an identity and status equal to that of its members. Thus, to start a new meta-organization in order to compete with another meta-organization would be of little value unless all its members switched to the new organization.

Almost all IGOs gravitate towards a monopoly position. Although some have started to compete with states or INGOs, we rarely see IGOs competing with each other in the same functional and regional domain. (See Alter & Meunier, 2009: 19.) A clear division of labour characterizes the UN organizations. Functional overlap is the exception even among international environmental 'regime complexes', and it is usually not created deliberately by the member states (Gehring & Oberthür, 2011). Whenever IGOs do perform similar tasks, it is detrimental to their effectiveness as they lose influence over their member states (Drezner, 2009). Thus, IMF policies, designed to promote long-term economic development, have been seen as a problematic intrusion into the domain of the World Bank. The European Economic Community (EEC) and the European Free Trade Association (EFTA) once had identical purposes of promoting free trade in Western Europe. Yet, over time, the two trading blocs have co-operated so closely that they have become indistinguishable for all practical purposes.

The establishment of an IGO changes the environment for both members and non-members. Even if it were in the interest of non-members to resist the establishment of the IGO, their environment has now changed in such a way that they may be interested in joining it. Furthermore, a monopoly puts the meta-organization into a powerful position relative to prospective new members. Once an IGO has been established as the only one in a certain area, potential members have only two options: to become a member or not. Not becoming a member eliminates any opportunity of influencing the organization's future direction. A state that is interested in influence and what an IGO can offer is in a weak negotiating position, and can often be persuaded to adapt to the special member requirements for that organization. It is exactly at the moment when a potential member applies for membership that the IGO is in its most powerful position.

IGOs have used this power position on various occasions to a greater or lesser extent. One strategy has been to recruit as many states as possible that are willing to become members, in order to eliminate a large part of the environment – a strategy followed by the UN. Another strategy, applied by such international organizations as the EU, Organisation for Economic Co-operation and Development (OECD), and the WTO is the exercise of selectivity in accepting new members and placing strong demands on any new member regarding its constitution, economic performance, and political systems. The first strategy, to include as many members as possible, encompasses a larger part of the environment, but at the cost of reducing the IGO's power over the new members.

The second, selective, strategy tends to leave a greater part of the environment unorganized. On the other hand, the IGO is able to place stronger demands on new members. Sometimes a limited membership is granted as a first step, in order to make the fulfilment of IGO demands seem less dramatic, and commitment to them is secured over time. Prospective members are first admitted as associate members (as in the EU or WTO) until they have fulfilled the required criteria for membership. The Financial Action Task Force on Money Laundering (FATF) has sought to increase its control over offshore financial centres by encouraging them to become members of FATF-style regional bodies. Membership in these regional bodies does not include the right for these countries to participate in decision making (Hülsse & Kerwer, 2007).

Transforming Members

Members of organizations are influenced not only by the use of organizational elements, but also by more indirect processes connected to their membership. Because of the difficulties of using the organizational elements, meta-organizations must rely to a large extent on these indirect ways of influencing their members. A time perspective is critical here. We suggest that the strengths of meta-organizations vis-à-vis their existing members can be revealed only in the long run, and membership tends to be a long-term affair. Like most other meta-organizations, IGOs often have considerable staying power, and the turnover of their members is extremely low. Belonging to an IGO may eventually lead to processes over which the members have less control, and which reinforce the IGO at the expense of its members. Although IGOs appear to be resistant to planned change in the form of reform attempts, they are likely to change in other ways.

We identify three processes observable in IGOs and other meta-organizations. One is the *successive adding and sedimentation of decisions*. Over time, even if decision making is slow and tedious, an IGO is likely to have accumulated a substantial number of valid decisions on organizational elements. The IGO has become more organized. After a decade or so, the members may find that they have agreed to many rules, monitoring activities, and sanction systems, some of which may even be binding. And abolishing these elements requires new decisions that are difficult to make.

A second process is one of *mutual adaptation* – a fundamental ordering that is based on no organizational decision other than membership, but that is common in organizations, because of their role as an arena where members meet (Lindblom, 2001). When representatives of an IGO member state, whether politicians or administrators, work closely together with representatives from other states, they may be socialized into ways of running the business of an international organization (Checkel, 2005; Schimmelfennig, Engert, & Knobel, 2006). There is a process of learning. Member states learn from other members how they can influence IGO decision making and how they can best comply with the IGO's decisions (Jacobsson & Sundström, 2006). As they do so, the awareness of member states about the common decision-making agenda will increase, which may lead to national policies becoming more compatible with that agenda.

Finally, the *boundaries between a meta-organization and its members may become blurred,* because both the members and the organization of which they are members constitute the same type of social construction. This ontological affinity easily leads to unclear or permeable boundaries. As the members become involved in and adjust themselves to the decision-making procedures of the meta-organization, the boundaries can dissolve – when the administration of the member organization is integrated into the administration of the meta-organization, for instance, or the other way around. This is not an unusual process for members of such international organizations as the EU, OECD, and WTO. The administrative staff of the IGO delegates tasks directly to some or all of its members. Consequently, some administrative divisions of a member state can be regarded as 'enclaves' of the IGO; in this sense, some member ministries and authorities can be considered enclaves of the EU (Vifell, 2006; Wessels, 1997; Trondal, 2010).

Common policies and operations and a number of common rules and monitoring activities facilitate co-operation and exchange among IGO members. If there is an increase in interaction within trade, education, or research, for instance, the members will become more dependent on their membership. It would require strong mobilization to achieve the same things outside the IGO. Thus, members prefer to remain members. And over time they are likely to become more willing to adapt to their IGO's requirements as their status and identity become associated more strongly with it.

The sedimentation of decisions, the mutual adjustment among members, the blurring of boundaries, and the ensuing increased member dependence may, in the long run, undermine members' actorhood and increase the actorhood of the meta-organization. If this development goes too far, the members may become more like departments or divisions, and the meta-organization may become more like an organization with individual members. Finally, it may even be transformed into an individual-based organization. This development has been observed in other types of meta-organizations, but it may take place in IGOs as well. During the 19th century, for instance, the German Customs Union was transformed into a single German state. European federalists expect the EU to be transformed into a single state as well – albeit without any wars of unification.

VARIATION

So far, we have explained some general characteristics of IGOs. But there are exceptions to the general trend and there are *variations among* IGOs. At a certain point, some IGOs are more autonomous, powerful, or changeable than others are, whereas others function as little more than arenas, in rough accordance with the way authors in the realist tradition have treated them. In line with the arguments presented in this chapter, we predict that an IGO will become a stronger actor the more resources it controls, the more similar its members, and less the need of members to demonstrate their autonomy. In addition, the IGO's influence over its present and future members can be expected to be stronger the closer it is to a monopoly and the more selective it can afford to be in choosing its members. Furthermore, the older the organization, the more likely it is that its members become more and more similar, which in turn increases the organization's chances for stronger actorhood. Yet there may be counteracting forces. A new IGO that begins by refraining from difficult decisions may gain strength relatively quickly, whereas an established IGO with ambitious management and many organization activities may at some point trigger strong resistance from its member states.

Similarly, we need to consider *variation over time*. We believe that it is critical to consider the dynamics of IGOs. Their present state is the result of on-going development, in which the role of the members varies over time. Due to their paradoxical construction, meta-organizations have built-in problems and tensions that tend to prevent equilibria and steady states. Observed stability in IGOs requires as much explanation as observed change does. It is crucial to understand the processes that reinforce the IGO. Rather than merely analysing the activities and effects of large secretariats, for example, one can ask what helps large secretariats to grow and what hinders their growth within IGOs. And what are the processes by which IGOs gain control over large resources? Individual-based organizations may be not only the beginning, but also the end of an IGO. What processes would favour the dissolution of an IGO, a return to a set of non-organized, separate states, or its transformation into one individual-based state?

Finally, we contend that our arguments cast new light on the perennial question of *how much IGOs can matter*. The two theories discussed in the introduction to this chapter share the assumption that IGOs can become relatively powerful with the help of secretariats. By contrast, we see principle limitations to IGOs ever attaining great levels of power as long as they remain meta-organizations and do not become individual based. Although we acknowledge sources of influence other than powerful actorhood, we come somewhat closer to the realist position than does either of the other two approaches.

As mentioned in the introduction to this chapter, realists are sceptics regarding IGOs because they view the international system as an anarchical one, in which the survival of a state is constantly jeopardized. States that invest too much trust in IGOs, the sceptics say, risk their security and ultimately their survival. But the international system is often not a maligned Hobbesian world; it can be a more benign Lockean world of co-operation or even a Kantian international society of norms (Wendt, 1999). Consequently, the realist scepticism may seem overblown. Yet, our analysis in this chapter suggests that this is not entirely the case. Rather, if we generalize the realist scepticism to today's more benign worlds of international relations, relying on IGOs does entail a risk for a state's autonomy. But in contrast to realism, this risk is not one of being conquered by another state; rather, it is the risk of losing autonomy to the IGO. For this reason, there will be limits to the amount that member states will be prepared to delegate to

IGOs, even when they do not need to operate in a Hobbesian international environment. If this reasoning is correct, any deficits in the power of IGOs are a matter not merely of design, but of principle, and we need to adjust our expectations of the possible role of IGOs in contemporary global governance accordingly.

IGOs are lacking in actorhood; yet they lead to some taming of member-state actorhood. They obstruct or retard the decision making of members. But the loss of some actorhood among member states does not mean that IGOs become actors that are as strong as states can be. The decrease of members' actorhood is not fully compensated by the increase of the IGO's actorhood. The result may well be a general reduction of actorhood. But in a world that has already witnessed too much actorhood by nation states and empires, reduced actorhood is perhaps more of a solution than a problem.

REFERENCES

Abbott, K. & Snidal, D. (1998) Why States Act Through Formal International Organizations. *Journal of Conflict Resolution* 42(1): 3–32.

Ahrne, G. (1994) *Social Organizations: Interaction inside, outside, and between Organizations*. Thousand Oaks: SAGE.

Ahrne, G. & Brunsson, N. (2005) Organizations and Meta-Organizations. *Scandinavian Journal of Management* 21(4): 429–49.

Ahrne, G. & Brunsson, N. (2008) *Meta-Organizations*. Cheltenham: Edward Elgar.

Ahrne, G. & Brunsson, N. (2011) Organization outside Organizations: The Significance of Partial Organization. *Organization* 18(1): 83–104.

Ahrne, G., Brunsson, N., & Kerwer, D. (2016) The Paradox of Organizing States: A Meta-Organization Perspective on International Organizations. *Journal of International Organizations Studies* 7(1): 5–24.

Alter, K. J. (2001) *Establishing the Supremacy of European Law: The Making of an International Rule of Law in Europe*. Oxford: Oxford University Press.

Alter, K. J. & Meunier, S. (2009) The Politics of International Regime Complexity. *Perspectives on Politics* 7(1): 13–24.

Barnett, M. N. (2002) *Eyewitness to a Genocide: The United Nations and Rwanda*. Ithaca: Cornell University Press.

Barnett, M. N. & Finnemore, M. (1999) The Politics, Power, and Pathologies of International Organizations. *International Organization* 53(4): 699–732.

Barnett, M. N. & Finnemore, M. (2004) *Rules for the World: International Organizations in Global Politics.* Ithaca: Cornell University Press.

Berkowitz, H. & Dumez, H. (2015) La dynamique des dispositifs d'action collective entre firmes: le cas des méta-organisations dans le secteur pétrolier. *L'Année sociologique* 65(2): 333–56.

Biermann, F. & Siebenhüner, B. (2009) *Managers of Global Change: The Influence of International Environmental Bureaucracies.* Cambridge, MA: MIT Press.

Biersteker, T. J. & Weber, C. (1996) *State Sovereignty as Social Construct.* Cambridge, MA: Cambridge University Press.

Boli, J. & Thomas, G. M. (1999) INGOs and the Organization of World Culture. In J. Boli and G. M. Thomas (eds.), *Constructing World Culture: International Nongovernmental Organizations Since 1875.* Stanford: Stanford University Press. 13–49.

Borrás, S. & Jacobsson, K. (2004) The Open Method of Co-Ordination and New Governance Patterns in the EU. *Journal of European Public Policy* 11(2): 185–208.

Brunsson, N. (2007) Organized Hypocrisy. In N. Brunsson (ed.), *The Consequences of Decision-Making.* Oxford: Oxford University Press. 111–34.

Brunsson, N. & Jacobsson, B. (2000) *A World of Standards.* Oxford: Oxford University Press.

Brütsch, C. & Lehmkuhl, D. (eds.) (2007) *Law and Legalization in Transnational Relations.* London: Routledge.

Carreau, D. (1994) Why Not Merge the International Monetary Fund (IMF) with the International Bank for Reconstruction and Development (World Bank)? *Fordham Law Review* 62(7): 1989–2000.

Checkel, J. T. (2005) International Institutions and Socialization in Europe: Introduction and Framework. *International Organization* 59(3): 801–26.

Chwieroth, J. M. (2010) *Capital Ideas: The IMF and the Rise of Financial Liberalization.* Princeton: Princeton University Press.

Codding, G. A. & Rutkowski, A. M. (1982) *The International Telecommunication Union in a Changing World.* Dedham: Artech House.

Cox, R.W. and Jacobson, H. K. (eds.) (1973) *The Anatomy of Influence: Decision Making in International Organization.* New Haven: Yale University Press.

Deitelhoff, N. (2009) The Discursive Process of Legalization: Charting Islands of Persuasion in the ICC Case. *International Organization* 63(1): 33–65.

Drezner, D. W. (2009) The Power and Peril of International Regime Complexity. *Perspectives on Politics* 7(1): 65–70.

Drori, G. S., Meyer, J. W., & Hwang, H. (2006) Introduction. In G. S. Drori, J. W. Meyer, & H. Hwang (eds.), *Globalization and Organization: World Society and Organizational Change.* Oxford, New York: Oxford University Press. 1–22.

Dryzek, J. S. (2006) *Deliberative Global Politics: Discourse and Democracy in a Divided World.* Cambridge: Polity.

Ellis, D. C. (2010) The Organizational Turn in International Organization Theory. *Journal of International Organizations Studies* 1(1): 11–28.

Finke, D., Koenig, T., Proksch, S. O., & Tsebelis, G. (2012) *Reforming the European Union: Realizing the Impossible.* Princeton: Princeton University Press.

The Globe and Mail (2011) www.theglobeandmail.com/news/politics/canada-formally-abandons-kyoto-protocol-on-climate-change/article4180809/

Goldstein, J., Kahler, M., Keohane, R. O., & Slaughter, A.-M. (eds.) (2001) *Legalization and World Politics.* Cambridge, MA: MIT Press.

Grant, R. W. & Keohane, R. O. (2005) Accountability and Abuses of Power in World Politics. *American Political Science Review* 99(1): 29–43.

Hatch, M. J. (2011) *Organizations: A Very Short Introduction.* New York: Oxford University Press.

Hawkins, D. G., Lake, D. A., Nielson, D. L., & Tierney, M. J. (eds.) (2006) *Delegation and Agency in International Organizations.* Cambridge: Cambridge University Press.

Heidenreich, M. & Zeitlin, J. (2009) *Changing European Employment and Welfare Regimes: The Influence of the Open Method of Coordination on National Reforms.* London: Routledge.

Hill, C. & Smith, M. (2011) *International Relations and the European Union.* Oxford: Oxford University Press.

Hix, S. & Høyland, B. K. (2011) *The Political System of the European Union.* Basingstoke: Palgrave.

Hülsse, R. & Kerwer, D. (2007) Global Standards in Action: Insights from Anti-Money Laundering Regulation. *Organization* 14(5): 625–42.

Hurd, I. (2008) Myths of Membership: The Politics of Legitimation in UN Security Council Reform. *Global Governance* 14(2): 199–217.

Jacobsson, B. & Sundström, G. (2006) *Från hemvävd till invävd: europeiseringen av svensk förvaltning och politik.* Malmö: Liber.

Keohane, R. O. (1984) *After Hegemony: Cooperation and Discord in the World Political Economy.* Princeton: Princeton University Press.

Keohane, R. O. & Nye, J. S. (2002) The Club Model of Multilateral Cooperation and Problems of Democratic Legitimacy. In R. O. Keohane (ed.), *Power and Governance in a Partially Globalized World.* London: Routledge. 219–44.

Keohane, R. O., Macedo, S., & Moravcsik, A. (2009) Democracy-Enhancing Multilateralism. *International Organization* 63(1): 1–31.

Kerwer, D. (2013) International Organizations as Meta-Organizations: The Case of the European Union. *Journal of International Organizations Studies* 4 (Special Issue: Sociological Perspectives on International Organizations and the Construction of Global Order): 40–52.

Koch, M. (2009) Autonomization of IGOs. *International Political Sociology* 3(4): 431–48.

Krasner, S. D. (1983) *International Regimes*. Ithaca: Cornell University Press.

Krasner, S. D. (1999) *Sovereignty: Organized Hypocrisy*. Princeton: Princeton University Press.

Lake, D. A. (2003) The New Sovereignty in International Relations. *International Studies Review* 5(3): 303–23.

Lake, D. A. (2009) *Hierarchy in International Relations*. Ithaca: Cornell University Press.

Lindblom, C. E. (2001) *The Market System: What It Is, How It Works, and What to Make of It*. New Haven: Yale University Press.

Lindley-French, J. (2007) *The North Atlantic Treaty Organization: The Enduring Alliance*. New York: Routledge.

Lipson, M. (2007) Peacekeeping: Organized Hypocrisy? *European Journal of International Relations* 13(1): 5–34.

Luhmann, N. ([1964]1976) *Funktion und Folgen formaler Organisation*. Berlin: Duncker & Humblodt.

Luhmann, N. (2000) *Organisation und Entscheidung*. Wiesbaden: Westdeutscher Verlag.

Malone, D. M. (2007) Security Council. In T. G. Weiss & S. Daws (eds.), *The Oxford Handbook on the United Nations*. Oxford: Oxford University Press. 117–35.

March, J. G. & Simon, H. A. ([1958]1993) *Organizations*. Cambridge, MA: Blackwell.

Mearsheimer, J. J. (1994) The False Promise of International Institutions. *International Security* 19(3): 5–49.

Meyer, J. W., Boli, J., Thomas, G. M., & Ramirez, F. O. (1997) World Society and the Nation-State. *American Journal of Sociology* 103(1): 144–81.

Meyer, J. W., Drori, G. S., & Hwang, H. (2006) World Society and the Proliferation of Formal Organization. In G. S. Drori, J. W. Meyer, & H. Hwang (eds.), *Globalization and Organization: World Society and Organizational Change*. Oxford: Oxford University Press. 25–49.

Meyer, J. W. & Jepperson, R. L. (2000) The 'Actors' of Modern Society: The Cultural Construction of Social Agency. *Sociological Theory* 18(1): 100–20.

Moravcsik, A. (1998) *The Choice for Europe: Social Purpose and State Power from Messina to Maastricht*. Ithaca: Cornell University Press.

Mörth, U. (ed.) (2004) *Soft Law in Governance and Regulation: An Interdisciplinary Analysis*. Cheltenham: Edward Elgar.

Ness, G. D. & Brechin, S. R. (1988) Bridging the Gap: International Organizations as Organizations. *International Organization* 42(2): 245–73.

Oberthür, S. & Gehring, T. (2011) Institutional Interaction: Ten Years of Scholarly Development. In S. Oberthür & O. Schram Stokke (eds.), *Managing Institutional Complexity. Regime Interplay and Global Environmental Change*. Boston: MIT Press. 25–58.

Rittberger, V., Zangl, B., & Kruck, A. (2011) *International Organization: Polity, Politics and Policies*. Basingstoke: Palgrave.

Schäfer, A. (2006) A New Form of Governance? Comparing the Open Method of Co-ordination to Multilateral Surveillance by the IMF and the OECD. *Journal of European Public Policy* 13(1): 70–88.

Schimmelfennig, F. (2003) *The EU, NATO and the Integration of Europe: Rules and Rhetoric*. Cambridge: Cambridge University Press.

Schimmelfennig, F., Engert, S., & Knobel, H. (2006) *International Socialization in Europe: European Organizations, Political Conditionality, and Democratic Change*. Basingstoke: Palgrave.

Scott, W. R., Gerald, F. D. (2007) *Organizations and Organizing: Rational, Natural, and Open System Perspectives*. Upper Saddle River: Pearson.

Shanks, C., Jacobson, H. K., & Kaplan, J. H. (2009) Inertia and Change in the Constellation of International Governmental Organizations, 1981–1992. *International Organization* 50(4): 593–627.

Simon, H. A. ([1945]1997) *Administrative Behavior: A Study of Decision-Making Processes in Administrative Organizations*. New York: Free Press.

Steffek, J. (2010) Public Accountability and the Public Sphere of International Governance. *Ethics & International Affairs* 24(1): 45–68.

Trondal, J. (2010) *An Emergent European Executive Order*. New York: Oxford University Press.

Trondal J., Marcussen M, Larsson, T. & Veggeland, F. (2010) *Unpacking International Organizations: The Dynamics of Compound Bureaucracies*. Manchester: Manchester University Press.

Tsebelis, G. (2002) *Veto Players: How Political Institutions Work*. Princeton: Princeton University Press.

Usherwood, S. & Starting, N. (2013) Euroscepticism as a Persistent Phenomenon. *Journal of Common Market Studies* 51(1): 1–16.

Vifell, Å. (2006) *Enklaver i staten. Internationalisering, demokrati och den svenska statsförvaltningen.* Stockholm Studies in Politics 113. Stockholm University: Department of Political Science.

Waltz, K. N. (1979) *Theory of International Politics.* Reading, MA: Addison-Wesley.

Warren, M. (2001) *Democracy and Association.* Princeton: Princeton University Press.

Weaver, C. (2008) *Hypocrisy Trap: The World Bank and the Poverty of Reform.* Princeton: Princeton University Press.

Wendt, A. (1999) *Social Theory of International Politics.* Cambridge: Cambridge University Press.

Wessels, W. (1997) An Ever Closer Fusion? A Dynamic Macropolitical View on Integration Processes. *Journal of Common Market Studies* 35(2): 267–99.

Zürn, M. (2004) Global Governance and Legitimacy Problems. *Government and Opposition* 39(2): 260–87.

ACKNOWLEDGEMENT

This chapter is a shortened and somewhat edited version of Ahrne, Brunsson, and Kerwer (2016).

Conclusion

19 More and Less Organization

Göran Ahrne and Nils Brunsson

In Chapter 1, we argued that there has been a strong tendency in the social sciences to underestimate or hide organization, particularly organization outside formal organizations. To describe behaviour driven by institutions as following scripts or to describe the gender order as negotiated are not ways of emphasizing the existence of organization. Rather, they indicate the view that organization is so unimportant in social life that organizational concepts can be used not as analytical concepts, but as metaphors for something that is not organized at all.

But not only scholars avoid or fail to notice organization. Our cases show that many people that we considered as being involved in organization did not want to be seen in that way. People associated with social movements wanted to see those movements not as organizations or as being organized, but as consisting of individuals having spontaneous relationships with each other. (See Chapters 14 and 16.) Several terms that do not signal organization are popular even in cases of organization. 'Brotherhood' is a term indicating lack of organization, for instance; yet it is often an expression of organization (Chapter 13). The term 'sharing economy' does not signal organization, but it is used as a catchword by firms the very business concept of which is to organize buyers and sellers (Chapter 6).

The term 'network' is often more popular than the term 'organization'. Managers of the World Economic Forum (WEF) describe it as a network rather than an organization organizing other organizations (Chapter 10). Both practitioners and scholars refer to even strongly organized relationships among firms as 'networks' (Chapter 9). Because co-operation among firms, particularly among competitors, is often seen as problematic, firms have an interest in downplaying the organizational aspects of their relationships. Even formal organizations, such as meta-organizations, sometimes describe themselves as networks (Ahrne & Brunsson, 2008).

Students of the inner life of formal organizations have the opposite experience – that managers in these organizations often exaggerate the existence and salience of organization. Operations and results are explained by referring to the wise decisions of top management and to its ability to organize in the right way. There is a long tradition in organization theory of questioning such exaggerations – by pointing to the importance of institutions and networks for understanding what happens in formal organizations, for instance.

In general, students of organizations have less experience finding organization in contexts in which people do not talk about organization or have an interest in downplaying its existence, perhaps by exaggerating other aspects. It is more difficult in those contexts than it is in the context of formal organizations to notice the existence of organization. With this book, we hope to have convinced the reader that organization can be found in many social contexts where it has not traditionally been noted by the people involved or by observing scholars.

ORIGINS AND MOTIVES FOR PARTIAL ORGANIZATION

Both individuals and organizations organize. Individuals can partially organize their family life and sometimes their network of friends (Chapter 11). They can try to form a social movement and then find a need for organization, albeit for partial organization only (Chapters 14, 15, and 16). Organizations such as firms or states often want to organize their immediate environments (e.g., Chapters 5, 9, and 18); they do not want the environmental order to be determined merely by mutual adaptation, network dynamics, or institutions. Furthermore, there are countless organizations the main task of which is to organize other organizations in order to favour themselves or others. Apart from the standardizers, certifiers, accreditors, rankers, and prize givers that we have discussed in this book, there are rating institutes and a large number of organizations, such as Amnesty International, World Wildlife Fund, or Human Rights Watch that are based on idealistic principles and set rules and monitor and sanction firms and states via reports to the mass media. They constitute a large part of the organizations that John Meyer (1996) has called 'others'.

For both individuals and organizations, there are many possible motives for organizing. The preceding chapters illustrate how organization can be a means for trying to achieve better coordination among people or organizations, to make them do the right thing, to create similarities among them, to make an order more transparent, to influence status orders, or to change the distribution of power. Participating in organization activities can also be a way of attracting attention to oneself – by distributing prizes, for example (Chapter 3) or to earn money – by selling certifications, for example (Chapter 7). The starting points for organization vary as well, from a perceived lack of order to the organizers wanting to change an existing order.

Organizing the unordered

The 'tragedy of the commons' is a concept denoting that without some form of order, common resources tend to become over-used, even if it is not in the interest of anyone using them. Ostrom (1990) demonstrated that this tragedy can be avoided by organization and has been avoided in many historical and more recent cases. (See Chapter 1.) Organization has led from disorder to order and to a coordination of individual behaviour that improves the situation for everyone.

As we indicated in Chapter 1, it is difficult to explain the contemporary high degree of global order without considering the extensiveness of partial organization at a global level. Without organization, the world would be much more chaotic. Organization is less dependent on local conditions and cultural values than institutions and pure networks are.

There are few institutions that are shared across the globe. We believe that one can explain some forms of partial organization as a way for people and organizations to respond to and handle such institutional diversity. Different economies have somewhat different conceptions of what a firm is (Hall & Soskice, 2003), but international accounting standards help investors to judge the economic situation of firms around the world. There are still varying local institutions for family life, but they are challenged in marriages across cultural boundaries. A decision about membership has always been necessary to start a new family, but in a global world with increasing migration and more cross-cultural marriages, couples starting a new family will have more decisions to make.

With the increasing globalization of social relationships, it is likely that partially organized networks will become even more common. The Internet offers many opportunities to form social relationships, even among people from different parts of the world who have had no previous contact with each other. Such networks lack the local embeddedness that used to be seen as the prerequisite to networking (Thompson, 2003: 144) – meaning that the relationships emerged and were reproduced without any decisions when people met regularly in their neighbourhood in such places as churches or schools. But in a network lacking local embeddedness, keeping the network together requires decisions – decisions about membership or hierarchy, for instance. Chapters 6, 15, and 16 demonstrate how interaction and social relationships on the Internet can be partially organized. In another study, partial organization on the Internet has been found in connection with crowd funding (Roed Nielsen, 2018).

The type of 'sustainability standards' described in Chapter 2 can be seen as attempts to move from an unordered situation in which organizations behave differently to a highly ordered situation of all firms behaving in a similar way. Many of these standards are global. Here the main argument is that the standards shall initiate the behaviour that is morally right, which implies similarity rather than differences. Through organization, one creates a moral order without having to wait for (the unlikely event that) the moral right to become institutionalized in all organizations.

The global development of systems for certification and accreditation, which has expanded into more and more areas (Chapter 7), is intended to contribute to increased transparency, so that consumers and organizations can trust that other organizations actually comply with the standards they have accepted. Such organization is expected to increase trust and confidence, thereby facilitating trade or other forms of interaction among people and organizations at great distances, in situations in which the parties have little knowledge about each other.

Many rankings and prizes are global in scope and may create global status orders in areas that once contained only national ones (Chapter 3). Many contemporary prizes within science, art, and sport can be given to people or organizations from any country (Chapter 3), and some national prizes have a special category for foreigners, even when they are awarded in a national context. Today there are global rankings for almost everything. Rankers decide on the best university in the world; the best states for human rights, economic policy, and employment; and the best firms for customer satisfaction. Ranking lists are reports from monitoring activities, and they can be defined only as that. But if the people or organizations that are ranked become interested in their ranking position, ranking becomes a sanction as well – a positive sanction if one is placed high and a negative sanction if one is placed low. Rankings then become similar to prizes, although with prizes the primary factor is the sanction rather than the (possible) monitoring.

The development of the WEF (Chapter 10) provides an example of global organization of people and firms, some of which may have had some contact in other contexts, but which are now organized in a new way and in different constellations. There are many instances of co-operation among firms across national borders (Chapter 9), and thousands of meta-organizations that partially organize states, firms, or associations across national borders (Chapter 18). Most global meta-organizations are created by national meta-organizations that express the striving for a global order similar to the national ones. The specific division into national industries reflected in national industry associations is most often recreated in international industry associations or vice versa. Meta-organizations for business schools have sprung up over the years, comprising not only those that operate under the Anglo-American idea of a business school, but also those that originally did not.

Last but not least, many 'others' organize other organizations irrespective of national borders. Human Rights Watch monitors all states in the world. And standardization is now almost completely transnational and fundamental in creating global order in a host of technical areas. Many rankings and prizes have created global status orders that did not exist previously, as exemplified by universities on opposite sides of the globe that would never have heard of each other without rankings.

Organization instead of or in addition to another order

In other cases, partial organization does not begin with a lack of order, but with a certain order that the organizers want to reinforce or change. We have pointed to institutional orders as one example. Queues are formed according to patterns of behaviour that are taken for granted. But queues can also be organized in a way that reinforces the institutional order or in order to break with it (Chapter 8). Organization within families is necessary because traditional institutions have been weakened; old patterns are questioned, and new patterns have not yet been institutionalized (Chapter 11). Or organization can be driven by institutional insufficiency: Because not all aspects of family life are institutionalized, the institution must be supplemented by organization.

Prizes and rankings are sometimes attempts at influencing an existing institutionalized status order (Chapter 3). A common idea behind prizes is that one wants to make people aware of achievements that would otherwise have passed unnoticed. Rankings may be an attempt to change a taken-for-granted status order among universities.

Markets are based on a fundamental market institution of property rights that make an ordered exchange among people and organizations possible, but organization is a way of creating a more specific order in various markets (Chapter 5). Standards, perhaps in combination with certifications and accreditations (Chapters 2 and 7), facilitate an exchange among firms; this organization does not challenge the fundamental market institution but adds to it. And for a market to function well, the market institution is insufficient; organization is also required (Chapter 5).

In other cases, organization starts from a network order, relatively stable interactions, and relationships among people or organizations. Common in markets are networks of production firms with exchange relationships. Chapter 9 described how such networks are organized. Even firms that have a competitive relationship can be organized in so-called alliances (e.g., among airlines), which involve various degrees of organization. The classic example of such organization is cartels, which were particularly common in the early years of capitalism, and in which all organizational elements were commonly used (Strandqvist, 2018). In Chapter 6, the authors demonstrated how firms organized markets in which private persons were engaged as sellers.

Social movements often begin as networks that must later be organized in order to create continuity and achieve the common purpose of the participants (den Hond, de Bakker, & Smith, 2015). Chapter 14 demonstrated how striving for dialogue from an external party served as a force towards more organization. At a minimum, external parties can demand hierarchy, so that they can communicate with people who represent the movement and have responsibility for movement activities.

THE DIVERSITY AND DYNAMICS OF PARTIAL ORGANIZATION

The empirical studies in previous chapters have demonstrated that every organizational element can be applied independent of any other element. In many situations, an organizer does not need to or does not want to decide about more than one element. In other cases, organizers are not able to introduce more than one element. In yet other cases, the same organizer uses more elements or other organizers add more elements. Elements can also be dropped, as when management dispenses with hierarchy in order to make room for innovations (Chapter 17). Sometimes, some elements can be mobilized during a certain period or at special events (Chapter 15), only to be dropped later.

We have not found any order of priority or definite pattern for the way organizational elements are combined. Membership can later be completed with rules or with hierarchy (e.g., in gangs; see Chapter 12). But in other cases, membership can be added after rules or monitoring (Chapter 7). Sanctions can be complemented with rules in prizes (Chapter 3), but in many examples of standardization, rules come first and sanctions are added later (Chapter 2).

Little organization

Organization may meet with resistance, because individuals do not want to subordinate themselves to others or be forced to behave like others. Subordination and similarities go against prevalent ideas that individuals are or ought to be independent and unique. And subordination is a threat to the very existence of a formal organization. In such situations, the fewer the organizational elements that must be taken into account, the easier it is to organize.

There is evidence that the diffusion of standards is facilitated when other organizational elements are missing (Chapter 2); the plasticity of the standards increases, and the followers have more freedom in interpreting the rules in their own way.

An organizer who wishes to award a prize for outstanding achievement does not need any members. No hierarchy is required because it is taken for granted that the receiver of a prize will accept it with pleasure. Demands for more organization, such as rules and monitoring, can be avoided if the organizer provides an explanatory statement for why the prize is awarded and if the decision making is transparent (Chapter 3).

Many individuals may be reluctant to participate in organized actions if they have to become members who are expected to be available for future commitments. An organizer may acquire more participants merely by establishing rules for how and where someone can participate. Instead of members, there are contributors (Chapter 4, 15, 16) who can participate without necessarily sharing an identity or ideology with the organizer. In some of these cases, however, it turned out that there were contributors who did not follow the rules. But this did not lead to the introduction of membership; rather, it led to a decision that certain individuals were no longer allowed to participate. Instead of creating a closed social relationship, a negative social relationship was established.

In some of these examples, membership could be replaced by rules. In other cases, however, there is membership without any rules. In the organized network of the WEF, membership is combined with monitoring from the beginning (Chapter 10). But the organizers do not want to decide about rules; that would give the impression of too much control. The idea is that the notion of what is the right thing to do or say in WEF must emerge by itself.

Hierarchy is an organizational element that triggers a great deal of resistance. In the social movement initiative, Helsinki Timebank, one aim of the members was to create an alternative 'prefigurative' social order without organization and decisions for others (Chapter 14). Although a group of members clearly saw the need for some form of hierarchy, the resistance from other members was too strong to implement this element. The need for organizations to appear sovereign is an obstacle to hierarchy in both inter-firm networks and meta-organizations (Chapters 9 and 18).

Reluctance and resistance alone cannot explain the absence of hierarchy; a functional equivalent may already exist that makes decisions about hierarchy redundant. A decision order is often taken for granted from the start. Status is a source of power in street gangs and in kinship (Chapters 11 and 12). In an inter-firm network, it is taken for granted that a dominant corporation has the right to make decisions (Chapter 9). In the *We do what we can* movement, some people had access to the administrative function in Facebook, which gave them the power to decide about crucial issues without this power having been decided (Chapter 16).

There are also institutional impediments against organization. An institutional order may be complemented by organizational elements, but it cannot be organized in any possible way if people continue to define it in the same way. There is a risk that a queue will be perceived as something else if an organizer makes decisions that would revoke its order of priority or makes decisions about queue membership (Chapter 8). Decisions about membership are not compatible with the notion of friendship (Chapter 11), which explains why a brotherhood is a type of relationship that differs from friendship (Chapter 13).

More organization

An organizer can realize from the start that several organizational elements will be required, yet will begin with only one element in order to favour compliance. Some of the standardizers described in Chapter 2 started with a standard, but later monitoring and sanctions were introduced in order to make the standard more trustworthy. In the Helsinki Timebank (Chapter 14), members were supposed to learn from each other how to co-operate without organization. But as membership grew, this strategy no longer worked, and a rulebook proved necessary.

Affected individuals often demand more organization. In the beginning there was no organization in the *We do what we can* initiative (Chapter 16), but when the activists realized how much money had been collected, they demanded monitoring. Contemporary families are likely to discover before long that many more decisions than the fundamental one about membership have to be made (Chapter 11).

Initiatives for more organization may also come from external parties that are neither organizers nor organized. In Chapter 2, the authors describe how the legitimacy of a standard was threatened by criticism from several NGOs, which forced the organizers to introduce hierarchy, membership, and monitoring.

Decisions by one organizer easily provide incentives for others to add organizational elements because they do not agree and want to keep the existing order or change it in another way. Alternatively, others see the opportunity to add elements that support and extend previous elements. One example is the system of standards, certifications, and accreditations described in Chapter 7. For every new organizational element, new organizers appeared. Monitoring was conducted by certification organizations, which were monitored by accreditation organizations. The element of membership was added later through the creation of a number of interconnected meta-organizations.

WHY NOT FORMAL ORGANIZATION?

One may well ask why organization outside organizations can persist. Why does it not always lead over time to the creation of a formal organization in which the organizers and the organized are the members? Formal organization is, after all, a well-known institution that offers a readymade form for organizing. From the organizer's point of view, formal organization has one major advantage: It is expected to be organized. In contrast to organization outside organizations, it is more likely in formal organizations that one must justify the lack rather than the existence of organization. In the industrial firm described in Chapter 17, considerable effort had to be spent in order to *avoid* organization.

Organizing ambitions sometimes do lead to the creation of formal organizations. Over time, many social movements turn into formal organizations (Meyer & Tarrow, 1998). The goal of organizing markets may, in fact, lead to the creation of exchanges – placing markets in such formal organizations may be the only realistic way of making them work in reasonable accordance with the ideal of the 'perfect' or the 'perfectly organized' market (Chapter 5).

The preceding chapters illustrate several reasons for organizers to avoid the formation of a formal organization, however. In some cases, a formal organization lies beyond our imagination. Can a queue become a formal organization? A family can hardly become a formal organization and still be seen as a family.

In other cases, a formal organization is a possible option, but is still avoided by the organizers. Perhaps it is possible to create enough organization without a formal organization; in some cases, the organizers have no *need* for a formal organization in order to reach their purposes. Sometimes all organizational elements can be used outside organizations; organization may be 'complete' (Ahrne & Brunsson, 2011) outside a formal organization as well (Chapter 2). Many markets provide an example (Chapter 5). Inter-organizational networks may be more organized than the corporations that participate in them (Chapter 9). Besides, our example of meta-organizations demonstrates that a formal organization is no guarantee of achieving complete organization (Chapter 18).

In other cases, it is an *advantage* that organization remains outside a formal organization. The purposes of organization can be more easily reached and be easier to legitimate. If prizes are given to members of one's own organization, their impact on a wider status order is seriously weakened (Chapter 3). In Chapter 7, we demonstrated that auditors, certifiers, and accreditors consider it a fundamental value that they belong to a different organization and are 'independent from' the organizations they monitor. They may also prefer to earn their money from business rather than from salaries in the monitored organizations. Although markets are sometimes turned into formal organizations, and formal organizations sometimes arrange 'internal markets', it is usually advantageous for the organizers to keep or create the general market order in which sellers and buyers are sovereign individuals or organizations with property rights (Chapter 6).

A formal organization may have troublesome or negative effects that can be avoided by organizing outside organizations. Members of formal organizations tend to have rights that may provide obstacles to organizers realizing their intentions. States must handle members they have not selected (Chapter 11), and members of meta-organizations are keen to keep most of their autonomy (Chapter 18). In contrast, organizers of digital platforms (Chapter 6) could sidestep the issue of troublesome participants because they avoided making them members of their organization. The idea of 'contributors' rather than members facilitated the organization of work with refugees (Chapter 4).

Formal organizations are also expected to have a hierarchy: constitutions that regulate who can make decisions and in what way. Constitutions limit the amount of organization and provide a hindrance to the organizing plans of most would-be organizers.

The creation of formal organizations may also demand more time and administrative work than does organization outside organizations. The *We do what we can* initiative (Chapter 16) gave rise almost overnight to the devotion of thousands of people, who quickly contributed with large resources. Creating and registering a formal organization with a certain constitution and a certain membership would have been a much slower process.

In the social initiatives *We do what we can* (Chapter 16) and Helsinki Timebank (Chapter 14), there was a strong *scepticism* over the formal organization. In the case of *We do what we can*, the reasons were practical and familiar in the debate about organizations: putative inertness, excessive administration, and the risk of corruption in formal organizations. In Helsinki Timebank, the resistance was more ideologically motivated and was directed towards organization in general. Scepticism over formal organizations may have the same background as resistance to organization in general – that organization provides obstacles to the realization of individuality, spontaneity, and genuine commitment. Even if a formal organization is not necessarily more organized than a context outside formal organizations, it tends to make the existence of organization more explicit and clear. A combination of scepticism over organization and the need for organization provides an excellent breeding ground for compromise: organization without the formation of a formal organization.

External parties may be more interested than organizers are in organization being placed within a formal organization. Creating a formal organization means creating a social unit that can act and make statements, that can own things, and that can be attributed responsibility. External parties can have a relationship to and interact with this unit instead of having to relate to a bunch of people whose status may be unclear. It was the city authorities that wanted Helsinki Timebank to create an organization they could register, discuss with, and, not least, tax (Chapter 14).

The organized may prefer a formal organization because they find it easier to establish hierarchy and membership there – a hierarchy that can reduce the number of organizers and perhaps reduce the amount of organization in general, and a membership that gives them greater influence over what is organized and how. Organizations that do not like all the standards and monitoring they have been exposed to sometimes create meta-organizations. The meta-organization can decide on rules and monitoring systems that better fit the members. Or people and organizations that are exposed to organization may prefer a formal organization because they prefer transparency and responsibility concentration; even if all decided orders are stronger in these respects than emergent orders are, they are likely to be reinforced by placing organization within a formal organization.

IS ORGANIZATION OUTSIDE ORGANIZATIONS ON THE RISE?

Partial organization outside organizations can hardly be considered a new social innovation; as Ostrom's (1990) studies indicate, it existed a thousand years ago. Partial organization also seems to have been part of such primordial forms of social relations as marriage and kinship; even if most of the behaviour in these relationships has been highly institutionalized, options and a need for decisions have existed. How should kinship be defined at the margins? Which sanctions should affect individuals and which should affect families? Even in cultures in which women and men are expected to marry their cousins, a decision still has to be made about which cousin.

Formal organization as it currently exists constitutes a relatively recent and now abundant social phenomenon: entities that can exist without bonds to families or relatives and are able to choose their own members, hierarchy, rules, monitoring systems, and sanctions. The existence of such a large number of these organizations is, in fact, a major trait of contemporary social life; the modern society is a 'society of organizations' (Perrow, 1991). Much organization has become internalized into formal organizations. Many needs and opportunities for organization have been handled by the creation of formal organizations.

One may speculate that the increase and reinforcement of formal organizations during the industrialization of the 19th century reduced existing organization outside organizations and moved it into these new formal organizations. The invention of the limited liability company increased the number of formal organizations. Organization was facilitated by the spread of the factory system, which moved production to one place owned and controlled by one formal organization. Many new associations were founded during that period, including labour unions, political parties, churches, temperance societies, and sports clubs (Geijer, 1980; Tocqueville, 1961). Mergers and the creation of multidivisional business structures were the main strategies for growth during the first seven decades of the 20th century (Chandler, 1977). During the second half of the 20th century, the scope of the welfare state increased dramatically in a development that has been called 'the public revolution' (Tarschys, 1983).

The tendency to range organization into formal organizations does not necessarily reduce the total extent of organization outside organizations, however. In some respects, the development creates new needs and opportunities for such organization. Formal organizations are interdependent, often need to be coordinated in some way, and are power centres that many others are interested in organizing. Moreover, they are actors with the ability to organize not only their inner life, but also their environment.

Formal organizations often exhibit an interest in organizing their immediate environment, while maintaining it as an environment – not incorporating it into their own organization. The founding of standardization organizations around 1900 provides a historical example. Standards were a response to the discovery that organization within all the new industrial firms was not enough; the need for coordination among firms created the need for organization among them as well. By creating technical standards, products from one firm could be made to fit the products of other firms without merging these firms. Similarly, the last few decades have seen strong tendencies towards marketization, outsourcing, and privatization, involving the division of large organizations into smaller ones (Davis 2013, 2017; Pallesen, 2011), without necessarily leading to a reduction in dependence or the need for organization among the units. Thus much organization is likely to have moved from formal organizations into the spaces between them.

The context of many formal organizations also creates opportunities for new formal organizations with the task of organizing the others. As mentioned in this chapter and exemplified in other chapters in this book, standardization organizations are far from the only organizations that organize other organizations. These 'others' reduce the opportunity for managers in organizations such as firms and states to organize their own organizations; these managers have less need and fewer opportunities for organization than they would have in a world with less organization outside them. Even if some states and firms control enormous resources and employ thousands of people, they may have less autonomy and power than their own politicians and managers claim.

As we have indicated, globalization is likely to increase organization outside organizations. Maybe the great salience of formal organizations as arenas for organization is tied to the 19th and 20th centuries, when nation states were more important than they are now. The forms for formal organizations were decided by national law, and the organizations lived in symbiosis with the nation states, which, through their laws, monitoring, and sanctions took care of much of the organizing. In today's more globalized world there is no world state to fill this role, but because the need for organization has increased rather than decreased, opportunities for organization are grasped by a great number of organizations with the task of organizing other organizations. Furthermore, partial organization 'travels' easier than formal organizations do (Ahrne & Brunsson, 2014); it takes more time and effort to expand the operations of a multinational corporation to new parts of the world than for a global standard or ranking to have global effects.

Maybe the period is over when one finds the most organization within firms and states. Rather, the world is organized by tens of thousands of global standards, millions of certifications, and extensive monitoring, most of which is implemented by social movements and idealistic associations and by some 10,000 international meta-organizations, many of which are only partially organized. And the organizers are almost always formal organizations. Contemporary society is marked by a large number of formal organizations and by an extensive organization between and outside these organizations; in both respects, it is an 'organizational society'. 'Hyper-organization' (Bromley & Meyer, 2015) is a concept that can be used to denote both of these phenomena.

THE RELEVANCE OF PARTIAL ORGANIZATION

Research about organization began a large expansion in the 1950s and 1960s, after a long period during which formal organizations had become more and more common and salient. No wonder scholars concentrated on organization within formal organizations, where most organization seemed to take place. Today's situation makes it easier to observe organization outside the context of formal organizations. So much knowledge about the inner life of formal organizations has been produced over the decades that it has become more difficult to find new fundamental issues for research. Accordingly, students of organization have directed more of their attention to organizational environments, including networks consisting of several organizations and, not least, the societal institutions that form organizations and their inner life. Network theories and institutional theories are currently in vogue. Institutional theory can even be seen as a fundamental criticism of the relevance of organization within formal organizations; many organizational decisions can be understood as reflections of institutions and should be explained with reference to a more general context than that of the individual organization.

We have not rejected these ideas in this book, but we have argued that other aspects of organizational environments can be understood as organized and that more classical theories about organization as a decided order can be fruitfully used for analysing these aspects. Furthermore, because most organization outside organizations is performed by formal organizations, the functioning of these organizing organizations should be a significant research topic. There is a need for more research on standardizers, certifiers, award givers, and the like, rather than intensifying the study of industrial firms, which have been so much in focus in organization studies over the past few decades.

Research on organization outside organizations is relevant from a normative point of view as well. Organization, whether inside or outside formal organizations, is problematic in many ways, but it has some advantages over networks and institutions. Organization is more visible and transparent than either networks or institutions are. In an organized context, norms are replaced with rules; gossip and rumours are replaced with the results of monitoring; bullying is replaced by sanctions; and connections are replaced by membership.

And all these decisions must normally be motivated by referring to values that many people find acceptable. They point not only to their content, but also to their options and the fact that the order could be different, thus stimulating criticism. Decision making also requires decision makers – people who can be held responsible and be the focus of debate. And there is something optimistic about organization: It consists of attempts to change environments instead of taking them for granted, to make things happen rather than waiting for something to happen, to create an order when it is lacking, or to change an existing order.

Organization outside organizations opens large, rich firms and states to influence from sources other than its managers or politicians. As the influence from many successful 'others' illustrates, it is possible to have an impact on modern global society even with few resources.

Organization may be perceived as too dynamic, however. The fact that an organized order can be easily contested introduces possibilities for new organization with another content (cf. Brunsson, 2009, Ch. 5). Using organization to try to change previous orders implies that a seed for continued change is sown: Even if one organizes to exactly mirror a previous form of order, the probability for change increases. This may be a greater problem in organization outside organizations than it is in formal organizations. Formal organization is contained in one specific and local context that is lacking outside that organization. Outside formal organizations, new organization may mean additional elements, but it may also mean that more organizers are making new decisions about elements that have already been decided, leading to several different rules for the same thing, rankings with differing results, and a plethora of monitoring systems covering almost every aspect of life. There is a risk that rather than creating a new order, partial organization creates chaotic disorder, thereby introducing obscureness rather than clarity.

For at least a century there has been an on-going discussion about the way formal organizations could be made to function better with respect to issues like responsibility, transparency, democracy, and the rights of those who are organized – a discussion that has generated many suggestions, ideas, and reforms. How such values can be secured in organization outside organizations is more uncertain. More descriptive and explanatory knowledge about such organization will be useful for making this normative discussion productive.

REFERENCES

Ahrne, G. & Brunsson, N. (2008) *Meta-Organizations*. Cheltenham: Edward Elgar.

Ahrne, G. & Brunsson, N. (2011) Organization outside Organizations: The Significance of Partial Organization. *Organization* 18(1): 83–104.

Ahrne, G. & Brunsson, N. (2014) The Travel of Organization. In G. S. Drori, M. A. Höllerer, & P. Walgenbach (eds.), *Global Themes and Local Variations in Organization and Management*. London: Routledge. 39–51.

Bromley, P. & Meyer, J. (2015) *Hyper-Organization. Global Organizational Expansion*. Oxford: Oxford University Press.

Brunsson, N. (2009) *Reform as Routine. Organizational Change and Stability in the Modern World*. Oxford: Oxford University Press.

Chandler, A. (1977) *The Visible Hand: The Managerial Revolution in American Business*. Cambridge, MA: Belknap.

Davis, G. (2013) After the Corporation. *Politics and Society* 41(2): 283–308.

Davis, G. (2017) Organization Theory and the Dilemmas of a Post-Corporate Economy. *Research in the Sociology of Organizations* 48B: 311–22.

den Hond, F., de Bakker, F. G. A., & Smith, N. (2015) Social Movements and Organizational Analysis. In M. Diani & D. della Porta (eds.), *The Oxford Handbook of Social Movements*. Oxford: Oxford University Press. 291–305.

Geijer, E. G. (1980) *Om vår tids inre samhällsförhållanden*. Historiska skrifter i urval och med kommentarer av Thorsten Nybom. Stockholm: Tidens förlag.

Hall, P. A. & Soskice, D. (2003) *Varieties of Capitalism: The Institutional Foundations of Comparative Advantage*. Oxford: Oxford University Press.

Meyer, D. S. & Tarrow, S. G. (1998) A Movement Society: Contentious Politics for a New Century. In D. S. Meyer & S. G. Tarrow (eds.), *The Social Movement Society: Contentious Politics for a New Century*. Lanham: Rowman & Littlefield. 1–28.

Meyer, J. (1996) Otherhood, the Promulgation and Transmission of Ideas of the Modern Organizational Environment. In B. Czarniawska & G. Sevon (eds.), *Translating Organizational Change*. New York: Walter de Gruyter. 241–52.

Ostrom, E. (1990) *Governing the Commons. The Evolution of Institutions for Collective Action*. Cambridge: Cambridge University Press.

Pallesen, T. (2011) Privatization. In T. Christensen & P. Lægreid (eds.), *The Ashgate Research Companion to New Public Management*. Farnham: Ashgate. 251–64.

Perrow, C. (1991) A Society of Organizations. *Theory and Society* 20(6): 725–62.

Roed Nielsen, K. (2018) Crowdfunding through a partial organization lens – The co-dependent organization. *European Management Journal* 36:6: 695–707.

Strandqvist, K. (2018) From a Free Market to a Pure Market. The History of Organizing the Swedish Pipe and Tube Market. In N. Brunsson & M. Jutterström (eds.), *Organizing and Reorganizing Markets*. Oxford: Oxford University Press. 232–48.

Tarschys, D. (1983) *Den offentliga revolutionen*. 2nd edition. Stockholm: Liber.

Thompson, G. F. (2003) *Between Hierarchies and Markets. The Logic and Limits of Network Forms of Organization*. Oxford: Oxford University Press.

Tocqueville, A. (1961) *Democracy in America*. Volume 2. New York: Schocken Books.

Index

Printed in the United States
by Baker & Taylor Publisher Services